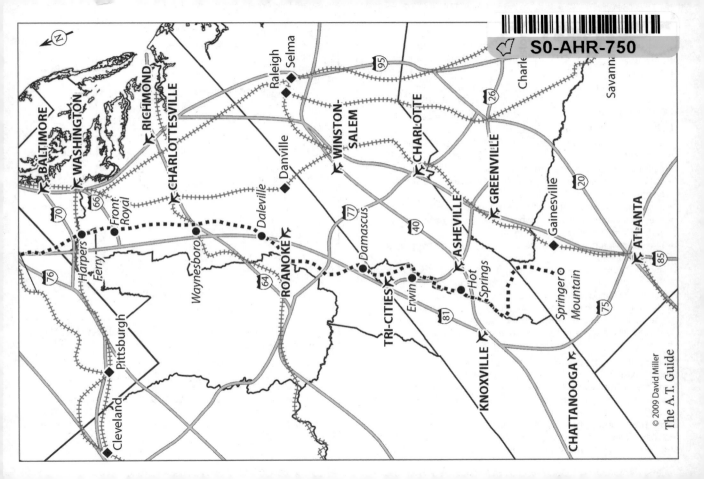

S0-AHR-750

© 2009 David Miller

The A.T. Guide

Maildrop Guidelines

Packages sent to PO:

> John Doe
> C/O General Delivery
> Trail Town, VA 12345
>
> Please hold for AT hiker
> ETA May 16, 2016

Packages sent to businesses:

> John Doe
> C/O Hiker Hostel
> 2176 Appalachian Way
> Trail Town, VA 12345
> Please hold for AT hiker
> ETA May 16, 2016

▶ Use your real name (not a trail name), include an ETA & return address.
▶ Only send "General Delivery" mail to a Post office.
▶ FedEx and UPS packages cannot be addressed to PO boxes.
▶ USPS will forward unopened general delivery mail for free if it was shipped by Priority Mail.
▶ Be prepared to show an ID when you retrieve your mail.
▶ The "C/O" name is essential when mailing to a business's PO Box; without it, they may not be able to retrieve your mail.
▶ When sending mail somewhere other than a PO, it's best to call first. Hostels and outfitters go out of business. Consider adding your phone number or email so they have a way to contact you about your mail.
▶ Send maildrops to a lodging facility only if you plan to stay there. If your plans change, offer to pay for the service of holding your mail.
▶ Many outfitters hold maildrops. Although none have rules about what you send, it's bad form to buy from an on-line retailer and have it shipped to a store where you could have bought it.

Maildrop services: these businesses offer small quantities of typical resupply items, packaged and mailed to you on the AT:
Son Driven Outfitters 276-781-6994 ⟨www.SonDriven.com⟩ Gear, food & toiletries. Free shipping any CONUS address on orders over $39.99, no sales tax.
Zero Day Resupply ⟨www.ZeroDayResupply.com⟩ Mail drop resupply for thru-hikers. No sales tax, no handling fee, next day shipping. Eat what you want, where you want, when you want it.

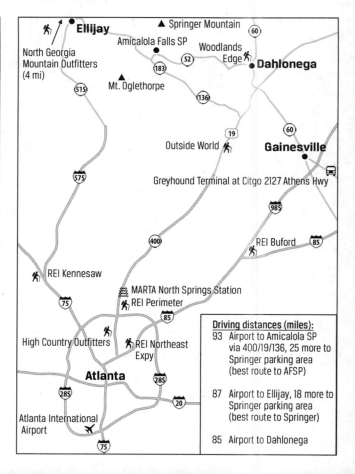

Driving distances (miles):
93 Airport to Amicalola SP via 400/19/136, 25 more to Springer parking area (best route to AFSP)

87 Airport to Ellijay, 18 more to Springer parking area (best route to Springer)

85 Airport to Dahlonega

Getting to Springer Mountain

The southern terminus of the AT on Springer Mountain is accessible only by foot. The 8.8-mi. Approach Trail originating at the Visitor Center in Amicalola Falls SP is one means of getting there. Or you can drive to Springer Parking area on USFS 42, a dirt road passable by most vehicles unless there is bad-weather washout. From the parking area, hike south 1 mi. on the AT to Springer Mtn. Your hike would begin by retracing your steps. (See Start of Trail map pg. 10)

The closest major city is Atlanta, GA, 82 miles south. If you fly or take AMTRAK into Atlanta, take the MARTA rail system to the North Springs Station; shuttlers pickup from there. There is also Greyhound bus service to Gainesville, GA, 38 miles from the park.

🚌 **Hiker Hostel** Package deal including shuttle, see pg. 11.
🚌 ⊛ **Ron Brown** Cell: 706.669.0919, Home: 706.636.2825 hikershuttles@outlook.com. Flat rate shuttles to/from the AT or trail towns up to Fontana, including Amicalola Falls SP, Atlanta airport, & Gainesville, GA. Dogs welcome; extra stops OK. Fuel on request.
🚌 **Sam Duke** 706.994.6633 In Blairsville; range Atlanta-Fontana.
🚌 **Henry Carter** 678.525.3497 Ranging from Atlanta-all of GA.

✖ Which two maps in this book contain the flora symbol?

Due to increasing **bear/human interactions**, the Appalachian Trail Conservancy strongly recommends the use of **bear canisters** for food storage while overnight camping along the A.T. in GA, NC, & TN. Recommended canisters: http://sierrawild.gov/bears/food-storage

Solid, non-pliable "bear canisters" are required if you camp in GA between Jarrard Gap & Neel Gap from March 1 to June 1.

Within the Great Smoky Mtn NP all food must be hung from cables; even food within bear canisters.

Outfitters Near the Southern Terminus

🚶 **Mountain Crossings** 706.745.6095 (see pg. 11)
🚶 **North Georgia Mountain Outfitters** 706.698.4453 ⟨hikeNorthGeorgia.com⟩ 14244 Hwy 515N, Suite 1200, Ellijay, GA 30536 Full service outfitter. Tu-Sa 10-6
🚶 **Woodlands Edge** 706.864.5358 Open 10-5, 363 days a year (closed Easter and Christmas Day). Full service outfitter, fuel/oz, ask about shuttles. 36 North Park Street Dahlonega, GA 30533
🚶 **Outside World** 706.265.4500 471 Quill Drive, Dawsonville, GA 30534
🚶 **Half Moon Outfitters** 404.249.7921 1034 N. Highland Ave. NE, Atlanta, GA 30306
🚶 **High Country Outfitters** 404.814.0999 3906 Roswell Rd. #B, Atlanta, GA 30342
🚶 **REI** Four Atlanta area stores:
1800 Northeast Expy NE, Atlanta, GA 30329, 404.633.6508
1165 Perimeter Ctr W Suite 200, Atlanta, GA 30338, 770.901.9200
740 Barrett Parkway Suite 450, Kennesaw, GA 30144, 770.425.4480
1600 Mall of Georgia Blvd, Buford, GA 30519, 770.831.0676

ATC's **voluntary thru-hiker registration** helps prospective thru-hikers to choose start dates that best avoid the impacts of overcrowding. **Section hikers**, even though you will not register, make use of the information to avoid peak dates. http://appalachiantrail.org/home/explore-the-trail/thru-hiking

⚠ Water Sources

Be aware of trail conditions before heading out, and tune in to advice from outfitters and other hikers. The trail gets re-routed, springs dry up, streams alter their course. Be prepared to deal with changes, particularly late in the season. Never carry just enough water to reach the next spring.

AMICALOLA FALLS STATE PARK

⟨www.www.amicalolafallslodge.com⟩
706.265.8888 Hikers may use lot across from the visitor center for long-term parking ($50 for 2 weeks or more, even for the duration of a thru-hike) if you plan to leave your car overnight. There is $5 fee to park anywhere in the park. Dogs are allowed, but must be leashed.

🛏 🔥 🚶 🛜 ✉ The Lodge at Amicalola Falls

Rooms in the lodge and cottages throughout the park. Rates are seasonal; reservations strongly recommended. Many campsites are also available; most hold 2 tents and up to 6 persons. Pets allowed in campsites and in designated cottages. WiFi in Lodge common area only. Mail: Arriving hiker "your name", 418 Amicalola Falls Lodge Rd, Dawsonville, GA 30534.

Amicalola Falls are the highest east of the Mississippi River.

Reflection Pool

Stairs

🛏 The Len Foote Hike Inn (5 mi.)

800.581.8032 ⟨www.hike-inn.com⟩ Currently $117S $170D (higher on Saturdays & holidays). Includes hearty family-style dinner & breakfast. 20 rooms with bunkbeds & common bath areas. Reservations recommended and can be made on-line. Check in at Amicalola Falls Visitor Center by 2pm; arrive early enough for 5pm orientation and 6pm dinner. This is an eco-friendly facility accessible only by foot. There are hot showers and electricity, but no outlets in the rooms. No Pets. Please do not use cell phones, beepers or radios. Open year round.

↑ Approach Trail

← *Max Epperson Shelter (free, for use by thru-hikers only)*

↑ Approach Trail

⟵ Archway

🛏 📞 🚶 **Visitor Center** Carries guidebooks, maps and a small selection of cold drinks and snacks. There is a hiker register inside and a pack scale outside.

Appalachian Trail Kick-Off (ATKO) March 4-6. Enjoy demonstrations and workshops by hikers and retailers covering gear and trip preparation.

Springer Mtn (7 mi from edge of map)

↑ Approach Trail

Parking

Tenting

Cabins

Ampitheater

Cabins

P

34.5578, -84.25
Mag. Dec. 5.23° W

⊕ **N**

Amicalola Creek

Dahlonega 18 mi

1.0 mi

Ellijay 19.7 mi

(52)

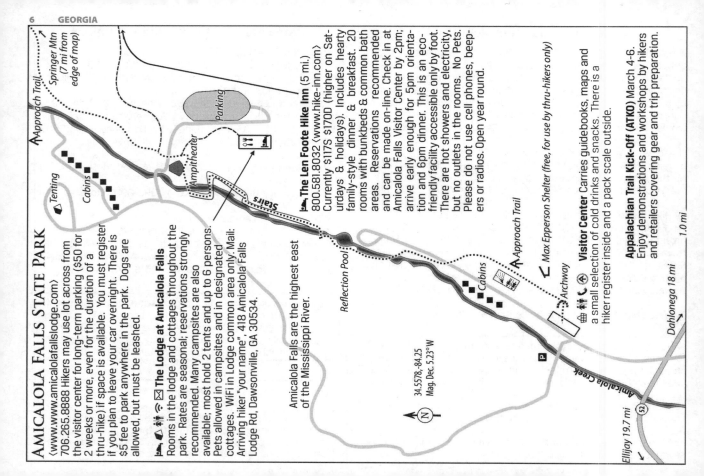

The Approach Trail

SoBo	NoBo	The Approach Trail	Elev
8.8	0.0	**Amicalola Falls State Park**, archway behind Visitor Center	1800
8.7	0.1	**Max Epperson Shelter**, for thru-hiker use only	1858
8.4	0.4	Reflection Pond at base of falls	2003
8.1	0.7	Staircase - 604 steps to the top of the Falls	2216
7.7	1.1	Parking, side trail to Lodge	2639
7.6	1.2	Lodge Road (lodge to east)	2642
7.5	1.3	Trail to **Len Foote Hike Inn** (5.0E) blazed lime-green	2656
7.3	1.5	USFS Road 46, steps on north side	2584
5.6	3.2	High Shoals Road	2841
4.0	4.8	Frosty Mountain. Spring (0.2E) is unreliable.	3384
3.7	5.1	Frosty Mountain Road, USFS Road 46	3178
3.4	5.4	Trail to **Len Foote Hike Inn** (1.0E) blazed lime-green.	3353
3.1	5.7	Woody Knob.	3406
2.8	6.0	Nimblewill Gap, USFS Road 28	3100
2.6	6.2	Spring (left of trail), unreliable	3419
1.5	7.3	**Black Gap Shelter** (0.1W). Spring is on opposite side of the Approach Trail (0.1E).	3300
0.0	8.8	Springer Mountain	3782

SoBo	NoBo		Elev
2189.1	0.0	Springer Mountain southern terminus, register on back of rock with plaque. [icon]	3782
2188.9	0.2	**Springer Mountain Shelter** (0.2E) Tent pads.)●◭(18) ⊂(12)	3720
		0.0◀0.0◀0.0◀▶2.6▶7.9▶15.6 150 yards north, Benton MacKaye Trail to east.	
2188.1	1.0	Big Stamp Gap, USFS 42 . . . 34.6376,-84.1954 P	3350
2187.1	2.0	Benton MacKaye Trail.	3268
2186.4	2.7	Footbridge, stream	2918
2186.3	2.8	**Stover Creek Shelter** (0.1E) (2006).)●◭(3) ⊂(14)	2916
		0.0◀0.0◀2.6◀▶5.3▶13.0▶25.3	
2186.2	2.9	Footbridge, stream	2873
2185.7	3.4	Stream.	2693
2184.9	4.2	Benton MacKaye / Duncan Ridge Trail to east	2586
2184.8	4.3	Three Forks, USFS 58, footbridge	2530
2183.9	5.2	Benton MacKaye / Duncan Ridge Trail to west Trail to Long Creek Falls	2800
2182.9	6.2	Dirt road, 0.2W to Hickory Flats Cemetery, pavilion	3081
2181.7	7.4	Hawk Mountain campsite (0.2W) 30 designated tent pads . . .)◭(30)	3220
2181.0	8.1	**Hawk Mountain Shelter** (0.2W) (1993) limited camping in 2016. .)◭(12) ⊂(12)	3194
		0.0◀7.9◀5.3◀▶7.7▶20.0▶21.2 Water south on AT and 0.1 mile behind shelter.	
2180.5	8.6	Hightower Gap, junction USFS 42 & 69 . . . 34.6635,-84.1297 P	2854
2178.6	10.5	Horse Gap	2681
2177.6	11.5	Sassafras Mountain	3347
2176.8	12.3	Cooper Gap, USFS 15, 42 & 80 . . . 34.653,-84.0846 P	2929
2176.3	12.8	Justus Mountain	3219
2175.6	13.5	Dirt road	2752
2174.7	14.4	Justus Creek. Use designated campsites north of creek, to west . . . ●◭(6)	2589
2174.2	14.9	Stream.	2636
2173.6	15.5	Blackwell Creek.	2656
2173.3	15.8	**Gooch Mountain Shelter** (0.1W) (2001) Water behind shelter)●◭(6) ⊂(14)	2789
		15.6◀13.0◀7.7◀▶12.3▶13.5▶22.6 Designated tentsites, cables.	
2172.2	16.9	Spring to the east	2831
2171.9	17.2	Gooch Gap, USFS 42 (gravel) . . . 34.652,-84.0323 P	2824
		Suches, GA (2.7W - see Woody Gap entry) water north of rd 0.1E on marked trail	
2170.9	18.2	Roadbed.	2939
2170.7	18.4	Liss Gap.	3052
2170.1	19.0	Ramrock Mountain . . . [icon]	3222

NoBo
SoBo

(elevation profile: 5000 — 3000 — 1000)

SoBo	NoBo	Description	Elev.
2168.7	20.4	Seasonal springs. △	3208
2168.3	20.8	Woody Gap, GA 60 . . . 34.6777,-84.0000 P 🏛️ 🚻 ♦ (pg. 11)	3198
		Suches, GA (2.0W); Hostel (6.0E); spring north of road 0.2W.	
2167.3	21.8	Preaching Rock, view to east. Woody Lake in Suches in view to west. 📷	3593
2167.0	22.1	Big Cedar Mountain, rock ledges and views. 📷	3737
2166.8	22.3	Spring to west. ♦	3659
2166.0	23.1	Spring to west ♦	3325
2165.2	23.9	Dockery Lake Trail	3050
2164.8	24.3	Lance Creek, camp in designated sites north of footbridge ♦ ◁(6)	2865
2164.0	25.1	Henry Gap (unmarked) is 70 yards west on side trail, woods road to GA 180. P	3083

⚠️ A hard-shell bear-resistant canister is required for hikers overnighting between Jarrard Gap and Neel Gap from Mar 1 - Jun 1. No fires (year-round) from Slaughter Creek Trail to Neel Gap.

SoBo	NoBo	Description	Elev.
2162.4	26.7	Jarrard Gap, dirt road. ♦ (0.3W) (pg. 11)	3250
2162.2	26.9	Gaddis Mountain	3402
2161.0	28.1	Turkey Stamp	3742
2160.9	28.2	**Woods Hole Shelter** (0.2W) 25.3◀20.0◀12.3▶12►10.3▶15.1 🚻 △ ♦ ⊏(7)	3662
		Bird Gap, Freeman Trail east bypasses Blood Mtn & rejoins AT at Flatrock Gap	
2160.6	28.5	Slaughter Creek Trail, Coosa Trail to west on AT, campsite 0.1 south on AT ♦ ◁(8)	3800
2160.2	28.9	Duncan Ridge Trail, Coosa Trail to west.	4168
2159.8	29.3	**Blood Mountain Shelter** (1934) 21.2◀13.5◀1.2◀▶9.1▶8.9▶21.2 🚻 ⊃ ⊏(8)	4457
		Privy 50 yards south. No fires. Stream (0.8S). Many views from AT south of shelter	
2158.5	30.6	Flatrock Gap, Freeman Trail east bypasses Blood Mtn; west. P ♦ (0.2W)	3487
		to Byron Reece parking area. Balance Rock 150 yards north.	
2157.4	31.7	Neel Gap, US 19 . . . 34.7411,-83.9206 P (pg. 11)	3125
2156.3	32.8	Bull Gap, spring 0.1W. ♦	3685
2155.7	33.4	Levelland Mountain, view 📷	3870
2154.5	34.6	Swaim Gap, spring to west. ♦	3536
2153.8	35.3	Wolf Laurel Top, views to east 📷	3780

✽ **Mayapple** – White flower ball dangling under an umbrella of broad leaves. Plant is about a foot tall.

SoBo	NoBo	Description	Elev.
2152.4	36.7	Cowrock Mountain 📷	3842
2151.4	37.7	Tesnatee Gap, GA 348, Russell Hwy . . . 34.7262,-83.8476 P (pg. 11)	3138
2150.9	38.2	Wildcat Mountain. ♦	3637
2150.7	38.4	**Whitley Gap Shelter** (1.2E) Spring 0.3 mi. behind shelter. 🚻 ⊃ ♦ ◁(3) ⊏(7)	3625
		22.6◀10.3◀9.1◀▶4.8▶12.1▶20.2 Campsite 0.1E with view just beyond.	
2150.5	38.6	Hogpen Gap, GA 348, Water S of rd, E of AT. . . 34.7259,-83.8399 P ♦ (pg. 11)	3444

NoBo
SoBo

Temperature decreases about 3.5° Fahrenheit for every 1000' gain in elevation. The decrease is even greater in clear weather. If you see a forecast of 50° for Dahlonega (1450'), expect temperatures below 40° on Blood Mountain (4461').

Check weather conditions anywhere on the AT: ⟨www.atweather.org⟩

Vogel SP 11.6 mi. from Suches

High Valley Resort

Jarrard Gap

Wolfpen Gap Country Store

Suches

Woody Gap

Hightower Gap

USFS 58

Three Forks

Hawk Mtn Shelter

Horse Gap

Cooper Gap

Big Creek Rd

52 to USFS 42 11.8 mi.

Double Gap Rd

Double Gap Rd to parking 6.5 mi.

USFS 42

Stover Creek Shelter

USFS 42

Cooper Gap to parking 10 mi. on USFS 42

Gooch Gap

Gooch Mtn Shelter

60

Roy Rd

52

Stanley's Chevron

Ellijay 6.1 mi. from Big Creek Rd

P

Springer Mtn Shelter

Black Gap Shelter

Camp Merrill

FS 80/Cooper Gap Rd (3 mi.)

Hiker Hostel

19

52

Amicalola to Roy Rd. 13.6 mi.

Approach Trail

Len Foote Hike Inn

Winding Stair Gap Rd

FS 28-1

Camp Wahsega Rd (9 mi.)

19

9

Amicalola Falls S.P.

Lodge

Max Epperson Shelter

Nimblewill Church

Mystic Country Cupboard

60

52

Grizzle's Store

9

183

136

Approximately 27 mi. of the AT are shown on this map.

Dahlonega

60

26 mi

20.8 Woody Gap, GA Hwy 60

🛏️🏠⛺🚐🛜🖥️✉️ (6.0E) **Hiker Hostel** 770.312.7342 ⟨www.hikerhostel.com⟩ hikerhostel@yahoo.com Open year-round. $19PP Bunks, $45 Private room for 2, $55-$65 Private Cabin for 2. Stay includes breakfast, bed linens, towel & shower. Computer w/internet & wireless. Laundry $3. SPECIAL(Feb 24-Apr 20): $85 pickup from Atlanta North Springs MARTA Station or Gainesville, overnight stay bunk, breakfast, shuttle to Amicalola or Springer, 8oz of white gas/alcohol. Canister fuel and limited gear available for purchase. Feb 24-Apr 27 5pm FREE daily pickup at Woody Gap. Shuttles from Atlanta & Gainesville and to all trailheads in GA by reservation for hostel guests. Mail: (USPS) PO Box 802 or (FedEx/UPS) 7693 Hwy 19N, Dahlonega, GA 30533.

🧍🏚️ (0.5W) **Woody Gap Outfitters** 678.262.8406 ⟨woodygapoutfitters.com⟩ Full service discount outfitter specializing in thru-hiker needs. Pack shakedowns by triple-crowner Bob "Sir-Packs-Alot" Gabrielsen, resupply, pizza & snacks. Open daily 10-4, Feb 15 - June 1. Easy downhill road walk to store on corner of Hwy 60 & Caldwell Mt. Rd or call for pickup.

Suches, GA 30572 (2W) (pronounced "such-is")

📮 M-F 12:15-4:15, 706.747.2611

🛏️🏠🍴🏚️💲⛺🛜✉️ **Wolfpen Gap Country Store** 706.747.2271 M-Sat 8-8, Su 9-6, later in summer. Bunks $20. Laundry $5/load. Beer, soda, hiker foods, pizza, BBQ. Coleman/oz & canisters. Free pickup for overnight guests at Woody or Gooch Gap. Accepts Visa/MC/Disc. Mail: 41 Wolf Pen Gap Rd, Suches, GA 30572.

🛌🛏️◐⛺🛜 **High Valley Resort** (0.7W) of PO, 404.720.0087 ⟨www.highvalleyresort.com⟩ Open Apr-Oct. Camping $15PP, bunkhouse $55PP, both have access to bathhouse, showers and lodge with satellite TV. Cabins $125/night Su-Wed; $165 Th-Sat, some sleep 4, some sleep up to 8 persons.

🛌🛏️◐🍴🏚️ **Wildcat Lodge and Campground** 706.973.0321. (7W) $15 bunkroom, $12 camping. Lodge room sleeps 8 $100D, $25EAP. Camp store has Coleman & canisters. Diner serves B/L.

🚐 **Wes Wisson** 706.747.2671, 706.781.4333 Shuttles covering trailheads in north Georgia.

➕ **Don Pruitt** 706.747.1421, M-W 9-4, walk-ins before 10am.

26.7 Jarrard Gap

◐🌿 (1.0W) **Lake Winfield Scott Recreation Area** tent sites $12 for up to 5 persons, showers & bathrooms, leash dogs.

31.7 Neel Gap, US 19

🧍🛏️🏠🚐🌿⛺✉️ **Mountain Crossings** 706.745.6095 ⟨www.mountaincrossings.com⟩ Full-service outfitter, full resupply, gear shakedown, alcohol/oz, bunkroom $18PP includes shower w/towel. No Pets. Shower without stay $5. Laundry $5. Ask about shuttles. Outgoing shipping available. Maildrops (USPS/UPS/FedEx) held for 2 weeks, $1 fee at pickup, 12471 Gainesville Hwy, Blairsville, GA 30512. ✂️What shoe is over the hostel door?

🛌⛺ (0.3E) **Blood Mountain Cabins** ⟨www.bloodmountain.com⟩ 706.745.9454 Thru-hiker rate $72. Cabin w/ kitchen and satellite TV, holds 4 adults & 2 children under the age of 13. Laundry free w/ stay. WiFi at lodge. No pets.

🛌◐🏚️🌿⛺🅿️ (3W) **Vogel State Park** 706.745.2628 Primitive tent sites $25, cabins for 2-10 persons $100-$200. $2 shower for tenters & visitors. Long term parking $5. ⟨www.gastateparks.org⟩

🛌🚐 (3.5W) **Goose Creek Cabins** 706.781.8593, 706.745.5111 Cabins and shuttles available, call for details.

Blairsville, GA 30514 (14W) All major services.

🛌⛺🛜 **Misty Mtn Inn** 706.745.4786 B&B rooms $108 ($98 w/o breakfast), cabins for 2-10 price $105-$125. Free pickup/return from Neel, Tesnatee or Hogpen Gap. Slackpacking with multi-night stay.

🍴 **Jim's Smokin' BBQ** Th-Sa 11-8.

🧍 **Blairsville Hikes and Bikes** 706.745.8141 Packs, poles, fuel & hiker food. Open 10-5:30.

🚐 **Sam Duke** 706.994.6633 Shuttle range Atlanta-Fontana.

Dahlonega, GA 30597 (17E) All major services.

37.7 Tesnatee Gap,

38.6 Hogpen Gap, **Blairsville, GA 30514** (14W) listings above.

> ⚠ Get the most out of your guidebook: pay attention to lines that end with a page number. The page that is referenced will list the services available at or near the trailhead.

SoBo	NoBo	Description	Elev.
2149.6	39.5	White Oak Stamp	3470
2148.6	40.6	Poor Mountain	3620
2146.8	42.3	Sheep Rock Top	3558
2145.9	43.2	**Low Gap Shelter** 15.1◄13.9◄4.8◄►7.3►15.4►22.8 ♪◑◣(4)⊂(7) Water 30 yards in front of shelter. Cables. Privy on steep hill beyond shelter.	3024
2145.5	43.6	Stream. ●	3183
2144.5	44.6	Poplar Stamp Gap, spring 0.1E, gap and side trail unmarked. ●◣	3345
2143.8	45.3	Spring to west. ●	3550
2142.5	46.6	Stream with cascade, several streams in area. ●	3464
2142.0	47.1	Cold Springs Gap	3495
2140.9	48.2	Chattahoochee Gap, Jacks Gap Trail to west, spring 0.5E ●	3583
2140.2	48.9	Red Clay Gap (pg.14)	3485
2139.6	49.5	Site of former Rocky Knob Shelter. ●	3630
2139.3	49.8	Spring west of trail down slope ●	3606
2138.6	50.5	**Blue Mountain Shelter** 21.2◄12.1◄7.3◄►8.1►15.5►23.6 ♪●◣(4)⊂(7) Bear cables. Spring on AT (0.1S), camping west of AT, south of shelter.	3880
2137.7	51.4	Blue Mountain	4025
2136.2	52.9	Unicoi Gap, GA 75, **Helen, GA** (9.0E) 34.8017,-83.7428 P (pg.14) **Hiawassee, GA** (12.0W)	2949
2135.5	53.6	Stream. ●	3502
2135.3	53.8	Rocky Mountain Trail to west. ●	3715
2134.8	54.3	Rocky Mountain, views from AT 0.1 north of summit 📷◣	4017
2133.5	55.6	Indian Grave Gap, USFS 283 34.7927,-83.7143 P Andrews Cove Trail to east.	3113
2132.8	56.3	Tray Mountain Rd (gravel), USFS 79, piped stream east on road. ●	3480
2132.5	56.6	Cheese factory site, water (0.1W) on blue-blazed trail ●◣	3579
2131.8	57.3	Tray Gap, Tray Mountain Rd, USFS 79 34.7993,-83.691 P	3847
2131.0	58.1	Tray Mountain. 📷	4430

NoBo
SoBo

SoBo	NoBo	Feature	Elev.
2130.5	58.6	**Tray Mountain Shelter** (0.2W) ☽◆⛺(3) 20.2◄15.4◄8.1◄▶7.4▶15.5▶22.8 Spring 0.1 mile behind shelter. Cables. ⟅(7)	4193
2129.3	59.8	Wolfpen Gap	3550
2128.8	60.3	Steeltrap Gap, water 0.5E ◆	3448
2128.2	60.9	Young Lick Knob	3748
2126.9	62.2	Swag of the Blue Ridge	3451
2125.8	63.3	Sassafras Gap, water 0.2E on steep blue-blazed trail ◆◇	3500
2124.9	64.2	Addis Gap ◆◇ Campsite 0.5E down old fire road, stream to right of campsite.	3304
2123.9	65.2	Kelly Knob, trail skirts summit	4126
		📶 *No phone signal at Dicks Creek Gap. If you need ride, call from Shelter or Powell Mtn.*	
2123.1	66.0	**Deep Gap Shelter** (0.3E) 22.8◄15.5◄7.4◄▶8.1▶15.4▶20.3 ☽◆◇⟅(4)⟅(12) Water 0.1 before shelter.	3554
2122.0	67.1	"Vista" blue-blaze leads 0.1E to campsite. ◇	3886
2121.7	67.4	Powell Mountain	3850
2120.5	68.6	Moreland Gap, water to east ◆	3015
2119.5	69.6	Dicks Creek Gap, US 76 34.9121,-83.6188 🚻🅿(pg.14) Water, picnic tables at the gap, **Hiawassee, GA** (11.0W)	2675
2118.5	70.6	Campsite, 200 yards to water ◆◇	3177
2117.7	71.4	Cowart Gap ◇	2900
2116.3	72.8	Buzzard Knob	3679
2116.2	72.9	Bull Gap	3541
2115.5	73.6	Spring ◆	3317
2115.0	74.1	**Plumorchard Gap Shelter** (0.2E) Privy 0.2 mi down steep tr. ☽◆◇⟅(6)⟅(14) 23.6◄15.5◄8.1◄▶7.3▶12.2▶19.8 Creek on trail to shelter & spring (0.1W) of AT.	3144
2114.3	74.8	As Knob	3460
2113.8	75.3	Blue Ridge Gap, dirt road (no longer passable by car)	3090
2112.8	76.3	Spring to west, campsite ◆◇	3403
2112.1	77.0	Rich Cove Gap	3532
2111.9	77.2	Rocky Knob	3574

NoBo

SoBo

48.9   Red Clay Gap

🛏️�́🚗⊙ ⛺ 🏠 ✉ **Enota Mountain Retreat** 706.896.9966, 1.4W from Red Clay Gap. No sign & trail not blazed; be certain of location if you walk. Marked on some maps by its previous name "Camp Pioneer." Trail is downhill to Joel's Creek and follows creek into camp. Driving from Unicoi Gap: 2.4W on Hwy 17, then left 2.4 mi. on Hwy 180. Rides sometimes available. Tentsites, cabins, bunkrooms ($25), and laundry. Store with snacks and small gear items. Dining room open when there is enough guests. Beautiful waterfall, trout pond, work for stay possible on organic farm. Mail (guests only): 1000 Highway 180 Hiawassee, GA 30546

52.9   Unicoi Gap, GA 75
        Enota Mountain Retreat (4.8W, see listing above)
        Helen, GA 30545 (9E) Lodging tax 15%
🏠 M–F 9–12:30 & 1:30-4, Sa 9-12, 706.878.2422
Tourist town with many hotels, restaurants, gift shops, ice cream shops, river rafting and tubing rentals. Visitor Center on Bruckenstrasse (near the PO) has information about places to stay and a free phone for making reservations.

🛏️🚃 ⊙ 🖥 **Best Western Motel** 706.878.2111 Hiker rate Mar 15-Apr 30; $50S + $5EAP up to 4. Includes breakfast buffet. Ride to/from trail weekdays only when staff is available.

🛏️ ⛺ ⊙ 🖥 **Helendorf River Inn** 800.445.2271 Prices 1 or 2 persons Su-Th; Nov-Mar $44, Apr-May $54, Jun-Aug $84, +tax, $10EAP. Weekend rates higher. Pets $20. Includes cont B. Visa/MC/Disc accepted.

🛏️ ⊙ 🖥 **Super 8 Motel** 706.878.2191, ask for hiker room $49+tax for 1 or 2 persons, pet fee $25.

🛏️ ⊙ 🖥 **Econo Lodge** 706.878.8000   Weekdays $60, weekends higher, includes cont. b'fast. Pets under 20 pounds with $20 fee.

🛏️ ⛺ ⊙ 🖥 **Country Inn and Suites** 706.878.9000 Call for rates, stay includes full hot b'fast, indoor pool & hot tub.

🏪 **Betty's Country Store** 706.878.2943 Open Su-Th 7-8, F-Sa 7-9.
⛺ laundromat

Hiawassee, GA 30545 (12E) *(see Dicks Creek Gap)*

69.6   Dicks Creek Gap, US 76
🛏️🚃 ⊙ 🏠 ⛺ 🚌 ⊙ 🖥 ✉ (0.5W) **Top of Georgia Hostel & Hiking Center** 706.982.3252 ⟨www.topofgeorgiahostel.com⟩ Open year-round 7-7. Downhill blue-blazed road walk (NoBo left / SoBo right). Full service discount outfitter. Delivery of gear where you need it when you need it. Full resupply. Bunk & shower $25. Overflow tenting $12PP includes shower & use of full hostel kitchen. Free shuttles year-round to Hiawassee, Dicks Creek Gap & Unicoi Gap for all overnight guests. Slackpacking options & shuttles ranging from Springer to NOC for a fee. Hearty, hot breakfast $6. Pizza & snacks available. Laundry $5/load. Computer, free Wi-fi. Free (Appalachian Trail School) nightly seminar "11 Keys for a Successful Thru-Hike". Pack shakedowns by proprietor, Triple Crowner and guide Bob "Sir-Packs-Alot" Gabrielsen. Separate suite for hikers with pets. No alcohol or drugs. Mail ($1 fee) held for 30 days; ID required: 7675 US Hwy 76 E., Hiawassee GA 30546.

🛏️ ⛺ 🚌 🅿 ⊙ 🖥 ✉ **Henson Cove B&B** (5W) 800.714.5542 relax@henson-cove-place.com. Small cabin for 1-6 persons, full kitchen, 3 beds, 1.5 baths. $100 for 3 people, $120 for 6. Breakfast $8PP. Standard B&B rooms $100D, breakfast included. All stays include free ride to/from AT from Dick's Creek Gap or Unicoi Gap, or into town for provisions, free laundry & internet. Credit cards OK, well behaved pets OK. Shuttles, parking for section hikers. Mail drops: 1137 Car Miles Rd, Hiawassee, GA 30546.

Hiawassee, GA 30546 (11W)
Hiker Fool Bash March 25-26 at the Budget Inn. Food, fun & games.
🛏️ ⊙ ⛺ 🚌 ⊙ 🖥 ✉ **Budget Inn** 706.896.4121
⟨hiawasseebudgetinn.com⟩ $39.99S, $5EAP, pets $10, coin laundry. For guests, free ride to/from Dick's Creek Gap or Unicoi Gap (9 & 11am) Mar-Apr. Non-guest shuttles for a fee. **Three Eagles**

Satellite on-site. Accepts Visa/MC. Complimentary guest maildrop transfer to Franklin Budget or Sapphire Inn. Mail: 193 South Main Street, Hiawassee, GA 30546.

🛏🚈📶📧 **Mull's Inn** 706.896.4195 $45/up, no pets, shuttles by arrangement. Guest Mail: 213 N Main St, Hiawassee, GA 30546.

🛏⛄📶💻📧 **Holiday Inn Express** 706.896.8884 $79/up, accepts all major credit cards. Full hot breakfast included, indoor pool and hot tub, no pets. Mail: 300 Big Sky Drive, Hiawassee, GA 30546.

🛏🍴⛄📶💻 **Lake Chatugue Lodge** 706.896.5253 $89/up includes continental breakfast. **Chophouse Restaurant** on site.

🏃 **Three Eagles Satellite** (call Franklin store) Open Mar-Apr 8:30-1:30, 7 days. Footwear, hiking gear, clothing, fuel/oz, food, shipping services, free "bumps" to Franklin store.

🏃 **Mountain Roots Outfitters** 706.896.1873 M-Sa 11-5 Canister fuel, freeze-dried meals, small gear items.

🛒🍴🏪 **Ingles** 706.896.8312 7-10, 7 days. Pharmacy, **Starbucks**, deli, bakery, salad bar.

◼ **Goin' Postal** 706.896.1844 FedEx and UPS shipping 10-5 M-F.

85.4 Deep Gap, USFS 71
(3.7W) **Standing Indian Campground** (See Rock Gap)

106.1 Rock Gap
◣🏪🚻🚿 (1.5W) **Standing Indian Campground** 828.369.0442 or 828.524.6441. Campsites $16, open Apr 1 - Nov 30. Camp store (season is shorter) has small selection of foods.
🚌 **Macon County Transit** See entry pg. 18.

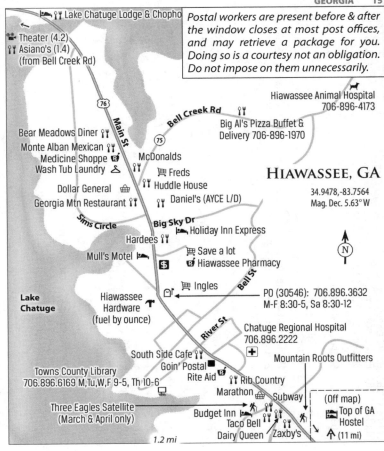

Postal workers are present before & after the window closes at most post offices, and may retrieve a package for you. Doing so is a courtesy not an obligation. Do not impose on them unnecessarily.

Lake Chatuge Lodge & Chopho
Theater (4.2)
Asiano's (1.4)
(from Bell Creek Rd)

Hiawassee Animal Hospital
706-896-4173

Bell Creek Rd
Big Al's Pizza Buffet & Delivery 706-896-1970

Bear Meadows Diner
Monte Alban Mexican
Medicine Shoppe
Wash Tub Laundry
McDonalds
Freds
Huddle House
Dollar General
Georgia Mtn Restaurant
Daniel's (AYCE L/D)
Main St

HIAWASSEE, GA
34.9478,-83.7564
Mag. Dec. 5.63°W

Sims Circle
Big Sky Dr
Hardees
Holiday Inn Express
Mull's Motel
Save a lot
Hiawassee Pharmacy
Ingles
Bell St
PO (30546): 706.896.3632
M-F 8:30-5, Sa 8:30-12

Lake Chatuge
Hiawassee Hardware (fuel by ounce)
River St
Chatuge Regional Hospital 706.896.2222
Mountain Roots Outfitters

South Side Cafe
Goin' Postal
Rite Aid
Rib Country
Towns County Library 706.896.6169 M,Tu,W,F 9-5, Th 10-6
Marathon
Subway
(Off map)
Top of GA Hostel
(11 mi)
Three Eagles Satellite (March & April only)
Budget Inn
Taco Bell
Dairy Queen
Zaxby's
1.2 mi

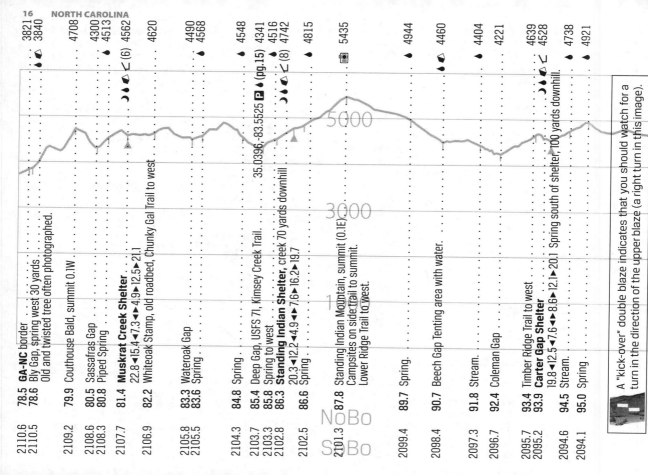

NoBo	SoBo	Feature	Elevation
2110.6	78.5	**GA-NC** border	3821
2110.5	78.6	Bly Gap, spring west 30 yards ◖ ◢	3840
		Old and twisted tree often photographed.	
2109.2	79.9	Couthouse Bald, summit 0.1W	4708
2108.6	80.5	Sassafras Gap	4300
2108.3	80.8	Piped Spring ◢	4513
2107.7	81.4	**Muskrat Creek Shelter** ◖◢◄⌐(6)	4562
		22.8◄15.4◄7.3◄►4.9►12.5►21.1	
2106.9	82.2	Whiteoak Stamp, old roadbed, Chunky Gal Trail to west	4620
2105.8	83.3	Wateroak Gap	4490
2105.5	83.6	Spring ◢	4558
2104.3	84.8	Spring ◢	4548
2103.7	85.4	Deep Gap, USFS 71, Kimsey Creek Trail. 35.0396, -83.5525 **P** ◢ (pg.15)	4341
2103.3	85.8	Spring to west	4516
2102.8	86.3	**Standing Indian Shelter,** creek 70 yards downhill ◖◢◄⌐(8)	4742
		20.3◄12.2◄4.9◄►7.6►16.2►19.7	
2102.5	86.6	Spring ◢	4815
2101.3	87.8	Standing Indian Mountain, summit (0.1E)📷	5435
		Campsites on side trail to summit.	
		Lower Ridge Trail to west.	
2099.4	89.7	Spring. ◢	4944
2098.4	90.7	Beech Gap Tenting area with water. ◖◢	4460
2097.3	91.8	Stream. ◢	4404
2096.7	92.4	Coleman Gap	4221
2095.7	93.4	Timber Ridge Trail to west	4639
2095.2	93.9	**Carter Gap Shelter** ◖◢◄⌐	4528
		19.8◄12.5◄7.6◄►8.6►12.1►20.1 Spring south of shelter, 100 yards downhill.	
2094.6	94.5	Stream. ◢	4738
2094.1	95.0	Spring. ◢	4921
2091.5	97.6	Betty Creek Gap. ◖◢	4300

A "kick-over" double blaze indicates that you should watch for a turn in the direction of the upper blaze (a right turn in this image).

NoBo	Description	SoBo	Elev
98.4	Mooney Gap, USFS 83, Ball Creek Rd, stream 0.1 north.	2090.7	4498
99.8	USFS 67, To bypass Albert Mt, take road 0.2W to parking area, then take side trail 0.2 from parking area back to AT north of summit	2089.3	4843
100.1	Albert Mountain, fire tower. ▣ 🅐	2089.0	5250
100.3	Albert Mountain bypass, west 0.2 to parking on USFS 67 🅿	2088.8	5052
100.7	Site of former Big Spring Shelter. Land reclamation underway, no camping	2088.4	4978
102.5	**Long Branch Shelter** (0.1W)(2012) four tent pads. ● ☽ 🍴 ⊂ (16) 21.1◀16.2◀8.6◀▶3.5▶11.5▶18.3	2086.6	4479
103.3	Glassmine Gap, Long Branch Trail 2.0W to USFS 67 ●	2085.8	4185

🅐 White blazes on the north side of trees are identical to the blazes on the south side. Make sure you are headed in the right direction, especially when sleepily leaving shelters in the morning.

NoBo	Description	SoBo	Elev
106.0	**Rock Gap Shelter** (1965) 19.7◀12.1◀3.5◀▶8.0▶14.8▶19.6. ☽●⊂(8)	2083.1	3772
106.1	Rock Gap, 0.7E to Wasalik Poplar and water. 35.094,-83.5226 🅿 (pg.15)	2083.0	3732
106.7	Wallace Gap, W. Old Murphy Rd, stream to north. ●	2082.4	3738
109.8	Winding Stair Gap, US 64. 35.1196,-83.548 🅿 ● (pg.18)	2079.3	3690
110.0	piped spring east of steps, **Franklin, NC** (10.0E) ●	2079.1	3727
110.1	Forest Service road, waterfall ●	2079.0	3812
110.4	Stream, campsite.	2078.7	4026
110.9	Logging road Swinging Lick Gap	2078.2	4100
111.8	Panther Gap	2077.3	4480
114.0	**Siler Bald Shelter** (0.5E steep), south end of shelter loop trail ● ☽●🍴⊂(8) 20.1◀11.5◀8.0◀▶6.8▶11.6▶17.4	2075.1	4769
114.7	Siler Bald, summit (0.2W), shelter (0.3E), north end of shelter loop trail ▣ ●🍴	2074.7	5001
115.2	Piped spring	2073.9	4481
115.5	Footbridge, stream	2073.6	4374
115.6	Wayah Crest Picnic Area (0.1W) 35.154,-83.5807 🅿 ● (pg.18)	2073.5	4258
115.7	Wayah Gap, Wayah Rd	2073.4	4180
116.1	AT skirts USFS 69.	2073.0	4352
116.5	USFS 69, meadow	2072.6	4480
116.9	Wilson Lick Trail, 0.2W to historic site.	2072.2	4630

NoBo

SoBo

109.8   Winding Stair Gap, US 64   *Franklin, NC* (10E)

⊨🏠⊛🔥⛺🛏🖵✉ **Haven's Budget Inn** 828.524.4403 ⟨www.budgetinnoffranklin.com⟩ $39.99S, $5EAP, $50 pet deposit. Bunkroom $20. Owner Ron Haven makes trips at 9 & 11am Mar-Apr to drop-off/pickup at Rock, Wallace & Winding Stair Gaps. Motel guests may call for free pickup Mar-Apr, and get 4pm shuttle around town for errands. Internet & coin laundry on-site. Print Smokies permit for free. Shower w/o stay $5. Mail: 433 East Palmer Street, Franklin, NC 28734.

🏠⦿🔥🛏🅿🛜✉ **Gooder Grove AT & Adventure Hostel** 828.332.0228 Bunks $23, private room $43, tent/hammock $13PP. If you pay $3 for Macon Transit it'll be deducted from prices above. Shuttles, slackpacking, section hiker parking. Lounge with movie library, many activities on-site, coupons for local discounts. Pet friendly. Mail: 130 Hayes Circle, Franklin, NC 28734.

🛏⦿🛜✉ **Sapphire Inn** 828.524.4406, $49.95S/D, $59.95 (up to four), pet fee $15. Prices good Spring only. Mail: 761 East Main Street, Bus 441, Franklin, NC 28734.

🛏🛜🖵✉ **Microtel Inn & Suites** 888.403.1700 Prices vary, cont. breakfast, pet fee $20. Mail: 81 Allman Dr, Franklin, NC 28734

🛏🔥🛜🖵✉ **Comfort Inn** 828.369.9200 10% thru-hiker discount, hot breakfast, laundry on-site. Call in advance if you need pet-friendly room. Mail: 313 Cunningham Rd. Franklin, NC 28734

🍴⦿**1st Baptist Church** Free Breakfast daily from Mar 14 - Apr 16.

🍺🖵🛜⦿ **Lazy Hiker Brewing Co.** Food Truck, computer/printer, pet friendly. Please sign taproom wall, ask about summit card. Spring/Summer M-Th 12-9, F/Sa 12-11, Su 12-6.

🔥⦿🚌🛜🖵✉ **Outdoor 76** 828.349.7676 ⟨www.outdoor76.com⟩ Open M-Sa 10-7. Specialty AT hiking store with lightweight gear, food, fuel & draft beer, right in center of town. Footwear experts with trained staff to deal with injuries and various foot issues. Spend $50 get a $10 gift card for local restaurant. 10% off for thru-hikers. Shipping services, free internet, ask about shuttles. No charge for Mail: 35 East Main Street, Franklin, NC 28734.

🍺🛜 **Rock House Lodge** taproom inside Outdoor 76, M-Sa 10-9. Beer on tap & wine. 10% hiker discount. Live entertainment.

🔥⦿🍴🛜🖵✉ **Three Eagles Outfitters** 828.524.9061 ⟨www.threeeaglesoutfitters.net⟩ Full-service outfitter serving AT hikers for over 20 years. 10% discount for thru-hikers & free shuttle to store from anywhere in town. Gear, footwear specialist, clothing, hiker food, white gas/alcohol/oz. Open M-Sa 9-6, Su 12-5. **Trail Tree Cafe and Expresso Bar** inside; free coffee & internet access for hikers. UPS/USPS shipping services. Mail: 78 Siler Rd, Franklin, NC 28734.

🚌 **Macon County Transit** 828.349.2222 Shuttles M-F from Feb 15-May 27. Stops: Winding Stair Gap 9:30, 12:30, & 3:30; Rock Gap 9:45, 12:45, 3:45. $3PP per ride. Multiple pick-up locations in town at 9, 12 & 3. Call day ahead to arrange pickup.

🚌 **Beverly Carini** 850.572.7352 shuttle range approx 100 mi.

🚌 **Chuck Allen** 828.371.6460, Springer to Fontana, call after 1pm.

🚌 **City Taxi** 828.369.5042 Rides up to 6pm, later by appt.

🚌 **Roadrunner Driving Services** 706.201.7719 where2@mac.com Long distance shuttles covering Atlanta to Damascus.

🚌 **Larry's Taxi Service** 828.421.4987, shuttles anywhere.

🐾 **Lenzo Animal Hospital** 828.369.2635 M-F 8:30-5:00, Sa 8:30-noon. Emergency clinic 828.665.4399.

ℹ **Visitor Center** (Chamber of Commerce) 828.524.3161 M-F 9-5 year-round, Sa 10-4 (May-Oct). List of hiker services & shuttles.

115.7   Wayah Gap, Wayah Rd.
124.4   Burningtown Gap, NC 1397
129.2   Tellico Gap, Otter Creek Rd.

🛏⊨⦿🍴🏠🔥🛏🅿🛜✉ **Nantahala Mtn Lodge** 828.321.2340 ⟨www.aquonecabins.com/at.html⟩ Run by 2010 thru-hiker "Wiggy". Open Feb 20 - Jun 1. Bunks $25PP (clean bedding, towels, soap, shampoo), private room $50D, cabin $100. Rides from/ to Burningtown, Wayah or Tellico $5PP per trip. Home cooked breakfast $6, 3-course dinner $12.50. Laundry $5. Short term resupply; candy, sodas, packaged meals, some gear. Slackpacking from Franklin to Fontana with reservations. Safe parking for section hikers. No pets. $3 surcharge for CC. Shipping from nearby village PO. Mail (guests only): 63 Britannia Dr, Aquone, NC 28781.

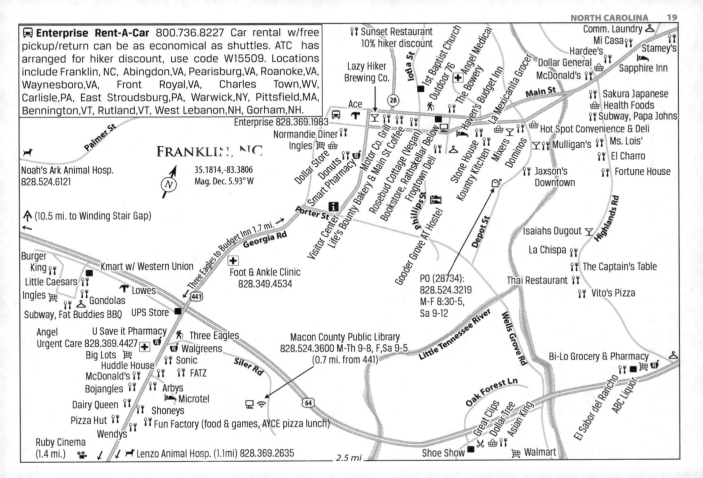

Enterprise Rent-A-Car 800.736.8227 Car rental w/free pickup/return can be as economical as shuttles. ATC has arranged for hiker discount, use code W15509. Locations include Franklin, NC, Abingdon,VA, Pearisburg,VA, Roanoke,VA, Waynesboro,VA, Front Royal,VA, Charles Town,WV, Carlisle,PA, East Stroudsburg,PA, Warwick,NY, Pittsfield,MA, Bennington,VT, Rutland,VT, West Lebanon,NH, Gorham,NH.

Enterprise 828.369.1983

FRANKLIN, NC
35.1814,-83.3806
Mag. Dec. 5.93°W

Sunset Restaurant
10% hiker discount

Comm. Laundry
Mi Casa
Hardee's
Stamey's
Dollar General
Sapphire Inn
McDonald's

1st Baptist Church
Angel Medical
The Bowery
Haven's Budget Inn
La Mexicanita Grocery
Main St
Iota St

Lazy Hiker Brewing Co.
Ace
Outdoor 76

Sakura Japanese
Health Foods
Subway, Papa Johns

Normandie Diner
Ingles
Dollar Store
Donuts
Smart Pharmacy

Motor Co. Grill
Rosebud Cottage (Vegan)
Frogtown Deli
Bookstore, Rathskellar Below
Life's Bounty Bakery & Main St Coffee

Stone House
Kountry Kitchen
Mixers
Dominos

Hot Spot Convenience & Deli
Mulligan's
Ms. Lois'
El Charro
Fortune House
Jaxson's Downtown

Noah's Ark Animal Hosp.
828.524.6121

Porter St
Visitor Center
Phillips St
Gooder Grove AT Hostel
Depot St

Isaiahs Dugout
La Chispa
The Captain's Table
Thai Restaurant
Vito's Pizza

(10.5 mi. to Winding Stair Gap)

Three Eagles to Budget Inn 1.7 mi.
Georgia Rd

PO (28734):
828.524.3219
M-F 8:30-5,
Sa 9-12

Highlands Rd

Burger King
Little Caesars
Ingles
Gondolas
Subway, Fat Buddies BBQ

Kmart w/ Western Union
Lowes
UPS Store
Foot & Ankle Clinic
828.349.4534

Macon County Public Library
828.524.3600 M-Th 9-8, F,Sa 9-5
(0.7 mi. from 441)

Little Tennessee River
Wells Grove Rd
Bi-Lo Grocery & Pharmacy

Angel Urgent Care 828.369.4427
Big Lots
Huddle House
McDonald's
Bojangles
Dairy Queen
Pizza Hut
Wendys
Ruby Cinema
(1.4 mi.)

U Save it Pharmacy
Three Eagles
Walgreens
Sonic
FATZ
Arbys
Microtel
Shoneys
Fun Factory (food & games, AYCE pizza lunch)

Siler Rd

Oak Forest Ln
Great Clips
Dollar Tree
Asian King
Shoe Show
Walmart

El Sabor del Rancho
ABC Liquor

Lenzo Animal Hosp. (1.1mi) 828.369.2635

2.5 mi

NoBo	Feature	Elev.
117.4	USFS 69, piped spring to east	4993
117.8	Bartram Trail to west	5236
118.0	0.1E to Wine Spring Rd, meadow, campsites 0.1E, water on west side of AT	5290
119.5	USFS 69	5188
119.7	Paved footpath to latrines and parking . . . . 35.179,-83.5622 P	5298
119.9	Wayah Bald, stone tower and paved footpath	5342
120.5	⚠ NoBos: AT to left, Bartram Trail to east, campsite, spring to west of trail	4887
120.8	**Wayah Bald Shelter**, east to shelter, west 0.2 to water	4712
	18.3◄14.8◄6.8◄▶4.8▶10.6▶15.5	
122.1	Licklog Gap	4440
123.5	Intersection with old roadbed and side trails, AT turns to east	4515
124.1	Stream.	4323
124.4	Burningtown Gap, NC 1397 . . . . 35.2223,-83.5622 P (pg.18)	4236
124.8	Spring	4511
125.6	**Cold Spring Shelter**.	4926
	19.6◄11.6◄4.8◄▶5.8▶10.7▶18.4 Trail to tentsites 0.1N on AT.	
126.3	Copper Ridge Bald, views	5080
127.5	Side trail 0.1E to Rocky Bald, views	5030
129.2	Tellico Gap, NC 1365 Otter Creek Rd . . . . . . 35.268,-83.5726 P (pg.18)	3850
130.6	Wesser Bald, east 40 yards to observation tower, panoramic views	4627
131.3	Spring-fed stone cistern on blue-blazed trail (0.1E)	4208
131.4	**Wesser Bald Shelter** (0.1W)	4092
	17.4◄10.6◄5.8◄▶4.9▶12.6▶21.7 Spring 0.1S on AT (at switchback).	
	Cables. Just north of shelter trail, Wesser Creek Trail to east.	
133.0	The Jumpoff, views	3940
134.7	Weak spring.	3008
136.3	**A. Rufus Morgan Shelter**.	2184
	15.5◄10.7◄4.9◄▶7.7▶16.8▶22.9 Shelter in view to east, stream west of AT.	
136.8	Multiple streams and footbridges.	1997

SoBo: 2071.7, 2071.3, 2071.1, 2069.6, 2069.4, 2069.2, 2068.6, 2068.3, 2067.0, 2065.6, 2065.0, 2064.7, 2064.3, 2063.5, 2062.8, 2061.6, 2059.9, 2058.5, 2057.8, 2057.7, 2056.1, 2054.4, 2052.8, 2052.3

NoBo / SoBo

NoBo	Feature	Elev	SoBo
137.3	US 19 & 74, **Nantahala Outdoor Center** · 35.3312,-83.5922 **P** (pg.24)	1732	2051.8
137.4	Side trail to bunkhouse	1771	2051.7
138.8	Wright Gap, dirt road	2403	2050.3
139.7	Grassy Gap, Grassy Gap Trail to west	2979	2049.4
140.0	Wade Sutton Memorial	3012	2049.1
141.3	Spring	3575	2047.8
141.9	The Jump-up, views to Nantahala Gorge	3814	2047.2
143.1	Swim Bald	4710	2046.0
144.0	**Sassafras Gap Shelter** (0.1W) (2002) Reliable spring front-right of shelter. 18.4◄12.6◄7.7◄▶9.1▶15.2▶21.9	4391	2045.1
145.2	Cheoah Bald	5062	2043.9
145.4	Bartram Trail to west	4911	2043.7
147.7	Locust Cove Gap, water to west	3642	2041.4
148.8	Simp Gap	3558	2040.3
150.7	Stecoah Gap, NC 143, · 35.3582,-83.7179 **P** ⛺ ◆ (pg.24) Sweetwater Cr Rd (paved). Hostel, B&B. Blue-blaze west 200 ft on NC 143, then left 250 ft on abandoned road to water.	3165	2038.4
151.7	Sweetwater Gap, start of "Jacob's Ladder"	3270	2037.4
152.3	Cliff, west 20 yards to view.	3868	2036.8
153.1	**Brown Fork Gap Shelter** Reliable spring to right of shelter. 21.7◄16.8◄9.1◄▶6.1▶12.8▶24.2	3813	2036.0
153.3	Brown Fork Gap	3600	2035.8
153.8	Brushnell Knob	3928	2035.3
155.2	Hogback Gap	3500	2033.9
156.0	Cody Gap, water 0.2W	3620	2033.1

Rocks that glitter are embedded with **mica**. North Carolina leads the nation in production of the mineral.

NoBo

SoBo

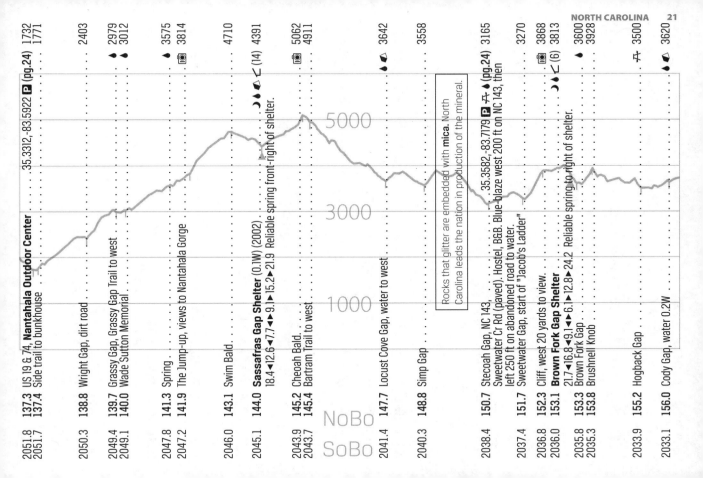

NoBo	SoBo	Feature	Elev.
2031.1	158.0	Yellow Creek Gap, stream	3255
2030.7	158.4	County Rd 1242, Yellow Creek Mountain Rd . . . . 35.4105, -83.7657 **P** (pg.25)	2954
2029.9	159.2	**Cable Gap Shelter**. 22.9◄15.2◄6.1◄►6.7►18.1►21.2 Stream in front of shelter.	2878
2028.5	160.6	Black Gum Gap	3403
2027.1	162.0	Walker Gap	3450
2026.8	162.3	Footbridge, stream	3266
2025.1	164.0	Spring	2287
2024.4	164.7	NC 28 (paved). **Fontana 28 AT Crossing, Fontana Dam, NC** (2.0W) . . . 35.4414, -83.7968 **P** (pg.25)	1756
2023.2	165.9	**Fontana Dam Shelter** "Fontana Hilton" (0.1E). 21.9◄12.8◄6.7◄►11.4►14.5►17.3	1853
2022.8	166.3	**Dam Visitor Center** . . . . 35.452, -83.8013 **P** **H** (pg.25)	1700
2021.7	167.4	Great Smoky Mountains National Park southern boundary . . . . (pg.28) NoBo reenter woods, SoBo join road. Benton MacKaye Trail northbound diverges from the AT and follows road to east. The BMT reconnects with the AT at Davenport Gap in approximately 100 miles (BMT miles).	1862
2019.7	169.4	Boulder jumble, throne-shaped rock	3314
2019.4	169.7	Stream.	3487
2018.3	170.8	Shuckstack, fire tower 0.1E.	3889
2017.9	171.2	Sassafras Gap	3667
2017.0	172.1	Birch Spring Gap . . . . Campsite west 100 yards down slope, tent pads, cables, spring unreliable.	3736
2015.1	174.0	Side trail 3.1W to Gregory Bald.	4443
2014.9	174.2	Doe Knob, NoBo follow NC/TN border; SoBo enter NC.	4520
2014.6	174.5	Mud Gap.	4325
2013.5	175.6	Ekaneetlee Gap	3842

❋ **Sarvis Tree** – Also called "serviceberry." Blooms with plentiful petite white-petaled flowers.

SoBo	NoBo	Feature		Elev
2011.8	177.3	**Mollies Ridge Shelter,** spring 24.2◄18.1◄11.4◄▶3.1▶5.9▶12.0	△ ⊂(12)	4586
2011.1	178.0	Devils Tater Patch.		4775
2010.1	179.0	Little Abrams Gap		4120
2009.7	179.4	Big Abrams Gap		4115
2008.7	180.4	**Russell Field Shelter,** spring 0.1W 21.2◄14.5◄3.1◄▶5.9▶14.6	◆ ⊂(14)	4348
2007.3	181.8	Stream.	◆	4747
2005.9	183.2	**Spence Field Shelter** (0.2E) on Eagle Creek Trail 17.3◄5.9▶2.8◄6.1▶11.8▶13.5 100 yards north, Bote Mountain Trail to west.	☽ △ ⊂(12)	4916
2005.5	183.6	Jenkins Ridge trail to east.		4948
2004.7	184.4	Rocky Top, views	📷	5440
2004.1	185.0	Thunderhead Mountain		5527
2003.4	185.7	Water to west.	◆	4964
2001.5	187.6	Starkey Gap.		4552
2000.8	188.3	Sugar Tree Gap.		4435
1999.8	189.3	**Derrick Knob Shelter** 12.0◄8.9◄6.1◄▶5.7▶7.4▶13.5 Reliable spring near shelter. Cables.	◆ ⊂(12)	4882
1999.5	189.6	Sams Gap, water 100 yards west, on left side of Greenbrier Ridge Trail	◆	4758
1997.4	191.7	Cold Spring Knob		5203
1997.1	192.0	Miry Ridge Trail to west.		4944
1996.9	192.2	Buckeye Gap.		4817
1994.1	195.0	**Silers Bald Shelter,** spring 75 yds right of shelter. 14.6◄11.8◄5.7◄▶1.7▶7.8▶15.1	◆ ⊂(12)	5453
1993.9	195.2	Silers Bald, survey mark on boulder, AT turns to east	📷	5607

NoBo
SoBo

5000 · 3000 · 1000

⚙️🍴⛺🚐📶 **Nantahala Outdoor Center** 888.905.7238 ⟨www.noc.com⟩ Complex w/lodging, food, gear & whitewater rafting. Non-guest coin-op showers Apr-Oct. In-season office hours 8-5. Reservations recommended, even for hostel. Walk-ins w/out reservation, check-in at General Store or **River's End Restaurant**. CC accepted. Campus wide WiFi.

Events at NOC: Southern Ruck Jan 15-18. **Trail Magic Festival** Apr 8-9 Movies, soda & popcorn Friday, thru-hiker dinner Sat. Live music, lightweight backpacking, cooking, & ATC clinics, fun & giveaways, gear reps for support & repairs. Extended restaurant & store hours.

🛏 Motel rooms $69.99/up. Prices higher mid-summer, weekends & holidays. Basic rooms do not have TV or phone. Rooms w/ more amenities can be economical for groups; ask about prices.

🛏 **Base Camp Bunkhouse** $39.99/2 persons, $79.99/4, $109.99/6, $139.99/8 includes shower, common area & kitchen.

🍴📶 **River's End Restaurant** (B/L/D); **Big Wesser BBQ/ Pourover Pub** Live music, opens mid-April.

🚶🚐🚐📧 **NOC Outfitters** Full line of gear, trail food, fuel/oz. Gear shakedowns. Open daily, extended hours in summer. Can print Smokies permits. Ask about shuttles. Thru-hikers 10% off 1 full price item. Mail: dated & marked "Hold for AT Hiker", 13077 Hwy 19W, Bryson City, NC 28713.

🏪 **Wesser General Store** Open Mar-Oct.

🛏⚙️🏪 **Nantahala General Store & Lodge** (0.9E) 828.488.4559 Camping Cabins (up to 4) with mini-kitchen $69.95, offseason (Nov-May) $49.95. 3-bedroom cabins (up to 8) $129. Free pickup/return for guests.

🚐 **Jude Julius** 828.736.0086 In Bryson City, NC. Shuttle range Hiawassee, GA to Newfound Gap.

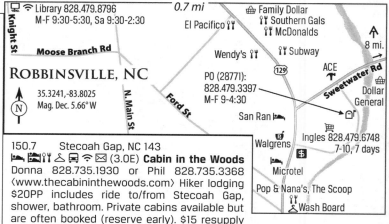

ROBBINSVILLE, NC

📺📶 Library 828.479.8796 M-F 9:30-5:30, Sa 9:30-2:30

Moose Branch Rd

35.3241,-83.8025 Mag. Dec. 5.66°W

Knight St

N. Main St

Ford St

El Pacifico 🍴

Wendy's 🍴

PO (28771): 828.479.3397 M-F 9-4:30

San Ran 🛏

Walgrens

Microtel

Pop & Nana's, The Scoop 🍴

🏪 Family Dollar 🍴 Southern Gals 🍴 McDonalds

🍴 Subway

ACE

Sweetwater Rd

Dollar General

Ingles 828.479.6748 7-10, 7 days

🚶⛺ Wash Board

0.7 mi

8 mi.

150.7   Stecoah Gap, NC 143

🛏🏠🍴⛺🚐📶📧 (3.0E) **Cabin in the Woods** Donna 828.735.1930 or Phil 828.735.3368 ⟨www.thecabininthewoods.com⟩ Hiker lodging $20PP includes ride to/from Stecoah Gap, shower, bathroom. Private cabins available but are often booked (reserve early). $15 resupply trip to Robbinsville. For-fee shuttles ranging from Amicalola to Hot Springs or to Knoxville/Asheville bus stations & airports. Family style breakfast $5, dinner $8, laundry $3/load. Cash or check only, no CC. Mail: 301 Stecoah Heights Rd. Robbinsville, NC 28771.

🛏⛺📶📧 (19.0W) **Buffalo Creek B&B** 828.479.3892 RobMason@rocketmail. com. Hiker rate (no drive-ins) $60S, $100D, $45PP for 3-4. Includes Stecoah Gap pickup/return, Robbinsville resupply stop, laundry, breakfast, hot tub, free home brew. Open Apr-Oct, call for availability in other months. Print Smokies permit here. Mail (guests only): 4989 W. Buffalo Rd, Robbinsville, NC 28771.

🛏⛺📶 (1.2E) **Appalachian Inn** 828.735.1792 Luxurious log cabin with great views $130-150 double, 1.2E from Stecoah Gap. Includes pickup/return from Stecoah Gap, laundry and full country breakfast. Additional charge for lunch/ dinner. Some rooms have jacuzzi tubs. Cash/check only.

Robbinsville, NC (8W from Stecoah Gap)

🛏📶 **San Ran Motel** 828.479.3256 Fridge & m'wave. No smoking, no pets.

🛏📶 **Microtel** 828.479.6772 Nov-Mar $64.95D $74.95(4), Apr-Oct $69.95D 79.95(4) rates $10 higher on wknds. Pet fee $50.

158.4 Yellow Creek Mountain Rd.

🏠⚫⛺🚆📶✉ **(1.8W) Creekside Paradise on the A.T.** 828.346.1076 Cynthia/Jeff,postandwilson@gmail.com. Room: $60PP, $45PP if 2+per room. Camping $10. Stays include pickup/return from Yellow Creek Gap, resupply trip to Robbinsville, laundry, hot tub, & free slackpack. Breakfast included w/room rental, $10 for campers. Dinner $15PP. Pickup/return from Stecoah Gap/Fontana $5, NOC $15. Pets welcome. Mail: 259 Upper Cove Rd, Robbinsville, NC, 28771.

164.7 NC 28 🚻 **Fontana 28 AT Crossing** Bathrooms, vending machines, GSMNP maps ($1), house phone to call for shuttle. Snacks & canned meats available from bait store on dock 0.1E.

🚌 **Fontana Shuttle** 828.498.2211 Shuttle $3PP each way between AT Crossing (Marina) or Visitor Center and Fontana Village. 8:30-6 daily Feb 15- May 15. Call for availability of rides outside these dates.

Fontana Village, NC (2W from NC 28) For all facilities contact: 800.849.2258 or 828.498.2211

🏠✉🖥📶🏨 **Fontana Lodge** Ask for thru-hiker rate $69(up to 4), no pets. Price higher on high-demand nights. Cabins $99/up pets welcome. Computer & printer in lobby can be used for Smokies permit. Mail ($5 non-guest fee): Fontana Village Resort, ATTN: Front Desk, 300 Woods Rd., Fontana Dam, NC 28733.

🚆🛒 **General Store** Grocery store, freeze-dried food, Coleman/alcohol/oz, canister fuel during thru-hiker season, small selection of gear items. Open Mar 10-Thanksgiving.

⛩🍴 **Fontana Pit Stop** Hot dogs, microwave fare, soda & coffee. Stocks hiker food & fuel when General Store closed. Open daily 9-5, later in summer.

🍴 **Mountainview Bistro, Wildwood Grill** Apr-Sept.

⛺ **Laundromat** 7 days, open year-round, detergent available at General Store.

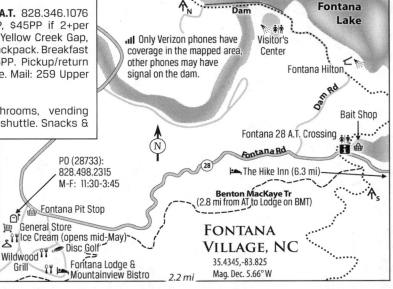

ıll Only Verizon phones have coverage in the mapped area, other phones may have signal on the dam.

PO (28733):
828.498.2315
M-F: 11:30-3:45

Fontana Pit Stop

General Store
Ice Cream (opens mid-May)
Disc Golf
Wildwood Grill
Fontana Lodge &
Mountainview Bistro   *2.2 mi*

FONTANA VILLAGE, NC
35.4345,-83.825
Mag. Dec. 5.66°W

Benton MacKaye Tr
(2.8 mi from AT to Lodge on BMT)

🚌 **Smoky Mtn Adventures** 828.736.7501, 828.479.9608 Licensed shuttle range Hiawasee-Hot Springs and 3 area airports. Slackpacking services.

166.3   Fontana Dam Visitor Center

🏨♿🚻🚿 828.498.2234 Soda machine outside, ice cream sold inside when open (9am-6pm daily May-Oct), free showers.

🏠⛺🚆 **(6.3E) The Hike Inn** 828.479.3677 hikeinn@graham.main.nc.us www.thehikeinn.com. A hiker-only service run by Jeff & Nancy Hoch since 1993. BY RESERVATION ONLY. We ask that all long distance hikers call us pre-hike so that we can better accommodate you. Open year-round for accommodations & transportation. Please call, e-mail or visit our website for more information, reservations and directions.

SoBo	NoBo	Elev	Feature
1993.7	195.4	5444	Welch Ridge Trail to east.
1992.4	196.7	5510	**Double Spring Gap Shelter** 13.5◀7.4◀1.7◀▶6.1▶13.4▶20.6. Best water 15 yards from crest on NC side. Water is also 35 yards down TN side.
1991.8	197.3	5778	Goshen Prong Trail to west.
1990.0	199.1	6590	Mt Buckley
1989.9	199.2	6518	Trail 0.5E to Clingman's parking area ⚠ NoBo: AT is left fork of this intersection
1989.7	199.4	6643	Clingmans Tower Path, paved path between tower and parking area
1989.6	199.5	6667	Clingmans Dome, tower to east (pg.28)
1989.0	200.1	6446	Mt Love
1987.7	201.4	5750	Collins Gap
1986.7	202.4	6187	Mt Collins
1986.3	202.8	5962	Sugarland Mtn Trail, **Mt Collins Shelter** (0.5W). 13.5◀7.8◀6.1◀▶7.3▶14.5▶19.4 Cables. Small spring 0.1 beyond shelter.
1986.0	203.1	5882	Fork Mountain Trail east ot Clingmans Dome Rd
1985.2	203.9	5628	Spring
1983.6	205.5	5273	Road Prong Trail, AT skirts Clingmans Dome Rd. 35.6094, -83.4467 P
1983.3	205.8	5437	Mingus Ridge, two wild hog containment bridges
1982.0	207.1	5045	Newfound Gap, US 441. 35.6112, -83.4257 P (pg.28) Large parking area, restrooms. No potable water. **Gatlinburg, TN** (15.0W)
1980.3	208.8	5821	Sweat Heifer Creek Trail to east
1979.8	209.8	6036	0.2W to Mt Kephart, 0.6W to Jumpoff (views), Blvd Trail 5.5W to Mt LeConte
1979.0	210.1	5935	**Icewater Spring Shelter** to east. 15.1◀13.4◀7.3◀▶7.2▶12.1▶19.8 Spring 75 yards north on AT.
1978.1	211.0	5522	South end of Charlies Bunion Loop Trail (0.1W)
1978.0	211.1	5475	North end of Charlies Bunion Loop Trail
1977.8	211.3	5420	Unmarked side trail 0.1W to original Charlies Bunion.
1977.6	211.5	5398	Dry Sluice Gap Trail to east
1977.0	212.1	5400	The Sawteeth
1976.7	212.4	5364	Porters Gap

NoBo

SoBo

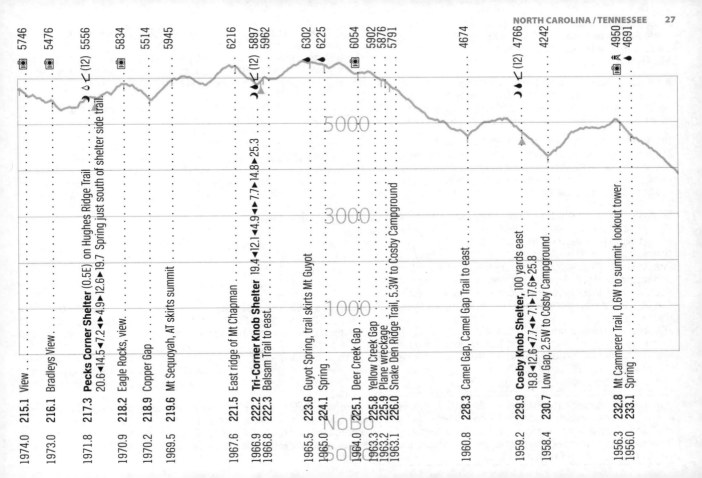

Elevation	NoBo	Feature	SoBo
5746	215.1	View	1974.0
5476	216.1	Bradleys View	1973.0
5556	217.3	**Pecks Corner Shelter** (0.5E) on Hughes Ridge Trail 20.6◄14.5◄7.2◄▶4.9▶12.6▶19.7 Spring just south of shelter side trail	1971.8
5834	218.2	Eagle Rocks, view	1970.9
5514	218.9	Copper Gap	1970.2
5945	219.6	Mt Sequoyah, AT skirts summit	1969.5
6216	221.5	East ridge of Mt Chapman	1967.6
5897	222.2	**Tri-Corner Knob Shelter** 19.4◄12.1◄4.9◄▶7.7▶14.8▶25.3	1966.9
5962	222.3	Balsam Trail to east	1966.8
6302	223.6	Guyot Spring, trail skirts Mt Guyot	1965.5
6225	224.1	Spring	1965.0
6054	225.1	Deer Creek Gap	1964.0
5902	225.8	Yellow Creek Gap	1963.3
5876	225.9	Plane wreckage	1963.2
5791	226.0	Snake Den Ridge Trail, 5.3W to Cosby Campground	1963.1
4674	228.3	Camel Gap, Camel Gap Trail to east	1960.8
4766	229.9	**Cosby Knob Shelter**, 100 yards east 19.8◄12.6◄7.7◄▶7.1▶17.6▶25.8	1959.2
4242	230.7	Low Gap, 2.5W to Cosby Campground	1958.4
4950	232.8	Mt Cammerer Trail, 0.6W to summit, lookout tower	1956.3
4691	233.1	Spring	1956.0

Great Smoky Mountains NP ⟨www.nps.gov/grsm⟩
Backcountry Info: 865.436.1297
Reservations: 865.436.1231

A permit is required and there is a backcountry fee -
$4PP per night or $20PP flat rate fee for up to 8 nights.
An on-line system allows you to pay and print a permit up
to 30 days in advance ⟨www.smokiespermits.nps.gov⟩

Shelters - The only near-trail campsite is Birch Spring,
otherwise hikers must stay in shelters. Reservations
required for section hikers. If the shelter is full, thru-hikers
must give up bunk space and tent in the vicinity of the
shelter. Hikers must use bear cables to secure food.

No pets - Dogs are not permitted in the park. Below are
kenneling options, vaccination records often required:
🐾 ✉ **Loving Care Kennels** 865.453.2028
⟨www.LovingCareKennels.com⟩ 3779 Tinker Hollow Rd,
Pigeon Forge, TN 37863. Pickup your dog at Fontana Dam
and return him/her to Davenport Gap. $350 for one dog,
$500 for two. Will deliver maildrops upon pickup/return.
Call at least 2 days in advance (preferably from NOC if
NoBo).
🐾 **Barks and Recreation** 865.325.8245
⟨www.barksandrecgatlinburg.com⟩ Does not offer rides,
but you can drop-off/pickup from 2159 East Parkway
Gatlinburg, TN. M-Sa 7am-8pm, Su 10-6.
🐾 **Standing Bear Farm** (see pg. 34)

⚠ Prices are subject to change, particularly at hotels.
Prices published in this guidebook were given in fall of
2015 and often represent a significant discount for hikers.
Businesses *intend* to keep these prices throughout
2016, but they are not obliged to do so.

199.5 **Clingmans Dome** 35.5572,-83.4939 🅿 🚻 Highest point on the AT.
Parking lot & restrooms 0.5E on a paved walkway. There are no sinks in
the restrooms. Gift shop near parking area sells drinks & snacks 10am-
6pm Apr 1-Nov 30. It's 7 mi. from the parking area to Newfound Gap on
Clingmans Dome Rd; the road is closed to cars Dec 1 - Apr 1.

207.1 Newfound Gap, US 441 (📶weak AT&T signal) *Gatlinburg, TN* (15W)
🛏☆🚗📶🖥 **Grand Prix Motel** 865.436.4561 ⟨www.grandprixmotel.com⟩
$39, coin laundry. Shuttle up to 8 to Newfound Gap $30; Clingmans Dome
$40. No Sunday shuttles. Mail: 235 Ski Mtn Rd, Gatlinburg, TN 37738.
🛏📶✉ **Microtel Gatlinburg** 865.436.0107 $44.95/up, cont B, pets $10.
Maildrop with reservation: 211 Historic Nature Trail, Gatlinburg, TN 37738.
🛏📶✉ **Motel 6** 865.436.7813 Reasonable rates. Pool, pets under 25 lbs
free, 26-50 lbs $10, 50+lbs $20. Trolley stops at the front door. All major CC.
Mail: 309 Ownby St, Gatlinburg, TN 37738.
🛏📶 **Days Inn** 865.436.5811
🛏📶 **Best Western** 865.436.5121
🚶🍽✉ **NOC Great Outpost** 865.277.8209 Open 7 days 10-9, (Jan-May 10-
6). Full line of gear, white gas/denatured/oz. Free showers & pack storage.
Mail: 1138 Parkway, Gatlinburg, TN 37738.
🚶 **The Day Hiker** 865.430.0970 Small shop w/shoes & fuel. Hours vary by
season.
🚐**Highlands Shuttle Service** (Ron McGaha) 423.625.0739 or
865.322.2752 mdron@bellsouth.net, shuttles from Standing Indian (NC)
to Damascus, VA. Also pickup/drop-off at Knoxville and Asheville airports
and bus stations.
🚐 **A Walk in the Woods** 865.436.8283 ⟨www.aWalkintheWoods.com⟩
Guides Vesna & Erik Plakanis resupply & shuttling (hikers & dogs). Shuttle
range Springer to Damascus (company based in Gatlinburg). Special thru-
hiker rates.
🚐 **Cherokee Cab** 828.269.8621 Short and long distance shuttles 24/7
covering all trailheads in the Smokies and nearby cities. Call for rates.
🚐 **Cherokee Transit** 866.388.6071 ⟨www.cherokeetransit.com⟩
■ **Roger Bailey, LMT** 865.250.0676 Special thru-hiker rate $60/hr
massage.

Cherokee, NC (21E) Large town, many services.

🛌🏕️🚐📞📶💻📧 **Microtel Inn & Suites** 828.497.7800 $65, higher on wkends, includes breakfast, free local/long distance phone. Coin laundry, pool. Adjacent supermarket, fast-food, shoe store. Mail: (Fed Ex/UPS only): 674 Casino Trail Cherokee, NC 28719.

237.9   Davenport Gap *(See map pg. 34)*, **Great Smoky Mountain NP**
🔋🏕️ (2.3E) **Big Creek Campground** 865.436.1261 $14/site, no showers or electricity. Open Apr 10 - Oct 31. Chestnut Branch Tr (2.0mi) connects campground to AT 0.1S of Davenport Gap Shelter.

239.8   I-40
🚐 **Highlands Shuttle Service** (Ron McGaha) 423.625.0739 or 865.322.2752 mdron@bellsouth.net, shuttles from Standing Indian (NC) to Damascus, VA, Knoxville and Asheville airports and bus stations.

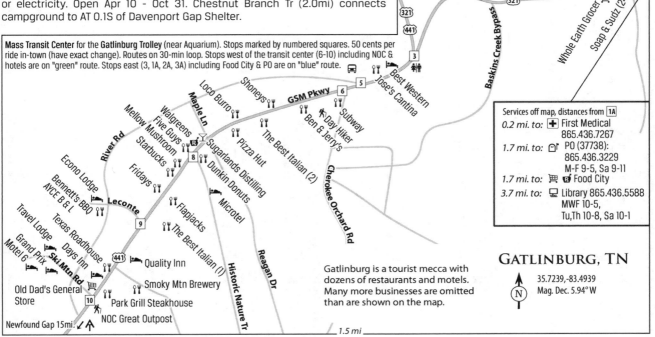

Mass Transit Center for the **Gatlinburg Trolley** (near Aquarium). Stops marked by numbered squares. 50 cents per ride in-town (have exact change). Routes on 30-min loop. Stops west of the transit center (6-10) including NOC & hotels are on "green" route. Stops east (3, 1A, 2A, 3A) including Food City & PO are on "blue" route.

Alamo Steakhouse
East Pkwy
Baskins Creek Bypass
321
441
Whole Earth Grocer
Soap & Sudz (24 hr)
1A
3

Shoneys
Loco Burro
Maple Ln
GSM Pkwy
Subway
Day Hiker
Ben & Jerry's
Jose's Cantina
Best Western
5
6

River Rd
Walgreens
Five Guys
Mellow Mushroom
Starbucks
Fridays
Sugarlands Distilling
Pizza Hut
The Best Italian (2)
Cherokee Orchard Rd
8

Econo Lodge
Bennett's BBQ AYCE B & L
Leconte
Texas Roadhouse
Dunkin Donuts
Microtel
Flapjacks
The Best Italian (1)
9

Travel Lodge
Grand Prix
Motel 6
Ski Mtn Rd
Days Inn
441
Quality Inn
Smoky Mtn Brewery
Reagan Dr
Historic Nature Tr

Old Dad's General Store
10
Park Grill Steakhouse
NOC Great Outpost
Newfound Gap 15mi.

Gatlinburg is a tourist mecca with dozens of restaurants and motels. Many more businesses are omitted than are shown on the map.

Services off map, distances from 1A
0.2 mi. to: ✚ First Medical 865.436.7267
1.7 mi. to: 🏠 PO (37738): 865.436.3229 M-F 9-5, Sa 9-11
1.7 mi. to: 🏪 Food City
3.7 mi. to: 💻 Library 865.436.5588 MWF 10-5, Tu,Th 10-8, Sa 10-1

GATLINBURG, TN
N
35.7239,-83.4939
Mag. Dec. 5.94° W

1.5 mi

NoBo	Mile	Description	Elev.
1954.1	235.0	Lower Mt Cammerer Trail, Cosby Campground (7.8W)	3468
1953.1	236.1	Chestnut Branch Trail, 2.1E to parking at Big Creek Ranger Station and north end of BMT. 35.7593,-83.1069 P (2.0E)	2876
1952.9	236.2	Spring	2823 ◆ ⌂(12)
1952.1	237.0	**Davenport Gap Shelter**, spring to left of shelter 19.7◄14.8◄7.1◄►10.5►18.7►23.6	2591
1951.2	237.9	TN 32, NC 284, Davenport Gap, cross road where pavement ends (pg.29) Great Smoky Mountains National Park northern boundary	1975
1950.1	239.0	Stateline Branch, multiple crossings	1698 ◆
1949.6	239.5	Pigeon River Bridge.	1373
1949.3	239.8	I-40 underpass	1439
1949.1	240.0	Stream (pg.29)	1569
1948.5	240.6	Green Corner Rd (gravel) hostel to west. (pg.34)	1788 ◆
1946.4	242.7	Painter Branch, cross branch to campsites.	2844 ◆◒
1946.1	243.0	Blue-blazed trail east across Painter Creek to campsite and spring. Stream.	3098 ◆
1945.5	243.6	Spanish Oak Gap, trail joins old roadbed	3470
1944.1	245.0	Snowbird Mountain, grassy bald, side trail 50 yards to FAA tower on summit.	4263 📷🖼
1943.3	245.8	Wildcat Spring uphill from trail	4065 ◆
1942.6	246.5	Turkey Gap	3648
1941.8	247.3	Spring	3034 ◆
1941.6	247.5	Deep Gap, **Groundhog Creek Shelter** (0.2E) 25.3◄17.6◄10.5◄►8.2►13.1►23.0 Stone shelter, reliable spring to left. Cables.	2911 ☾◆⌂(6)
1939.8	249.3	Spring downhill, east 30 yards	3563 ◆
1939.3	249.8	Rube Rock Trail to Hawks Roost	3853
1938.7	250.4	Brown Gap, USFS 148A	3500
1936.2	252.9	Cherry Creek Trail, water 0.3E	4341 ◆
1935.9	253.2	SR 1182, Max Patch Rd, stream to north.	4259 ◆
1935.6	253.5	Dirt road, west to parking, east to Buckeye Ridge 35.7963,-82.9627 P	4397
1935.2	253.9	Max Patch Summit (no fires) ⚠ NoBos turn right at north end of bald	4629 📷

"Max Patch" is a homophone that replaced the original name "Mack's Patch". The summit was cleared for cattle and is maintained as a bald.

NoBo
SoBo

SOBO	Mile	Feature	Elev.
1934.7	254.4	Stream.	4384
1934.3	254.8	Roadbed, Buckeye Ridge Trail to east.	4215
1933.7	255.4	Stream.	4121
1933.5	255.6	Water to east (signed)	4026
1933.4	255.7	**Roaring Fork Shelter,** water 0.1S or 0.4N, 7 tent pads, cables ☾ ● ◖ ⌂ (10) 25.8◄18.7◄8.2◄▶4.9▶14.8▶29.0	4019
1933.0	256.1	Footbridge, stream	3936
1932.2	256.9	Footbridge	3742
1931.9	257.2	Stream (many in area)	3639
1931.1	258.0	Two streams about 0.1 mile apart	3455
1930.3	258.9	Footbridge	3558
1930.0	259.1	Footbridge, stream	3496
1929.8	259.3	Lemon Gap, NC 1182, TN 107	3550
1929.1	260.0	Stream.	3951
1928.6	260.5	Walnut Mountain, grassy clearing	4293
1928.5	260.6	**Walnut Mountain Shelter** 23.6◄13.1◄4.9◄▶9.9▶24.1▶32.7 ☾ ● ◖ ⌂ (6) Walnut Mt tr. to west. Cables. Water 0.1 behind, campsite in field beyond water.	4245
1927.8	261.3	Kale Gap, campsite 125 yards north on AT	3700
1927.1	262.0	Catpen Gap, 0.1 east to campsite atop small knoll ◖	4130
1926.7	262.4	Streams	4262
1926.4	262.7	Unnamed gap.	4452
1926.1	263.0	Bluff Mountain	4686
1925.4	263.7	Spring 50 yards west. ●	4195
1924.8	264.3	Old roadbed, spring	3921
1924.5	264.6	Big Rock Spring located in ravine	3730
1923.9	265.2	Dirt road.	3407
1923.3	265.8	Brook with cascades ●	2978
1922.9	266.2	Old Rd	2710
1922.0	267.1	Garenflo Gap, Shut-In Trail to west . . . 35.8534, -82.8759 **P**	2500
1921.3	267.8	Taylor Hollow Gap, two footbridges, one over a stream ●	2639
1918.6	270.5	**Deer Park Mountain Shelter** (0.2E) water at gap west of AT ☾ ● ◖ ⌂ (5) 23.0◄14.8◄9.9◄▶14.2▶22.8▶29.6 Cables. Gragg Gap 0.1 north on AT.	2319
1917.8	271.3	Deer Park Mountain.	2571

NOBO
SOBO

NoBo	SoBo	Elev	Description
273.7	1915.4	1326	NC 209 + US 25/70, **Hot Springs, NC** . . . . . . 35.8895, -82.8323 P (pg.34)
274.1	1915.0	1339	French Broad River, US 25/70 bridge.
			NoBo turn east through gap in guardrail immediately after crossing river.
275.0	1914.1	1686	Lovers Leap Rock, several rock outcroppings, Silver Mine Trail to west.
277.0	1912.1	2130	Pump Gap, trail crossing
277.4	1911.7	2299	Springs
277.9	1911.2	2410	North intersection with Pump Gap Loop Trail
278.5	1910.6	2467	Pond with boxed spring, campsite.
278.8	1910.3	2604	NoBo: AT 0.3W on dirt road. Cross Mill Ridge to gravel road. (double-blazed oak tree). Go 0.1W on gravel road and reenter woods to east.
279.3	1909.8	2429	Stream.
279.6	1909.5	2270	Tanyard Gap, US 25/70 overpass. . . . . . . 35.91, -82.791 P
281.0	1908.1	3039	Piped spring
281.5	1907.6	3237	Roundtop Ridge Trail west 3.5 miles to Hot Springs (former path of AT)
282.0	1907.1	3532	Side trail 0.1W to campsite, Rich Mountain Lookout Tower, piped spring north on AT.
282.5	1906.6	3202	Spring
282.9	1906.2	2968	Hurricane Gap, northmost of two gravel road crossings.
283.2	1905.9	2983	Grave stone.
284.7	1904.4	3538 (5)	**Spring Mountain Shelter** 29.0◄24.1◄14.2◄▶8.6▶15.4▶21.7
			Water 75 yards down blue-blazed trail on east side of AT. Cables.
286.5	1902.6	2892	Deep Gap, Little Paint Creek Trail, west 200 yards to spring
287.9	1901.2	2757	Spring in ravine 30 yards west
288.5	1900.6	2223	NC 208, TN 70, Allen Gap, Paint Creek 0.2W
289.5	1899.6	2338	AT skirts gravel road
290.0	1899.1	2371	Log Cabin Drive, hostel to west. (pg.35)
			Private home in view to east, please do not trespass.

*Peter Barr ("Whippersnap" GA-ME 2010), author of **Hiking North Carolina's Lookout Towers**, recorded the track and landmarks that are the core of this book.*

SoBo	NoBo	Feature	Services	Elev
1895.8	293.3	**Little Laurel Shelter** 32.7◀22.8◀8.6▶6.8▶13▶21.9. Boxed spring 100 yards down blue-blazed trail behind shelter. Campsites west side of AT, south of shelter. Cables.	☽ ◖ ◢ ⊏(5)	3656
1894.5	294.6	Pounding Mill Trail to east. 0.2W to Camp Creek Bald Lookout-lower. Tower is beyond first cluster of buildings and catwalk is locked (no view).	🏠	4750
1893.7	295.4	Jones Meadow, spring 100 yards south.	◆	4450
1892.7	296.4	Trail west to Jones Meadow, 30 yards east to Whiterock Cliff.		4465
1892.5	296.6	0.1W to view from Blackstack Cliffs	📷	4496
1892.3	296.8	Bearwallow Gap, Jerry Miller Trail to east, Firescald bypass to west reconnects with AT 1.5 miles north. AT between bypass points is rocky and strenuous.		4432
1891.6	297.5	Big Firescald Knob	📷	4544
1890.7	298.4	Firescald bypass to west, reconnects with AT 1.5 miles south.		4182
1890.0	299.1	Round Knob Trail to west.		4284
1889.2	299.9	Fork Ridge Trail to east.	☽ ◆ ⊏(6)	4274
1889.0	300.1	Chestnut Log Gap, **Jerry Cabin Shelter.** 29.6◀15.4◀6.8◀6.3▶15.1▶25.2 Water opposite shelter. Cables.		4148
1888.2	300.9	Bald Ridge		4543
1887.8	301.3	Sarvis Cove Trail to west.		4569
1887.4	301.7	Howard C. Bassett Memorial, old roadbed before and after		4687
1887.1	302.0	Big Butt Mountain, summit to west, short bypass trail		4812
1886.7	302.4	Blue-blazed trail to west.		4674
1885.5	303.6	Shelton Gravesite to east.		4451
		⚠ AT northbound from Flint Gap to Rice Gap is compass south.		
1884.1	305.0	Cross stream	◆	3941
1883.4	305.7	Flint Gap.		3449
1882.7	306.4	**Flint Mountain Shelter,** water on AT 50 yards north of shelter. 21.7◀13.1◀6.3◀8.8▶18.9▶29.5	☽ ◆ ⊏(8)	3557
1882.6	306.5	Spring	◆	3564
1881.7	307.4	Spring	◆	3374
1881.3	307.8	AT + roadbed south end	◆	3280
1881.2	307.9	Spring	◆	3272
1880.6	308.5	AT + roadbed north end.		3309
1880.2	308.9	Devil Fork Gap, NC 212, hostel & resupply 2.5E 36.0105,-82.6086 🅿 (pg.35)	◆	3104
1879.7	309.4	Rector Laurel Rd, spring north on AT. 36.0065,-82.607 🅿	◆	2938
1879.3	309.8	Stream	◆	3205
1879.0	310.1	Cascade	◆	3399
1878.8	310.3	Stream	◆	3565
1878.2	310.9	Sugarloaf Gap.		4036
1876.8	312.3	Lick Rock		4541

NoBo
oBo

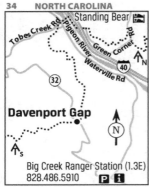

Standing Bear
Davenport Gap
Big Creek Ranger Station (1.3E)
828.486.5910

240.6   Green Corner Rd
Standing Bear Farm (0.1W) 423.487.0014 Open year-round, hosted by Maria. Bunk $20, Tenting $15PP, Cabin or treehouse $25. Reasonably-priced resupply, beer, cook-yourself meals. All stove fuel. Daypacks for slackpackers. Shuttles anywhere. Kennel service & dog shuttle for hike through Smokies, $250. Directions (see map): Green Corner Rd is unsigned gravel road 1.0 north of I-40, go west 200 yards to white farmhouse. Parking $5/car/day. Credit cards accepted. Mail: 4255 Green Corner Rd, Hartford, TN 37753.

273.7   NC 209, US 25/70 *Hot Springs, NC* 11.5% tax added to all Hot Springs lodging prices. **Trailfest** Apr 15-17; Friday dinner $5 at the Comm. Center, activities all day, Sat & Sun pancake breakfast $4. ✘How many AT diamonds are embedded in the sidewalk between Walnut St and Spring St?

Elmers Sunnybank Inn 828.622.7206 ⟨www.sunnybankretreatassociation.org⟩ Located across from Dollar General, at 26 Walnut St. Traditional thru-hikers $20PP private room, includes linens, towel & shower. Guests only can purchase breakfast $6 and dinner $12; gourmet organic vegetarian meals. No pets, no smoking, no credit cards. Historic Sunnybank Inn has offered hospitality to AT hikers since 1947. Staffed by former thru-hikers, the Inn offers an extensive library & well-equipped music room. Work exchange possible. Mail: PO Box 233, Hot Springs, NC 28743.

Hostel at Laughing Heart Lodge 828.206.8487 $20pp bunks, $25 semi-private, $30 single private, $45D private (one full-size bed). Open year-round. All rooms include morning coffee, shower & towel, movies, hiker kitchen, WiFi. Pets $5 in limted rooms. Tenting with shower $10S $15D (one tent). Shower only $5. Laundry $5 includes soap. Quiet time 10pm-7am. Lodge rooms $75-100 include continental breakfast, call 828.622.0165 to reserve. Mail: 289 NW Hwy 25/70, Hot Springs, NC 28743.

Iron Horse Station 866.402.9377 Hiker rate $65D. Restaurant, tavern and coffee shop. Serves L/D, and offers some vegetarian options. Live music Tu, Wed, Fri, Sat, Sun.

Little Bird Cabins 828-206-1487 ⟨www.littlebirdcabinrentals.com⟩ nataliedmarsh@hotmail.com Rental cabin sleeps 6, includes kitchenette. Please call/email in advance. Pet fee $15. Credit cards accepted. Open year-round.

HOT SPRINGS, NC
35.895,-82.8286
Mag. Dec. 6.43°W
No AT&T
PO (28743):
828.622.3242
M-F 9-11:30 & 1-4,
Sa 9-10:30
Hot Springs Medical Center
828.622.3245
Hillbilly Market
Dollar General
Smoky Mtn Diner
Elmer's Sunnybank Inn
Little Bird Cabins
Hostel at Laughing Heart Lodge
Mountain Magnolia Inn
Hot Springs Resort and Campground
Hiker's Ridge Ministries
Spring Creek Tavern
Creekside Court
Hot Springs BBQ
Bill Whitten Comm. Center
Wash Tub
Artisun Gallery
Iron Horse Station Inn and Restaurant
Spring Brook Cottages
French Broad River
Take Out Grill
Bridge St
Alpine Court
Welcome Center
Gentry Hardware
Bluff Mtn Outfitter & Natural Foods
Spring St
Andrews Ave
L&K's
Walnut St
Library:
828.622.3584
M,Tu,Th 10-6,
F 10-5, W,Sa 10-2
Restrooms, WiFi. Look for Earl Shaffer Memorial
Surpentine Ave.
0.7 mi

🛏🍴🛜 **Mountain Magnolia Inn** 800.914.9306 〈www.mountainmagnoliainn.com〉 Discount hiker rates $65 $95D when rooms available includes AYCE breakfast. Dinner Th-M open to all. Mail: 204 Lawson St, Hot Springs, NC 28743.

🛏🛜 **Creekside Court** 828.215.1261 〈www.lodginghotspringsnc.com〉 Su-Th $50S $75D, Fr-Sa $65S $90D, ask for hiker discount, pets allowed.

🛏🛁🚿🍴🛜 **Hot Springs Resort & Spa** 828.622.7676 〈www.nchotsprings.com〉 Tenting $24 up to 4. Camping cabins (no TV, no linens, common bath/showers) tax-included prices; $55.88 sleeps 5, $73.76 sleeps 8. Pets $10. Motel-style room (linens, TV, some with mineral water bath) $120-$300. Mineral water spa $15S before 6pm; 3-person rate $30 before 6pm, $35 after 6pm. Camp store carries snacks & supplies; **Take Out Grill** inside the campstore has outstanding food. Also offers massage therapy. Accepts CC.

🛏🚿🍴🛜 **Spring Creek Tavern** 828.622.0187 〈www.thespringcreektavern.com〉 Su-Th 11-10, F-Sa 11-11. 50 varieties of beer, special AT burger, outdoor deck, live music F-Sa nights. 3 rooms for rent, call for availability.

🛏 **Alpine Court Motel** 423.721.0450 Tax-included prices; $57S, $67D, $79(3). No CC.

🍴 **Smoky Mountain Diner** 828.622.7571 Hiker special 12 oz burger.

🍴🛜✉ **ArtiSun Gallery** 828.622.3573 Open 7 days 9-4. Coffee, baked goods, ice cream, AT hiker artwork. May use phone. FedEx/ UPS Mail: 16 S. Andrews Ave, Hot Springs, NC 28743.

ℹ🚶🛜 **Visitor Center** 828-622-9932 WiFi signal accessible outside after hours.

🚶🚿🛜🖥 **Hiker's Ridge Ministries Resource Center** 〈www.hikersridge.com〉 Open M-Sa 9-3, Mar 21 - May. Place to relax, coffee, drinks, snacks, restroom.

🚶🚐💲🚌🚿🛜🖥✉ **Bluff Mountain Outfitters** 828.622.7162 〈www.bluffmountain.com〉 daily 9-5 (seasonally 9-6) Full service outfitter, fuel/oz. Complete resupply, natural foods grocery & hiker foods. Free 20 min. computer/internet access, ask about WiFi. ATM & scale inside. Shuttles Springer-Roanoke and area airports & bus stations. SoBo hikers can print GSMNP permits. Ships UPS packages. Mail: (USPS) PO Box 114 Hot Springs, NC 28743 or (FedEx/UPS) 152 Bridge St.

◼ **Glenda Dolbeare, LMT** 603-204-7893, will come to **Laughing Heart** for massage services.

290.0   Log Cabin Drive (dirt/gravel road)

🛏🚐🛁🚿🍴🚂💥🅿🚌🛜✉(0.7W) **Hemlock Hollow Inn & Paint Creek Cafe** 423.787.1736 〈www.hemlockhollowinn.com〉 Open year-round. West on Log Cabin Dr. to paved Viking Mtn Rd. Bunkroom $25PP w/linens, $20 w/out. Upgraded bunkroom $30 (larger mattress, linens included). Cabin for couples w/linens $60. All rooms heated. Tent site $12PP. Pets $5. All stays include shower, free return ride to trail. Non-guest shower & towel for $5. Camp store stocked with long term resupply, some gear, cold drinks, foods, fruit, stove fuels. Cafe open 7 days in hiker season only; open off-season with call-ahead reservation. Shuttles available, slackpacking welcomed. Parking free for guests, fee for non-guests. WiFi available for a fee. Credit cards accepted. Mail (ETA mandatory): 645 Chandler Circle, Greeneville, TN 37743.

308.9   Devil Fork Gap, NC 212

⚠ AT northbound is due south; trading post is "trail east" (to the right for northbounders) but compass west.

🚐🛁🚿💥⛺ (2.5E) **Laurel Trading Post** 828.656.2016 Open 7 days 7-7 year-round. Bunkroom $25, tenting $10, shower included with stay, laundry $5, shower & towel w/o stay $5. Full kitchen & plenty of resupply. Free shuttle to store & return to trail. CC accepted.

317.6   Sams Gap, US 23

🍴 **Little Creek Cafe** (2.8E) 828.689.2307 M-Th & Sa 6-2, F 6-3.

🚿💲 **Wolf Creek Market** (3.3E) Open M-F 6-2, Sa 7-2.

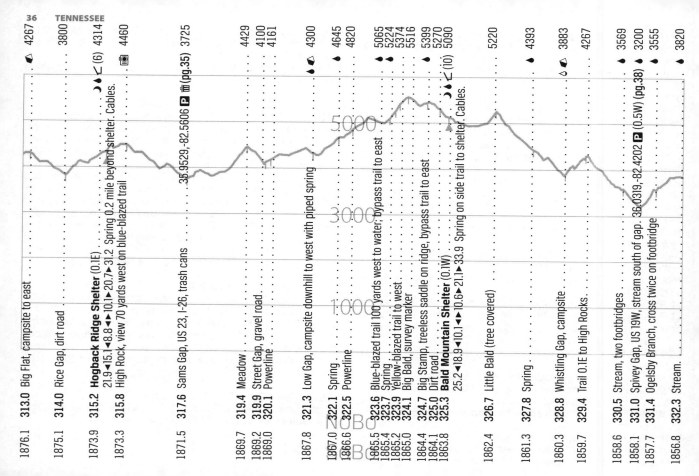

NoBo	NoBo	Mile	Feature	Elev
1876.1		313.0	Big Flat, campsite to east	4267
1875.1		314.0	Rice Gap, dirt road	3800
1873.9		315.2	**Hogback Ridge Shelter** (0.1E) 21.9◀15.1◀8.8▲10.1▶20.7▶31.2 Spring 0.2 mile beyond shelter. Cables.	4314
1873.3		315.8	High Rock, view 70 yards west on blue-blazed trail	4460
1871.5		317.6	Sams Gap, US 23, I-26, trash cans 35.9529,-82.5606 **P** 🏛 (pg.35)	3725
1869.7		319.4	Meadow	4429
1869.2		319.9	Street Gap, gravel road	4100
1869.0		320.1	Powerline	4161
1867.8		321.3	Low Gap, campsite downhill to west with piped spring	4300
1867.0		322.1	Spring	4645
1866.6		322.5	Powerline	4820
1865.5		323.6	Blue-blazed trail 100 yards west to water; bypass trail to east	5065
1865.4		323.7	Spring	5224
1865.2		323.9	Yellow-blazed trail to west	5374
1865.0		324.1	Big Bald, survey marker	5516
1864.4		324.7	Big Stamp, treeless saddle on ridge, bypass trail to east	5399
1864.1		325.0	Dirt road	5270
1863.8		325.3	**Bald Mountain Shelter** (0.1W) 25.2◀18.9◀10.1▲10.6▶21.1▶33.9 Spring on side trail to shelter. Cables.	5090
1862.4		326.7	Little Bald (tree covered)	5220
1861.3		327.8	Spring	4393
1860.3		328.8	Whistling Gap, campsite	3883
1859.7		329.4	Trail 0.1E to High Rocks	4267
1858.6		330.5	Stream, two footbridges	3569
1858.1		331.0	Spivey Gap, US 19W, stream south of gap. 36.0319,-82.4202 **P** (0.5W) (pg.38)	3200
1857.7		331.4	Ogelsby Branch, cross twice on footbridge	3555
1856.8		332.3	Stream.	3820

NoBo	Feature	Elev	SoBo
332.5	Devils Creek Gap, dirt road	3769	1856.6
334.7	Stream.	3036	1854.4
334.8	Stream.	2998	1854.3
335.6	Stream.	3047	1853.5
335.9	**No Business Knob Shelter** Reliable water on AT 0.3S of shelter. △ ⚑ ⌂ (6) 29.5◄20.7◄10.6◄►10.5►23.3►32.4	3171	1853.2
338.3	Temple Hill Gap, Temple Hill Trail	2850	1850.8
340.4	Views to Erwin	2648 📷	1848.7
342.1	River Rd, Unaka Springs Rd, 36.1042,-82.467 **P** (pg.38) **Erwin, TN** (3.8W) AT to east, crossing Nolichucky River on bridge	1673	1847.0
342.4	Railroad tracks	1706	1846.7
343.4	Side trail to Nolichucky Gorge Campground before footbridge	1729 ●(pg.39)	1845.7
343.8	Footbridge, stream	1790	1845.3
344.2	Footbridge, stream	1910	1844.9
344.5	Stream.	2008	1844.5
344.9	Footbridge	2101	1844.2
345.1	Footbridge	2217	1844.0
346.4	**Curley Maple Gap Shelter**, water south of shelter 31.2◄21.1◄10.5◄►12.8►21.9►30.4	3063	1842.7
346.9	Spring.	3219	1842.2
347.5	Stream	3290	1841.6
347.7	Stream	3302	1841.4
350.5	Indian Grave Gap, TN 395 36.1096,-82.3616 **P** ●(pg.39)	3350	1838.6
351.0	Water 0.1E outside of curve in road.	3704	1838.1
351.2	Survey marker (USFS 38I-28)	3745	1837.9
351.6	Powerline USFS 230, Red Fork Rd (gravel)	3767	1837.5

NoBo

SoBo

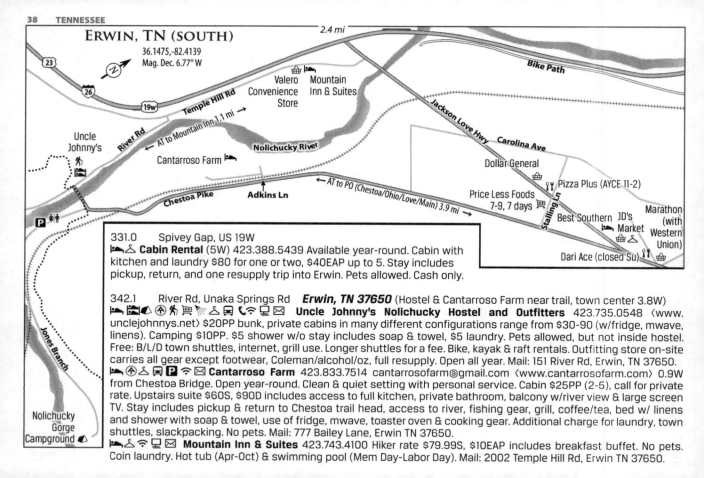

ERWIN, TN (SOUTH)

36.1475,-82.4139
Mag. Dec. 6.77° W

2.4 mi

Bike Path

23

26

19w

Temple Hill Rd →

Valero Convenience Store

Mountain Inn & Suites

Jackson Love Hwy

Carolina Ave

River Rd

AT to Mountain Inn 1.1 mi →

Uncle Johnny's

Nolichucky River

Cantarroso Farm

Dollar General

Pizza Plus (AYCE 11-2)

Price Less Foods 7-9, 7 days

Stalling Ln

← AT to PO (Chestoa/Ohio/Love/Main) 3.9 mi →

Chestoa Pike

Adkins Ln

Best Southern

JD's Market

Marathon (with Western Union)

P

Dari Ace (closed Su)

Jones Branch

Nolichucky Gorge Campground

331.0   Spivey Gap, US 19W
⛺ **Cabin Rental** (5W) 423.388.5439 Available year-round. Cabin with kitchen and laundry $80 for one or two, $40EAP up to 5. Stay includes pickup, return, and one resupply trip into Erwin. Pets allowed. Cash only.

342.1   River Rd, Unaka Springs Rd   Erwin, TN 37650 (Hostel & Cantarroso Farm near trail, town center 3.8W)
Uncle Johnny's Nolichucky Hostel and Outfitters 423.735.0548 ⟨www.unclejohnnys.net⟩ $20PP bunk, private cabins in many different configurations range from $30-90 (w/fridge, mwave, linens). Camping $10PP. $5 shower w/o stay includes soap & towel, $5 laundry. Pets allowed, but not inside hostel. Free: B/L/D town shuttles, internet, grill use. Longer shuttles for a fee. Bike, kayak & raft rentals. Outfitting store on-site carries all gear except footwear, Coleman/alcohol/oz, full resupply. Open all year. Mail: 151 River Rd, Erwin, TN 37650.
Cantarroso Farm 423.833.7514 cantarrosofarm@gmail.com ⟨www.cantarrosofarm.com⟩ 0.9W from Chestoa Bridge. Open year-round. Clean & quiet setting with personal service. Cabin $25PP (2-5), call for private rate. Upstairs suite $60S, $90D includes access to full kitchen, private bathroom, balcony w/river view & large screen TV. Stay includes pickup & return to Chestoa trail head, access to river, fishing gear, grill, coffee/tea, bed w/ linens and shower with soap & towel, use of fridge, mwave, toaster oven & cooking gear. Additional charge for laundry, town shuttles, slackpacking. No pets. Mail: 777 Bailey Lane, Erwin TN 37650.
Mountain Inn & Suites 423.743.4100 Hiker rate $79.99S, $10EAP includes breakfast buffet. No pets. Coin laundry. Hot tub (Apr-Oct) & swimming pool (Mem Day-Labor Day). Mail: 2002 Temple Hill Rd, Erwin TN 37650.

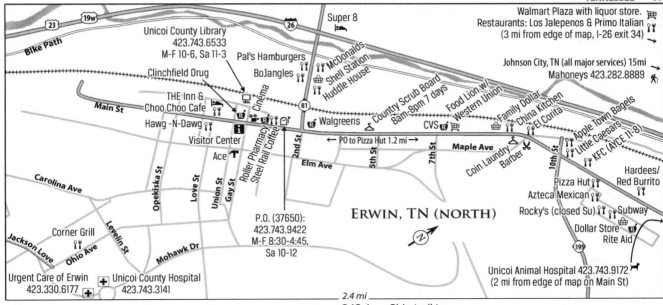

ERWIN, TN (NORTH)

2.4 mi

Best Southern 423.743.6438 $49.99S/D, pet fee $10, Mail (guests only): 1315 Jackson Love Hwy, Erwin, TN 37650.

Super 8 423.743.0200, $49.99S, $59.99D, $10EAP, max 4, includes b'fast, no pets. Mail: 1101 N Buffalo St, Erwin TN 37650.

THE Inn 423.743.0700 One luxurious room for up to 3 $122.50.

Primo (near Unicoi Walmart) BYOB.

Shuttles by Tom 423.330.7416, 910.409.2509 ⟨www.hikershuttles.com⟩ Owners Tom (10-K) and Marie (J-Walker) Bradford, licensed and insured. Shuttles to all area trailheads, bus stations, airports, outfitters, etc... from Springer-Harpers Ferry.

Baker's Shoe Repair 423-743-5421 Also repairs jackets & packs.

343.4   Side trail to:
Nolichucky Gorge Campground 423.743.8876, ⟨www.nolichucky.com⟩ Tent or bunkroom (when available) $10, includes shower. Cabin $80/up. Well-behaved pets okay. Small camp store. CC accepted.

350.5   Indian Grave Gap
(3.3W) **Rock Creek Recreation Area (USFS)** 423.638.4109 Tent site $12, Open May-Nov.
(5.4E) **Poplar Creek Farm** 828.688.1653 Prices range from $45D to $135 for 8, two night min., includes pickup/return. Laundry $2. Cable TV, common kitchen, some food items for sale on-site.

NoBo	Elev	Feature	SoBo
353.9	4323 [P] 36.1163,-82.3372	Beauty Spot Gap, clearing. Parking to west, trail parallel to USFS 230 from here north to Deep Gap.	1835.2
354.7	◆ 4115	Piped spring & campsites 100 yards west across USFS 230.	1834.7
354.8	4559	AT skirts Red Fork Rd.	1834.3
355.9	5180	Unaka Mountain, dense spruce forest.	1833.2
358.1	△ 3900	Low Gap, campsite, weak stream 0.1W.	1831.0
359.0	◆ 4122	Footbridge, stream.	1830.1
359.2	⊏(6) 3988	**Cherry Gap Shelter** 33.9◄23.3◄12.8◄▶9.1▶17.6▶22.8	1829.9
359.5	3908	Spring 120 yards on blue-blazed trail behind shelter to the left. Unmarked trail crossing.	1829.5
360.6	◆ 4337	Little Bald Knob, trail skirts summit.	1828.5
360.8	4286	Stream.	1828.3
362.3	3723 [P] 36.1433,-82.2332 (pg.42)	Iron Mountain Gap, TN 107, NC 226	1826.8
363.6	◆ 4023	Campsite, water 0.1W from signpost near north end of clearing	1825.5
364.7	4434	Rock pillar.	1824.4
366.4	4034	Greasy Creek Gap, campsite at gap, water 0.2W, (pg.42) **Greasy Creek Hostel** 0.6E	1822.7
367.2	△ 4134	Campsite, weak spring 0.1W.	1821.9
368.3	◆ ⊏(10) 4496	**Clyde Smith Shelter** (1976) (0.1W) 32.4◄21.9◄9.1◄▶8.5▶13.7▶15.6 Water 0.1 left of shelter, tent sites behind.	1820.8
369.5	4918 📷	Little Rock Knob, views to west, south of summit.	1819.6
369.8	◆ 4749	Stream. *Here north to Roan parking, NoBo trail bearing is compass south.*	1819.3
370.6	4375	Stream.	1818.5

✽ **Golden ragwort** – Small flower with yellow center and small floppy petals. "Field flower" that can create a sea of yellow

NoBo

SoBo

SoBo	NoBo	Description	Elevation
1817.4	**371.7**	Hughes Gap, TN 1330, Hughes Gap Rd.	4040 ◙ ♦
1817.0	**372.1**	Water 50 yards east	4288 ♦
1814.4	**374.7**	Ash Gap, campsite at gap, water 0.1E	5350 △ ◁
1813.0	**376.1**	Toll House Gap, saddle between Roan. 36.104,-82.1331 ◙	6212 ◙ 🏛 🅿 🚻
1812.9	**376.2**	High Bluff & Knob, 0.1E to parking, picnic area, open Mem day - Oct 1.	6134 ♦ ◁
1812.3	**376.8**	Chimney (remnant)	6193 ◁ (15)
		Roan High Knob Shelter (0.1E). Piped spring, highest shelter on AT.	
1811.5	**377.6**	30.4◀17.6◀8.5◀▶5.2▶7.1▶25.1 △ NoBo: watch for AT turning west off of the wide treadway	5784 ♦
1810.9	**378.2**	Several footbridges, streams	5525 ♦
1810.8	**378.3**	Carvers Gap, TN 143, NC 261 . 36.1068,-82.1106 🅿	5512 🅿 ♪
1810.1	**379.0**	Access road to summit (1.9mi) open approx. Memorial day - Oct 1	5813 ◙
1809.3	**379.8**	Round Bald, 30 yards east to summit, views	5790 ◙
1808.7	**380.4**	Jane Bald, big rock slab, views back to Roan Mtn	5891 ◙
1808.5	**380.6**	Side trail 0.5E to Grassy Ridge Bald and views, AT to west.	5864 ◙
		Springs	
1807.8	**381.3**	Campsite to west	5373 △ ◁
		Stan Murray Shelter	
1807.1	**382.0**	22.8◀13.7◀5.2◀▶1.9▶19.9▶29.5	5045 △ ⊂ (6)
		Spring on blue-blazed trail opposite shelter.	
1805.2	**383.9**	**Overmountain Shelter** (0.3E) Yellow Mountain Gap	4657 ◙ ♪ ♦ ⊂ (20)
		15.6◀7.1◀1.9◀▶18.0▶27.6▶36.2 Converted barn. Water on way to shelter.	
1804.2	**384.9**	Two intersections with old roadbed	5180
1804.0	**385.1**	Side trail 0.1E to Big Yellow Mountain	5271
1803.6	**385.5**	Little Hump Mountain, clearing	5459 ◙
1802.9	**386.2**	Piped spring, campsites to north and south	5177 ♦
1802.3	**386.8**	Bradley Gap, spring east 100 yards	4950 ♦
1801.7	**387.4**	Fence	5406 ♦
1801.4	**387.7**	Hump Mountain, Stan Murray plaque, NoBo have several false summits	5587 ◙
1800.6	**388.5**	Fence	5226
1800.0	**389.1**	Spring	5007 ♦
1799.7	**389.4**	Spring	4857 ♦
1799.0	**390.1**	Doll Flats, **NC-TN** border	4600 ♦ 🚻
1798.7	**390.4**	Stone steps, view.	4321 ♦
1798.4	**390.7**	Spring west of trail, massive stone wall.	4085 ♦

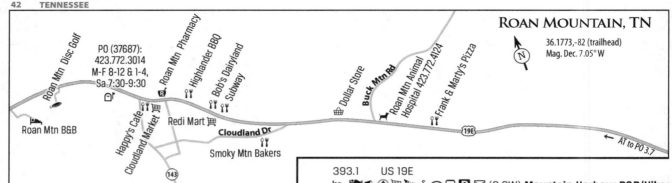

ROAN MOUNTAIN, TN

36.1773,-82 (trailhead)
Mag. Dec. 7.05° W

N

Roan Mtn Disc Golf

PO (37687):
423.772.3014
M-F 8-12 & 1-4,
Sa 7:30-9:30

Roan Mtn Pharmacy

Highlander BBQ

Bob's Dairyland
Subway

Roan Mtn B&B

Happy's Cafe

Cloudland Market

Redi Mart

Cloudland Dr

Smoky Mtn Bakers

143

Dollar Store

Buck Mtn Rd

Roan Mtn Animal
Hospital 423.772.4124

Frank & Marty's Pizza

19E

← AT to PO 3.7

_3.8 mi_

362.3 Iron Mountain Gap, TN 107, NC 226 **Buladean, NC** (4.1E)
🍴 **Mountain Grill** 828.688.9061 Cash only, M-Sa 11-8.

366.4   Greasy Creek Gap
🏠🛍️⊕🍴🏠🗽⚹☂🚗🅿🖥️✉ (0.6E) **Greasy Creek Friendly**
828.688.9948 All room prices include tax: $10PP bunkhouse,
$15PP/up indoor beds, $7.50PP tenting includes shower.
Shower without stay $3. Pets okay outside. Open year-round
(call ahead Dec-Feb), self serve during the Sabbath (sundown
Friday to sundown Saturday). Home cooked meals, including
vegetarian options. Limited kitchen privileges. Store of goods
for multi-day resupply including snacks, meals, Coleman/
alcohol/oz. Shuttles Hot Springs to Damascus. Parking $2/
night. Free long distance calls within US. Credit cards accepted.
Directions: take old woods road east (trail east, not compass
east), follow curve to the left, then take the first right. You
should be going downhill all the way. Hostel is first house to
your right. Mail: 1827 Greasy Creek Rd, Bakersville, NC 28705.

393.1   US 19E
🛏️🍴🛍️⊕🏠🗽⚹☂🚗🅿✉ (0.3W) **Mountain Harbour B&B/Hiker
Hostel** 866.772.9494 ⟨www.mountainharbour.net⟩ Hostel over barn
overlooking creek $25PP, semi-private king bed $55D, treehouse
$75D, includes linens, shower, towel, full kitchen, wood burning
stove, video library. Tenting with shower $10, non-guest shower w/
towel $4, laundry w/soap $6, telephone w/calling card. Breakfast $12
when available. B&B rooms $125-165 includes breakfast, separate
shower & fireplace, A/C, refrigerator, cable TV/DVD. Free white gas/
denatured alcohol. **General Store** on-site, open also to non-guests,
sells fuel canisters and full resupply. Slackpack/long distance
shuttles by arrangement. Secured parking $5/day or $2/day with
shuttle. Open year-round. Mail: (non-guests $5) 9151 Hwy 19E, Roan
Mountain, TN 37687.
          Roan Mountain, TN 37687 (3.5W)
🛏️⊕🗽🚗☂🅿 **Roan Mountain B&B** 423.772.3207
⟨www.roanmtbb.com⟩ Open year-round. Hiker rate $65S, $85D does
not include b'fast. Free pickup/return at Hwy 19E & 5pm town shuttle.
Pets okay, no alcohol, no smoking inside. Do-it-yourself laundry $5.
Some resupply items on-site. Shuttles & slackpacking Erwin to
Watauga Lake. Parking for section hikers. CC accepted.
    🍴☂ **Happy's Cafe** 423.772.3400 7am-3pm 7 days. Hikers who come
in for breakfast get ride (when staff avail) to 19E trailhead.

🍴 **Bob's Dairyland** 423.772.3641 daily 6am-9pm

🍴 **Smoky Mountain Bakers** 423.957.1202 Tu-Sa 8-8, fresh bread, wood-fired pizza.

🍴 **Frank & Marty's Pizza** 423.772.3083, closed Su & M.

🛒 🟥 **Redi Mart** 423.772.3032 M-Sa 8-10, Su 9-10.

🛒 **Cloudland Market** 423.772.3201 M-Sa 8-7.

Elk Park, NC 28622 (see services on map)

Newland, NC (7E, 19E to NC 194)

🛏🛜🖥 **The Shady Lawn Lodge** 828.733.9006, Thru-hikers get 10% off regular room rates, which are approx. $80D ($5 extra on weekends). Free pickup & return when driver is available. Laundry and restaurants nearby.

Banner Elk, NC

🛏🛜🅿 **Harmony Hostel** 828.898.6200 Comfortable semi-private bed $45PP, includes pickup/return from US 19E, resupply stop, morning coffee & toast. No smoking, no alcohol. Section hiker parking.

405.8 Upper Laurel Fork. (0.3W) Blue-blazed side trail to hostel originates at the hand-railed footbridge. Follow side trail along creek (drinking creek water is not recommended).

🛏🍴🛁🛜🍺⚒🔺🛜🖥✉ (0.2W) **Vango/Abby Memorial Hostel** 423.772.3450 vangoabby@gmail.com. Run by "Scotty", Trekkie, engineer, trail maintainer with over 14,000 trail miles. Open year-round with 24 hour advance call. Cash or paypal only. Bunkrooms with/without heat $10/$5 night, includes shower. "Astronaut" upper private room & deck, queen bed w/linens, heat, $20S/$30D. Free tenting. Privy only, no hiker toilet. Shower w/o stay $2. Slackpack special from 19E: $40S, $60D (2 nights lodging & 2 rides to 19E). Resupply available daily 4-8: beverages, pizza, B&J ice cream & stove fuels. Hike-in/out only; no yellow-blazers, no parking. No illegal drugs. Pets okay. WiFi, porch piano, guitar & fiddle. Maildrops held free if they do not require special trip to post office: PO Box 185, Roan Mtn, TN 37687.

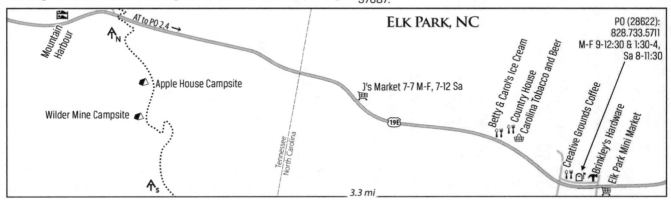

ELK PARK, NC

AT to PO 2.4 →

Mountain Harbour

Apple House Campsite

Wilder Mine Campsite

Tennessee
North Carolina

J's Market 7-7 M-F, 7-12 Sa

19E

Betty & Carol's Ice Cream

Country House

Carolina Tobacco and Beer

Creative Grounds Coffee

Brinkley's Hardware

Elk Park Mini Market

PO (28622):
828.733.5711
M-F 9-12:30 & 1:30-4,
Sa 8-11:30

3.3 mi

NOBO	SOBO	Feature	Elev.
1796.8	392.3	Stream	3268
1796.6	392.5	Wilder Mine Group campsite, piped spring	3111
1796.5	392.6	Apple House Tentsite	3052
1796.4	393.1	US 19E **Elk Park, NC** (2.4E) **Roan Mtn, TN** (3.5W) (pg.42)	2895
1795.8	393.3	Bear Branch Rd, streams north of road 36.1794,-82.0128 **P**	2900
1795.0	394.1	AT + Jeep Path, south end, stream	3219
1794.6	394.5	AT + Jeep Path, north end	3434
1794.4	394.7	Barbwire fence	3553
1793.6	395.5	Open ridge with views to east and west	3766
1793.1	396.0	Isaacs Cemetery	3600
1792.7	396.4	Buck Mountain Rd, water at church 0.1E 36.204,-81.9975 **P**	3501
1792.4	396.7	Campbell Hollow Rd, streams south of road	3396
1792.1	397.0	Footbridge at bottom of ravine	3408
1791.7	397.4	Footbridge, stream	3432
1790.6	398.5	Side trail 0.1E to Jones Falls	2985
1789.9	399.2	Campsite, Elk River 0.1E	2736
1789.5	399.6	Stream	2697
1788.5	400.6	Stream (cross twice)	2831
1787.7	401.4	Footbridge, stream	3020
1787.3	401.8	Mountaineer Falls to west	3110
1787.2	401.9	**Mountaineer Shelter,** water 70 yards from shelter 25.1◄19.9◄18.0◄▶9.6▶18.2▶26.8 ⊏(14)	3173
1786.4	402.7	Campsite to east	3244
1786.0	403.1	Slide Hollow Stream, footbridge	3348
1785.8	403.3	Roadbed	3520
1785.6	403.5	Walnut Mountain Rd	3603
1784.7	404.4	Footbridge, stream (many in area)	3453
1783.9	405.2	Bench, view	3509
1783.3	405.8	Upper Laurel Fork, side trail to hostel (pg.43)	3314
1782.6	406.5	Footbridge, stream	3445
1782.4	406.7	USFS 293 (gravel), waterfall south on AT	3457
1781.7	407.4	Spring	3341
1781.4	407.7	Spring	3378
1781.0	408.1	Footbridge, stream	3436
1780.6	408.5	Hardcore Cascades	3391
1779.8	409.3	Stream	3633
1779.3	409.8	Campsite, several streams and footbridges	3563

NOBO
SOBO

NoBo	SoBo	Feature	Elev
1777.7	411.4	Rock outcropping, views	3933
1777.6	411.5	**Moreland Gap Shelter** 29.5◄27.6◄9.6◄►8.6►17.2►24.4 Water source long way downhill across from shelter.	⌂(6) 3798
1775.3	413.8	Piped spring	3806
1774.8	414.3	Forest Service road.	3773
1774.0	415.1	Trail skirts White Rocks Mountain	3977
1772.7	416.4	Trail to Coon Den Falls 0.8E downhill	3419
1771.6	417.5	Stream.	2849
1771.1	418.0	Barn.	2594
1770.9	418.2	Dennis Cove Rd, USFS 50, hostels 36.2643, -82.1231 P (pg.47)	2491
1770.1	419.0	Footbridge	2427
1769.8	419.3	Switchback. Path straight ahead is high water bypass, reconnects at L.F. Shltr	2395
1769.6	419.5	Laurel Falls. Do not swim close to falls, there is a dangerous whirlpool	2120
1769.0	420.1	**Laurel Fork Shelter** 36.2◄18.2◄8.6◄►8.6►15.8►22.6	⌂(8) 2162
1768.6	420.5	Waycaster Spring, two footbridges over Laurel Fork	1983
1768.1	421.0	Side trail to **Hampton, TN** US 321 (1.0W) Hampton is west on 321. (pg.47)	1959
1765.5	423.6	Pond Flats, campsite, spring 0.1N on AT.	3693
1762.7	426.4	Campsite to east	2298
1762.4	426.7	NoBo: east on Shook Branch Rd	2019
1762.3	426.8	US 321, **Hampton, TN** (2.6W) 36.3019, -82.129 P NoBo: turn west after crossing 321 **Shook Branch Recreation Area**, picnic area, sandy beach. No Camping. (pg.47)	1990
1760.8	428.3	Griffith Branch	2040
1760.4	428.7	**Watauga Lake Shelter** 26.8◄17.2◄8.6◄►7.2►14.0►21.6 Water south of shelter on AT. Re-opened after two-year closure because of bear activity. Cook away from shelter and properly store your food (bear pole).	⌂(6) 2063
1759.2	429.9	Watauga Dam, AT on road for 0.4 mi south & north of dam, sparsely blazed..	1975

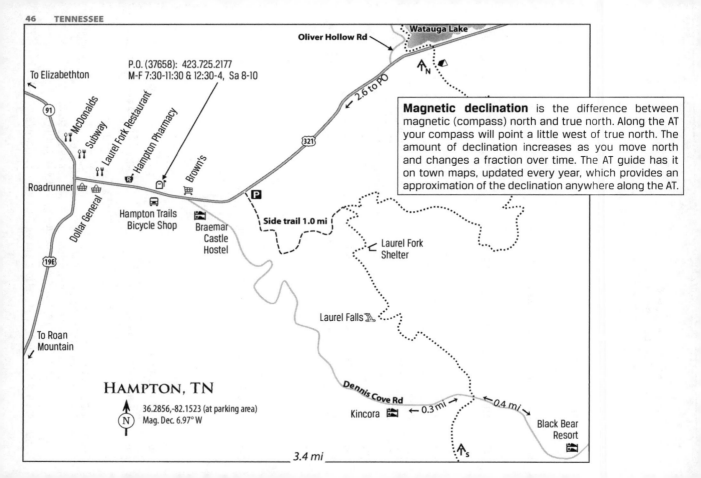

Watauga Lake

Oliver Hollow Rd

P.O. (37658): 423.725.2177
M-F 7:30-11:30 & 12:30-4, Sa 8-10

N

To Elizabethton

91

McDonalds

Subway

Laurel Fork Restaurant

Hampton Pharmacy

Brown's

2.6 to PO

321

Magnetic declination is the difference between magnetic (compass) north and true north. Along the AT your compass will point a little west of true north. The amount of declination increases as you move north and changes a fraction over time. The AT guide has it on town maps, updated every year, which provides an approximation of the declination anywhere along the AT.

Roadrunner

Dollar General

Hampton Trails
Bicycle Shop

Braemar
Castle
Hostel

P

Side trail 1.0 mi

Laurel Fork
Shelter

19E

Laurel Falls

To Roan
Mountain

Dennis Cove Rd

HAMPTON, TN

N 36.2856,-82.1523 (at parking area)
   Mag. Dec. 6.97° W

Kincora   ← 0.3 mi →   ← 0.4 mi →

Black Bear
Resort

S

3.4 mi

418.2 Dennis Cove Rd, USFS 50

🏠🛍️⟁⊛⁕⟑ ⟁🚐⊠ (0.3W) **Kincora Hiking Hostel** 423.725.4409 Cooking facilities, laundry, $5 per night suggested donation. No dogs, 3 night limit. Coleman/alcohol/oz. Long-time owner Bob Peoples is very active in trail maintenance; if you have interest in working on the trail, ask about opportunities. Maildrops (non-guest fee $5): 1278 Dennis Cove Rd, Hampton, TN 37658.

🏠🛍️⟁⊛⟖⟁🚐🖥⊠ (0.4E) **Black Bear Resort** 423.725.5988 ⟨www.blackbearresorttn.com⟩ Open Mar 1 - Oct 31. Clean and spacious creekside resort with bunkroom $18, upper bunkroom $25, tenting $10PP. Cabin $45/$60 for up to 4 people, $18EAP, 6-person max. Courtesy phone, computer, movies (DVD) and free morning coffee for all guests. Camp store with long-term resupply items (freeze-dried meals), snacks, sodas, pizza, beer, ice cream and food that can be prepared on-site with microwave/stove. Laundry $4. Fuel/oz & canister fuel. Pet friendly. CC accepted. Long and short distance shuttles. Parking free for section-hiking guests, $3/night for non-guests. Maildrops (non-guest fee $5): 1511 Dennis Cove Rd, Hampton, TN 37658.

421.0 Side trail to Hampton (1.0W) see **Hampton, TN** below
426.8 US 321

🛍️⟑ (0.8E) **Dividing Ridge Campground** 423.957.0821, 1219 US Hwy 321. Open year-round $15PP includes shower, charging stations, TV in pavillion, wash tub, morning coffee, once-daily town shuttle. No arrival after 9pm, pets okay.

Hampton, TN (2.6W)

🏪 🏠⊛🚐 ⟑ **Brown's Grocery & Braemar Castle Hostel** 423.725.2411 423.725.2262 Open year-round. Both operated by Sutton Brown; check-in at grocery to stay at the hostel or for shuttles. Store open M-Sa 8-6, closed Sunday. Store accepts CC; hostel is cash only. Pets okay and WiFi at hostel only.

🚐 **Hampton Trails Bicycle Shop** 423.725.5000 ⟨www.hamptontrails.com⟩ brian@hamptontrails.com

Elizabethton, TN (services 5 mi. north of Hampton)

🏠⟑🖥⊠ **Americourt** 423.542.4466 $59.95 plus tax, up to 4 in room, includes hot breakfast. Pets $20. Not available on race weekends. Mail: 1515 Hwy 19 East, Elizabethton, TN 37643.

🍴 **Little Caesars, Arbys, Lone Star Steakhouse**
🛒 **Food City, Ingles, Big Lots**
🎬 **State Line Drive-in** 423.542.5422 Open seasonally. Showings F, Sa & Su.

Bulter, TN

🏠⟁🚐⟑🖥⊠ **Iron Mountain Inn** 423.768.2446 ⟨www.creeksidechalet.net⟩ Open year-round. 10 miles from Hampton, but you can call for pickup or for directions. Fee for pickup/return. B&B room includes breakfast for $100S/$150D. Log cabin with hot tub under the stars, $50PP, no breakfast. CC accepted but with 5% fee. Free laundry. Shuttles from Watauga Lake to Damascus. Pets okay. Mail: c/o Woods, 268 Moreland Dr, Butler, TN 37640.

447.3 TN 91   1.9E to Sluder Rd hostel, 2.6E to Wallace Road campground, and 4.5E to **Shady Valley** (listed at US 421).

🏠⊠ (1.9E) **PB Farm** 423.739.3015 Walk in or call for ride. Mail for guests: 2293 Sluder Rd. Shady Valley, TN 37688

🏠🛍️⟁ (2.6E) **Switchback Creek Campground** 407.484.3388 Open Apr 1 - Oct 31. 1.8E to Sluder Rd, turn right for 0.2mi, then right on Wallace Rd. 0.6mi to 570 Wallace Rd, Shady Valley, TN 37688. Cabin for two $40, campsite $12+tax, cash only. Showers, laundry, call for ride at TN91/Low Gap. Pets allowed for camping only.

453.8 Low Gap, US 421

Shady Valley, TN 37688 (2.7E)

🏤 M-F 8-12, Sa 8-10, 423.739.2073

⟖🍴 **Shady Valley Country Store & Deli** 423.739.2325 May 1-Oct 31: M-F 6-8, Sa 8-8, Su 9-6. Closes earlier in winter. Deli serves burgers and sandwiches. Coleman fuel.

🍴 **Raceway Restaurant** 423.739.2499 Open 7-8 all days except W 7-2 & Su 8-2.

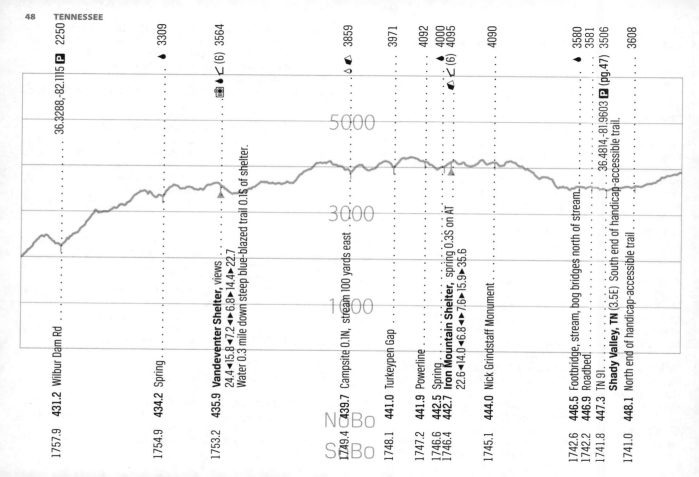

2250	36.3288,-82.1115 ⓟ	
3309	♦	
3564	🖼 ♦ ⌐ (6)	
3859	◊ ♠	
3971		
4092		
4000	♠	
4095	⌐ (6)	
4090		
3580	♦	
3581		
3506	36.4814,-81.9603 ⓟ (pg.47)	
3608		

Vandeventer Shelter, views
24.4◄15.8◄7.2◄►6.8►14.4►22.7
Water 0.3 mile down steep blue-blazed trail 0.1S of shelter.

Iron Mountain Shelter, spring 0.3S on AT
22.6◄14.0◄6.8◄►7.6►15.9►35.6

NOBo		SOBo
431.2	Wilbur Dam Rd	1757.9
434.2	Spring	1754.9
435.9	**Vandeventer Shelter,** views	1753.2
439.7	Campsite 0.1N, stream 100 yards east	1749.4
441.0	Turkeypen Gap	1748.1
441.9	Powerline	1747.2
442.5	Spring	1746.6
442.7	**Iron Mountain Shelter,** spring 0.3S on AT	1746.4
444.0	Nick Grindstaff Monument	1745.1
446.5	Footbridge, stream, bog bridges north of stream.	1742.6
446.9	Roadbed.	1742.2
447.3	TN 91.	1741.8
	Shady Valley, TN (3.5E) South end of handicap-accessible trail.	
448.1	North end of handicap-accessible trail	1741.0

NoBo	SoBo	Elev	Description
450.3	1738.8	♦ ⊏ (6) 4073	**Double Springs Shelter** . . . 21.6◄14.4◄7.6◄►8.3►28.0►34.5 Spring 80 yards left of shelter. Rich Knob to south, Holston Mtn Trail to north.
451.9	1737.2	3615	Locust Knob.
453.8	1735.3	36.5386,-81.9489 P ♦ (pg.47) 3384	Low Gap, US 421 Piped spring on south side of road. **Shady Valley, TN** (2.7E)
455.2	1733.9	3574	Low stone wall on east side of AT
455.7	1733.4	◣ 3542	Double Spring Gap, campsite
456.1	1733.0	◁ 3657	Weak, muddy spring east side of AT.
457.1	1732.0	3900	McQueens Knob, disused shelter 0.1N.
457.5	1731.6	36.5743,-81.932 P 3680	McQueens Gap, USFS 69.
458.6	1730.5	♦ ⊏ (5) 3780	**Abingdon Gap Shelter** . . . 22.7◄15.9◄8.3◄►19.7►26.2►38.5 Piped spring 0.2 mile behind shelter on blue-blazed trail.
462.6	1726.5	3667	Unnamed gap.
463.7	1725.4	3487	Backbone Rock Trail leads 2.3E to USFS recreation area.
465.1	1724.0	3210	TN-VA border.
466.7	1722.4	♦◣ 2768	Campsite, Spring 0.1E on blue-blazed trail
468.5	1720.6	36.636,-81.7896 P (pg.52) 1919	**Damascus, VA** (south), Water St, welcome sign.
469.0	1720.1	(pg.52) 1911	**Damascus, VA** (Laurel and Shady)

Leave campsites better than you found them; carry in carry out your own trash and any you find on the AT.

NoBo
SoBo

NoBo	Feature	Elev	SoBo
469.9	**Damascus, VA** (north), (pg.52) US 58, AT follows Virginia Creeper Trail for 0.4 mile.	1974	1719.2
470.4	Campsite to west	2339	1718.7
470.8	Spring	2505	1718.3
472.3	Iron Mountain Trail to west.	2913	1716.8
473.8	Beech Grove Gap Trail to west, streams and footbridges in area	2302	1715.3
474.3	Feathercamp Trail to west, stream, campsite.	2232	1714.8
474.7	US 58, Feathercamp Branch 36.6449, -81.7366	2200	1714.7
474.8	Stream.	2180	1714.3
475.2	Stream.	2205	1713.9
476.0	Footbridge, campsite.	2287	1713.1
476.7	Taylors Valley Trail	2407	1712.4
478.3	**Saunders Shelter** (0.2W) 35.6◀28.0◀19.7◀▶6.5▶18.8▶24.0 Reliable spring on right behind shelter and down road.	(8) 3359	1710.8
478.7	North shelter side trail	3344	1710.4
480.6	Beatree Gap Trail, 3.0W to Beatree Recreation Area	3050	1708.5
480.7	Pond, campsite.	3016	1708.4
481.3	Stream.	2978	1707.8
481.8	Footbridge, stream.	2913	1707.3
482.3	AT + Creeper Trail (south end) 36.6494, -81.6724	2688	1706.8
483.0	Luther Hassinger Memorial Bridge, AT + Creeper Trail (north end), VA 728.	2781	1706.1
483.4	Stream.	2813	1705.7
483.6	VA 859, Grassy Creek Rd (gravel)	2943	1705.5
483.8	Streams	3034	1705.3
484.8	**Lost Mountain Shelter** 34.5◀26.2◀6.5◀▶12.3▶17.5▶24.2 Water source on trail to left of shelter.	(8) 3381	1704.3
485.9	US 58, footbridge, stream 36.6398, -81.6654	3160	1703.2
486.2	Stream, campsite	3231	1702.9
486.7	Spring	3345	1702.4
486.9	Fence stile	3451	1702.2
487.2	VA 601, Beech Mountain Rd 36.6373, -81.6404	3526	1701.9
487.7	Fence stile, 50 yards north of road is sign for spring to west. Spring	3707	1701.4

NoBo
SoBo

SOBO	NOBO	Feature	Elev.
1699.4	**489.7**	Buzzard Rock, Side trail west to Whitetop Mtn Rd, summit of Whitetop Mountain..	5080
1698.6	**490.5**	Piped spring on east side of trail	5082
1698.5	**490.6**	Whitetop Mtn Rd, USFS 89 ♦ P	5087
		Campsites just after road.	
1697.8	491.3	Stream.	5172
1696.1	**493.0**	VA 600, Elk Garden, views, spring south on AT 36.6462,-81.5832 P 📷	4448
1695.8	493.3	View, bench to west	4582
1695.5	493.6	Fence, enter Lewis Fork Wilderness	4672
1694.0	495.1	Deep Gap, spring 0.1 south and north.	5015
1693.0	**496.1**	Brier Ridge	5215
1692.6	**496.5**	Spring	5191
1692.1	**497.0**	Side trail 0.5W to Mt Rogers, Virginia's highest peak at 5,729 ft.	5430
1692.0	**497.1**	**Thomas Knob Shelter** 38.5◀18.8◀12.3◀▶5.2▶11.9▶16.1	5413
1691.7	497.4	Campsite	5397
1691.0	**498.1**	Rhododendron Gap, Pine Mountain Trail to west	5398
1690.5	**498.6**	Wilburn Ridge Trail 0.3E to rock outcropping, view	5447
1690.2	498.9	Fatman Squeeze (rock tunnel).	5358
1689.5	499.6	Grayson Highlands State Park (south end), fence (pg.53)	4999
		Horse trail crosses AT. No tenting in GHSP.	
1688.2	**500.9**	Massie Gap, 0.2E to parking area 🚻 🏛 P	4890
1687.6	**501.5**	GHSP boundary, two fence stiles	4595
1687.0	**502.0**	Stream.	4420
1686.8	**502.3**	**Wise Shelter** 24.0◀17.5◀5.2◀▶6.7▶10.9▶20.1	4409
1686.7	502.4	East fork of Big Wilson Creek, footbridge, stream, fence stile	4390
		Grayson Highlands State Park (north end)	
1686.3	502.8	Horse trail	4357
1684.8	504.3	Bearpen Trail	4662
1684.2	504.9	Stone Mountain, views	4820
1683.6	**505.5**	The Scales livestock corral. 36.6697,-81.4872 P	4648
		First Peak Trail to east, Crest Trail to west.	
1682.4	506.7	Fence stiles, Pine Mountain Trail to west	4950

NOBO SOBO

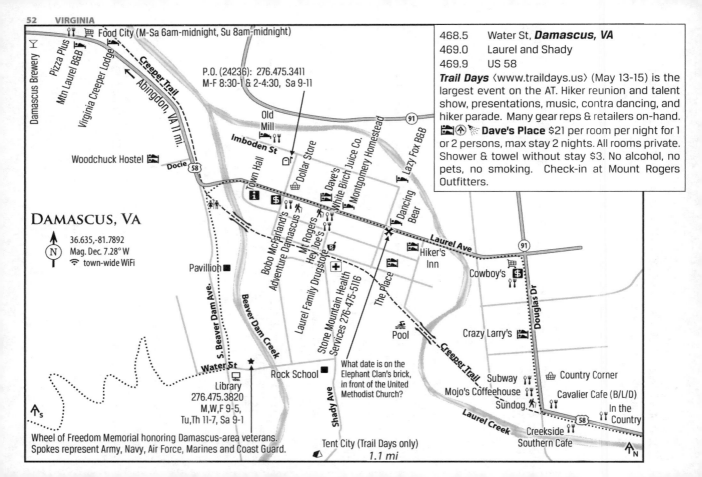

Food City (M-Sa 6am-midnight, Su 8am-midnight)

Damascus Brewery
Pizza Plus
Mtn Laurel B&B
Virginia Creeper Lodge

Creeper Trail

Abingdon, VA 11 mi.

P.O. (24236): 276.475.3411
M-F 8:30-1 & 2-4:30, Sa 9-11

Old Mill

Imboden St

Woodchuck Hostel

Docie

58

Town Hall

Dollar Store

Dave's
White Birch Juice Co.
Montgomery Homestead

91

Lazy Fox B&B

DAMASCUS, VA

N
36.635,-81.7892
Mag. Dec. 7.28° W
town-wide WiFi

Bobo McFarland's
Adventure Damascus
Mt Rogers
Hey Joe's
Laurel Family Drugstore
Stone Mountain Health
Services 276-475-5116

Dancing Bear

Laurel Ave

91

Pavillion

Hiker's Inn

Cowboy's

The Place

Pool

Crazy Larry's

Douglas Dr

S. Beaver Dam Ave.

Beaver Dam Creek

Creeper Trail

Subway
Mojo's Coffeehouse
Sundog

Country Corner

Cavalier Cafe (B/L/D)

Water St

Rock School

Library
276.475.3820
M,W,F 9-5,
Tu,Th 11-7, Sa 9-1

What date is on the
Elephant Clan's brick,
in front of the United
Methodist Church?

Shady Ave

In the Country

Laurel Creek

58

N

Creekside
Southern Cafe

Wheel of Freedom Memorial honoring Damascus-area veterans.
Spokes represent Army, Navy, Air Force, Marines and Coast Guard.

Tent City (Trail Days only)
1.1 mi

468.5   Water St, **Damascus, VA**
469.0   Laurel and Shady
469.9   US 58

Trail Days ⟨www.traildays.us⟩ (May 13-15) is the
largest event on the AT. Hiker reunion and talent
show, presentations, music, contra dancing, and
hiker parade. Many gear reps & retailers on-hand.

Dave's Place $21 per room per night for 1
or 2 persons, max stay 2 nights. All rooms private.
Shower & towel without stay $3. No alcohol, no
pets, no smoking. Check-in at Mount Rogers
Outfitters.

🛏️🖼️😊⛺📶 **Hikers Inn** 276.475.3788, $25 bunks, hostel private room $50. Rooms in house $75; $65/night for multi-night stays, tax included. Guest laundry $5. Run by Lee and Paul (2010 thru-hiker "Skink"). A/C in all rooms. Smoking outside, dogs allowed in hostel, cash or check only. Closed in winter.

🖼️🛒😊🦺 **The Place** 276.492.3983 Methodist Church-run bunkrooms, tenting, pavilion, showers with towel & soap. Suggested donation $7. Seasonal caretaker, please help to keep the bunkroom clean. No pets, alcohol or smoking anywhere on the premises. Two night max unless sick/injured. Check-in from 1-10pm. Open early Mar until mid-Nov (depending on weather). No vehicle-assisted hikers (except during Trail Days).

🖼️🛒😊🚗✉️ **Crazy Larry's** 276.274.3637 Hostel $20, tenting $10, Shower & morning coffee included with stay, hostel has A/C & heat. Breakfast $7, Laundry $8. Shuttles for a fee. No reservations. Mail: 209 Douglas Drive, Damascus, VA 24236.

🖼️🛒😊🚗🦺✉️ **Woodchuck Hostel** 406.407.1272. Open year-round. Bed w/linens $25. One private cabin $45S $55D. Teepee $15. Tent or hammock $10. Hot breakfast w/stay ($2 extra for tenter or hammocker). Laundry $5. Shower without stay $3. Kitchen privileges, common area, large yard, pavilion with gas grill. Dogs welcome. Alcohol/oz, cold drinks and snacks available. Free shuttles to Food City, other shuttles by arrangement. No drugs or Alcohol. Mail: P.O.Box 752, Damascus Va. 24236.

🛏️✉️😊⛺ **Montgomery Homestead Inn** 276.492.6283 $70/up includes laundry. No smoking, no alcohol, no pets. Open Mar-Oct, cash or check only. Mail (guest only): (USPS) PO Box 12, (FedEx/UPS) 103 E. Laurel Ave, Damascus, VA 24236.

🛏️📶✉️ **Dancing Bear B&B** 423.571.1830, $65-$140+tax. Cash or check only. Includes b'fast. No smoking, no pets. Mail (guest only): PO Box 252, 203 E Laurel Ave, Damascus, VA 24236.

🛏️✉️ **Lazy Fox B&B** 276.475.5838 $75/up includes tax & breakfast. Check or cash only. Open year-round. No pets, no smoking. Guest Mail: PO Box 757, 133 Imboden St, Damascus, VA 24236.

🛏️ **Mountain Laurel B&B** 276.475.5956

🛏️⛺📶 **Virginia Creeper Lodge** 276.492.1143 〈www.virginiacreeperlodge.com〉 $75/per room hiker rate (most rooms sleep 6). Shared kitchen, common area, satellite TV, pet friendly. Coin laundry. 702 W. Beaverdam Ave. Damascus, VA 24236

🖼️⛺📶 **Appalachian Folk School** 423.341.1843 〈www.warrendoyle.com〉 Non-profit run by Warren Doyle (17 AT traverses) offers work-for-stay weeknights (M-Th) only (2-3 hrs/night) for all hikers who have a spiritual/poetic connection to the trail. Open Mar-July and mid-Sept-Nov. Kitchen privileges, shower, wireless, laundry and rides to/from the AT between Rt. 321 (Hampton) and VA 603 (Fox Creek).

🛒🛒 **Food City** (0.5W on US 58) 276.475.3653, 7 days.

🎒😊🛍️🦺🚗🅿️✉️ **Mt. Rogers Outfitters** 276.475.5416 〈www.mtrogersoutfitters.com〉 Full service backpacking store, fuel/oz. Shuttles, parking for section hikers $5/day. Shower w/ towel $3. Mail: PO Box 546, 110 W Laurel Ave, Damascus, VA 24236.

🎒😊🛍️🦺🚗✉️ **Adventure Damascus** 888.595.2453 or 276.475.6262 〈www.AdventureDamascus.com〉 Catering to thru-hikers with backpacking gear, hiker foods, alcohol/Coleman/oz, other fuels, bike rentals, shuttles to area trailheads by arrangement, $3 showers, open 7 days year-round. USPS and UPS Mail: PO Box 1113, 128 W. Laurel Ave. Damascus, VA 24236.

🎒😊🛍️🚗✉️📶 **Sundog Outfitter** 276.475.6252 〈www.sundogoutfitter.com〉 Backpacking gear and clothing, repairs, hiker food, Coleman/alcohol/oz, other fuels, shuttles to area trailheads by arrangement, open 7 days a week. Mail: PO Box 1113 or 331 Douglas Dr, Damascus, VA 24236.

🖥️ **Library** 276.475.3820, M,W,F 9-5, T,Th 11-7, Sa 9-1, internet 1 hr.

499.6　　Grayson Highlands State Park

⛵🚗🦺　276.579.7092 Blue-blazed trail (0.5E) to parking; campground 1.5 mi. farther east on road. Park closed in cold weather; call ahead if possible. Camp store with courtesy phone, tent site w/ shower $21, shower only $5. May 1 - mid Oct.

NoBo	SoBo	Description	Elev
1680.6	508.5	Spring	4240
1680.1	509.0	**Old Orchard Shelter** 24.2◀11.9◀6.7▶4.2▶13.4▶23.2	4066
		Water 100 yards on blue-blazed trail to right. Privy 50 yards behind shelter.	
1679.3	509.8	Old Orchard Trail	3782
1678.4	510.7	Fox Creek, VA 603 . . . . 36.6966, -81.5066	3480
		Footbridges and streams 0.1 to north and to south.	
		100 yards east to parking and porta-potty.	
1676.8	512.3	Chestnut Flats, Iron Mountain Trail to west	4240
1675.9	513.2	**Hurricane Mtn Shelter** (0.1W)	3788
		16.1◀10.9◀4.2▶5.0▶19.0▶26.0 Creek and tentsites opposite side of trail.	
1675.3	513.8	Hurricane Creek Trail 0.3W to USFS 84, AT to east	3451
1674.8	514.3	Spring	3146
1674.1	515.0	Powerline, stream just north on AT	3208
1673.6	515.5	Stream.	3004
1673.1	516.0	Stream.	2968
1672.8	516.3	Dickey Gap Trail to **USFS Hurricane Creek Campground** (0.7W)	2941
		276.783.5196 Tent site $16, shower $2. Open mid Apr–Oct. Restroom & shower.	
1672.0	517.1	Comers Creek (drinking not advised), footbridge, cascades.	3310
1670.8	518.3	Dickey Gap, AT crosses VA 650 (gravel), east 50 yards to (pg.58)	3300
		VA 16 (paved Sugar Grove Hwy), **Troutdale, VA** 2.6 south on VA-16	
1669.9	519.2	Horse trail.	3485
1669.2	519.9	Bobby's Trail (blue-blazed), campsite and spring (0.2E)	3698
1666.7	522.4	**Trimpi Shelter** (0.1E)	2985
		20.1◀13.4◀9.2▶9.8▶16.8▶36.1	
1665.9	523.2	Fence stiles 0.2 apart, cattle graze in area, close gates behind you	2684
1665.5	523.6	VA 672 (gravel)	2608
1664.6	524.5	VA 670, South Fork Holston River . . . . . . 36.7631, -81.4939	2450
1663.6	525.5	Stream, intermittent	2602
1663.1	526.0	Campsite on west side of trail	2861

NoBo
SoBo

500
300
100

NoBo	SoBo	Feature	Coordinates / Notes	Elev
1660.7	528.4	VA 601 (gravel), limited parking	36.7994,-81.4575 P	3269
1659.2	529.9	Powerline		3318
1658.3	530.8	Footbridge, stream	●	3011
1656.9	532.2	**Partnership Shelter,** showers, tenting not allowed near shelter. ☽ ● ⊆ (16) 23.2◄19.0◄9.8▼►7.0►26.3►35.7 Can call for pizza from Visitor Center.		3242
1656.7	532.4	VA 16, Mt Rogers Visitor Center **Sugar Grove, VA,** 24375 (3.2E), **Marion, VA** 24354 (5.9W)	36.8814,-81.4204 P (pg.58)	3220
1656.0	533.1	VA 622		3270
1652.7	536.4	USFS 86, Glade Mountain Rd. Private road, permission required, may not be suitable for passenger cars.	36.8348,-81.3708 P	3650
1651.4	537.7	Glade Mountain		4113
1650.4	538.7	Spring	●	3513
1650.1	539.0	Stream	●	3287
1649.9	539.2	**Chatfield Shelter** 26.0◄16.8◄7.0▼►19.3►28.7►39.4	☽ ● ⊆ (6)	3173
1649.6	539.5	USFS 644 (dirt), streams to north and south		3046
1649.3	539.8	Footbridge, stream	●	2929
1649.0	540.1	Stream	●	2775
1648.3	540.8	Two powerlines	●	2698
1648.1	541.0	VA 615, Lindamood School Settlers Museum 0.1E (276.686.4401) parking available at farm. (Apr 1-Nov 15)	36.8708,-81.3577 P	2596
1647.6	541.5	VA 729		2537
1646.8	542.3	Fence stile		2708
1646.1	543.0	Middle Fork of the Holston River, footbridge, RR tracks just north of river	●	2436
1645.3	543.8	VA 683, US 11, I-81, **Atkins, VA**	(pg.59)	2420
1644.9	544.2	I-81 underpass		2419
1644.0	545.1	VA 617, Davis Cemetery	36.8973,-81.3691 P	2450
1643.4	545.7	Fence stile, end of field	●	2566
1643.2	545.9	Blue-blazed trail 0.1E to water at Davis Hollow	☽ ●	2539
1641.9	547.2	Davis Path campsite and privy.	☽ ●	2874

NoBo	Feature	Elev	GPS / Notes	SoBo
549.4	Gullion (Little Brushy) Mountain	3300		1639.7
549.9	Virginia Horse Trail	3185		1639.2
550.6	Crawfish Trail to east, campsite and stream on AT south of here	2600		1638.5
551.6	Stream	3024		1637.5
552.2	Spring	3347		1636.9
552.4	Tilson Gap, crest of Walker Mtn	3432		1636.7
553.2	Spring, fence	2948		1635.9
553.9	VA 610, Old Rich Valley Rd. Fence stiles here and to south	2700	(pg.59)	1635.2
554.7	Fence stile	2770		1634.4
555.3	VA 742, Holston River Bridge	2474		1633.8
555.8	Stream	2518		1633.3
556.3	VA 42, O'Lystery Pavilion (private, do-not use) Campsite just north of trail to parking area	2536	36.9833,-81.4064 P	1632.8
557.3	Brushy Mountain	3200		1631.8
558.5	**Knot Maul Branch Shelter,** water 0.1N on AT 36.1◄26.3◄19.3◄►9.4►20.1►33.6	2757	(8)	1630.6
559.2	Footbridge, stream	2597		1629.9
559.9	Lynn Camp Creek, footbridge, campsite	2400		1629.2
561.0	Lynn Camp Mountain	3035		1628.1
562.2	Lick Creek, footbridge	2268		1626.9
563.2	Stream	2318		1625.9
563.4	VA 625, USFS 222 (gravel)	2326	37.0226,-81.4262 P	1625.7
564.6	Stream	3096		1624.5
565.8	Chestnut Ridge, south end, start of clearing	3780		1623.3
566.1	Pond, spring at north end, best water source for Chestnut Knob Shelter	3896		1623.0

NoBo
SoBo

Elevation profile (NoBo / SoBo), with feature descriptions:

NoBo	SoBo	Feature	Coordinates / Notes	Elevation
1622.2	566.9	Views from open ridgeline	📷	4177
1621.3	567.8	Spring 0.1E on unmarked roadbed	△	4315
1621.2	567.9	**Chestnut Knob Shelter** 35.7◄28.7◄9.4◄►10.7►24.2►33.9 Concrete block shelter, fully enclosed with door.	☾ ⊂(8)	4393
1619.8	569.3	Walker Gap, dirt road 100 yards south	37.0544,-81.3789 P ◆	3520
1618.8	570.3	Garden Mountain, rock outcropping		3869
1615.0	574.1	VA 623	37.077,-81.3071 P	3867
1614.0	575.1	Davis Farm Campsite (0.5W)	△ ◖	3850
1611.4	577.7	Stream (unreliable)	△	2889
1610.5	578.6	**Jenkins Shelter,** creek 100 yards north on AT 39.4◄20.|◄10.7◄►13.5►23.2►37.7	☾ ◆ ◖ ⊂(8)	2400
1606.1	583.0	Laurel Creek, VA 615 (gravel) Intersection with Trail Boss Trail. Campsite just north of road.	37.1025,-81.2022 P ◆ ◖	2450
1604.2	584.9	Trail Boss Trail to west		3099

✳ **Mountain Laurel** – Shrub similar to the rhododendron. Grows five to ten feet high and blossoms with abundant cup-shaped white flowers.

518.3   Dickey Gap, VA 650, **_Troutdale, VA 24378_** (2.6E)

🥾🍴🚿🏕 (2.6E) **Troutdale Church Hostel** 276.677.4092 bunkhouse with microwave, tenting, shower. Pets outside, no alcohol. Mar15-Nov15, donations appreciated. Hikers welcome to service in hiker attire. Pastor Ken Riggins. NO maildrops; 62 Sapphire Lane, Troutdale.
🏪 **Fox Creek Store** 4mi. south on Rte 16, 276.579.6033 M-F 7-7, Sa 7-6.

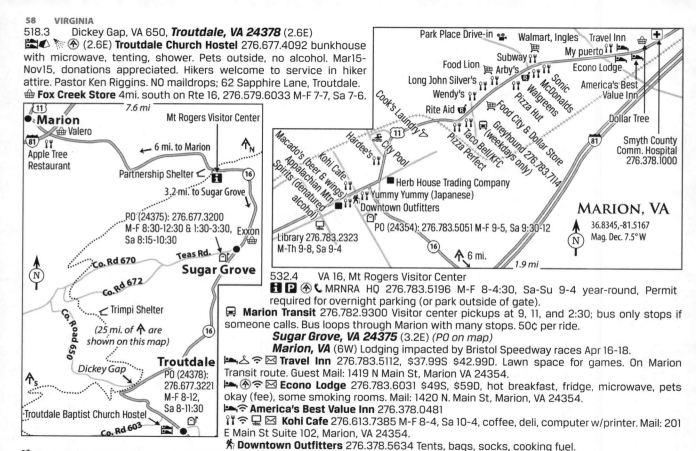

532.4   VA 16, Mt Rogers Visitor Center

🚻 🅿 ♿ 🔌 **MRNRA HQ** 276.783.5196 M-F 8-4:30, Sa-Su 9-4 year-round, Permit required for overnight parking (or park outside of gate).

🚌 **Marion Transit** 276.782.9300 Visitor center pickups at 9, 11, and 2:30; bus only stops if someone calls. Bus loops through Marion with many stops. 50¢ per ride.

Sugar Grove, VA 24375 (3.2E) (PO on map)

Marion, VA (6W) Lodging impacted by Bristol Speedway races Apr 16-18.

🛏🏕📶✉ **Travel Inn** 276.783.5112, $37.99S $42.99D. Lawn space for games. On Marion Transit route. Guest Mail: 1419 N Main St, Marion VA 24354.

🛏♿📶✉ **Econo Lodge** 276.783.6031 $49S, $59D, hot breakfast, fridge, microwave, pets okay (fee), some smoking rooms. Mail: 1420 N. Main St, Marion, VA 24354.

🛏📶 **America's Best Value Inn** 276.378.0481

🍴📶💻✉ **Kohi Cafe** 276.613.7385 M-F 8-4, Sa 10-4, coffee, deli, computer w/printer. Mail: 201 E Main St Suite 102, Marion, VA 24354.

🥾 **Downtown Outfitters** 276.378.5634 Tents, bags, socks, cooking fuel.

🍦 **Park Place Drive-In** 276.781.2222 Walk-ins welcome. Also has mini-golf, arcade, and ice cream shop. Open seasonally.

■ 🛜 **Herb House Trading Co.** 276.356.9832 Tu-Sa 10-6 Welcomes hikers. Ice cream and local baked goods.

543.8   VA 683, US 11, I-81 **Atkins, VA 24311** Intersection is between Atkins & Rural Retreat in the township of Groseclose.

🛏📐🖥📶🛜📨 **Relax Inn** 276.783.5811 $45S $50D, $5EAP (max 4), pets $10. Parking $3/day. Call for shuttle availability. Mail for guests (limit 2 boxes): Relax Inn, 7253 Lee Hwy, Rural Retreat, VA 24368.

🍴⊛ 🅿 📨 **The Barn Restaurant** 276.686.6222 M-Sa 7-8, Su 7-3, 16oz hiker burger, Sunday buffet 11-2, parking for section hikers $5/day, $25/wk. Mail: 7412 Lee Highway Rural Retreat, VA 24368.

🏠 🛒 **Shell Convenience Store** 24hr, ATM inside.

■ **Rambunny & Aqua** 276.783.3754 Shuttle referrals & other help.

🚌 **Skip** 276.783.3604 By appt, covers Damascus to Pearisburg.

🛏📶🖥📨 **Comfort Inn** (3.7W) 276.783.2144 Get hotel discount book coupon at Exxon or ask for hiker rate, usually $79.95D. Cont. breakfast. Guest Mail: 5558 Lee Hwy, Atkins, VA 24311.

553.9   VA 610, Old Rich Valley Rd

🛏📐⊛📐🏠🅿 **Quarter Way Inn** (0.8W) 276.522.4603 tina@quarterwayinn.com ⟨www.quarterwayinn.com⟩ Renovated 1910 farmhouse, run by 2009 thru-hiker Tina (Chunky). $28 suggested donation includes bunk, shower, laundry, phone, movie library, morning coffee & cereal. Tenting $17 includes same. Resupply (snacks, fuel, mountain house, pasta sides, oatmeal, etc.), pizza, sodas & ice cream. NoBo slackpacking often available from Partnership Shelter, Settler's Museum, or The Barn (Atkins) – call in advance. No drugs, alcohol, shenanigans. Parking $3/day. Open April-June, but closed from May 11-18.

589.9   US 52, North Scenic Hwy, **Bland, VA 24315** (3E to PO or Citgo, 4E to hotel & restaurants)

🏚 M-F 8:30-11:30 & 12-4, Sa 9 -11, 276.688.3751

🛏📶📨 **Big Walker Motel** 276.688.3331 $64.33(1-2), $69(3-4), pets okay. Fridge & microwave. Guest Mail: (UPS) 70 Skyview Lane, Bland VA 24315, (USPS) PO Box 155, Bland VA 24315.

🍴 **Subway, Dairy Queen**

🛒 **Grants Supermarket** 276.688.0314 M-Sa 8-8, Su 10-6

🏠🍴📞🛒 **Citgo, Bland Square Grill** 276.688.3851 Open 7 days 6:30-7 year-round. Groceries, Canister fuel & Heet, Grill serves B/L/D.

🏠 **Dollar General** 7 days 8-10

➕ **Bland Family Clinic** 276.688.0500 M 10-6, Tu 11-7, Th 9-5, F 10-2. Call ahead: sometimes closes early.

🖥 **Bland County Library** 276.688.3737 M,W,F,Sa 10-4:30, T,Th 10-7:30, 697 Main Street.

🚌 **Bubba's Shuttles** 276.266.6147 barnes.james43@yahoo.com Shuttles from Damascus to Pearisburg & Roanoke Airport.

Bastian, VA 24314 (3W)

🏚 M-F 8-12, Sa 9:15-11:15, 276.688.4631

🍴 **Pizza Plus** 276.688.3332 Su-Th 11am-9pm, F-Sa 11am-10pm.🛒 **Kangaroo Express** 276.488.4363 24 hours, ATM.

💊 **Bland Pharmacy** 276.688.4204 M,W-F 9-5, Tu 9-8, Sa 9-12.

➕ **Bland County Medical Clinic** 276.688.4331 M 8-6, Tu-Th 8-8, F 8-5, 12301 Grapfield Rd. ⟨www.blandclinic.com⟩

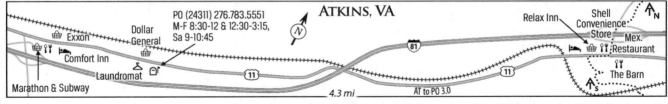

ATKINS, VA

PO (24311) 276.783.5551 M-F 8:30-12 & 12:30-3:15, Sa 9-10:45

Exxon · Dollar General · Comfort Inn · Laundromat · Marathon & Subway

Relax Inn · Shell Convenience Store · Mex. Restaurant · The Barn

4.3 mi · AT to PO 3.0

SoBo	NoBo	Feature	Elev
1602.2	586.9	Views to west.	2996
1601.3	587.8	Powerline	2721
1599.8	589.3	AT on gravel road from here north to US 52	3088
1599.2	589.9	US 52 (North Scenic Hwy), **Bland, VA** (2.5E), **Bastian, VA** (3W) (pg.59)	2905
1598.8	590.3	AT crosses over I-77 on VA 612.	2780
1598.4	590.7	VA 612 parking, Kimberling Creek, drinking discouraged . 37.1389,-81.1266 **P** ◊	2600
1597.0	592.1	**Helveys Mill Shelter** (0.3E). 33.6◄24.2◄13.5◄▶9.7▶24.2▶33.7 Water source 0.3 mile down switch-backed trail in front of shelter.	☽♦∈(6) 3121
1590.4	598.7	VA 611 (gravel). 37.1453,-81.0094 **P** ◊	2820
1590.1	599.0	Stream, unreliable.	2679
1589.0	600.1	Brushy Mountain	3101
1587.3	601.8	**Jenny Knob Shelter,** spring near shelter. 33.9◄23.2◄9.7◄▶14.5▶24.0▶39.7	☽♦∈(6) 2668
1586.6	602.5	Stream.	2328
1586.3	602.8	Stream, campsite.	2264
1586.1	603.0	Lickskillet Hollow, VA 608, footbridge 37.1569,-80.9614 **P** ♦	2200
1584.9	604.2	Powerline	2771

❋ **Rhododendron** – 10-15 foot tall shrubs with broad waxy leaves. Grows in thick stands that the AT sometimes tunnels through. Flowers grow in large bouquets of ruffled pink.

5000

3000

1000

NoBo
SoBo

NOBO	Description	Elev.	SOBO
608.2	Kimberling Creek, suspension bridge	2025	1580.9
608.3	VA 606, parking to east . . . 37.1757, -80.9083 P (pg.64) **Trent's Grocery** (0.5W)	2041	1580.8
610.1	Dismal Falls Trail, 0.3W to waterfall, camping on side trail.	2343	1579.0
610.4	Road on other side of falls sometimes brings visitors by car. Stream, campsite.	2273	1578.7
611.8	Footbridge	2365	1577.3
612.0	Footbridge, stream	2390	1577.1
612.3	Two streams	2453	1576.8
612.9	Woods road	2585	1576.2
613.4	Streams, footbridge	2528	1575.7
613.8	Footbridge, stream (2)	2453	1575.3
614.0	Dismal Creek, gravel road, campsite, footbridge to north	2447	1575.1
614.2	Ribble Trail 3.0W connects with AT near Big Horse Gap	2452	1574.9
614.8	Center of one-mile stretch with at least 6 stream crossings by footbridge.	2477	1574.3
615.5	Clearing, side trail to west	2513	1573.6
615.7	Footbridge, stream(2)	2516	1573.4
616.1	Dirt road	2580	1573.0
616.3	**Wapiti Shelter** (0.1E) 37.7◄24.2◄14.5◄▶9.5▶25.2▶37.8	2603 (5)	1572.8
616.5	Stream.	2651	1572.6
616.9	Stream.	2802	1572.2
617.6	Spring	3342	1571.5
618.9	View.	3896	1570.2
621.2	Side trail 0.1E to radio tower, views from ledge in front of tower	4027	1567.9
621.8	Ribble Trail west, wide grassy path, reconnects with AT south of Wapiti Shelter.	3800	1567.3
621.9	Big Horse Gap, USFS 103 Sometimes confused with Sugar Run Gap, which is 1.5N. There is a short sign south of road, west of AT	3749	1567.2
623.1	Woods road.	3485	1566.0
623.5	Sugar Run Gap, Sugar Run Rd (gravel), road fork in view to east . . . (pg.64) **Woods Hole Hostel** (0.5E)	3395	1565.6
624.9	View, 30 yards east.	3910	1564.2

SoBo	NoBo	Description	Elev
1563.4	625.7	Side trail to forest service road	3557
1563.3	625.8	**Docs Knob Shelter,** reliable spring to left of shelter ☽♦⊂(8) 33.7◄24.0◄9.5◄►15.7►28.3►32.2	3541
1562.1	627.0	Spring ♦	3399
1560.3	628.8	Spring ♦	3150
1559.6	629.5	Powerline, view 📷	3431

� **Fire Pink** – Scarlet-colored flower with five snake-tongued petals.

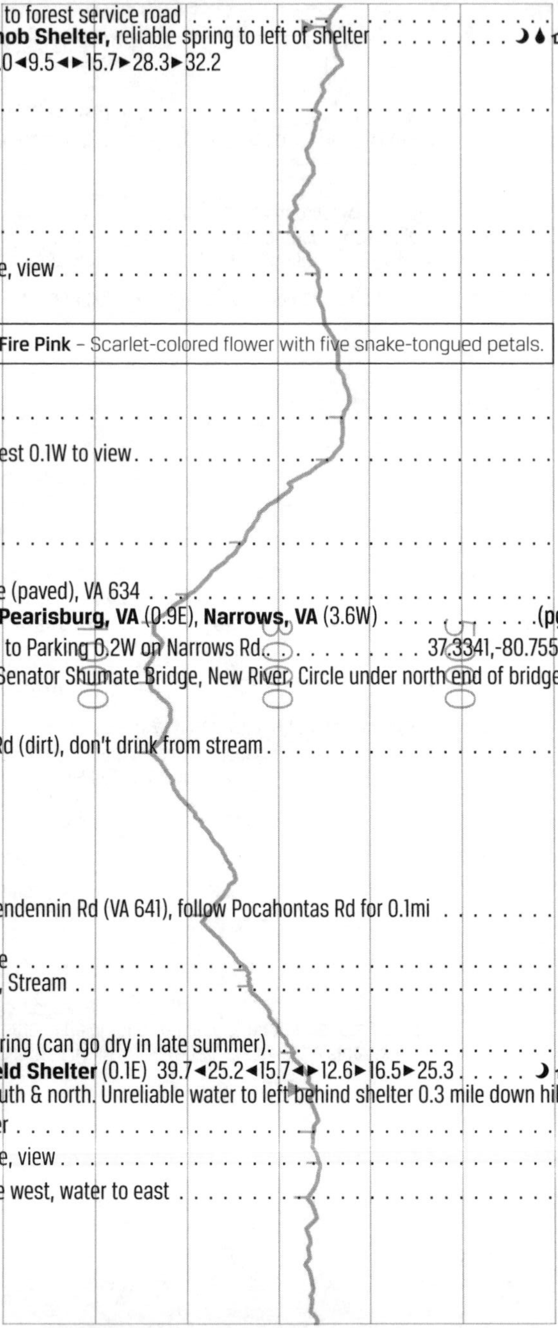

SoBo	NoBo	Description	Elev
1557.5	631.6	View 📷	3693
1556.9	632.2	Angels Rest 0.1W to view 📷	3550
1555.7	633.4	Roadbed	2603
1554.9	634.2	Cross Ave (paved), VA 634	2019
1554.5	634.6	Lane St, **Pearisburg, VA** (0.9E), **Narrows, VA** (3.6W) (pg.64)	1650
1554.0	635.1	Side trail to Parking 0.2W on Narrows Rd 37.3341,-80.7553 **P**	1647
1553.6	635.5	US 460, Senator Shumate Bridge, New River, Circle under north end of bridge.	1602
1552.6	636.5	Landfill Rd (dirt), don't drink from stream	1597
1550.2	638.9	Cross Clendennin Rd (VA 641), follow Pocahontas Rd for 0.1mi	2196
1549.4	639.7	Powerline ♦	2641
1549.1	640.0	Dirt road, Stream ♦	2688
1548.1	641.0	Piped spring (can go dry in late summer). △	3159
1547.6	641.5	**Rice Field Shelter** (0.1E) 39.7◄25.2◄15.7◄►12.6►16.5►25.3 ☽⊂(7) Stiles south & north. Unreliable water to left behind shelter 0.3 mile down hill.	3375
1547.0	642.1	Cell tower	3368
1546.5	642.6	Powerline, view 📷	3435
1546.0	643.1	Campsite west, water to east ♦△	3300

NOBO	Feature	Elev.	SOBO
646.6	Symms Gap, campsite to west.	3320	1542.5
647.6	Groundhog Trail to west	3421	1541.5
648.4	Campsite	3388	1540.7
649.2	Dickenson Gap	3300	1539.9
651.6	Allegheny Trail to west	3726	1537.5
653.5	Streams	2964	1535.6
654.1	**Pine Swamp Branch Shelter** 37.8◄28.3◄12.6◄▶3.9▶12.7▶18.5	2532	1535.0
654.4	Stony Creek Valley, 0.1E to parking on VA 635. 37.191,-80.6046	2381	1534.7
654.9	Stream.	2400	1534.2
655.3	Camping at "The Captain's" place 30 yards east	2410	1533.8
655.5	Footbridge, stream.	2435	1533.6
656.5	Bridge over Stony Creek, VA 635, don't drink water from creek	2450	1532.6
657.5	Gravel road	3121	1531.6
657.8	Spring 100 yards east	3362	1531.3
658.0	**Bailey Gap Shelter** 32.2◄16.5◄3.9▶8.8▶14.6▶21.0 Water 0.2S on AT, then east down blue-blazed trail.	3510	1531.1
659.0	Spring	3721	1530.1
660.6	Spring	3760	1528.5
661.7	VA 613 (gravel), Mountain Lake Rd	3950	1527.4
661.9	Wind Rock, view, campsite.	4100	1527.2
662.7	Woods road	4054	1526.4
664.3	Lone Pine Peak	4026	1524.8

608.3 VA 606

🛶🏠🍴🅱🌾⛺🚐📬 **Trent's Grocery** (0.5W) 276.928.1349
Open year-round M-Sa 7-8, Sun 9-8. Deli with pizza, hamburgers, hot dogs and more. Camping $6, shower $3, laundry $3. Coleman/alcohol/oz and canister fuel. Accepts credit cards. Soda machines outside. Shuttles. Mail: 900 Wilderness Rd, Bland, VA 24315.

🚐 **Larry Richardson** 540.921.4724 Shuttle range Bland to Pearisburg.

623.5 Sugar Run Gap, Sugar Run Rd

🛏🚌🛶👤🍴🏠🌾⛺🚐💻📬 **Woods Hole Hostel** (0.5E) 540.921.3444
⟨www.woodsholehostel.com⟩ Open year-round. A "Slice of heaven, not to be missed." The 1880's chestnut-log cabin was discovered by Roy & Tillie Wood, who opened the hostel in 1986. Their granddaughter, Neville, continues the legacy with husband Michael, with emphasis on sustainable living through beekeeping, farming, organic gardening, yoga, & massage therapy. Directions: NoBo right on dirt road at Sugar Run Gap, SoBo turn left. Bear left at fork, go downhill 0.5 mile to hostel on right. Offers massage, healing arts, & retreats. Bunkhouse $16PP has mattresses, electricity, hot shower, and coffee/tea in the morning. Camping $12PP. Pet fee. Indoor rooms: $28PP shared / $55 private (thru-hiker rate). Guests often invited to share local/organic communal meals. Dinner $13, breakfast $8. Please call to inquire or reserve. Shuttles for a fee, computer access, laundry, smoothies, cheese & baked goods. Coleman/alcohol/oz, fuel canisters, limited resupply. Credit or cash(discount). Maildrops for guests: Woods Hole Hostel, 3696 Sugar Run Rd, Pearisburg, VA 24134.

634.6 Lane St, **Pearisburg, VA 24134** (0.9E)

🚌🛏👤🅱⛺🛜📬 **Holiday Motor Lodge** 540.921.1551 Open May 1-Sept 30. Prices include tax: $20 bunkroom with WiFi, TV, pets free. Limited economy rooms $39, other rooms $50, $10 pet fee. Pool. Mail: 401 N Main St, Pearisburg, VA 24134.

🛏⛺🛜💻📬 **Plaza Motel** 540.921.2591 $44S $55D includes tax, no pets, accepts credit cards. Mail: 415. N. Main St, Pearisburg, VA 24134.

🚌🛶🌾 **Holy Family Hostel** 540.626.3337 Volunteer caretaker Patrick Muldoon please do NOT call for a ride. Check-in directions posted. Suggested donation $10PP, 2 night max. Open Mar-Nov; otherwise call.

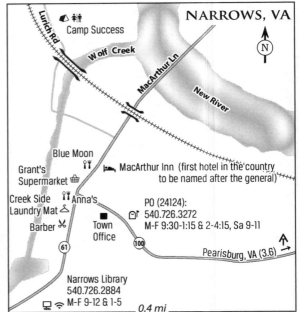

NARROWS, VA

Lurich Rd
Camp Success
Wolf Creek
MacArthur Ln
New River
Blue Moon
Grant's Supermarket
🛏 MacArthur Inn (first hotel in the country to be named after the general)
Creek Side Laundry Mat 🍴Anna's
Barber ✂
Town Office
61
100
PO (24124):
📮 540.726.3272
M-F 9:30-1:15 & 2-4:15, Sa 9-11
Pearisburg, VA (3.6)
Narrows Library
540.726.2884
💻🛜 M-F 9-12 & 1-5
_0.4 mi_

Hot shower, fridge, grill. Keep hostel clean & noise down (church in residential area). No pets or alcohol.

🏠🚐 **Pearis Mercantile** 540.921.2260 M-Sa 10-5:30 Selection of hiker foods, small gear items, fuel.

🔧 **Harvey Electronics and Hardware** 540.921.1456 M-F 9-5, Sa 10-4. Cell phones & supplies, canister fuel, alcohol/oz, tent repair kits.

➕ **Community Health Center** 540.921.3502 M-F 8-4:30 Quick, low-cost healthcare, hikers welcome.

🚐 **Don Raines** 540.921.7433 ⟨ratface20724@aol.com⟩

PEARISBURG, VA

Distances from (100) & Main:
0.8 to Food Lion
1.4 to Pizza Hut
2.7 to Wal Mart

37.3225,-80.7267
Mag. Dec. 8.13° W

Blacksburg, Va 24 mi →

In Blacksburg:
Backcountry Ski &
Sports 540.552.6400

Shortcut to Hospital & Walmart plaza

Narrows, VA 3.6 mi

(100)

Main St

Hardees

Clover Dew

Lucky Star Chinese (AYCE)

Food Lion (7-11)

Pizza Plus

Dairy Queen

Plaza Motel

La Barranca Mex. Grill

Holy Family Hostel
(0.7 from Wenonah)

Giles Memorial
Hospital
540.921.6000

Cross Ave

Holiday Motor Lodge

Harvey Electronics & Hardware

EZ Way Laundromat M-Sa 6-9, Su 6-8

Hale St

Gale Rd

Queen's Pizza

Walmart

Mt. Lake Ave

Campo Verde

Pearis Mercantile

Star Mart & Quiznos

Wendy's

McDonald's

PO (24134): 540.921.1100
M-F 9-4:30, Sa 10-12

Rite-Aid 540.921.1284

Wenonah Ave

Friends & Family

Animal
Care Center
540.921.3707

Melinda's

Pap's Pizza

Pizza Hut

Dollar General

Grant's

Pearisburg Library 540.921.2556
M 12-8, Tu 12-5, W 9-5, Th 9-8,
F 9-5, Sa 9-1

Community Health Center

2.7 mi

Anytime, anywhere. Slackpacking available.

Tom Hoffman 540.921.1184 ⟨gopullman@aol.com⟩ mid-range shuttles centered in Pearisburg.

Narrows, VA (3.6W on VA 100)

MacArthur Inn 540.726.7510 $45D/up. Call for ride from Pearisburg area trailheads, ride $5 each way. Longer shuttles and slackpacking can be arranged. Free long distance phone, cable TV and WiFi. In center of town with all services (restaurants, laundry, PO, grocery) in close walking distance. Shower only $8. On-site restaurant serves breakfast 6am-11am M-Sa, and dinner F & Su 5-8. Shop with dried foods, socks, small gear items. Mail: 117 MacArthur Lane, Narrows, VA 24124.

Camp Success Camping $5 tent/night, no showers. Check-in at Town Office 540.726.3020 M-F 9-5. Call ahead for after-hours arrivals or print permit from ⟨www.townofnarrows.org⟩.

Grants Supermarket 540.726.2303 M-Sa 8-8, Sun 9-8

Anna's Restaurant 540.726.3545 Tu-Su 11-8 L/D.

655.3   The Captain's

Camping available at 4464 Big Stony Creek Rd, 30 yards east of AT. Use zip line to cross the creek. *This is not a hostel; do not enter the house.* You may camp even when no one is home. Dogs bark but are friendly & are contained by an invisible electric fence. If it rains, you may stay on back porch. Hiker Feed two weeks after Trail Days.

SoBo	NoBo	Feature	Elevation
664.8	1524.3	War Branch Trail to east	3507
665.2	1523.9	Spring	3267 ◆
666.8	1522.3	**War Spur Shelter,** spring north on AT. 25.3◀12.7◀8.8◀▶5.8▶12.2▶18.2	2361 ☾◆⊏(6)
667.6	1521.5	VA 632, cross Johns Creek on footbridge	2080 ◆
667.7	1521.4	Footbridge, stream, campsite	2058 ◗
668.7	1520.4	Spring	2627 ◆
669.6	1519.5	Rocky Gap, VA 601 (gravel)	3264
670.2	1518.9	Johns Creek Mountain Trail to west	3782
671.4	1517.7	Kelly Knob, view.	3730 ▣
672.6	1516.5	**Laurel Creek Shelter** 18.5◀14.6◀5.8◀▶6.4▶12.4▶22.5. Water 60 yards north of shelter junction and west of AT.	2798 ☾⊏(6)
672.8	1516.3	Stream	2753 ◆
673.2	1515.9	Piney Ridge	2614
674.7	1514.4	Pasture, several fence stiles.	2227
675.1	1514.0	Footbridge, Sinking Creek, VA 42, **Newport, VA** (8.0E) (pg.70) "Trail east" is compass west (NoBo right, SoBo left to town).	2097
675.9	1513.2	VA 630 (paved), chimney, and footbridge close together	2145 ◆
676.3	1512.8	Keffer Oak, largest oak tree on AT in south, over 18' around, over 300 yrs old Dover Oak along AT in NY is slightly larger.	2322
676.7	1512.4	Powerline	2526
678.1	1511.0	Powerline	3223
678.8	1510.3	Bruisers Knob	3417 ☾◆⊏(6)
679.0	1510.1	**Sarver Hollow Shelter** (0.4E) (2002) 21.0◀12.2◀6.4◀▶6.0▶16.1▶29.7	3402
680.9	1508.2	View	3381 ▣▣
681.2	1507.9	View	3354 ▣▣
682.3	1506.8	North end of ridge crest on Sinking Creek Mountain, Eastern Continental Divide West is old route of AT leading 2.5 miles to Old Hall Rd.	3368
683.9	1505.2	Stream.	2703 △

NoBo		Feature		Elev
1504.1	**685.0**	**Niday Shelter,** water on opposite side of AT	☽⬥◭⌐(6)	1988
		18.2◄12.4◄6.0◄►10.1►23.7►24.7		
1502.7	686.4	VA 621, Craig Creek Rd	37.3793,-80.25 🅿	1547
1502.2	686.9	Many footbridges crossing Craig Creek and feeder streams. within a mile north of road	⬥	1583
1499.7	689.4	Bench at southern crest of Brush Mountain		2988
1499.0	690.1	Audie Murphy Monument		3100
		Murphy was most decorated American soldier of World War II. Monument on blue-blazed trail to west.		
1495.2	693.9	Footbridge, Trout Creek, VA 620 (gravel)	⬥	1548
1494.8	694.3	Powerline		1749
1494.0	695.1	**Pickle Branch Shelter** (0.3E)	☽⬥◭⌐(6)	1951
		22.5◄16.1◄10.1◄►13.6►14.6►17.0 Tenting along trail to shelter. Water on steep trail 0.2 mile downhill from shelter.		
1493.0	696.1	View	📷	2392

⚠ The AT is mostly on National Park Service Land from Newport Rd to Mtn Pass Rd (roughly from Catawba through Troutville). Camping permitted only in designated locations (at the shelters; Lamberts Meadow Campsite and the Pig Farm Campsite).

NoBo		Feature		Elev
1490.1	699.0	View	📷📷	2963
1489.8	699.3	Cove Mountain		3020
		Trail 0.1E to Dragons Tooth (stone monolith), views.		
1489.0	700.1	Lost Spectacles Gap	📷📷	2520
1488.6	700.5	Rawies Rest, view		2482
1488.4	700.7	View		2307
1487.7	701.4	Scout Trail west to Dragons Tooth Parking	🅿	2039
1487.3	701.8	VA 624, Newport Rd	(pg.70)	1810
1486.5	702.6	Footbridge		1816
1486.0	703.1	Fence stile		1842
1485.7	703.4	VA 785, Blacksburg Rd		1790

NoBo
SoBo

NoBo	SoBo		Elevation

1485.4	703.7	Footbridge, Catawba Creek, fence stile, treat water	1770
1481.4	707.7	VA 311, **Catawba, VA** (1.0W) . . . . 37.3801, -80.0898 **P** (pg.70)	1990
1480.8	708.3	Footbridge	2030
1480.4	708.7	**Johns Spring Shelter** (2003) 29.7◄23.7◄13.6◄▶1.0▶3.4▶9.4	1957
		Unreliable spring 25 yrds left front of shelter.	
1480.0	709.1	Footbridge	2110
1479.4	709.7	**Catawba Mountain Shelter** (1984) Camping to north	2203
		24.7◄14.6◄1.0◄▶2.4▶8.4▶22.8	
		Blue-blaze to water 100 yards from front of shelter.	
1477.7	711.4	McAfee Knob; excellent views, no camping.	3197
1477.2	711.9	Powerline	2781
1477.1	712.0	Water to east, Pig Farm campsite, same water source as shelter	2682
1477.0	712.1	**Campbell Shelter** (1989), water behind shelter	2636
		17.0◄3.4◄2.4◄▶6.0▶20.4▶26.6	
1473.9	715.2	Brickeys Gap, Lamberts Meadow Trail to east	2194
1472.1	717.0	Tinker Cliffs, 0.5 mile cliff walk, views back to McAfee Knob.	3000
1471.6	717.5	Scorched Earth Gap, Andy Layne Trail to west	2600
1471.0	718.1	**Lamberts Meadow Shelter** 9.4◄8.4◄6.0◄▶14.4▶20.6▶27.9	2126
1470.7	718.4	Lamberts Meadow Campsite, Sawmill Run	2000
		Footbridge, stream. North of footbridge an east trail rejoins AT at Brickeys Gap.	
1468.5	720.6	Blue-blazed trail west to view	2217
1466.6	722.5	Angels Gap	1692
1466.3	722.8	Powerline	1840

SoBo	NoBo	Feature	Elev
1465.6	723.5	Hay Rock, view	1955
1464.4	724.7	Powerline, view	1920
1463.6	725.5	Powerline	1959
1462.8	726.3	Powerline	1386
1462.2	726.9	Powerline, railroad tracks, bridge	1165
1461.6	727.5	US 220, **Daleville, VA** (pg.70)	1253
1460.4	728.7	I-81, trail passes under on VA 779	1400
1460.1	729.0	US 11, RR tracks, **Troutville, VA** (0.8W) 37.4045,-79.8895 P (pg.70)	1300
1459.8	729.3	Fence stile	1497
1459.5	729.5	VA 652, Mountain Pass Rd	1450
1459.3	729.8	Fence	1521
1456.6	732.5	**Fullhardt Knob Shelter** (0.1E) 22.8◄20.4◄14.4◄►6.2►13.5►20.0 Treat water from cistern.	2632
1453.8	735.3	Salt Pond Rd, USFS 191	2248
1453.0	736.1	Curry Creek, Curry Creek Trail to west	1572
1452.2	736.9	Stream.	1670
1450.9	738.2	Wilson Creek, Colliers Pit historical marker to north	1549
1450.4	738.7	**Wilson Creek Shelter** 26.6◄20.6◄6.2►7.3►13.8►20.8 Reliable stream 0.3 mile downhill in front of shelter.	1854
1449.9	739.2	Spring	2000
1448.0	741.1	Blackhorse Gap, dirt road, Blue Ridge Parkway (BRP) mile 97.7 to east.	2404
1447.3	741.8	BRP 97.0, Taylors Mountain Overlook	2350

NoBo
SoBo

675.1   VA 42, Sinking Creek, Trail "east" here is compass west.

🏠(1.0W) **Sublett Place** 540.544.3099 Home and cottage for rent, prices seasonal. ⟨www.thesublettplace.com⟩

🏛 (1.0W) **Joe's Trees** 540.544.7303 ⟨www.joestrees.com⟩ Limited summer/fall hours (call ahead), 7 days Nov 15-Dec 21, closed Dec 22-Apr. Drinks, jerky, cheese, jams.

Newport, VA 24128 (8E)
Store, post office and restaurant near intersection of 42 and 460.
🏤 M-F 8:15-11:30 & 12:30-3:15, Sa 9-11, 540.544.7415
🛒 **Super Val-U** 540.544.7702 Su-Th 6-10, F-Sa 6-10:30

701.8   VA 624, Newport Rd

🏠🏍🚗⛺☂🖥📧 (0.3E) **Four Pines Hostel**   Owner Joe Mitchell cell: 540.309.8615 Hostel is a 3-bay garage with shower; please leave a donation, open year-round. Laundry $3 wash/$3 dry. Pet friendly. Shuttles to/from The Homeplace Restaurant (Th-Su) and to Catawba Grocery. Longer shuttles for a fee. Mail: 6164 Newport Rd. Catawba VA 24070.
🛒🍴 **Catawba Grocery**   540.384.8050 West 0.3 mile to VA 311 and then left 0.1 mile to store, 7 days/week 6am-10pm. Grill serves breakfast, pizza, burgers, ice cream.

707.7   VA 311, *Catawba, VA 24070* (1W)
🏤 (1.0W) M-F 9-12 & 1-4, Sa 8:30-10:30, 540.384.6011
🍴 (1.4W) **Homeplace Restaurant** 540.384.7252 Th-F 4-8, Sa 3-8, Su 11-6, Popular AYCE family-style meals including drink and tax; $14 (two meats) $15 (three meats), $8 (kids 3-11).

727.5   US 220, *Daleville, VA*
729.0   US 11, *Troutville, VA*

Troutville Trail Days June 3-4 at Town Park. Free hiker dinner, gear repair, live music, food, vendors, & 5K race.

🔥🏕🌲⛺☂ **Troutville Park & Fire Station** Free camping at town park, no pets. Free laundry and showers at fire station.

🏠🏍⛺☂🖥📧💲 **Howard Johnson Express** 540.992.1234 $49.95 hiker rate, cont. breakfast. Game room and pool. Pets $10.

Mail: 437 Roanoke Road, Daleville, VA 24083.

🏠⛺☂🖥 **Super 8** 540.992.3000 $59.36 + tax, cont B, pool, accepts major credit cards, no pets.

🏠☂🖥 **Comfort Inn** 540.992.5600 hiker rate $49.99D, $10EAP, continental breakfast, pets $25.

🏠☂🖥 **Quality Inn** 540.992.5335 $71/up, pets $25.

🏠⛺☂🖥📧 **Holiday Inn Express** 540.966.4444 $109-119, no pets. Mail: 3200 Lee Hwy, Troutville, VA 24175.

🏠 **Red Roof Inn** 540.992.5055

🏠⛺☂ **Motel 6** 540.992.6700 $39.99D $6EAP, pets ok (no fee).

🍴⊕ **Three Li'l Pigs** 540.966.0165 Open year-round, extended summer hours M-Th 11-9:30, F-Sa 11-10:30, Su 11-9, Hiker friendly, hand-chopped BBQ ribs and wings, large selection of beer, some locally-brewed. Thru-hikers get free banana pudding dessert Mid-April to June 1.

🛒🍴 **Kroger Grocery Store and Pharmacy** 540.992.4920 24hr, pharmacy M-F 8-9, Sa 9-6, Su 12-6.

🚶⊕🚗☂🖥📧 **Outdoor Trails**   540.992.5850 Full service outfitter. White gas & denatured alcohol by oz. Computer for internet use, shuttler service. Open M-F 9-8, Sat 9-6 during hiking season (Apr 25-Jul 2); open M-F 10-8, Sat 10-6 the rest of the year. Mail: Botetourt Commons, 28 Kingston Dr, Daleville, VA 24083.
🚗 **Homer Witcher** 540.266.4849 Trail maintainer & 2002 thru-hiker.

🍺 **Flying Mouse Brewery** 540.254.0636 Open Th 5-7, F 4-8, Sa 2-8, Su 1-5. Check ⟨www.flyingmousebrewery.com⟩ for beer tasting events. 0.4W to Precast Way, then right 0.1mi.

Roanoke, VA (13E)
✈ A large city with an airport approx 13 miles from the AT.
🚶 (5E) **Gander Mountain** 540.362.3658, 8195 Gander Way.
🚶 (10E) **Sportsman's Warehouse** 540.366.9700, 3550 Ferncliff Ave NW. Full service outfitter with full line of gear including fuel, freeze dried foods, boots, clothes and trekking poles.

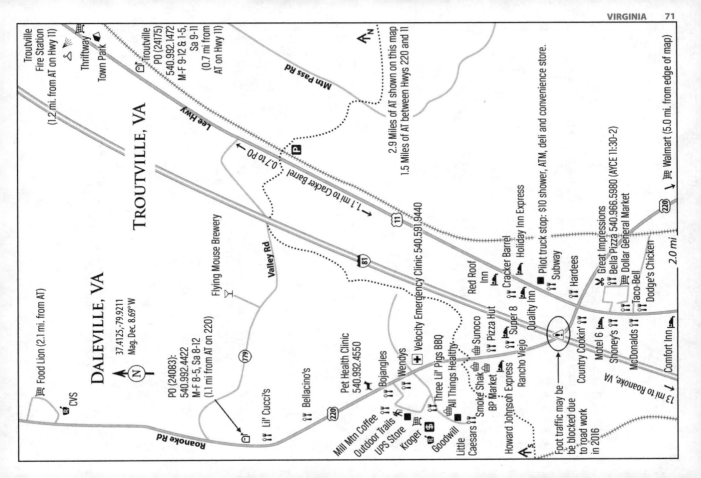

TROUTVILLE, VA

DALEVILLE, VA

Troutville Fire Station (1.2 mi. from AT on Hwy 11)

Thriftway
Town Park

Troutville PO (24175) 540.992.1472 M-F 9-12 & I-5, Sa 9-11 (0.7 mi from AT on Hwy 11)

Mtn Pass Rd

Lee Hwy

N

2.9 Miles of AT shown on this map
1.5 Miles of AT between Hwys 220 and 11

0.7 to PO

1.1 mi to Cracker Barrel

11

81

Flying Mouse Brewery

Valley Rd

37.4125,-79.9211
Mag. Dec. 8.69°W

PO (24083):
540.992.4422
M-F 8-5, Sa 8-12
(1.1 mi from AT on 220)

N

79

Velocity Emergency Clinic 540.591.9440

Pilot truck stop: $10 shower, ATM, deli and convenience store.

Great Impressions
Bella Pizza 540.966.5980 (AYCE 11:30-2)
Dollar General Market
Taco Bell
Dodge's Chicken

220

2.0 mi

Red Roof Inn
Cracker Barrel
Holiday Inn Express
Subway
Hardees

Pizza Hut
Super 8
Quality Inn

Sunoco
Rancho Viejo

Pet Health Clinic
540.992.4550

Bellacino's

Bojangles
Wendys

Three Lil Pigs BBQ
All Things Healthy
Smoke Shak
BP Market

Howard Johnson Express

Food Lion (2.1 mi. from AT)

CVS

Lil' Cucci's

Roanoke Rd

220

Mill Mtn Coffee
Outdoor Trails
UPS Store
Kroger
Goodwill
Little Caesars

Country Cookin'

Motel 6
Shoney's
McDonalds

Comfort Inn

13 mi to Roanoke, VA

Foot traffic may be be blocked due to road work in 2016

S

Walmart (5.0 mi. from edge of map)

NoBo		Description		Elev
1445.5	743.6	BRP 95.3, Harveys Knob Overlook	⛊	2527
1443.8	745.3	Hammond Hollow Trail to west		2327
1443.1	746.0	**Bobblets Gap Shelter** (0.2W) 27.9◄13.5◄7.3◄▶6.5▶13.5▶18.4	☾◢⊏ (6)	2086
		If spring to left of shelter dry, look farther downstream.		
1442.3	746.8	BRP 92.5, Peaks of Otter Overlook	◙	2341
1441.7	747.4	BRP 91.8, Mills Gap Overlook	⛊◙	2450
1440.0	749.1	Bearwallow Gap, footbridge, stream, VA 43, 0.2E to BRP 90.9	△ (pg.74)	2228
		Buchanan, VA (5.0W)		
1438.4	750.7	Cove Mountain		2720
1438.0	751.1	Little Cove Mountain Trail to east		2517
1436.6	752.5	**Cove Mountain Shelter** 20.0◄13.8◄6.5◄▶7.0▶11.9▶17.2	☾◢⊏ (6)	1942
1436.4	752.7	View	◙	1970
1434.9	754.2	Buchanan Trail		1790
1433.4	755.7	Cross Jennings Creek on VA 614 bridge . . . . . 37.5291, -79.6225 [P]◢ (pg.74)		951
		Swimming hole, campsites. **Buchanan, VA** (5.0W)		
		⚠ Bearing of NoBo AT in this area is more south than north.		
1431.8	757.3	Fork Mountain.		2042
1430.6	758.5	Stream south of powerline	◣	1239
1430.3	758.8	Stream.	◣	1271
1429.9	759.2	Stream.	◣	1192
1429.6	759.5	**Bryant Ridge Shelter**	☾◢⊏ (20)	1277
		20.8◄13.5◄7.0◄▶4.9▶0.2▶22.6 Stream on trail to shelter.		
		Blue-blazed trail 0.1N of shelter leads 0.5E to VA 714.		

5000

3000

1000

NoBo

SoBo

NoBo	Elev	Feature	SoBo
762.6	2937	Campsite, 0.1W to spring (signed).	1426.5
763.8	3560	Floyd Mountain	1425.3
764.4	3114	**Cornelius Creek Shelter** (0.1E)	1424.7
		18.4◄11.9◄4.9◄►5.3►17.7►21.6 Water on trail to shelter. Privy behind shelter.	
764.7	3027	Stream.	1424.4
765.3	3450	Black Rock Overlook, view 200' west	1423.8
765.6	3306	Footbridge, stream	1423.5
765.9	3224	Intersection with Cornelius Creek Trail	1423.2
767.0	3351	Apple Orchard Falls Trail 1.1W to 200' waterfall, 0.1E to Sunset Field, USFS 812 (Parkers Gap Rd) 0.1N on AT.	1422.1
768.5	4225	Apple Orchard Mountain, Federal Aviation Admin (FAA) tower, views	1420.6
768.8	4005	The Guillotine	1420.3
769.4	3900	BRP 76.3, spring 100 yards north, then east of AT	1419.7
769.7	3917	**Thunder Hill Shelter** 17.2◄10.2◄5.3◄►2.4►16.3►25.1 Poor water source, use spring south on AT, tentsites north of shelter	1419.4
770.7	3594	Hunting Creek Trail, BRP 74.9	1418.4
771.1	3501	0.1E to BRP 74.7 Thunder Ridge Overlook	1418.0
772.9	3307	Harrison Ground Spring	1416.2
773.5	2908	Spring.	1415.6
774.4	2369	Petites Gap, gravel road, BRP 71.0 to east.	1414.7
775.6	3064	Highcock Knob.	1413.5
776.6	2349	Marble Spring, campsite, spring 100 yards west	1412.5
777.1	2456	Sulphur Spring Trail south crossing	1412.0
778.9	2650	Gunter Ridge Trail, Hickory Stand	1410.2
779.4	2588	Sulphur Spring Trail north crossing	1409.7
780.2	1890	Big Cove Branch, stream.	1408.9

.ıll **(NoBo)** Poor cell reception at US 501, consider calling ahead if you need ride.

NoBo

SoBo

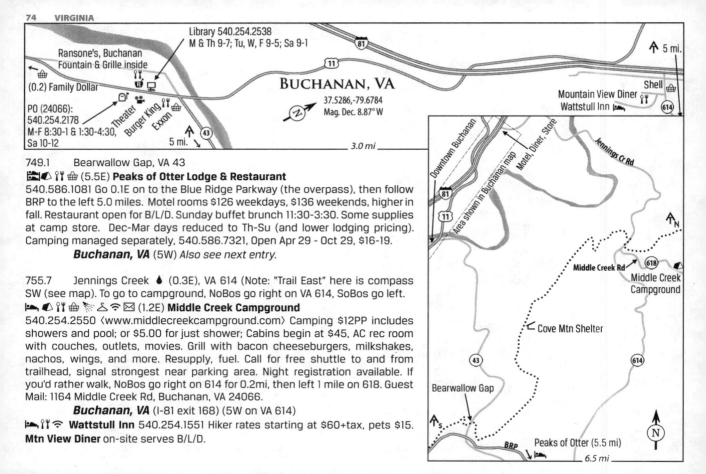

Library 540.254.2538
M & Th 9-7; Tu, W, F 9-5; Sa 9-1

Ransone's, Buchanan
Fountain & Grille inside

(0.2) Family Dollar

PO (24066):
540.254.2178
M-F 8:30-1 & 1:30-4:30,
Sa 10-12

Theater
Burger King
Exxon
5 mi.

BUCHANAN, VA
37.5286,-79.6784
Mag. Dec. 8.87° W

5 mi.

Shell
Mountain View Diner
Wattstull Inn
614

3.0 mi

749.1   Bearwallow Gap, VA 43

(5.5E) Peaks of Otter Lodge & Restaurant
540.586.1081 Go 0.1E on to the Blue Ridge Parkway (the overpass), then follow
BRP to the left 5.0 miles. Motel rooms $126 weekdays, $136 weekends, higher in
fall. Restaurant open for B/L/D. Sunday buffet brunch 11:30-3:30. Some supplies
at camp store. Dec-Mar days reduced to Th-Su (and lower lodging pricing).
Camping managed separately, 540.586.7321, Open Apr 29 - Oct 29, $16-19.

   Buchanan, VA (5W) *Also see next entry.*

755.7   Jennings Creek ♦ (0.3E), VA 614 (Note: "Trail East" here is compass
SW (see map). To go to campground, NoBos go right on VA 614, SoBos go left.

(1.2E) Middle Creek Campground
540.254.2550 ⟨www.middlecreekcampground.com⟩ Camping $12PP includes
showers and pool; or $5.00 for just shower; Cabins begin at $45, AC rec room
with couches, outlets, movies. Grill with bacon cheeseburgers, milkshakes,
nachos, wings, and more. Resupply, fuel. Call for free shuttle to and from
trailhead, signal strongest near parking area. Night registration available. If
you'd rather walk, NoBos go right on 614 for 0.2mi, then left 1 mile on 618. Guest
Mail: 1164 Middle Creek Rd, Buchanan, VA 24066.

   Buchanan, VA (I-81 exit 168) (5W on VA 614)

Wattstull Inn 540.254.1551 Hiker rates starting at $60+tax, pets $15.
Mtn View Diner on-site serves B/L/D.

Downtown Buchanan

Motel, Diner, Store

Jennings Cr Rd

Area shown in Buchanan map

N

Middle Creek Rd
618
Middle Creek
Campground

Cove Mtn Shelter

43

614

Bearwallow Gap

S

BRP
Peaks of Otter (5.5 mi)

N

6.5 mi

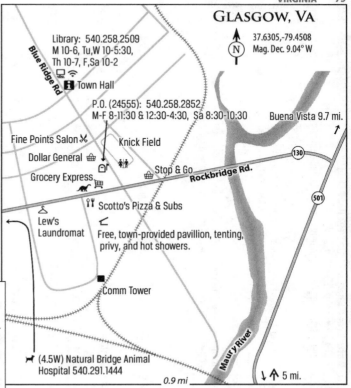

784.3   US 501, VA 130

🚐 **Ken Wallace** 434.609.2704 Range: Buchanan- Waynesboro.

Glasgow, VA 24555 (5.9W)

ℹ️ **Town Hall** 540.258.2246 Maintains shelter & Knick Field restrooms.

🛒 **Glasgow Grocery Express** 540.258.1818 M-Sa 6-11:30pm, Su 8-1130pm, Coleman/alcohol/oz.

🐾 **Natural Bridge Animal Hospital** 540.291.1444 4.5W of Glasgow on VA 130. M,W,F 8-5:30, T,Th 8-7.

🚐 **Gary Serra** 757.681.2254 Gary has completed the AT twice in sections and is familiar with all trailheads. Pickups at Glasgow & Buena Vista trailheads. Shuttles along AT, to Roanoke, Lynchburg and Charlottesville airports, and to Amtrak station. Will do long-distance shuttles. Sells fuel canisters.

Big Island, VA 24526 (5.6E)

🏠 M-F 8:15-12 & 1-4, Sa 8-10, 434.299.5072

🏪🍴✉️ **H&H Food Market** 434.299.5153 7 days 5:30-9, B/L/D served 6:30-8, Mail: 11619 Lee Jackson Hwy, Big Island, VA 24526.

➕ **Big Island Family Medical Center** 434.299.5951 M-Tu & Th-F 8:30-5.

DISPOSE OF WASTE PROPERLY 〈www.appalachiantrail.org/LNT〉
• Pack it in; pack it out. Leave any donated items at hiker boxes in town rather than at campsites or shelters.
• Walk at least 100 feet (40 steps) away from shelters, water sources and campsites to dispose of urine, toothpaste, cooking water and strained dishwater, and to wash bodies, dishes or clothing. Minimize any use of soap.
• Use the privy only for human waste and toilet paper. Pack out disposable wipes and hygiene products.
• If there is no privy, walk at least 200 feet (80 steps) away from campsites, shelters, trails and water sources to bury feces in a hole 6 to 8 inches deep. Bury or carry out toilet paper.

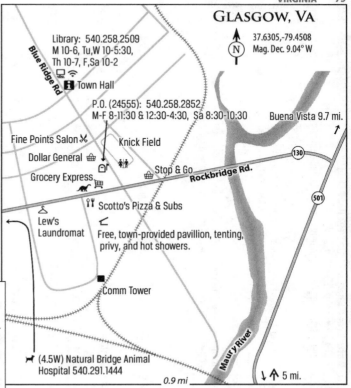

GLASGOW, VA

Ⓝ 37.6305,-79.4508
Mag. Dec. 9.04° W

Library: 540.258.2509
M 10-6, Tu,W 10-5:30,
Th 10-7, F,Sa 10-2
ℹ️ Town Hall

Blue Ridge Rd.

P.O. (24555): 540.258.2852
M-F 8-11:30 & 12:30-4:30, Sa 8:30-10:30

Buena Vista 9.7 mi.

Fine Points Salon ✂️

Knick Field

Dollar General 🏪

Grocery Express 🛒

Stop & Go

Rockbridge Rd.

🦕

🍴 Scotto's Pizza & Subs

Lew's Laundromat

Free, town-provided pavillion, tenting, privy, and hot showers.

Comm Tower

🐕 (4.5W) Natural Bridge Animal Hospital 540.291.1444

_0.9 mi._

Maury River

↓ 🔼 5 mi.

⚠️ Visit the website www.theATguide.com regularly to get updates, additions & corrections. Please let us know if you've found anything that should be added or corrected.

NoBo	SoBo	Description	Features	Elev
1407.0	782.1	**Matts Creek Shelter**, Matts Creek Trail 2.5E to US 501 22.6◀17.7◀12.4◀▶3.9▶12.7▶22.2	☾♦⊂(6)	848
1406.2	782.9	AT parallels James River from here north for 1.0 mile, no camping		695
1405.0	784.1	James River footbridge, longest foot-use-only bridge on AT		678
1404.8	784.3	US 501, VA 130, **Big Island VA** (5.6E), **Glasgow VA** (5.9W)	P (pg.75) ♦	680
1404.6	784.5	Lower Rocky Row Run Bridge, stream.	♦	679
1403.7	785.4	VA 812, USFS 36 (gravel) 37.6048,-79.3883	P	801
1403.3	785.8	Stream.		919
1403.1	786.0	**Johns Hollow Shelter** 21.6◀16.3◀3.9◀▶8.8▶18.3▶23.9 Springs to left and right of shelter.	☾♦⊂(6)	1021
1401.1	788.0	Little Rocky Row Trail to west, view just north on AT	📷	2416
1400.0	789.1	Big Rocky Row, view	📷	2992
		.ıll (SoBo) Poor cell reception at US 501, consider calling ahead if you need ride.		
1398.5	790.6	Saddle Gap, Saddle Gap Trail.		2600
1397.4	791.7	Saltlog Gap, Saltlog Gap Trail	♦(0.5W)	2573
1395.9	793.2	Bluff Mountain, Ottie Cline Powell monument, views.	📷	3372
1394.8	794.3	Punchbowl Mountain.		2850
1394.3	794.8	**Punchbowl Shelter** (0.2W), spring front left of shelter 25.1◀12.7◀8.8◀▶9.5▶15.1▶25.3	☾♦⊂(6)	2487
1393.9	795.2	BRP 51.7 Punchbowl Mtn Overlook, water north of road. 37.6738,-79.3347	P 🏛 ♦	2170
1393.6	795.5	VA 607, Robinson Gap Rd (gravel) **Buena Vista, VA** (6.0W) 37.6761,-79.332	P	2100
1391.7	797.4	Rice Mountain		2166
1391.1	798.0	Spring.	♦	1669
1390.7	798.4	Dirt road		1306
1389.8	799.3	Reservoir Rd (gravel), Pedlar River Bridge. 37.6705,-79.2845 campsite 0.2S of road.	P ♦ ◇	952
1388.1	801.0	Spring	♦	1164

NoBo
SoBo

NoBo	Feature	Elev	SoBo
801.8	Stream.	1116	1387.3
802.3	Swapping Camp Rd (gravel)	1286	1386.8
802.6	Stream.	1344	1386.5
804.3	**Brown Mountain Creek Shelter** 22.2◄18.3◄9.5◄▶5.6▶15.8▶22.4 Swimming hole. Camping opposite side of creek. In dry conditions, get water from Brown Mountain Creek south of shelter.	1358 (6)	1384.8
806.1	US 60, **Buena Vista, VA** (9.3W) 37.7234,-79.2506 P (pg.78)	2065	1383.0
807.0	USFS 507 (dirt)	2650	1382.1
808.9	Bald Knob, not actually bald	4059	1380.2
809.9	Hotel Trail, **Cow Camp Gap Shelter** (0.6E) 23.9◄15.1◄5.6◄▶10.2▶16.8▶24.4 Water source on blue-blazed trail left of shelter before small stream crossing.	3468 (8)	1379.2
811.1	Cole Mountain, views	4022	1378.0
812.4	Hog Camp Gap, USFS 48 (gravel), grassy meadow, many campsites. Signed spring just north of road crossing and 0.3 east. (pg.79)	3485	1376.7
813.3	Tar Jacket Ridge, view	3847	1375.8
814.6	Salt Log Gap, USFS 63, two gravel road crossings	3257	1374.5
815.8	USFS 246	3556	1373.3
816.3	Greasy Spring Rd, Lovington Spring Trail to west.	3600	1372.8
818.2	Piney River north fork.	3482	1370.9
819.4	Elk Pond Branch	3714	1369.7
820.1	**Seeley-Woodworth Shelter** 25.3◄15.8◄10.2◄▶6.6▶14.2▶20.4 Piped spring 0.1 mile downhill to right.	3806 (8)	1369.0
820.3	Stream.	3717	1368.8

NoBo
SoBo

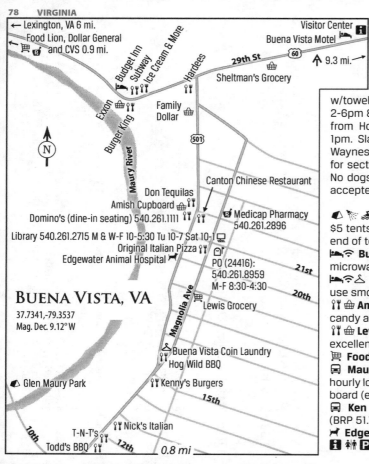

← Lexington, VA 6 mi.

Food Lion, Dollar General
and CVS 0.9 mi.

Budget Inn
Subway
Ice Cream & More

Visitor Center
Buena Vista Motel

29th St

↑ 9.3 mi. →

Hardees

Sheltman's Grocery

Exxon

Family
Dollar

Burger King

501

Canton Chinese Restaurant

Maury River

Don Tequilas

Amish Cupboard
Domino's (dine-in seating) 540.261.1111

Medicap Pharmacy
540.261.2896

Library 540.261.2715 M & W-F 10-5:30 Tu 10-7 Sat 10-1

Original Italian Pizza

Edgewater Animal Hospital

PO (24416):
540.261.8959
M-F 8:30-4:30

21st

20th

BUENA VISTA, VA

37.7341,-79.3537
Mag. Dec. 9.12°W

Magnolia Ave

Lewis Grocery

Buena Vista Coin Laundry
Hog Wild BBQ

Glen Maury Park

Kenny's Burgers

15th

T-N-T's

Nick's Italian

Todd's BBQ

12th

0.8 mi

806.1   US 60

(4.0W) **Three Springs Hostel Bunk & Breakfast** ⟨www.threespringshostel.com⟩ 434.922.7069 Open W-Su Apr 1-Jun 30 & Sep 15-Nov 15. Shuttles and mail drops year-round; mail pickup can be arranged even when hostel is closed. $49.99 bunk, full breakfast, shower w/towel & toiletries, laundry, free long distance calls, free pickup 2-6pm & return to US 60 or Hog Camp Gap. Easy 1.5mi walk downhill from Hog Camp Gap. Reservations recommended. Check-in after 1pm. Slackpacking (day packs available), shuttle range Daleville-Waynesboro VA, full resupply, snacks & sodas, alcohol/oz, parking for section hikers. Prepared food & ice cream for purchase for L/D. No dogs, alcohol, drugs, smoking, or firearms. Cash or credit cards accepted. Mail: 612 Wiggins Spring Road, Vesuvius, VA 24483.

Buena Vista, VA 24416 (9.3W)

Glen Maury Park Campground 540.261.7321 AT hiker special $5 tentsite. Sometimes WFS. Free shower, even without stay, South end of town across river. Maury River Fiddlers Convention mid-June.

Buena Vista Motel 540.261.2138 $44-$79 Rooms have fridge & microwave, free local calls. Shuttle to/from trail for a small fee.

Budget Inn 540.261.2156 $59.95-$99.95, pets $10 and must use smoking room.

Amish Cupboard 540.264.0215 Deli, Ice Cream, jerky, tons of candy and dried foods. M-F 10-7 (deli 10-6), Sa 10-5:30.

Lewis Grocery 540.261-6826 7 days 9-9, short order grill with excellent burger.

Food Lion 540.261.7672, 7 days 7-10.

Maury Express 800.964.5707 M-F 8-6, Sa 10-4 Area bus makes hourly loop though BV & connects with a Lexington loop bus. 50¢ per board (exact change required).

Ken Hawkins 540.817.9640 Shuttle range Punchbowl Overlook (BRP 51.7) to Reeds Gap.

Edgewater Animal Hospital 540.261.4114 M-F 8-6, Sa 8-12

Regional Visitor Center 540.261.8004 Multi-day parking.

Lexington, VA 24450 (15W of Buena Vista)

🛏🏕📶✉ **Brierley Hill B&B** 540.464.8421 relax@brierleyhill.com Open year-round. Thru-hiker special $75PP for double occupancy room. Includes breakfast, free use of laundry facilities, and WiFi. Shuttle to/from the AT (Rt. 60) for additional fee. No Pets. Mail: 985 Borden Rd, Lexington, VA 24450.

🛏🏕📶✉ **502 South Main B&B** 540.460.7353 info@502southmain.com. Open year-round. "Thru-hiker special" $75PP for 2 or 3 persons. Round trip to AT (Rt. 60) $10PP, free laundry, hearty breakfast. Restaurants & shops nearby. No pets, no smoking. Credit cards accepted. Mail: 502 S. Main St, Lexington VA 24450

🥾 **Walkabout Outfitter** 540.464.4453 M-Sa 10-5:30, Su 10-5 Full service outfitter owned by Kirk Miller (Flying Monkey '99). Fuel canisters.

812.4   Hog Camp Gap, USFS 48

🛏(1.5W) **Three Springs Hostel** See listing at US 60, pg. 78

822.4   Spy Rock Rd **Montebello, VA 24464**
2.4W to post office, general store. Go downhill on gravel road 1.1W to parking area on Fish Hatchery Rd. Watch for right turn 0.5 from AT, and watch for blue blazes. Follow F.H. Road (turn right at intersection) 0.9mi. to Crabtree Falls Hwy (VA 56). Go left on VA 56 0.4 miles to post office.

🏠 M-F 10-2, Sa 10-1, 540.377.9218

🍴🏠🏕 **Montebello Camping & General Store** 540.377.2650 Store open year-round 8-6 (summer 8-8, winter 9-5) camping & laundry Apr 1 - Oct 31. Thru-hiker rate on tentsite $14(1 person), $21(2), $28(3 or more) sometimes has fuel/oz.

🚐 **Earl Arnold** 540.377.2119 Shuttles James River to Rockfish Gap.

825.8   VA 826 (3.7 miles to Crabtree Falls Campground: 0.5W on 826 to Meadows parking area, 1.0 on blue-blaze trail to top of falls, 1.7 to bottom of falls, and 0.5 right on US 56.)

831.5   VA 56, Tye River (4W to Crabtree Falls Campground)
🛏🍴🏠🍳🏕✉ **Crabtree Falls Campground** 540.377.2066 ⟨www.crabtreefallscampground.com⟩ Cabins $50 four people, camping $26/site(2 tents). Laundry, free shower even w/o stay. Trail foods and snacks, ice cream, sodas. stove fuel. Mail (shoebox size or smaller): 11039 Crabtree Falls Hwy, Tyro, VA 22976.

840.5   Maupin Field Shelter
🛏🍴🍴🏠📶 **Royal Oaks Hostel** (1.7W) 540.943.7625 Cabin $60D (M-Th), $85D (F-Su), $15EAP up to 4. Tenting $20 up two. Cabin & tenting both include WiFi, shower w/towel. From Maupin Field Shelter, follow jeep road behind shelter west 1.2mi to the Blue Ridge Parkway (first paved road). Turn left on BRP for 0.5mi to Love Rd (814). Turn right for 100 yards to Royal Oaks. Call for shuttle from Reeds Gap. Store open year-round M-Sa 9-6, Su 12-6 (snacks, sodas, canned food) and deli on-site.

842.2   Reeds Gap, Rte 664 (5.0E to pub, 2.8W to Royal Oaks, listed previously)
🍴🏠🍴 **Devils Backbone Brewpub** 434.361.1001 ⟨www.dbbrewingcompany.com⟩ On Rte. 664 at intersection with Patrick Henry Hwy (151). Open 11:30 to 9 seven days, till 10 on weekends. Serves L/D and sometimes hiker-only breakfast for $5. Hikers welcome to camp on-site for free. Pickup rarely available, but morning return ride often provided.

SoBo	NoBo	Feature	Elevation
1367.9	821.2	Rock Spring, west 100 yards to campsite and spring ♦♠	3517
1366.7	822.4	Spy Rock Rd (formerly Fish Hatchery Rd, unpaved) (pg.79)	3454
1366.3	822.8	Campsite, Spy Rock 0.1E, rock outcrop requiring scramble, view ♠ 🏕	3781
1364.1	825.0	Cash Hollow Rd.	3280
1363.3	825.8	VA 826 (dirt road not easily passable). 0.5W to upper Crabtree Falls (pg.79) trailhead, parking area & privy. Falls Trail downhill 1.0 to major waterfall and 2.1 mi. to lower parking on VA 56 near **Crabtree Falls Campground.**	3350
1362.4	826.7	**The Priest Shelter** (0.1E) 22.4◄16.8◄6.6◄▶7.6▶13.8▶29.6. ♦☾⊏(8)	3885
1361.9	827.2	The Priest, views on AT south of summit	4063
1360.3	828.8	View 🏕	2933
1358.8	830.3	Cripple Creek ♠	1863
1357.6	831.5	VA 56, Tye River suspension bridge 37.8384,-79.0231 P (pg.79) 100 yards north, **Crabtree Falls Campground** (4.0W)	970
1356.4	832.7	Roadbed.	1667
1355.9	833.2	Mau-Har Trail to west, rejoins AT to the south at Maupin Field Shelter	2019
1355.0	834.1	Stream. ☾♠♦⊏(6)	1734
1354.8	834.3	**Harpers Creek Shelter** ▲ Harpers Creek in front of shelter. Privy uphill. 24.4◄14.2◄7.6◄▶6.2▶22.0▶34.7	1892
1353.3	835.8	View 🏕	2778
1352.9	836.2	Chimney Rock, view 🏕	3164
1351.5	837.6	Three Ridges Mountain.	3959
1350.7	838.4	Hanging Rock Overlook, view 🏕	3499

NoBo
SoBo

⚠️ Staying in or within 100 yards of any single AT shelter south of Waynesboro is limited to 3 nights in a 30-day period. This also applies to Davis Farm and Davis Path Campsites.

SoBo	NoBo	Description	Features	Elev.
1348.6	840.5	**Maupin Field Shelter** 20.4◄13.8◄6.2◄▶15.8▶28.5▶41.5 Piped spring behind shelter. Privy to right of shelter on unmarked path. Mau-Har Trail northern intersection. Jeep road leads 1.4mi. to BRP.	) ∆ ♠ ∠ (6) (pg.79)	2746
1346.9	842.2	Reeds Gap, VA 664, BRP 13.6 in view to west.	37.9016,-78.9853 P (pg.79)	2650
1346.4	842.7	Three Ridges Overlook, BRP 13.1	37.907,-78.9795 P 🏛	2700
1344.2	844.9	Stream	♦	2607
1343.4	845.7	Rock Point Overlook, view to west.	📷	2791
1342.6	846.5	Cedar Cliffs, view.	📷	2800
1342.1	847.0	Dripping Rock, BRP 9.6, spring	37.9411,-78.9369 P	2950
1341.8	847.3	Laurel Springs Gap, spring.	♦	2849
1340.9	848.2	Side trail 0.3W to Humpback picnic area		3215
1340.1	849.0	Campsite, view	📷 ⌂	3529
1339.3	849.8	Humpback Mountain		3628
1338.3	850.8	Trail 0.2W to view at The Rocks	📷	3263
1336.6	852.5	Spring	♦	2520
1335.6	853.5	Spring	♦	2335
1335.5	853.6	Side trail 0.2W to Humpback Gap, BRP 6.0		2328
1334.6	854.5	Glass Hollow Overlook, view to east.	📷	2250
1334.2	854.9	Side trail 1.3W to Humpback Visitor Center	37.9692,-78.8974 P H	2290
1334.1	855.0	Albright Loop Trail to west.	♦	2225
1332.8	856.3	**Paul C. Wolfe Shelter** 29.6◄22.0◄15.8◄▶12.7▶25.7▶38.9 Mill Creek 50 yards in front of shelter. Waterfall with pool 100 yards.	) ♦ ∠ (10)	1574
1332.0	857.1	Small cemetery		1860
1331.3	857.8	Cabin ruins, chimney.	♦	2068
1331.0	858.1	Spring	♦	2048
1329.7	859.4	Stream	♦	1873

NoBo
SoBo

5000

3000

1000

☘ Turks Cap Lily – Petals of this down-facing large flower curl back to form a bun shape (Turk's cap). Common color is flame orange and yellow, speckled with brown dots.

SOBO	NOBO	Feature	Elev	
1328.8	860.3	Stream	1735	♦
1327.8	861.3	US 250 + Blue Ridge Pkwy. ... 38.0311,-78.8591 ▣ ⊞ 🚻 ☏ (pg.84) Rockfish Gap, **Waynesboro, VA** (3.7W), I-64 overpass, south end of Skyline Dr.	1917	
1326.8	862.3	Shenandoah National Park (SNP) (pg.86) Entrance station and self-registration for overnight permits.	2221	
1324.1	865.0	Skyline 102.1, McCormick Gap	2450	
1322.8	866.3	Bears Den Mountain, communication towers, tractor seats	2885	
1322.3	866.8	Skyline 99.5, Beagle Gap ... 38.0729,-78.7935 ▣	2550	
1321.5	867.6	Little Calf Mountain	2917	📷
1320.8	868.3	Calf Mountain	2989	
1320.1	869.0	**Calf Mountain Shelter** (0.3W) 34.7◄28.5◄12.7◄▶13.0▶26.2▶34.4 Spring on way to shelter. Bear pole.	2668	☾ ◖ (0.2W) ⚑ ⊂ (6)
1319.6	869.5	Powerline	2293	
1319.5	869.6	Spring	2285	◖
1319.1	870.0	Gravel road 0.1W to Skyline 96.9, Jarman Gap	2248	
1318.9	870.2	Spring, just south of woods road	2143	◖
1317.3	871.8	Skyline 95.3, Sawmill Run Overlook	2200	📷
1315.9	873.2	Turk Mountain Trail to west.	2657	
1315.7	873.4	Skyline 94.1, Turk Gap ... 38.129,-78.7849 ▣	2600	
1313.7	875.4	Skyline 92.4	3009	
1313.4	875.7	Wildcat Ridge Trail east to Skyline 92.1 ... 38.1484,-78.7746 ▣	2914	
1310.7	878.4	Skyline 90.0, spur trail to east leads to Riprap parking area.	2752	▣
1310.3	878.8	Riprap Trail branches to west	2980	
1309.6	879.5	Skyline 88.9	2615	

SoBo	NoBo	Description	GPS / Notes	Elev.
1307.8	881.3	Skyline 87.4, Black Rock Gap, Paine Run Trail	38.2066,-78.7496 **P**	2321
1307.6	881.5	Skyline 87.2		2379
1307.1	882.0	**Blackrock Hut** (0.2E) 41.5◄25.7◄13.0◄▶13.2▶21.4▶33.8	38.2222,-78.7332 **P**	2743
1306.7	882.4	Trayfoot Mountain Trail to west		3076
1306.6	882.5	Blackrock, views from summit, which is skirted by the AT		3092
1306.0	883.1	Blackrock parking area.	38.2222,-78.7332 **P**	2923
1305.5	883.6	Skyline 84.3.		2800
1305.4	883.7	Jones Run parking	38.2301,-78.7263 **P**	2790
1304.8	884.3	Two trails west to Dundo Campground (primitive, reserved for group use)		2753
1304.1	885.0	Skyline 82.9, Browns Gap	38.2404,-78.7109 **P**	2576
1303.5	885.6	Big Run Loop Trail to west		2829
1303.2	885.9	Skyline 82.2.		2795
1302.7	886.4	West to Doyles River Parking Overlook, Skyline 81.9	38.2468,-78.6948	2854
1301.9	887.2	Doyles River Traill, west to Skyline 81.1, east to Doyles River Cabin (locked), 0.3E to spring, 1.2E to falls	38.2542,-78.683 **P**	2860
1301.1	888.0	Trail to Loft Mtn amphitheater	(pg.87)	3171
1301.0	888.1	Trail to **Loft Mtn Campground** (go here if camping)	(pg.87)	3259
1300.4	888.7	Trail to **Loft Mtn Campground**		3289
1300.0	889.1	Powerline	(pg.87)	3238
1299.8	889.3	Trail to **Loft Mtn Store** (in view to west)	(pg.87)	3159
1298.6	890.6	Frazier Discovery Trail 0.3W to **Loft Mtn Wayside**		3291
1298.5	890.5	Frazier Discovery Trail to west.		3299
1297.6	891.5	Trail to 0.5W to **Loft Mtn Wayside** (flatter than FDT), Ivy Creek spring 0.1W		2974
1297.0	892.1	Cross Ivy Creek		2560
1296.3	892.8	View to west		2949
1295.5	893.6	West to Skyline 77.5, Ivy Creek Overlook		2876
1293.9	895.2	**Pinefield Hut** (0.1E), Skyline Dr (0.1W). 38.9◄26.2◄13.2◄▶8.2▶20.6▶32.1 Spring on trail to shelter and 50 yards behind. Both unreliable. Campsites uphill, beyond shelter.		2474
1293.7	895.4	Skyline 75.2, Pinefield Gap.	38.2902,-78.6419 **P**	2590
1292.9	896.2	Weaver Mountain		2876
1291.8	897.3	Skyline 73.2, Simmons Gap Simmons Gap ranger station on paved road 0.2E from where AT crosses Skyline. Water available at pump outside buildings.		2250

NoBo

SoBo

861.3   Rockfish Gap

🅱 📞 🛜 🅿 Afton Mountain Visitor Center 540.943.5187 Open most days 9-5. Info on town services & trail angels. Many lodging facilities offer free pickup/return from here. Long-term parking okay; leave contact info & return date.

🛏 Inn at Afton 540.942.5201 Hiker rate $40+tax, pets allowed. Some restaurants deliver here.

🛏 ◐ △ 🛜 ✉ (0.5W on 250) Colony House Motel 540.942.4156 $42-70+tax, pets $10, some snacks sold on-site, rooms have micro & fridge. Ask about tenting on-site. Mail: 494 Three Notched Mtn Hwy, Waynesboro, VA 22980.

🍴 King's Gourmet Popcorn Mid-March through Nov. M-Th 9am-7pm; F 9-8, Sa,Su 8am-8pm; Dec-Mar open Thurs-Sun. Hot dogs, sodas, ice cream, coffee, kettle corn, and gourmet popcorn. CC accepted.

Waynesboro, VA 22980 (4.5W on I-64)

Hiker Fest on June 11, gather at Heritage On Main at 11am for food and a movie. Camping area has pavilion, grill, and solar charger; shower at YMCA nearby.

◐ ❋ YMCA 540.942.5107 Free camping & showers. Use of YMCA facilities $10. Check-in at front desk, need photo ID.

🛏 ◉ △ 🚗 🛜 🖥 Stanimal's 328 Hostel 540.290.4002 AdamStanley06@gmail.com $25 hiker-only hostel includes pickup/return to trail, mattress with clean linens, shower w/ towel, soap, laundry. Large private area including sunroom and finished basement, laptop, WiFi and DVDs. Fridge, freezer & microwave. Snacks, drinks, and ice cream for sale. Discounted slackpacking for multinight guests. Located in residential area but only 2 blocks from major hiker-valued businesses (grocery, restaurants). Please respect noise level. Hikers are required to call ahead and speak with owner prior to staying. Owned by Adam Stanley AT '04, PCT '10.

🛏 ◉ 🛜 🖥 Grace Hiker Hostel Supervised Lutheran Church hostel open May 16-June 19, closed Su nights, 2-night limit. Please do not call the church office. Check-in 5-8pm, check-out 9am; hikers staying over may leave packs. Cots in air-conditioned Fellowship Hall, showers, internet, big-screen TV & DVD, hiker lounge with kitchenette, snacks & breakfast foods. 20 hiker max. No pets, smoking, drugs, alcohol, firearms or foul language. Donations gratefully accepted. Congregation cooks free dinner Thur. nights followed by optional vespers service.

🛏 🛜 ✉ Tree Streets Inn 540.949.4484, $80S/D, includes breakfast, pool, snacks, no pets. Free pickup/return from Rockfish Gap with stay. Maildrops (pre-registered guests only): 421 Walnut Avenue, Waynesboro, VA 22980.

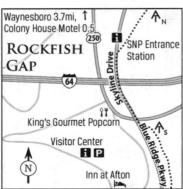

Waynesboro 3.7mi, ↑
Colony House Motel 0.5
ROCKFISH GAP
SNP Entrance Station
King's Gourmet Popcorn
Visitor Center
Inn at Afton

🛏 🛜 ✉ Belle Hearth B&B 540.943.1910 ⟨www.bellehearth.com⟩ $75S, $95D, higher on weekends, includes B, pool, pickup/return. No smoking, no alcohol, no pets. Guest Mail: 320 S. Wayne Ave, Waynesboro, VA 22980

🛏 🛜 🖥 Quality Inn 540.942.1171 Hiker rates $62S $67 up to 4 plus tax, pets $10. Includes continental breakfast.

🍴 Heritage on Main 540.946.6166 Hiker-friendly sports bar, beer, burgers, salads. M-Th 11am-12am, F,Sa 11-1am. Live music W&Sa, trivia Th.

🍴 Weasie's Kitchen 5:30am-8pm M-F, 5-2 weekends.

🍴 ◉ Ming Garden

🏃 ◉ Rockfish Gap Outfitters 540.943.1461 Full service outfitter, Coleman/alcohol/oz, other fuels, shuttle info. Freeze-dried foods. Located between town and trail; ask your ride to stop on the way. No aqua blaze.

🚗 Stanimal's Shuttle Service 540.290.4002 covers all of Virginia.

🚗 DuBose Egleston "Yellow Truck" 540.487.6388 shuttles Roanoke to Harpers Ferry.

⛏ Ace Hardware 540.949.8229 Coleman/oz.

🛶 Front Royal Outfitters 540.635.5440 Aquablaze options ranging from Port Republic to Snickers Gap; make arrangements from Waynesboro. Will store gear while you're on the river. Available Mar 15-Jun 30 (thru Oct 31 for SoBos). Please learn the rules for camping on the river.

Stanimal's Hostel (and more services)

0.9 mi from 340:
Budget Inn: 540.942.9551
Royal Inn: 540.949.8253

West 2.1 mi to interstate 64 interchange where there is:

Martin's, Wal-Mart, Target, and a dense cluster of restaurants and motels including:

Chick-fil-A, Cracker Barrel, McAlisters, Outback, Wendy's, Shoneys, KFC, Ruby Tuesdays, Buffalo Wild Wings, Applebees, Panera Bread

Best Western: 540.942.1100
Comfort Inn: 540.932.3060
Days Inn: 540.943.1101
Super 8: 540.943.3888
HI Express: 540.932.7170

Augusta Medical Clinic (inside Walmart) 540.245.7329

Zeus 8 Digital Movie Theater

McDonalds
Burger King
Gavid's
Little Caesars
Laundry Land
Dollar General
Papa Johns
Rite Aid
BP
Scotto's
Pizza Hut
Family Dollar
CVS
Tailgate Grill
Arbys
Subway
Cookout
Hardee's
Kline's Dairy Bar
New York Flying Pizza
Laundromat
Animal Hospital 540.943.3081
Ciro's

Magnolia Ave
Poplar Ave

Broad St

Healthy Habit
Waynesboro Area Learning Tree M-F 10-6
Green Leaf Grille
Blackjack's BBQ
Stella, Bella & Lucy
Heritage on Main
Constitution Park
BZ Laundromat
Weasie's Kitchen

Ace
Quality Inn
Jakes

Main St

Federal St

Mi Rancho

Maple Ave
Tree Streets Inn
Walnut Ave
11th St
Sam's Hot Dogs
Tourism Office
Graham's Shoe Services (also repairs gear) 540.943.7463

Ming Garden AYCE L/D
Kroger (24hrs) 540.943.3172

12th St

Market Ave
Arch Ave

PO (22980): 540.942.7320 M-F 9-5, Sa pickup (only) 8-12

WAYNESBORO, VA
38.0692,-78.8895
(N) Mag. Dec. 9.49°W

3.7 mi; Rockfish Gap Outfitters 0.8 mi

Belle Hearth B&B

14th St

Wayne Ave

Grace Lutheran

Royal Mart

South River Greenway (0.9 mile)
South River

Library 540.942.6746, M-F 9-9, Sa 9-5

YMCA showers

Hiker camping with hammock posts and solar powered charger

1.5 mi

Shenandoah National Park (SNP) 540.999.3500 ⟨www.nps.gov/shen⟩ Emegency line: 800.732.0911

Backcountry Permits are required for overnight hikes within the park. There is no charge for the permit and there is a fine for not having one. Permits are available from self-registration sites at the south and north entrance of the AT into SNP, from any park visitor center, or by mail (see contact information above).

Concrete 4"x4" signposts are used to mark intersections. Information is stamped into an aluminum band at the top of the post.

What is known as a "shelter" on most of the AT is called a "hut" in Shenandoah, and three-sided day-use-only structures are called "shelters." When overnighting in the park, please use the huts or designated campsites, which are usually near the huts.

Backcountry stay is limited to 14 consecutive nights; two at any one location. If you cannot tent in a designated campsite, follow LNT principles of dispersed camping. Tenting at a new location is limited to one night and must be:
- 20 yards from the trail (preferably out of view).
- One quarter mile from any park facility (roads, campgrounds, lodges, visitor centers, and picnic areas).
- 10 yards from any water source.
- 50 yards from other camping parties, building ruins, or "no camping" signs.
- Not within designated "no camping" locations.

Groups are limited to 10. Campfires are only permitted at pre-constructed fire rings at the huts. Pets must be leashed.

Lodges and campgrounds are typically full on weekends. A small number of unreserved walk-in tentsites are available on a first-come, first-served basis at all campgrounds except Lewis Mtn.

Delaware North Companies Parks & Resorts 877.247.9261 ⟨GoShenandoah.com⟩ operates the Skyland Resort, Big Meadows Lodge and Lewis Mountain Cabins, gift shops & camp stores and restaurants within Shenandoah National Park; many readily accessible from the trail.

The Park Service operates campgrounds. Call 877.444.6777 or visit ⟨www.recreation.gov⟩ to reserve campsites. All campsites accommodate 2 tents and up to 6 persons. All except Mathews Arm have coin operated laundry and showers. Many facilities are closed November-May and all are closed December-March.

🚕 **Yellow Cab of the Shenandoah** 540.692.9200 serves all of SNP (24/7). Pet friendly, accepts CC.

If You Plan to be a 2000-Miler

The ATC recognizes hikers who have completed the trail, all at once or in sections, with a "2000-miler" certificate. Your name will be printed in the Spring issue of ATC's member magazine, *AT Journeys*, and listed on ATC's website. The honor system application states that conditional bypasses and reroutes are acceptable and that "Issues of sequence, direction, length of time or whether one carries a pack are not considered." The number "2,000" is used out of tradition, and does not imply that hiking less than the full mileage qualifies. Feel free to set your own agenda on the AT, but if 2000-miler recognition is important to you keep in mind that the application will ask if you "have made an honest effort to walk the entire Trail."

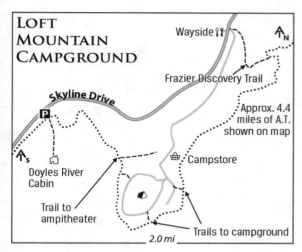

888.1, 888.7   Loft Mountain Campground
889.3   Loft Mountain Wayside

Loft Mountain Campground Campsites $15. AT skirts the campground, and several short side trails lead to campsites and the camp store. Showers, laundry and long term resupply available from camp store. Open May 4-Oct 30.

Loft Mountain Wayside 1.1 miles from camp store, serves B/L/D, short-order menu. Open Apr 8 - Nov 6, daily 9-7.

906.8   US 33, Swift Run Gap. US 33 is also known as Spotswood Trail. The AT crosses over US 33 on the Skyline Drive. North of the bridge, take access road to the west to reach US 33.

         (2.9W):

Country View Motel 540.298.0025 Room with 1 queen bed $75, two queen beds $91. No charge for laundry, but you must have detergent. Mail for guests: 19974 Spotswood Trail, Elkton, VA 22827.

         (3.2W):

Swift Run Camping 540.298.8086, $20 campsite, laundry, pool, and snack bar, open year-round.

Bear Mtn Grocery 540.298.9826 M-F 5am-8pm, Sa 6–8, Su 8-7.

         (6.5W): *Elkton, VA 22827*

M-F 8:30-4:30, Sa 9-11, 540.298.7772

Food Lion

Pizza Hut, several fast-food restaurants

Rite Aid

915.0, 915.1   Lewis Mountain Campground

Lewis Mountain Campground & Cabins 540.999.2255 Campsites $15, small bunkhouse, cabin rates seasonal. Open Apr 1 - Nov 6. Camp store open same dates, Su-Th 9-6, F-Sa 9-7. Reservations 877.247.9261.

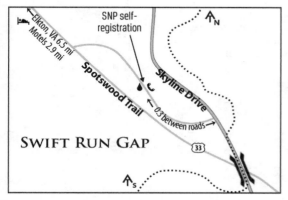

SoBo	NoBo	Feature	Elev
1289.0	900.1	View east to Powell Gap Hollow	2587
1288.5	900.6	Skyline 69.9, Powell Gap	2294
1286.9	902.2	Skyline 68.6, Smith Roach Gap	2600
1285.7	903.4	**Hightop Hut** (0.1W), reliable spring 0.1 from shelter ⟍ ♦ ⚒ (8) ⌐ (6) 34.4◄21.4◄8.2◄►12.4►23.9►34.8	3183
1285.2	903.9	Spring east of AT	3521
1285.0	904.1	View to west from flank of Hightop Mtn.	3514
1283.6	905.5	Skyline 66.7 38.3449,-78.5531 P	2650
1282.6	906.5	Stream.	2507
1282.3	906.8	Skyline 65.5, Swift Run Gap, **Elkton, VA** (6.4W) ♦ ☎ (pg.87) Bridge over US 33, access road north of bridge 0.1W to phone, water (treat), SNP self-registration	2367
1280.7	908.4	Saddleback Mtn Trail to east.	3019
1279.7	909.4	Trail 0.3E to spring at former South River Shelter site	2952
1279.2	909.9	South River Picnic Area 0.1W. 38.3817,-78.5192 P (0.1W) ⚒ Falls Trail to east.	2888
1278.8	910.3	South River Fire Road.	2878
1277.2	911.9	Baldface Mountain	3621
1276.0	913.1	Spring, Pocosin Cabin (locked), Parking on Skyline. 38.4136,-78.4897 P ♦	3150
1275.9	913.2	Trail west to parking on Skyline	3145
1274.1	915.0	West to **Lewis Mtn Campground & Cabins** P ⟍ ♦ (6) ⌐ 26.8 38.4372,-78.479 P (pg.87)	3431
1274.0	915.1	West to **Lewis Mtn Campground**.	3378
1273.3	915.8	**Bearfence Mountain Hut**. P ♦ (6) (0.2E; 0.1 on gravel rd, 0.1 on side trail 33.8◄20.6◄12.4◄►11.5►22.4►26.8	3194
1272.6	916.5	Bearfence Mountain Loop Trail, two intersections 0.2 mile apart, views 0.1E.	3511
1272.1	917.0	Skyline 56.4, Bearfence Mtn Trail, parking 0.1W. 38.4524,-78.4669	3386
1270.7	918.4	Skyline 55.1, Bootens Gap 38.4675,-78.4573 P	3243

NoBo
SoBo

SoBo	NoBo	Feature	Elev.
1270.2	918.9	Laurel Prong Trail to east.	3516
1269.8	919.3	Hazeltop.	3812
1267.9	921.2	Skyline 52.8, Milam Gap, parking to east · 38.4988,-78.4457 **P**	3300
1267.3	921.8	Spring, No camping in Big Meadows clearing within sight of Skyline Dr · ◆	3268
1266.8	922.3	Tanners Ridge Rd (gravel), cemetery	3329
1266.2	922.9	Lewis Spring & Road, Lewis Falls 0.5W · 38.4524,-78.4669 **P** ◆ (pg. 90)	3335
		Gravel road 0.2E to Skyline, then left 0.2 to **Big Meadows Wayside**	
1265.7	923.4	Rock outcropping, view	3621
1265.3	923.8	Trail to **Big Meadows Lodge,** Lewis Falls 0.5W · (pg.90)	3564
1264.9	924.2	Trail east to **Big Meadows Campground** · (pg.90)	3561
1264.7	924.7	David Spring 20 yards west · ◆	3490
1264.5	924.6	Stream. · ◆	3382
1263.7	925.4	Fishers Gap, Skyline 49.3 to east, maintenance road	3050
1263.5	925.6	Franklin Cliffs, view · ◙	3025
1262.4	926.7	Trail to Spitler Knoll parking, 4 cars (0.2W) · 38.5482,-78.4138 **P**	3226
1261.8	927.3	**Rock Spring Hut** (0.2W) ·) ◆ ⚲ (9) C (8)	3513
		32.1◄23.9◄11.5◄▶10.9▶15.3▶28.4 Locked cabin in front.	
1261.5	927.6	Trail east to Hawksbill Mountain, no camping anywhere above 3600'	3625
1260.5	928.6	Hawksbill Gap, parking to east. · 38.5629,-78.3825 **P**	3361
1260.0	929.1	Stream, trail to Crescent Rock Overlook, parking to east. · ◆	3408
1259.2	929.9	Spring. · ◆	3313
1258.3	930.8	Spring.	3438
1258.0	931.1	Skyland stables, service road	3550
1257.4	931.7	Trail to **Skyland Resort & Restaurant** (0.1W). · **P** (pg.90)	3747
1257.3	931.8	Skyland service road north. · 38.5926,-78.376 **P**	3693
1256.8	932.3	Trail to Stony Man Summit (0.2W) Highest point on the AT in SNP	3837
1256.2	932.9	Little Stony Man Cliffs, overlook to west.	3568
1256.0	933.1	Passamaquoddy Trail · ◙	3404
1255.7	933.4	Spur trail to parking · 38.6059,-78.3664 **P**	3225
1255.3	933.8	Stony Man Overlook · 38.6123,-78.3625 **P** ◙	3075
1254.9	934.2	Nicholson Hollow Trail	3096
1254.7	934.4	Crusher Ridge Trail	3179
1254.1	935.0	Corbin Cabin Trail	3120
1253.7	935.4	Powerline	3297
1253.0	936.1	Pinnacles Picnic Area & Parking, restrooms, water from faucet. · **P** 🚻 ☎	3387
1252.8	936.3	East to Skyline 36.4, side trail to Jewell Hollow Overlook.	3300
1252.5	936.6	Leading Ridge Trail to west. · ◙	3368
1251.9	937.2	The Pinnacle	3730
1250.9	938.2	**Byrds Nest #3 Hut,** spring 0.4E on service road. ·) ◆ C (8)	3259
		34.8◄24.4◄10.9◄▶4.4▶17.5▶28.0	

922.9   Lewis Spring Rd (See map for easiest access.)
923.8   Big Meadows Lodge

🍴🏠 **Big Meadows Wayside** B/L/D, Fuel/oz at gas station. Open Mar 24-Nov 13.

🛏🍴💲 **Big Meadows Lodge** Lodge rooms, cabins & suites, reservations required. Some pet-friendly rooms. B: 7:30-10:30, L: 12-2, D: 5:30-9. Open May 11 - Nov 6.

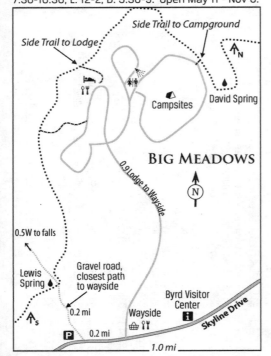

Side Trail to Campground

Side Trail to Lodge

Campsites

David Spring

BIG MEADOWS

0.9 Lodge to Wayside

0.5W to falls

Lewis Spring

Gravel road, closest path to wayside

Byrd Visitor Center

0.2 mi

Wayside

0.2 mi

Skyline Drive

1.0 mi

924.2   Big Meadows Campground 540.999.3231

🔋🏕🚿⛺ **Big Meadows Campground** $20 for 2 tents & 6 persons, self-register after-hours. Coin laundry & showers. Open Mar 25 - Nov 13.

931.7   Side trail to Skyland

🛏🍴💲🏕 **Skyland Resort and Restaurant** 540.999.2212
Rates seasonal, reservations required. Dining room hours B: 7:30-10:30, L: 12-2:30, D: 5:30-9, nightly entertainment. Snack foods & sodas sold at gift shop and vending machines. Open Mar 24 - Dec 4.

941.4   US 211, Thornton Gap

🛏🍴📶 (4.5W on US 211) to **Brookside Cabins & Restaurant** 540.743.5698 〈www.brooksidecabins.com〉 $85-$200 cabins open year-round, range in size (2-6 persons). A few have kitchen & hot tub, no TV or phone. Restaurant AYCE F-M, closed Dec-Mar.

🛏🔋🍴🏛⛺ (5.3W) **Yogi Bear's Jellystone Park** 540.743.4002 Cabins $63-$528 hold 4-15, summer wkend 2-night min (3 on holiday wkend). Tent sites $37-75, 2-night min. Open late Mar to late Nov. Pets at tentsites & some cabins. All stays include free water slide, paddle boat, mini golf. Memorial to Labor Day snack shop serving hamburgers, hot dogs, pizza. Coin laundry, camp store, pool. Showers for guests only.

🛏⛺📶💻 (6.9W) **Days Inn** 540.743.4521 $89.95-$109.95D, $10EAP, cont. B, pets under 50 lbs $15, pool.

Luray, VA 22835 (9W) Farmer's market held on Saturdays.

🏠🚿⛺🅿📶✉ **Open Arms at the Edge of Town** 540.244.5652 Call or text for availability. Open year-round, within a mile of town. Bunkroom $30, camping $15PP with shower & kitchen privileges. Breakfast, soda & snacks for sale on-site. Laundry $5/load. Pet friendly. Mail for guests: 1260 E. Main St., Luray, VA 22835

🛏📶💻✉ **Budget Inn** 540.743.5176 $59.95D/up, $10EAP, pets $10. Maildrops (non-guests $10): 320 W. Main St, Luray, VA 22835.

🛏📶✉ **Luray Caverns Motels** East & west buildings 540.743.4536, 888.941.4531, Su-Th $73, F-Sa $91. 20% discount coupon on food at Luray Caverns. No pets. Maildrops with reservation: 831 W. Main St, Luray, VA 22835.

🛏📶 **Cardinal Inn** 888.648.4633 Hiker rate: winter $55, summer $75.

🛏📶 **South Court Inn B&B** 540.843.0980 〈southcourtinn.com〉 Discounted rate for hikers $100S/D when rooms available, includes big breakfast. No pets, smoking outside only. Wir sprechen Deutsch.

🛏️🍴📶🖥️ **Best Western** 540.743.6511 Call for rates, pet fee $20.

🛏️ **Woodruff House & Victorian Inn B&B** 540.843.3200 ⟨www.woodruffhousebandb.com⟩

🛏️🍴 **Mimslyn Inn** 540.743.5105 ⟨www.mimslyninn.com⟩ Rooms $169/up, **Speakeasy** on-site, dinner 4-11pm, full bar and W-F entertainment.

🥾📶✉️ **Appalachian Outdoors Adventures** 540.743.7400 Full-service outfitter, Coleman/alcohol/oz, canisters, Dr. Bonner's/oz, freeze-dried foods. M-Th 10-6, F-Sa 10-8, Su 1-5. Mail: 2 West Main St, Luray, VA 22835.

ℹ️🚻📶 **Visitor Center** 540.743.3915 daily 9-5.

 5mi. north of town on Shenandoah River:

🛏️🛶 **Rock Tavern River Kamp** 540.843.4232 ⟨www.massanuttensprings.com⟩ Tentsites $45 for 4 (showers included), Yurt $110 (4 person), luxury cabins hold up to 10. Call in advance for availability.

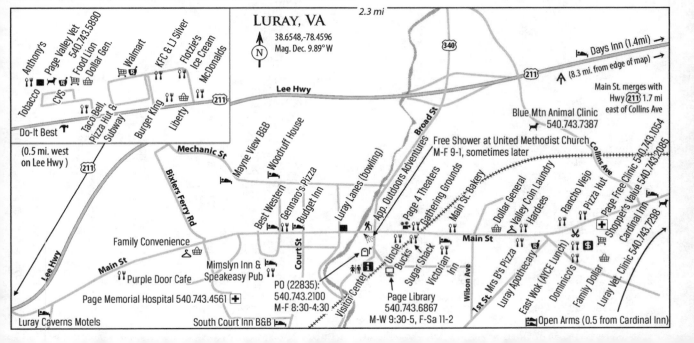

NoBo	SoBo	Description	Features	Elev
938.6	1250.5	View	● (0.3E)	3330
938.9	1250.2	Meadows Spring Trail to east	📷(0.3E)	3359
939.5	1249.6	Overlook, Mary's Rock to west	📷	3462
940.4	1248.7	Spring	●	2885
941.2	1247.9	Trail to Panorama RR parking, powerline	38.6605,-78.3221	2323
941.4	1247.7	US 211, Thornton Gap, **Luray, VA (9W)**.	🅿 ● (pg.90)	2224
941.5	1247.6	Skyline 31.2 .		2340
942.6	1246.5	**Pass Mountain Hut** (1939) (0.2E).	☽ ● ◣ ⊂(8)	2795
		26.8◀15.3◀4.4◀▶13.1▶23.6▶31.7 2 bear poles, 2 privies, and 8 tent sites.		
		Piped spring 15 yards behind shelter.		
943.4	1245.7	Pass Mountain		3052
944.5	1244.6	Beahms Gap Overlook, parking to east	🅿 📷	2490
944.9	1244.2	Spring to west	●	2437
945.8	1243.3	Neighbor Mtn Trail, Byrds Nest #4 day use picnic area.	●(0.5E)	2667
949.5	1239.6	Stream, Jeremys Run Trail	●	2226
950.0	1239.1	**Elkwallow Wayside** (and Gap) 0.1E on side trail or on Skyline 23.9.	👫 🍴	2480
		Grill B/L/D, limited groceries, vending outside, 9-7 Early April-Early Oct.		
950.7	1238.4	Frost-free pump at picnic area south of wayside. Range View Cabin (locked) 0.1E	●(0.1E)	2971
951.5	1237.6	Skyline 21.9, Rattlesnake Point Overlook	📷	3087
952.1	1237.0	Tuscarora Trail to **Mathews Arm Campground** (0.7W)	●	3400
		Primitive campground open May-Oct; no services. Tent sites $14.		
952.5	1236.6	Skyline 21.1, Hogback parking	🅿	3350
952.8	1236.3	Skyline 20.8, Hogback Overlook	📷	3350
954.0	1235.1	Skyline 19.7, Little Hogback parking 50 yards east	🅿	3025
954.1	1235.0	Little Hogback Mountain, view	📷	3050
954.7	1234.4	Skyline 18.8		2807
955.7	1233.4	**Gravel Springs Hut** (0.2E), spring en route to shelter	☽ ● ◣ ⊂(8)	2639
		28.4◀17.5◀13.1◀▶10.5▶18.6▶24.1		
955.9	1233.2	Skyline 17.7, Gravel Springs Gap	38.7678,-78.2335 🅿	2666
956.7	1232.4	View west		3071
957.0	1232.1	South Marshall Mountain		3212
957.5	1231.6	Skyline 15.9, parking to west.	🅿	3050

NoBo
SoBo

5000

3000

1000

SoBo	NoBo	Features	Elev
1230.9	958.2	North Marshall Mountain, view	3368
1229.9	959.9	Hogwallow Flat	2952
1229.4	959.7	Skyline 14.2, Hogwallow Gap. 38.7898,-78.1887 P	2739
1227.7	961.4	Skyline 12.3, Jenkins Gap, parking to east. 38.8065,-78.1808 P	2341
1226.8	962.3	Compton Springs	2700
1226.4	962.7	Compton Peak	2909
1225.6	963.5	Skyline 10.4, Compton Gap parking. 38.8236,-78.1706 P	2426
1223.8	965.3	Compton Gap Tr ("VA 610/Chester Gap" post), **Front Royal Hostel** (0.5E) (pg. 96)	2350
1223.6	965.5	SNP permit self-registration station	2335
1222.9	966.2	**Tom Floyd Shelter** 28.0◀23.6◀10.5◀▶8.1▶13.6▶18.1 bear pole, trail behind shelter and side trails north on AT lead to water. (6)	1944
1222.0	967.1	Trail 0.4W to N. Virginia 4H Center, parking.	1366
1221.4	967.7	VA 602, stream south of road.	1088
1220.0	969.1	US 522, **Front Royal, VA** (3.5W) P (pg.96)	950
1219.7	969.4	US 522 (east trailhead) **Mountain Home Cabbin** (0.1E). 38.878,-78.1507 P	974
1219.2	969.9	Bear Hollow Creek	1076
1218.1	971.0	Woods road	1558
1216.7	972.4	CCC Rd.	1800
1216.6	972.5	Sealock Spring, Mosby Campsite. Named after Colonel John Mosby	1749
1215.9	973.2	Powerline	1653
1214.8	974.3	**Jim & Molly Denton Shelter** Porch, chairs, solar shower. 31.7◀18.6◀8.1◀▶5.5▶10.0▶18.4 bear pole, piped spring 100 yards south. ✖ PVC pipe on outer wall of shower has printing on it. What city name is in red? (8)	1326
1213.8	975.3	Stream.	1048
1213.7	975.4	VA 638, powerline to south	1070
1213.0	976.1	Ridgetop clearing, bench view	1437
1211.8	977.3	VA 55 (John Marshall Hwy), Manassas Gap. 38.9092,-78.0533 P (pg.96) RR tracks to south, AT passes under I-66 on Tuckers Lane.	800

1211.6	977.5	Tuckers Lane parking, Footbridge, stream	38.9113,-78.053 ⚑P ◆	817
1210.3	978.8	Stone wall		1415
1209.3	979.8	**Manassas Gap Shelter** (0.1E) (1939) 24.1◄13.6◄5.5◄►4.5►12.9►19.8 Bear Pole. Reliable spring downhill to right of shelter on side trail. Blue-blazed trail south of shelter leads 0.9W to VA 638.	⌔◆◣⊏(6)	1669
1208.0	981.1	Spring	◆	1721
1207.3	981.8	Trico Tower Trail 0.3W to comm tower, parking on VA 638	38.9536,-78.0270 ⚑P	2080

> ❊ **Trillium** – Three-petal flower set upon three leaves. White and pink varieties are plentiful in the southern Appalachians.

1204.8	984.3	**Dicks Dome Shelter** (0.2E) 18.1◄10.0◄4.5◄►8.4►15.3►29.5 Whiskey Hollow Creek in front of shelter (treat water). Stream on AT 75 yards north of shelter side trail	⌔◆◣⊏(4)	1397
1204.4	984.7	Powerline		1607
1203.5	985.3	Spring	◆	1753
1203.6	985.5	Signal Knob parking on VA 638 / Fire Trail Rd 0.1W	38.9852,-77.9997 ⚑P	1837
1202.8	986.3	Boundary to Sky Meadows State Park		1832
1202.5	986.6	**Sky Meadows State Park Visitors Center** ⌕ ☰ ⚷ ◣ ◆ Bench, 1.7E to **Sky Meadows State Park.** 800.933.7275 Open W-Su 8-5, restrooms, soda machine, 12 sites & primitive group camping, $9PP, reservation required, campers must arrive before dusk.		1801
1201.7	987.4	View 0.4E on Ambassador Whitehouse Trail	📷	1578
1200.1	989.0	Two footbridges, streams	◆	888
1200.0	989.1	Ashby Gap, US 50/17		945
1199.8	989.3	Trail 0.1E to parking on VA 601, Blueridge Mtn Rd	39.0157,-77.962 ⚑P	1080
1198.6	990.5	Stream	◆	1137
1198.0	991.1	Stream	◆	1034
1197.7	991.4	Trail west to Myron Glaser Cabin (locked)		1127
1197.2	991.9	Stream	◆	997
1196.8	992.3	Fishers Hill Trail to west		1093
1196.4	992.7	**Rod Hollow Shelter** (0.1W) 18.4◄12.9◄8.4◄►6.9►21.1►36.7 Piped spring left of shelter. Stream on AT south of side trail.	⌔◆◣⊏(8)	891
1196.0	993.1	Stream, Fishers Hill Trail to west, south end of The Roller Coaster 13.5 miles of tightly packed ascents and descents.	◆	802
1194.7	994.4	Spring at Bolden Hollow		843
1193.1	996.0	Footbridge, Morgan Mill Stream, campsite	◆◣	775
1192.6	996.5	VA 605, Morgan Mill Rd (gravel)	39.0721,-77.912 ⚑P	1047

NoBo		Description		Elev
1191.9	997.2	Stream.	◆	1010
1191.0	998.1	Buzzard Hill, AT east of summit		1251
1190.4	998.7	Two streams	◆	804
1189.5	999.6	**Sam Moore Shelter** (1990) 19.8◄15.3◄6.9►14.2►29.8►33.9 ◗◆⊲(6)		904
		Springs in front of shelter and to the left. Several tent sites to left of shelter.		
1189.0	1000.1	Campsite	◢	1289
1188.2	1000.9	Spout Run Ravine, stream	◆	709
1187.0	1002.1	Footbridge, stream, campsite 60 yards north on AT	◆◢	830
1186.5	1002.6	Bears Den Rocks, **Bears Den Hostel** (0.2E), view north on AT ... ⌂ (pg. 96)		1265
1185.9	1003.2	Snickers Gap, VA 7 & 679 (Pine Grove Rd) ... 39.1153,-77.8475 **P** (pg.97)		1000
1185.1	1004.0	Stream.	◆	802
1183.7	1005.4	Stream.	◆	856
1183.4	1005.7	**VA-WV** border		1146
1183.2	1005.9	Raven Rocks, Crescent Rock 0.1E, view	⊚	1252
1183.0	1006.1	Campsite	◢	1365
1182.6	1006.5	The Roller Coaster (north end); 13.5 miles of ascents and descents	◆	1134
		Sand Spring to west, good water source, Devils Racecourse boulder field to north		
1179.7	1009.4	Wilson Gap		1380
1178.5	1010.6	Two trails 0.2E to **Blackburn AT Center** ... 39.1877,-77.7978 **P** (pg. 97)		1650
1176.8	1012.3	Laurel Springs, boardwalk	△	1449
1175.8	1013.3	Buzzard Rocks		1518
1175.3	1013.8	**David Lesser Memorial Shelter** (0.1E) 29.5◄21.1◄14.2►15.6►19.7►24.7 Overflow camping area below shelter.	◗◆◢⊲(6)	1421
		Spring 0.2 mile downhill from shelter.		
1174.0	1015.1	Roadbed.		1321

NoBo

965.3   Compton Gap Trail (post label "VA 610/Chester Gap")

🏠☀⚌🛏✉ **Front Royal Terrapin Station Hostel** (0.5E)
540.539.0509 At the last northbound concrete post in SNP, the AT turns left. NoBos go straight, follow Compton Gap Trail 0.5 mi. to paved road. Hostel is first home on left on paved road. Owned by Mike Evans, ⟨gratefulgg@hotmail.com⟩. Enter in back through marked gate. Open Apr 23-July 5, 2016. Hikers only, picture ID required, bunk only $25, shower w/soap & shampoo $3, laundry $3. One night hiker special $30 includes bunk, shower, laundry, pizza & soda. $50 Two-night special also includes slackpack and 2nd night but not 2nd dinner. All visits include free town shuttle. Other shuttles for fee. WiFi, charging stations, TV, library, music, room to chill. Reservations recommended. No dogs. Mail for overnight guests only: 304 Chester Gap Rd, Chester Gap, VA 22623.
⚌ **Mobile Mike's** 540.539.0509 shuttles and more (Mike Evans).

967.1   Side trail to:
🍴👫⚓🏕🅿 **Northern VA 4H Center** (0.4W) 540.635.7171 ⟨www.nova4h.com/appalachian-trail⟩ Swimming pool Mem-Labor Day, shower $1, concession stand. Free parking up to 30 days, register on-line or check in at office. Donations graciously accepted.

969.1, 969.4   US 522 (Remount Road) *Front Royal 22630* (4W)
🏁☀👫🛏 **Visitor Center** 540.635.5788 7 days, 9-5pm. Hiker goodie bags, hiker box, pack storage. Cold drinks for sale.
🏠☀🅿✉ **Mountain Home Cabbin** 540.692.6198
MountainHomeAT@gmail.com. Renovated "Cabbin" at historic home of Lisa & Scott (Possible AT'12) Jenkins, 3471 Remount Rd (US 522). NoBos: At US 522 trailhead, cross road, continuing on AT for 0.3 mi. parallel to 522. When trail turns north from 522, continue east on 522 for 120 yards. SoBos: Turn left on 522 as soon as you can. Mountain Home is first driveway on left with long stone wall. Cabbin is first small red brick building. Open year-round, call/email ahead suggested, drop-ins OK. Sleeps 6-8. $25PP includes bed, fresh linens, shower, hiker clothes, hiker box, breakfast, limited WiFi, town shuttle for laundry, dinner & resupply. Pizza, ice cream,

snacks & fuel for sale on site. All are welcome to lemonade, cookies, water from faucet on SW corner of cabbin. Max 1 dog per night for $5. Outdoor kennel avail. Parking $3/day for non-guests. Mail: 3471 Remount Rd., Front Royal, VA 22630.
🛏🍴🏕☀✉ **Quality Inn** 540.635.3161 $67S/D, $10EAP (up to 4) includes cont B. Pets $15. Pool. If you need ride back to AT in the morning, let them know when you check-in. **Thunwa Thai** on-site. Mail: 10 Commerce Avenue, Front Royal, VA 22630.
🛏☀ **Parkside Inn** 540.631.1153 Clean, hiker friendly: $50-75 w/ mini fridge & microwave. Trail pickup/drop-off when available.
🛏☀ **Woodward House B&B** 540.635.7010 Hiker rate $110D+tax w/b'fast, pickup & return to trail. Open year-round. CC accepted.
🛏☀🖥 **Super 8** 540.636.4888 10% hiker discount, pets $10.
🛏☀ **Scottish Inn** 540.636.6168 $50/up, pets $10.
🛏☀ **Budget Inn** 540.635.2196
🍴 **Lucky Star Lounge** L/D variety, some vegetarian, live music.

977.3   VA 55, Manassas Gap, *Linden, VA 22642* (1.2W)
🏤 M-F8-12&1-5,Sa8-12,540.636.9936,packagesheldonly15days.
🍴 **Apple House Restaurant** 540.636.6329 Tu-Su 7-8, M 7-5 year-round. Hiker specials, supplies and rides sometimes available.
🏪 **Monterey Convenience Store** 540.636.6791 Open till 8pm.

1002.6   Bears Den Rocks
🏁☀☀🏠🏕🅿🖥✉ **Bears Den Hostel** 540.554.8708 ⟨www.bearsdencenter.org⟩ A castle-like stone lodge, ATC owned and PATC operated. Bunk $20PP, tenting $12PP includes full house privileges. Hiker Special: Bunk, laundry, pizza, soda & pint of Ben & Jerry's ice cream $30PP. All stays include shower & self-serve pancake breakfast. CC accepted. Hiker room with TV, shower, Internet & sodas, accessible all day by entering a mileage code at the hostel door. Upper lodge, kitchen, camp store & office open 5-9pm daily. Check-out 9am. Slackpacking & shuttles may be available during summer months. Parking $3/day. Hosts the *Northern Ruck* Jan 22-24, 2016. No drugs or alcohol anywhere on the property. Pets welcome, but not allowed inside. Mail can

be picked up during office hours: Bears Den Hostel, 18393 Blue Ridge Mountain Rd, Bluemont, VA 20135. ✶What is the Virginia license plate number?

Purcellville, VA (6.0E of Bears Den)

🚶👁‍🗨🛜✉ **Appalachian Outdoor Readiness** 540.338.2437 〈www.appalachianreadiness.com〉 Full service outfitter, canisters, fuel/oz. Open summer 10-6, off-season 11-6. PO and many restaurants in Purcellville.

1003.2   Snickers Gap, VA 7 & 679 (Pine Grove Rd). AT crosses VA 7 at intersection with Pine Grove Rd. Take P.G. Rd. to anitque shop & restaurants. Take VA 7 0.8E, then right on route 734 for PO.

Bluemont, VA 20135

🏠 (1.7E) M-F 10-1 & 2-5, Sa 8:30-12, 540.554.4537
🏬🛜♦ (0.2W) **Snickers Gap Antiques** Hiker-friendly store with limited snacks & first aid items, WiFi, free water fill-up.
🍴 (0.3W) **Horseshoe Curve Restaurant** 540.554.8291 Tu,W 5-9; Th-Su 12-9. Live bands F & Sa. Good pub food.
🍴🅑🛜 (0.9W) **Pine Grove Restaurant** 540.554.8126 M-Sa 7-8, Su 7-2. Welcomes hikers, breakfast served all day.

1010.6 Side trails, both (0.27E) to:
🏠🛖👁‍🗨🔌♦ **Blackburn AT Center** 540.338.9028. PATC caretaker on-site. Hiker bunks in small cabin with wood-burning stove. On porch of main building: logbook, donation box, pay phone, and electrical outlets (welcome to charge devices). Solar shower on lawn, water from hose, picnic tables. Open year-round.

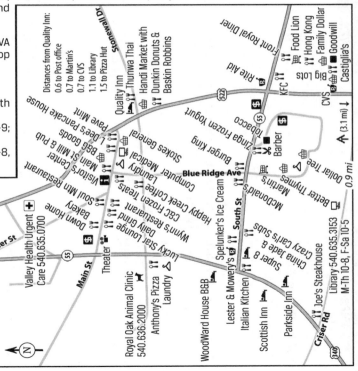

SoBo	NoBo	Description	Elev
1172.3	1016.8	Keys Gap, WV 9, markets 0.3E or W . . . . 39.2616,-77.7625 **P** (pg.100)	911
1170.8	1018.3	Powerline	916
1170.1	1019.0	Campsite ◭	1125
1168.4	1020.7	**VA-WV** border, Loudoun Heights, Loudoun Heights Trail to east	1117
1167.8	1021.3	WV 32, Chestnut Hill Rd	580
1166.9	1022.2	US 340, north end of Shenandoah River Bridge ⚠ No hitchhiking on 340 (pg.100)	319
1166.6	1022.5	Side trail to **Appalachian Trail Conservancy** (0.2W)	434
1166.2	1022.9	Jefferson Rock, view north to Potomac and Shenandoah Rivers	432
1166.0	1023.1	**Harpers Ferry, WV**, High Street . . . . . . 39.3165,-77.7558 📷 (pg.100)	274
1165.7	1023.4	Potomac River, Byron Memorial Footbridge, **WV-MD** border. North of river turn east on C&O Canal Towpath. No camping on AT section of towpath.	246
1164.6	1024.5	Pass under Sandy Hook Bridge (US 340)	248
1163.1	1026.0	C&O Canal Towpath north end, RR tracks, US 340 underpass . . . . . . (pg.102)	246
1162.5	1026.6	From Keep Tryst Rd: **Knoxville, MD** (1.0W), **Brunswick, MD** (2.5E) Weverton Rd . . . 39.333,-77.6832 **P**	371
1161.8	1027.3	Trail east to Weverton Cliffs, view 📷	859
1159.7	1029.4	**Ed Garvey Shelter** . . . . ☽ ◖ ⚑ ⌂ (12) 36.7◄29.8◄15.6◄▶4.1▶9.1▶16.6 Water on steep 0.4 mile trail in front of shelter. 2 tent sites north & south of shelter.	1083
1157.9	1031.2	Brownsville Gap, roadbed	1063
1156.0	1033.1	Gapland Rd, Gathland State Park, War Correspondents ♟ ⚑ (pg.102) Monument. Frost-free spigot by restrooms. No camping, no trash cans.	950
1155.6	1033.5	**Crampton Gap Shelter** (0.3E)(1941) . . . . ☽ △ ◖ ⌂ (6) 33.9◄19.7◄4.1▶5.0▶12.5▶20.7 Intermittent spring 0.1S on AT. NoBo: consider bringing water from Gathland SP in dry season (June-Sept).	1163

⚑ MD guidelines: camp only at designated campsites (where tent symbols are shown). Alcohol not permitted on AT lands in MD.

1153.0	1036.1	Spring 0.5E, trail to Bear Spring Cabin (locked)	◆ 1437
1152.4	1036.7	White Rock Cliff, view.	1579
1152.2	1036.9	Lambs Knoll 50 yards west to tower, view	1733
1151.1	1038.0	Lambs Knoll tower road (paved)	1347
1150.6	1038.5	**Rocky Run Shelters** (0.2W) 24.7◀9.1◀5.0◀▶7.5▶15.7▶20.6 ♪♦⌐(6)(16)	982
		Left fork on side trail to better water source & old shelter. Right to new shelter.	
1149.6	1039.5	Fox Gap, Reno Monument Rd (paved), **South Mountain Creamery** (2E). ♦	1068
1148.8	1040.3	**Dahlgren Backpack Campground**	980
		Large tenting area, picnic tables, restrooms; no fee. Note proximity to road.	
1148.5	1040.6	Turners Gap, US Alt 40, restaurant 0.1W, 39.4840,-77.6198 **P** (pg.102)	1080
		Boonsboro, MD (2.5W)	
1147.2	1041.9	Monument Rd.	1256
1146.9	1042.2	Washington Monument State Park, picnic tables, 39.4977,-77.6208 **P**	1358
		parking near entry, restrooms adjacent to visitor center.	
1146.6	1042.5	Washington Monument (0.1W)	1550
1146.3	1042.8	Powerline	1311
1144.5	1044.5	Boonsboro Mountain Rd, residential area.	1297
1144.2	1044.9	Bartman Hill Trail 0.6W to Greenbrier SP	1394
1143.8	1045.3	I-70 footbridge, US-40. 39.5353,-77.6035 **P** (pg.103)	1239
		Parking north end of footbridge 0.1E. Also cross Boonsboro Mtn Rd south of hwy.	
1143.1	1046.0	**Pine Knob Shelter** (0.1W) (1939), south end of loop trail ♪♦⌐(5)	1378
		16.6◀12.5◀7.5◀▶8.2▶13.1▶22.7 Piped spring next to shelter.	
1141.5	1047.6	Annapolis Rocks to west, campsite ♪♦(0.2W)♦(13)	1756
		Caretaker on site. Tentsites near outstanding overlook.	
1140.5	1048.6	Black Rock Cliffs to west.	1779
1140.1	1049.0	Black Rock Creek ◇	1597
1139.9	1049.2	**Pogo Memorial Campsite** ♪♦	1500
		Campsite east of AT, spring 100 yards west. Thurston Griggs Trail to west.	

✿ **Poison Ivy** – Vine that can grow as ground cover or that can cling to trees or other brush. Stems redden toward the end and terminate with 3 pointed-oval leaves.

1135.1	1054.0	Wolfsville Rd, MD 17, **Smithsburg, MD** (1.5W) (pg.103)	1340
1134.9	1054.2	**Ensign Cowall Shelter** (1999) 20.7◀15.7◀8.2◀▶4.9▶14.5▶16.9 ♪♦⌐(8)	1384
		Boxed spring, somewhat stagnant, south between shelter & road.	
1134.7	1054.4	Powerline	1500

1016.8 Keys Gap, WV 9

🏕 🍴 🛗 ✉ (0.3E) **Sweet Springs Country Store** 540.668.7200 M-Sa 4am-11pm, Su 7am-11pm. Good selection of hiker foods. Stove fuel. Mail: 34357 Charles Town Pike, Purcellville, VA 20132.

🏨 🍴 (0.3W veer left at intersection) **Mini-Mart & Torlone's Pizza**

🏚🍴⚲ (2.0E) **Stoney Brook Organic Farm** 703.622.7526, 571.442.2834, 540.668.9067 (Matt or Nathan) Run by a Twelve Tribes spiritual community. Offers WFS, meals, shower, laundry. Pickup/return from Bears Den, Blackburn Trail Center, Keys Gap, Harpers Ferry. Grocery and outfitter nearby. Mail: 37091 Charles Town Pike Hillsboro, VA 20132

1022.2 US 340, Shenandoah River Bridge

Go west on 340 to the Quality Hotel, KOA, or to Charles Town; east to Frederick. NoBos stay on the AT for better access to Harpers Ferry.

🛏⚲🛰🖥 **Econo Lodge** 304.535.6391 $89-$119 (peak rate mid-summer), 10% hiker discount, hot breakfast bar, no pets.

🔵🛏🍴🏨🔥⚲ (1.2W) **Harpers Ferry KOA** 304.535.6895 Camping $45/up, cabins $95/up, both prices for 2 persons, $8EAP. Coin laundry on-site, shower only $5. Cafe has limited hours.

🛏🍴⚲🛰🖥 (1.3W) **Quality Hotel** 304.535.6302 Pool, **Vista Tavern** on-site.

Charles Town, WV 25414 (6W) All major services.

🏪 🛒 **Walmart** with grocery and pharmacy 304.728.2720

➕ **Jefferson Urgent Care** 304.728.8533 M-F 8-8, Sa-Su 8-5

➕ **Winchester Foot & Ankle** 304.725.0084

🐾 **Jefferson Animal Hospital** 304.725.0428

Frederick, MD 21701 (20E) All major services.

1022.5 Side Trail to ATC HQ (0.2W)

🛗 ⚙🛰✉ **ATC HQ** 304.535.6331 ⟨www.appalachiantrail.org⟩ Open year-round, 7 days 9-5, Closed Thanksgiving, Christmas, New Year's Day. If you're thru-hiking or hiking the entire trail in sections, have your photo taken for the album; a postcard version of this photo may be purchased (first one free for ATC members).

Hiker lounge, register, scale, and cold & hot drinks inside, along with hats, shirts, maps, all ATC publications. Coleman/denatured alcohol/oz for donation. Information board on the front porch. Mail: (USPS) PO Box 807 or (FedEx/UPS) 799 Washington St, Harpers Ferry, WV 25425. ✘ This tree trunk has two blazes, but they're not white. On the AT they often surround you, just out of sight. What color are they and what are they for?

1023.1 *Harpers Ferry, WV 25425* (more services on map)

🏚⚙⚲🚗🛰🖥✉ **Teahorse Hostel** 304.535.6848 0.5W of ATC ⟨www.teahorsehostel.com⟩. $33 per bunk plus tax includes waffle breakfast. Laundry $6. No pets, alcohol or smoking. Shuttle range Thornton Gap to Duncannon and Dulles Airport. Call before sending maildrops in off-season (winter). Maildrops ($2 fee for non-guests): 1312 W. Washington St., Harpers Ferry, WV 25425.

🛏 🏚🍴🏨⚲🚗 **The Town's Inn** 304.932.0677 ⟨www.TheTownsInn.com⟩ Private room $110-$160 up to 4 persons, one pet room. Hostel $35PP. Laundry $5, shuttles $1/mile, no maildrops, Visa/MC accepted. Dining available 6am-10pm daily year-round. Shop stocked for hiker resupply.

🏚 **Harpers Ferry Hostel** (in Knoxville, MD see pg. 102)

🛏🛰 **Laurel Lodge** 304.535.2886 $150-195 for 2 includes big breakfast, view overlooking Potomac. Call about maildrops.

🥾⚙🏨 **The Outfitter at Harpers Ferry & Harpers Ferry General Store** 888.535.2087 Full service outfitter with good selection of shoes & trail food. Shuttle referrals. Open daily 10-6.

🛗 🅿 **Harpers Ferry National Historical Park** 304.535.6029 $6 entrance fee, parking up to 2 weeks (must register). Free shuttle bus to lower town. Gates open 8am-dusk.

🚐 **HostelHiker.com** 202.670.6323 Shuttles from Thorton Gap to Pen-Mar Park. Daily route to/from DC, Dulles & Baltimore. Insured.

🚐 **Mark "Strings" Cusic** 304.433.0028 mdcusic@frontier.com Shuttle range Rockfish Gap to Duncannon.

🚐 **Pan Tran** 304.263.0876 Route to Charles Town (Walmart) M-F 10:42, 12:03, 1:24 and 3:00, $2.50 each way.

■ **Chiropractic treatment & therapeutic massage** Dr Jenny Foster

301.371.3922 or 240.344.0066. Call ahead for possible ride from Harpers Ferry or from any trailhead in MD to therapy center. Sessions also done on-site. Best to get therapy at start of HF zero day(s).

🚆 **Amtrak** 800.872.7245 "Capitol Limited" daily HF to Washington DC Union Station 11:31am-1:05pm (depart-arrive), DC to HF 4:05-5:16pm. \$13 each way.

🚆 **Maryland Rail Commuter Service (MARC)** 410.539.5000 ⟨www.mta.maryland.gov/marc-train⟩. "Brunswick Line" M-F to Washington DC Union Station departs 5:25am, 5:50am and 6:50am, returns 4:25, 5:40 and 6:20pm. \$14 each way.

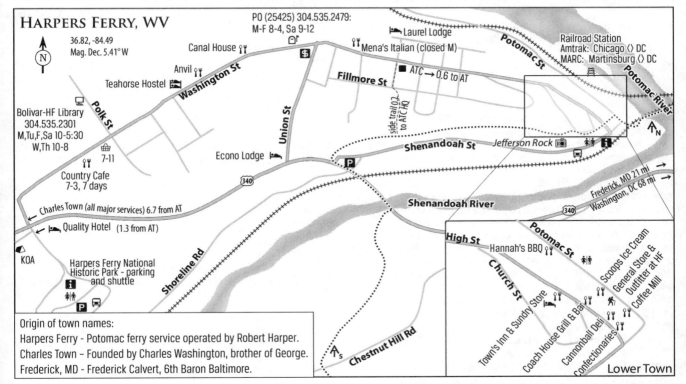

HARPERS FERRY, WV

36.82, -84.49
Mag. Dec. 5.41° W

PO (25425) 304.535.2479:
M-F 8-4, Sa 9-12

Laurel Lodge

Railroad Station
Amtrak: Chicago ⟨⟩ DC
MARC: Martinsburg ⟨⟩ DC

Canal House
Mena's Italian (closed M)
Anvil
Teahorse Hostel

Washington St

Fillmore St

ATC → 0.6 to AT

side trail 0.2 to ATC HQ

Bolivar-HF Library
304.535.2301
M,Tu,F,Sa 10-5:30
W,Th 10-8

Polk St

Union St

Shenandoah St

Jefferson Rock

7-11

Econo Lodge

Country Cafe
7-3, 7 days

340 (P)

Charles Town (all major services) 6.7 from AT

Quality Hotel (1.3 from AT)

Shoreline Rd

Shenandoah River

Frederick, MD 21 mi
Washington, DC 68 mi

340

KOA

Harpers Ferry National Historic Park - parking and shuttle

Chestnut Hill Rd

Lower Town

High St
Hannah's BBQ

Potomac St

Scoops Ice Cream
General Store & Outfitter at HF
Coffee Mill

Church St

Town's Inn & Sundry Store
Coach House Grill & Bar
Cannonball Deli
Confectionaries

Origin of town names:
Harpers Ferry - Potomac ferry service operated by Robert Harper.
Charles Town - Founded by Charles Washington, brother of George.
Frederick, MD - Frederick Calvert, 6th Baron Baltimore.

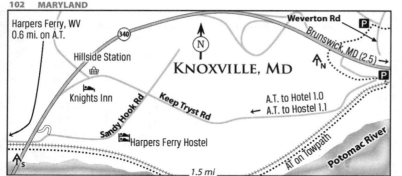

Harpers Ferry, WV
0.6 mi. on A.T.

KNOXVILLE, MD

Hillside Station

Knights Inn

Keep Tryst Rd

Sandy Hook Rd

Harpers Ferry Hostel

Weverton Rd

Brunswick, MD (2.5)

A.T. to Hotel 1.0
← A.T. to Hostel 1.1

AT on Towpath

Potomac River

1.5 mi

1026.0   US 340, Keep Tryst Rd, **_Knoxville, MD, 21758_** (1W)

🚌🛒⚡⛺⛽🚍🅿🛜🖥✉ **Harpers Ferry Hostel** 301.834.7652 ⟨www.harpersferryhostel.org⟩ ID required for any stay. Discounted thru-hiker rate $22.40 includes tax, shower, internet & WiFi, linens, A/C & heat, make-your-own breakfast & dinner. Call for trail angel help with rides. Laundry $4. Tenting $8PP, pay extra $5 for shower, $4 for breakfast. Campers permitted inside only for shower, laundry or breakfast. WiFi, soda machine and phone charging on back porch. Porta-potty, fire pits, grill on lawn. Service dogs okay inside, otherwise dogs on leash allowed only if tenting. Store with hiker snacks inside and there is often free food. Complimentary meals on Tu, Fr, & Sa. Netflix movies available. No drinking. Non-guest parking $5/day. Check-in 5-10pm, check-out 10am. Open May 1–Nov 15 for individuals, year-round for groups. NOT AVAILABLE 6/20/2016-7/1/2016. Mail: 19123 Sandy Hook Rd, Knoxville, MD 21758.

🛏⛺🛜 **Knights Inn** 301.660.3580 $59.99/king-2, $69.99/dbles-2, $89.99/ dbles-3, $99.99/dbles-4 includes fridge, mwave, cont B. Hiker laundry $5.

⛽🍴🅱 **Hillside Station** 301.834.5300 Convenience store with pizza, wings, and more. M-Sa 6-9, Su 7-7.

Brunswick, MD 21716 (2.5E from Keep Tryst Rd)
🏤 M-F 8-4:30, Sa 9-12, 301.834.9944
🍴 **Wing N' Pizza Shack** 301.834.5555 Delivers to HF Hostel.

1033.1   Gathland SP

⛺🏕 (0.4W) **Maple Tree Campground** 301.432.5585 ⟨www.TheTreehouseCamp.com⟩ $30 tentsite for 1 or 2, $10EAP. Campstore has candy bars, sodas, batteries & microwavable food. Open year-round. On Townsend Road which is to the right as you exit the park.

1040.6   Turners Gap, US Alt 40

🍴🍸 (0.1W) **Old South Mountain Inn** 301.432.6155 ⟨www.oldsouthmountaininn.com⟩ Tu-F 5-9, Sa 4-close, Su brunch 10:30-2, dinner 12-7:30. Men, no sleevless shirts. Please shower first. Dining reservations preferred.

Boonsboro, MD (2.5W)
🍴 **Vesta Pizzeria** 301.432.6166 M-Tu 11-9, W-Su 11-10.
🍴 **Mountainside Deli & Ice Cream** 301.432.6700 M-F 6-8, Sa 8-8, Su 11-6. Cash only.
🏕 **Cronise Market Place** 301.432.7377 M-F 9-7, Sa 9-6, Su 12-6.
🛜 🍴 **Turn the Page Book Store Café** 301.432.4588
🍴🏕 **Crawfords** 301.432.2903 M-F 7-5, Sa 7-3. Limited supplies.

1044.9   Bartman Hill Trail (0.6W) to:

🏕🚻🚿 **Greenbrier State Park** 301.791.4767 Camping first Fri of Apr to last full wkend in Oct. $5 entrance fee waived if camping or if you walk in on Bartman Trail. Prices listed as MD resident/nonresident. Tent sites with showers $26-30, higher wkends/holidays. Pets allowed at Dog Wood. Available Mem Day-Labor Day: lunch concession stand, lake swimming, row boat & paddle boat rentals.

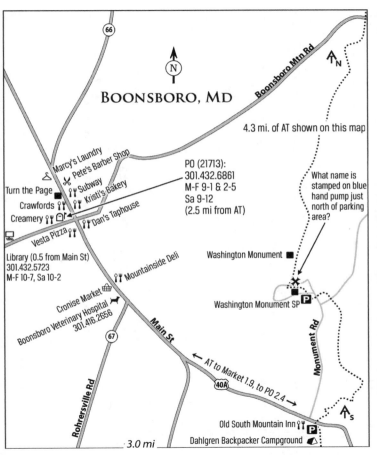

BOONSBORO, MD

4.3 mi. of AT shown on this map

Marcy's Laundry
Pete's Barber Shop
Turn the Page
Subway
Kristi's Bakery
Crawfords
Creamery
Dan's Taphouse
Vesta Pizza

PO (21713):
301.432.6861
M-F 9-1 & 2-5
Sa 9-12
(2.5 mi from AT)

What name is stamped on blue hand pump just north of parking area?

Library (0.5 from Main St)
301.432.5723
M-F 10-7, Sa 10-2

Mountainside Deli

Washington Monument

Cronise Market

Boonsboro Veterinary Hospital
301.416.2656

Washington Monument SP

Main St

AT to Market 1.9, to PO 2.4 →

Rohrersville Rd

Monument Rd

Old South Mountain Inn
Dahlgren Backpacker Campground

3.0 mi

1045.3   I-70, US 40: From US 40, it is 0.4W to entrance of **Greenbrier State Park,** (see previous entry) and an additional 0.7 to the visitor center, where the Bartman Trail enters the park. It's better to use the Bartman Trail.

1054.0   Wolfsville Rd, MD 17
🌢 (0.3E) If shelter water source is dry, you may get water from ranger's house. Go 0.1 east (compass south) to a gravel road on left, then 0.2 on gravel road to first house on left.

Smithsburg, MD 21783 (1.5W)

🏠 M-F 8:30-1 & 2-4:30, Sa 8:30-12, 301.824.2828
🏪 **Dollar General Store** 301.824.6940, daily 8-10
🏬 **Food Lion** 301.824.7011, daily 7-11
🍴 **Smithsburg Market** 301.824.2171, M-Sa 8-9, Su 10-9
🍴 **Rocky's Pizza** 301.824.2066, M-F 10:30-10, Sa 10:30-11, Su 11-10
🍴 **Vince's New York Pizza** 301.824.3939, daily 11-11
🍴 **Dixie Diner** 301.824.5224 Tu-F 7-8, Sa-Su 7-2, closed M.
🍴 **Subway** 301.824.3826, 24 hrs
🍴 **China 88** 301.824.7300, M-Th 11-10, F-Sa 11-10:30, Su 11:30-10
➕ **Smithsburg Emergency Medical** 301.824.3314
🐕 **Smithsburg Veterinary Clinic** 301.416.0888
💊 **Home Care Pharmacy**
💊 **Rite Aid** 301.824.2211, store 8-9, pharmacy 9-9
🛁 **Laundry**
🖥 **Library** 301.824.7722 M,W-F 10am-7pm, Tu 12-9pm, Sa 10am-2pm
🔨 **Ace Hardware**

SoBo	NoBo	Feature	Elev	Icons
1133.6	1055.5	Foxville Rd, MD 77, **Smithsburg, MD** (1.7W)	1590	
1132.4	1056.7	Spring	1325	♦
1132.2	1056.9	Powerline	1345	
1131.8	1057.3	Warner Gap Hollow, stream, Warner Gap Rd (gravel, AT to west).	1150	♦
1131.1	1058.0	Little Antietam Creek	1075	♦
1131.0	1058.1	Raven Rock Rd, MD 491	1062	
1130.7	1058.4	Raven Rock Cliff, view 100 yards east.	1288	
1130.0	1059.1	**Raven Rock Shelter** (0.1W) (2010), Ritchie (0.6E) 20.6◄13.1◄4.9◄►9.6►12.0►13.2 Two story shelter. Water on opposite side of AT (0.3E) on steep side trail.	1647	📷)♦⌂ (16)
1128.2	1060.9	Ends of High Rock Loop Trail 0.2 apart . . . 39.6948,-77.5232 P 📷 0.1E from either end to view and parking. Parking gated from dusk till 8am. 1.7 from parking area to Pen Mar Park via Pen Mar Rd.	1795	
1125.4	1063.7	Pen Mar County Park . . . 39.7164,-77.5072 P 📷 (pg.107)	1321	
1125.1	1064.0	**Cascade, MD** (1.4E), **Waynesboro, PA** (2.1W to Walmart, downtown 4.5)	1250	♦
1125.0	1064.1	**MD-PA** border, RR tracks, Mason-Dixon Line.	1240	♦
1124.5	1064.6	Pen Mar Rd · Falls Creek, footbridge, campsite	1068	♦⌂
1124.0	1065.1	Buena Vista Rd	1290	
1122.8	1066.2	Old PA 16	1278	
1122.5	1066.6	Footbridge, stream, PA 16, · · · 39.7414,-77.4905 P ♦ (pg.107)	1200	
1122.3	1066.8	**Blue Ridge Summit, PA** (1.2E) Mentzer Gap Rd, NoBo: turn west	1250	
1121.9	1067.2	Rattlesnake Run Rd (gravel)	1378	
1120.4	1068.7	**Deer Lick Shelters** 22.7◄14.5◄9.6◄►2.4►3.6►10.2. Spring 10 yards north on AT or (0.2E) on blue-blazed trail.	1406	)♦⌂ (2x5)
1120.1	1069.0	Pipeline clearing	1489	
1119.5	1069.6	Dirt road	1378	
1118.2	1070.9	Orange-blazed Chickadee Snowmobile Trail	909	
1118.0	1071.1	**Antietam Shelter** (1940). 16.9◄12.0◄2.4◄►12►7.8►13.4 Better to get water from Old Forge Park 0.1N	889	)♦⌂ (6)
1117.9	1071.2	Old Forge Picnic Area, Old Forge Rd · · · 39.8005,-77.4793 P ⊞⌕♦	898	
1116.8	1072.3	**Tumbling Run Shelters** 13.2◄3.6◄1.2◄►6.6►12.2►19.6 Piped water 75 yards right of shelter.	1082	)♦⌂ (2x4)
1115.5	1073.6	Chimney Rocks, view to east.	1900	📷
1114.6	1074.5	Pipeline clearing	1916	

5000

3000

1000

NoBo
SoBo

1113.5	1075.6	Powerline	2027
1112.8	1076.3	Snowy Mountain Rd	1703
1112.2	1076.9	Swamp Rd, **South Mountain, PA** 17261 (1.0E) (pg.107)	1560
1111.8	1077.3	PA 233, **South Mountain, PA** 17261 (1.2E) (pg.107)	1605
1110.2	1078.9	**Rocky Mountain Shelters** (0.2E)(1989) ☽ ◑ ⬟ ⊏ (2x4)	1662
		10.2◄7.8◄6.6◄►5.6►13.0►19.2	
		Piped spring 0.5 mile on trail to road, then right 75 yards.	

⚠ Many springs in PA run dry in June, July & August.

1107.2	1081.9	US 30, **Fayetteville, PA** (3.5W) 39.9059,-77.4786 **P** (0.6E)(pg.107)	960
		Overnight parking SW corner of US 30 & Pine Grove Rd, check-in at park HQ.	
1106.8	1082.3	Side trail to **Caledonia State Park**, pool area (pg.108)	934
1106.0	1083.1	Locust Gap Rd, Valley Trail to west	1334
1104.6	1084.5	**Quarry Gap Shelters** (1935) 13.4◄12.2◄5.6◄►7.4►13.6►24.5 ☽ ◑ ⬟ ⊏ (2x4)	1471
1104.3	1084.8	Footbridge, stream	1542
1103.9	1085.2	Hosack Run Trail to east	1819
1103.1	1086.0	5-way gravel road intersection	1984
1102.3	1086.8	Powerline	1867
1101.9	1087.2	Woods road	1986
1100.6	1088.5	Middle Ridge Road	2070
1100.0	1089.1	3 Points (intersecting gravel roads), campsite to north	1961
1099.6	1089.5	PATC Milesburn Cabin (locked), spring 100 yards west. ◑	1681
1099.3	1089.8	Ridge Rd (gravel), campsite north of road ◑	1907
1098.5	1090.6	Rocky Knob Trail (orange-blazed)	1902
1097.9	1091.2	Powerline, campsite to north ☽ ◑ ⬟	1913
1097.2	1091.9	**Birch Run Shelter** (2003) stream 75 yards north on AT ⊏ (8)	1800
		19.6◄13.0◄7.4◄►6.2►17.1►25.2	
1097.1	1092.0	Footbridge, stream ◑	1783
1095.9	1093.2	Shippensburg Rd 39.9972,-77.405 **P**	2040
1094.8	1094.3	Dead Woman Hollow Road (gravel)	1954
1094.6	1094.5	**AT Midpoint** (2016)	1991

Waynesboro, PA (western edge of town)

Rite Aid, Western Union
Hardees, Burger King
DQ

Cobblestone Hotel
Old City Buffet (AYCE L/D)
Olympia Sports (shoes)

Franks Pizza

Food Lion   Lowes
Dollar General
KFC
Red Run Grill

Applebees
Sheetz
Rolling Mill Tavern, Bobby-D's
Red Run Park

Keystone Family Restaurant (Th-Sa)

Mentzer Gap Rd

(16)

P.O. 2.0 → P.O. 1.3

39.7414, -77.4905 P

Old Rte 16

Waynesboro Walk-in Clinic

Vapor Club

Sunshine Lanes
Brothers Pizza

Blondie's

from edge of map:
➕ 1.0 Waynesboro Hospital
🛏 2.0 Days Inn & Burgundy Lane

Rouzerville PO (17250)
717.762.7050:
M-F 8:30-1 & 2-4:30,
Sa 8:30-11:30

Walmart Supercenter with groceries, pharmacy, and Subway

Blue Ridge Summit, PA

PO (17214) 717.794.2335 M-F 8-12, 1-4 Sa 9-11:30

Mountain Shadows

King's Pizza & Blue Ridge Food Mart

True Value

JJ's Laundromat

Unique Bar

Synergy Massage

Library 717.794.2240, M-Th 3-8, Sa 10-2

(418)

Midvale Rd

← 1.6 park to PO

Pen Mar Rd

(N)

Buena Vista Rd

Ft. Ritchie Rd

Military Rd

(550)

Harbaugh Church Rd

39° 43' 15"

Pennsylvania
Maryland

Sander's Market
301.241.3612

The AT crosses the Pennsylvania-Maryland line just north of PenMar Park and the railroad tracks. The border (244 miles of it) was defined by Charles Mason and Jeremiah Dixon in a survey that lasted four years and ended a long term boundary dispute. Mason and Dixon were commissioned to set the northern Maryland border on a line of latitude 15 miles south of the southernmost home in Philadelphia at the time of the survey.

PenMar Park - former site of amusement park, which was open 1877-1943; visit mini-museum in center of park.

↑ s

4.5 mi

← 1.3 park to Rocky's

Chocolate Park Liquors

Cascade, MD

Rocky's Pizza
Ft Ritchie Comm Center

PO (21719) 301.241.3403: M-F 10-1 & 2-5, Sa 8-12

↑ N Approximately 5 mi. of the AT are shown on this map.

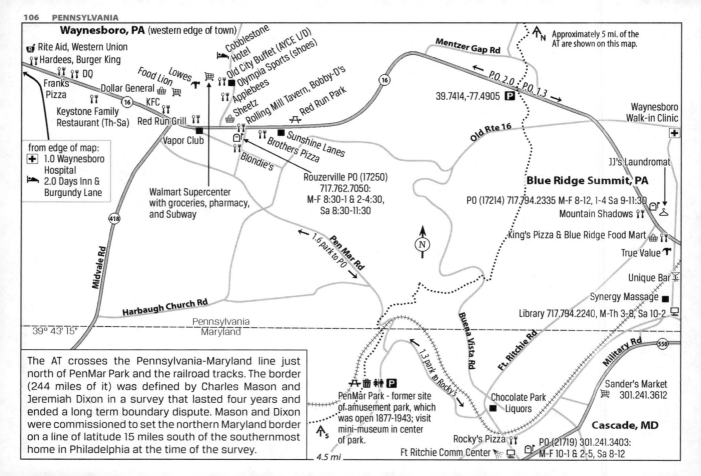

1063.7 **Pen Mar County Park** Open first Sunday in May to last Sunday in Oct. Vending & water; no camping. Restrooms locked when park closed. Bobby D's & other pizza places deliver. Pen Mar Rd passes in front of park, east of AT. Rouzerville PO is nearest to the AT. If intending to walk to town, do so from AT/Pen Mar Rd intersection 0.3N of park. Services available in multiple directions from the park & from PA 16. See map and listings for options.

🚐 **Dennis Sewell** 301.241.3176

Waynesboro, PA 17214

AT Festival June 18, 2016 at Red Run Park. 11am-4pm music & food.

🛏🛜🖵⛺ **Cobblestone Hotel** 717.765.0034 $80/up +tax, includes hot breakfast.

🍴 **Bobby D's Pizza** 717.762.0388

Also: Olympia Sports large selection of running shoes.

　　2.0W of Walmart:

🛏👁⛺🚐🛜🖵✉ **Burgundy Lane B&B** 717.762.8112 $90-105D w/full breakfast, free laundry & shuttle to trailhead or town stop. Longer shuttles for fee. Mail: 128 W Main St, Waynesboro, PA 17268.

🛏🛜🖵⛺ **Days Inn** 717.762.9113 $59S, $69D, $5EAP. Continental breakfast, $10 pet fee, laundry next door.

➕ **Waynesboro Hospital** 717.765.4000 501 E Main St.

🐾 **Wayne Heights Animal Hospital** 717.765.9636

　　Cascade, MD (1.4E on Pen Mar/High Rock Rd)

🏪 **Sanders Market** M–Sa 8:30–8, open till 9pm Tu and Sa.

🖵📷 **Ft Ritchie Comm Center** 301.241.5085 Showers, computer access, M-Th 6-9, F 6-6, Sa 9-5, Su 9:30-4.

1066.6　PA 16　***Blue Ridge Summit, PA 17214*** (1.2E)

➕ **Waynesboro Walk-in Clinic** 717.762.1700 M-F 8-5

◼ **Synergy Massage** 877.372.6617 〈www.synergymassage.com〉 Massage, hiker discount. Free outdoor shower, hot tub & pool.

🍴 **Unique Bar and Grill** 717.794.2565 live music.

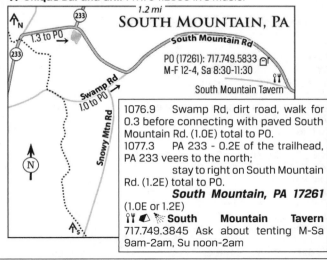

SOUTH MOUNTAIN, PA

1.2 mi

South Mountain Rd

1.3 to PO

PO (17261): 717.749.5833
M-F 12-4, Sa 8:30-11:30

South Mountain Tavern

Swamp Rd
1.0 to PO

Snowy Mtn Rd

1076.9　Swamp Rd, dirt road, walk for 0.3 before connecting with paved South Mountain Rd. (1.0E) total to PO.

1077.3　PA 233 - 0.2E of the trailhead, PA 233 veers to the north;
　　stay to right on South Mountain Rd. (1.2E) total to PO.

South Mountain, PA 17261

(1.0E or 1.2E)

🍴◣📷 **South Mountain Tavern** 717.749.3845 Ask about tenting M-Sa 9am-2am, Su noon-2am

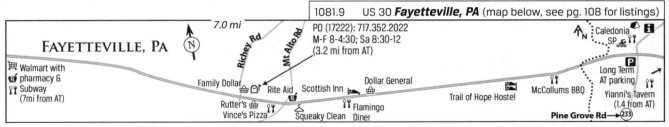

1081.9　US 30 ***Fayetteville, PA*** (map below, see pg. 108 for listings)

FAYETTEVILLE, PA

7.0 mi

Richey Rd

Mt Alto Rd

PO (17222): 717.352.2022
M-F 8-4:30; Sa 8:30-12
(3.2 mi from AT)

🏪 Walmart with
💊 pharmacy &
🍴 Subway
(7mi from AT)

Family Dollar
Rite Aid　Scottish Inn
Rutter's
Vince's Pizza　Squeaky Clean

Dollar General

Flamingo
Diner

Trail of Hope Hostel

McCollums BBQ

Caledonia
SP

Long Term
AT parking

Yianni's Tavern
(1.4 from AT)

Pine Grove Rd → 233

1081.9   US 30 **Fayetteville, PA** (see map pg. 107)

🏨🛒⛺✉ **Trail of Hope Hostel** 717.360.1481 or 717.352.2513 $22 bunk or $12 camping. Coin laundry, use of kitchen, resupply including white gas/denatured/oz and canister fuel. Mail: 7798 Lincoln Way East Fayetteville, PA 17222.

🛏🍴⛺📶✉ **Scottish Inn and Suites** 717.352.2144, 800.251.1962 $59S, $69D, $15 pets. $5PP for pickup or return to trail. $10 for ride to Walmart. Coin laundry. Guest Mail: 5651 Lincoln Way East, Fayetteville, PA 17222

🍴🏠📶 **Rutters** Convenience store with WiFi and deli.

🍴 **Flamingo Restaurant** Excellent large breakfast.

🍴 **Vince's Pizza** 717.401.0096

🚌 **Freeman's Shuttle Service** 717.352.2513 or 717.360.1481. Front Royal to DWG. Slackpacking Pen Mar to Duncannon.

1082.3   Side trail to **Caledonia State Park**

🛒🏠🍴⚡📞 **Caledonia SP** 717.352.2161 Open Apr 1 - Labor Day. Pool & snack bar open May 27-Labor Day 11-7, 7 days weather permitting. Campsites, $21 Su-Th, $25 F-Sa, $2 more for pets, $2 less for PA residents. $4.50 senior (62) discount. $4 shower only. Check-in at office for long term parking. Free local-call phone outside of office. Campsites will close in fall of 2016 for renovations.

🚌 **Gary Grant Shuttles** 717.706.2578 Can shuttle individuals and groups ranging from Caledonia SP to Duncannon, to local resupply (Walmart), Greyhound and Amtrak stations. Slackpacking, fuel on-hand.

1101.7   **Pine Grove Furnace State Park** (see map)

🏨🏠⛺📶🖥✉ **Ironmasters Mansion Hostel** 717.486.4108 ironmasterspinegrove@gmail.com. $25PP w/breakfast; $30 also includes pizza dinner. 5-9pm check-in, 9am check-out; closed 9am–5pm and Tu. nights. Call/email for reservations. Laundry $3. Open Apr

AT Museum - On the old halfway sign outside, what does diamond-shaped metal AT plaque commemorate?

PINE GROVE FURNACE SP

Fuller Lake & Beach

0.7 mi

1-Oct 31; sometimes closed for special events. Mail: Ironmasters Hostel, 1212 Pine Grove Rd, Gardners, PA 17324.

🏠🏠🍴💲 **Pine Grove General Store** 717.486.4920 Open daily 8am-7pm mid-May - Labor Day; weekends only mid-Apr - mid-May and Labor Day - Oct. Cold drinks, selection of hiking food, canister fuel, fuel/oz, socks, toiletries. Short-order grill. Soda machine outside. Home of **half gallon challenge.**

ℹ🏠 **A.T. Museum** ⟨www.atmuseum.org⟩ Hikers welcome to bring food to eat outside & relax. Artifacts and photos of past hikers, signs from Springer & Katahdin. Sells halfway patch & bandana. Open Mar 26-May 1 weekends only 12-4; May 7-July 17 every day 9-4; July 18-Aug 21 every day 12-4; Aug 24-Oct 30 W-Sun 12-4 **Hiker Festival** Jun 4.

🛒🚹🅿 **Pine Grove Furnace State Park** 717.486.7174 From end of Dec to end of Mar open weekdays only; open 7 days rest of year. Campsites start at $21 weekdays, $25 weekends, $2 off for PA residents. Dogs allowed in some sites. Restrooms throughout park. Check with park office before parking overnight; cars can be left for up to two weeks in lot compass south of Museum (interior of park). Beach/swimming area at Fuller Lake.

1107.8   Side trail (0.7W) to campground

🛏🛒🏠⛺ **Mountain Creek Campground** 717.486.7681 Open Apr-Nov, cabins $55+ tax, tentsites $28. Either holds 2 adults/4 children. Camp store has sodas & ice cream, short-order grill on weekends.

1110.2   PA 34, Hunters Run Rd,

🏠🍴💲 **Green Mtn Store** (0.2E) 717.486.4558 M-F 7am-8pm, Sa 8-8, Su 9-6. Good selection of hiker foods, prepared foods, ice cream, canister fuel, heet.

1112.2   PA 94 *Mt. Holly Springs, PA 17065* (2.5W) 5mi farther to 81 interchange with Walmart and movies at Carlisle Commons.
◖ M-F 8-1 & 2-4:30, Sa 9-12, 717.486.3468
🛏🍴🖥🛜 **Holly Inn, Restaurant and Tavern** 717.486.3823 $50S, $55D $5EAP, free ride to/from AT, $5 round trip from Pine Grove Furnace SP. Fri live music, Sa karaoke, Sun open mic. Restaurant open Su-Th 11:30-9, F-Sa 11:30-10.
⛪ **Sheetz, Dollar General, Family Dollar**
🍴 **Laura's** breakfast, lunch, ice cream.
🍴 **Subway**, **Sicilia Pizza**
💊 **Holly Pharmacy** 717.486.5321
🛁 **Dollie's Laundromat**

1112.5   Sheet Iron Roof Rd, 0.4W to campground
🛏♨🍴⛪🛁 **Deer   Run   Campground** 717.486.8168 Tent w/shower $10, cabin $75+tax.

1121.0   PA 174, *Boiling Springs, PA 17007*
♨ ☽ Free campsite & privy, see botton right corner of map. Railroad tracks pass near campsite.
🛏🍴🍸⛪🚻🛁🛜🖥 **Allenberry Resort Inn & Playhouse** ⟨www.allenberry.com⟩ 800.430.5468 Your zero-day oasis in PA: Hiker rate $40 double occupancy. Food service Tu-Su, bar open W-Su, general store open 7 days (snacks, beer & toiletries). Live theater $10, laundry $4, pool (in season), accepts credit cards. $5 fee for Mail: 1559 Boiling Springs Rd, Boiling Springs, PA 17007
🛏🛁🛜✉ **Gelinas Manor** 717.258.6584 ⟨www.gelinasmanor.com⟩ Room w/shared bath $99D/up. No pets, no packs inside. Full breakfast at 8:30. Laundry $6/load. CC accepted. Maildrops w/reservation: MUST say "in care of Gelinas Manor", 219 Front Street, Boiling Springs, PA 17007.

🛏🛜 **Red Cardinal B&B** 717.245.0823 Prices seasonal, queen bed room includes full breakfast & pickup/return from Boiling Springs (2mi away). No pets, no smoking.
🍴 **Karn's Quality Foods** 717.258.1458 Daily 7-10.
⛪🏧 **Gettys Food Mart** 717.241.6163 ATM inside.
🐾 **Boiling Springs Animal Hospital** 717.258.4575 M,W 8-7:30, Tu,Th-F 8-6, Sa 8-1
🍴 **Anile's Ristorante & Pizzeria** 717.258.5070 L/D subs, pizza. Daily 11-10.
🍴 **Boiling Springs Tavern** 717.258.3614 L/D 11:30-2, 5-9, closed Su-M.
🚿 **Boiling Springs Pool** 717.258.4121 Mem. Day-Labor Day, M-Su 11-7, $2 hot shower. If you want to swim, visit ATC Regional Office for $3 off the $12 admission.
🔥 **TCO Fly Shop** 610.678.1899 canister fuel and small hiking items.
🚐 **Mike's Shuttle Service** 717.497.6022
ℹ️ 🏛 **ATC Mid-Atlantic Regional Office** 717.258.5771 Open wkdays 8-5. Spigot on south side of building, may be off in winter. Staff & bulletin board provide info on trail conditions. Small shop with maps. Fuel/oz for donation.

BOILING SPRINGS, PA
N40 09.000, W77 07.633
Mag. Dec. 11° 0'W

Karn's Foods (0.9 mi from First St.)
Family Medical 717.249.8300
Benny's Pizza & Subs
Friendly Food Mart

PO (17007): 717.258.6668
M-F 9-12 & 1-4:30, Sa 9-12

Anile's
Boiling Springs Tavern
Getty Food Mart
Allenberry (0.4 mi from AT)
ATC Mid-Atlantic Regional Office
What manufacturer name is on the wrought iron benches?
Iron Works Long-term parking
Children's Lake
TCO Fly Shop
First St
Caffe 101 (B/L/D)
Walnut St
Gelinas
Third St
Front St
Bucher Hill Rd
Boiling Springs Pool
Campsite

← (5.0) Mt. Holly Springs
🛏 (2.0) Red Cardinal B&B
🐾 (1.4) Boiling Springs Animal Hospital
⚐ (2.0) Spring Meadows Disc Golf

Fourth St
0.7 mi

SoBo	NoBo	Description	Elev
1094.0	1095.1	Side trail to Michener Cabin (locked) ◆(0.3E)	1850
1093.4	1095.7	Woods road	1849
1092.1	1097.0	Woodrow Rd (gravel), campsite 0.1N	1779
1091.6	1097.5	Stream.	1538
1091.1	1098.0	Sunset Rocks Trail to east rejoins AT to north	1318
1091.0	1098.1	**Toms Run Shelter** (1936) 19.2◄13.6◄6.2◄10.9►19.0►37.2 Water behind shelter	1302
1090.8	1098.3	Stream.	1272
1089.8	1099.3	Michaux Rd	1330
1088.9	1100.2	Toms Run, footbridge, stream. Sunset Rocks Trail to east.	1020
1087.7	1101.4	PA 233 (paved), NoBo on road 0.1W, veer right on road into park	899
1087.4	1101.7	**Pine Grove Furnace SP, AT Museum** 40.0317,-77.3054 P (pg.108)	872
1086.9	1102.2	Fuller Lake, free showers, snack bar 11-7 daily Mem-Labor Day	841

⊘ No camping within one mile of PGF SP; camping within the park only at designated (paid) campsites. No overnight sleeping in pavilions.

SoBo	NoBo	Description	Elev
1085.0	1104.1	Campsite	1251
1084.8	1104.3	Pole Steeple Trail to west	1300
1083.8	1105.3	Campsite	1370
1081.6	1107.5	Roadbed	1049
1081.3	1107.8	Trail to **Mountain Creek Campground** (0.7W) signed & steep. (pg.108)	1015
1080.2	1108.9	Spring 50 yards west on marked trail	725
1080.1	1109.0	**James Fry (Tagg Run) Shelter** (0.2E), campsite west of AT 24.5◄17.1◄10.9►8.1►26.3►33.6 Spring uphill from shelter; water 0.2E farther.	699
1079.7	1109.4	Pine Grove Rd (paved)	664
1079.5	1109.6	Stream	639
1079.1	1110.0	⚠ Cross RR tracks; sharp east turn for NoBo, west for SoBo	633
1078.9	1110.2	PA 34, Hunters Run Rd, **Store & Deli** (0.2E) 40.0777,-77.1945 P (0.1E) (pg.108)	625
1076.9	1112.2	PA 94, **Mt Holly Springs, PA** (2.5W) (pg.109)	880
1076.6	1112.5	Sheet Iron Roof Rd, campground 0.4W 40.093,-77.1641 P (pg.109)	773
1076.2	1112.9	Footbridge, stream, campsite	687
1075.9	1113.2	Footbridge, stream	671
1075.5	1113.6	Old Town Rd (gravel)	736

SoBo	NoBo	Features	Elev
1074.9	1114.2	Rock maze	1186
1074.5	1114.6	Rock maze	1097
1074.1	1115.0	Whiskey Spring Rd, reliable water from spring ●	830
		No camping in Cumberland Valley between Alec Kennedy and Darlington Shelters, except at backpackers campsite south of Boiling Springs.	
1072.1	1117.0	Little Dogwood Run Campsite, orange-blazed trail 1.7E to BSA campground. ● ◢	870
1072.0	1117.1	**Alec Kennedy Shelter** (0.2E), spring behind shelter is unreliable. ⌒ ◁ ⊏ (7)	950
		25.2◄19.0◄8.1▶18.2▶25.5▶33.8	
1071.1	1118.0	Center Point Knob, original AT midpoint, White Rocks Trail 0.4E to view ▣	1060
1069.7	1119.4	Cornfield, south end	562
1069.2	1119.9	Leidigh Dr	553
1068.5	1120.6	Backpacker's Campsite (nearby railroad tracks can be noisy) ⌒ ◢	514
1068.3	1120.8	Bucher Hill Rd, get permit from ATC office to park overnight 40.1478,-77.1241 P	501
1068.1	1121.0	PA 174, First Street, ATC Mid-Atlantic Regional Office (pg.109)	500
		Boiling Springs, PA	
1066.6	1122.5	Stone wall	627
1066.0	1123.1	PA 74, York Rd 40.1731,-77.1211 P	573
1065.0	1124.1	Lisburn Rd	547
1064.5	1124.6	Byers Rd	556
1064.4	1124.7	Footbridge, stream ●	505
1064.0	1125.1	Trindle Rd, PA.641, kiosk 40.195,-77.1083 P (pg.114)	540
1062.8	1126.3	Ridge Rd, Biddle Rd. (pg.114)	471
1062.3	1126.8	Old Stone House Rd, footbridge, stream ●	474
1061.6	1127.5	Appalachian Dr	525
1061.3	1127.8	PA Turnpike (I-76) overpass	498
1060.7	1128.4	Railroad tracks	478
1060.1	1129.0	US 11, **Carlisle, PA** (0.5W) (pg.114)	490
1059.2	1129.9	Pass over I-81 on Bernheisel Rd	485
1058.6	1130.5	Fence stile (two)	465
1057.8	1131.3	Conodoguinet Creek, footbridge alongside road 40.2598,-77.1037 P ⚐ ⌒ ●	389
		Scott Farm Trail ATC Crew HQ Open May–Oct, picnic table, no camping.	
		The AT u-turns, passes under bridge, and heads north.	
1056.7	1132.4	Sherwood Drive, parking to east. 40.274,-77.0995 P ●	397
		Many footbridges, streams north and south of this road.	
1055.8	1133.3	PA 944 tunnel	480

NoBo
SoBo

5000

3000

1000

SoBo	NoBo	Description	Elev
1054.9	1134.2	Piped spring where AT crosses overgrown dirt road ◆ — NoBo planning stay at Darlington Shelter consider getting water here.	718
1054.2	1134.9	View 🄫	1102
1053.9	1135.3	Darlington Trail, Tuscarora Trail	1246
1053.8	1135.3	**Darlington Shelter** (0.1E) 37.2◀26.3◀18.2◀▶7.3▶15.6▶22.3 ◐⌂(5) (2005) Unreliable water on blue-blazed trail in front of shelter. Taj Mahal privy.	1221
1052.2	1136.9	Gravel road	725
1051.9	1137.2	Millers Gap Rd (paved)	684
1051.6	1137.5	PA 850 40.3218,-77.0781 P	673
1050.1	1139.0	Service road.	761
1049.9	1139.2	Footbridge, stream ◆	852
1049.1	1140.0	Pipeline, view, trail very rocky from here north to PA 274 🄫	1319
1047.4	1141.7	Blue-blazed trail 0.4W to service road	1259
1046.5	1142.6	**Cove Mountain Shelter** (0.2E)(2000) ☾◆⌂(8) 33.6◀25.5◀7.3◀▶8.3▶15.0▶33.0 Spring 0.1 mile on steep side trail.	1274
1044.5	1144.6	Hawk Rock, view 🄫	1052
1043.8	1145.3	⚠ Old trail to west, AT turns east (uphill for NoBo)	519
1043.4	1145.7	Inn Rd, trail very rocky from here south to pipeline.	380
1042.9	1146.2	PA 274, pass under US 11/15	385
1042.5	1146.6	**Duncannon, PA**, High St + Broadway (pg.114)	393
1041.4	1147.7	Juniata River bridge	366
1040.7	1148.4	Susquehanna River 40.396,-77.0085 P — North end of Clarks Ferry Bridge, US 22/322, railroad tracks	376
1039.8	1149.3	View 🄫	655
1038.4	1150.7	Susquehanna Trail to west ◆	1190
1038.2	1150.9	**Clarks Ferry Shelter** (0.1E)(1993) ☾◆◐⌂(8) 33.8◀15.6◀8.3◀▶6.7▶24.7▶38.1 Reliable piped spring just beyond shelter.	1211
1037.9	1151.2	Powerline 🄫	1331

NoBo

SoBo

Elevation profile with data points:

SoBo	NoBo	Feature	Elevation	Notes
1035.3	1153.8	Powerline	1225	
1034.4	1154.7	PA 225. **P**	1247	40.4119,-76.9299
1033.8	1155.3	Powerline	1282	
1032.4	1156.7	Table Rock, view	1333	
1031.5	1157.6	**Peters Mtn Shelter** (1994) 22.3◄15.0◄6.7◄►18.0►31.4►35.5. Weak spring 0.3 mile steeply downhill from shelter (300 rock steps).	1169	☾ ◁ ⌁ (16)
1030.5	1158.6	Victoria Trail. ⚠ See State Game Lands guidelines pg. 115	1196	
1029.9	1159.2	Whitetail Trail	1316	
1028.8	1160.3	Kinter View	1320	
1027.4	1161.7	Shikellimy Trail 0.9E to parking area.	1165	
1026.4	1162.7	Campsite	1369	40.4377,-76.8198
1025.1	1164.0	Spring 100 yards east on side trail	700	
1024.8	1164.3	PA 325, Clarks Creek north of road. **P**	550	40.4515,-76.7762
1024.5	1164.6	Spring.	606	
1024.4	1164.7	Henry Knauber Trail to east	685	
1023.1	1166.0	Spring	1251	
1021.5	1167.6	Horse-Shoe Trail to east	1650	
1020.8	1168.3	Rattling Run.	1504	
1018.2	1170.9	Yellow Springs Trail	1365	
1018.1	1171.0	Clearing with trail register, camping	1450	
		Yellow Springs Village Site, old coal mining settlement (0.7W).		
1017.2	1171.9	Spring.	1395	

NoBo
SoBo

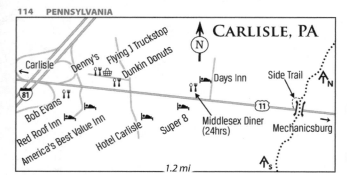

CARLISLE, PA

1.2 mi

1125.1   Trindle Rd
1126.3   Ridge Rd
⊨⚘🛜**Pheasant Field B&B** (0.5W) 717.258.0717 $135/up, free pickup & return with stay, big breakfast, laundry for fee, behaved pets ok. Call from Trindle Rd, or from Ridge Rd, go 0.25W to Hickory Town Rd, turn left on road, B&B on right.

1129.0   US 11 (Carlisle Pike), ***Carlisle, PA 17013*** (0.5W to hotels)
          The AT passes over the highway on a footbridge. A side trail down to the road is at the northwest corner of the overpass. Hotels run short of rooms (and go up in price) every other weekend when there is a car show.
⊨⚘🛜**Days Inn** 717.245.2242 Hiker rate $55.95, cont B, pets $20.
⊨⚘🛜✉ **Super 8 Motel** 717.249.7000 $54.99S, $59.99D, cont. breakfast, $10 pet fee. Guest Mail: 1800 Harrisburg Pike, Carlisle, PA 17013.
⊨**Red Roof Inn** 717.245.2400
⊨🛜**Americas Best Value Inn** 717.249.7775 $49.99/up + tax, cont B, $15 pet fee.
⊨⚘🛜🖳 **Hotel Carlisle** 717.243.1717 $15 pet fee.
🍴⚕🍴⚘ **Flying J Truckstop** 717.243.6659, 24hrs. Store, diner, pizza by the slice, showers $12 includes towel, laundry.

Mechanicsburg, PA 17050 (5.0E)
Large city with an abundance of services, most notably: 🏷 **CVS** (3.0E), 🏬 **Giant Food** (4.3E), 🏬 **Walmart** (4.6E), 🍸 **Appalachian Brewing Co** (4.9E), 🏬 **Wegmans** (5.4E) ⊨🍸 **Park Inn** (7.0E) 717.697.0321 restaurant & bars on-site.

1146.6   High St, ***Duncannon, PA 17020***
⊨⚛🍴🖳✉ **Doyle Hotel** 717.834.6789, $25S, $35D, $10EAP + tax, bar serves L/D. Pool Table. Coleman/alcohol/oz and canister fuel. Accepts Visa/MC/Disc. Mail: (USPS/UPS) 7 North Market Street, Duncannon, PA 17020.
⊨⚘ **Stardust Motel** 717.834.3191 $45S, $55D Sometimes pickup/ return rides available. No pets.
⊨⚘🛜 **Red Carpet Inn** 717.834.3320 $55S, $60D + tax. pickup and return from Duncannon for $10.
🔥🚐 **Riverfront Campground** 717.834.5252 Site & shower $5PP, check-in daylight till dark. Shuttles. Note proximity of railroad tracks.
🍴 **Sorrento Pizza** 717.834.5167
🍴 **Goodies** Breakfast 6am-11am
🍴 **Ranch House Restaurant** B/L/D, near Stardust Motel has dinner buffet F-Sa, breakfast on weekends.
🍴 **Lumberjack's Kitchen** 717.834.9099 Near Red Carpet Inn M-Th L/D, F-Sun B/L/D
🏬 **Mutzabaugh's Market** 717.834.3121 Hiker-friendly, open 7 days 6am-10pm. Pickup/return to Doyle 4pm daily.
🏷 **Rite Aid** next door to market.
⚕🍴🧺 **Pilot Travel Plaza** 717.834.3156, Open 24/7 $12 showers.
🐾 **Cove Mountain Animal Hospital** 717.834.5534
◼ **Christ Lutheran Church** Free hiker dinner Wednesdays in June & July 5pm-7pm. On Plum St + Church St one block west of High St.
🛜 **Presbyterian Church** Library with internet access W 1-4, Sa 10-2
🛜 **Store 34** M-F 12-7, Sa 10-4. High speed internet $3/30 min, $5/hr.
⛏ **Maguire's True Value Hardware** Coleman and Heet.
🚐⚛**Trail Angel Mary** 717.834.4706 2 Ann St, Duncannon, PA 17020
🏃 **Blue Mountain Outfitters** 717.957.2413 8mi south in Maryville, PA

DUNCANNON, PA

40.3947,-77.027
Mag. Dec. 11.16° W

Ⓝ N

Stardust Motel (2.0 mi)
Red Carpet Inn (3.6 mi)

Pilot Travel Plaza & Subway

Riviera Tavern 🍴

The Cabin

Riverfront Campground

Butchershop Rd

High St

Market St

Peregrine Falcon nesting area; they have been known to dive at hikers crossing bridge.

Municipal Building ℹ️ 🍴 3B Ice Cream

Cherry St

Susquehanna River

Christ Lutheran Church

PO (17020):
ID required
717.834.3332
M-F 8-11 & 12-4:30,
Sa 8:30-12:30

William Penn Hwy

The Pub 🍴 Sorrento's

Church / Library 🖥️ Store 34

The Doyle 🍴 Goodies

Quick-Mart

2nd St

Cumberland St

Locust

Zierdelli's 717.834.5167
Sunny Daze
Road Hawg BBQ (Th-Su)

Sunoco

274

Mutzabaugh's Market and Rite Aid (0.6 mi. from bridge)

322
22

Approx. 5.2 mi. of trail shown on map

Ⓝ N

Harrisburg, PA
(14 mi: all services)

Tubby's 🍴

1.5 mi

The AT is on **State Game Lands** in PA from north of Peters Mtn Shelter to Wind Gap, with the exception of small patches of land, mostly near major road crossings. Watch for posted regulations.

Primitive one-night camping is allowed:
- Only by hikers starting and ending at different locations.
- Within 200 feet of the AT, and
- 500 feet from water sources, trailheads, road crossings, and parking areas.
- Only small campfires are allowed, and only when the wildfire danger is less than "high."

Allentown, Bake Oven Knob Darlington, Cove Mtn, and Rausch Gap Shelters are on State Game Lands.

"Appalachee" is the name of an Indian tribe that once populated northwest Florida. Sixteenth century Spanish explorers used variants of the name to describe a region extending into the southern end of the mountain range. The place name, now morphed into "Appalachian," stuck to the mountains and moved north, leaving behind the flatlands where it originated.

SoBo	NoBo	Feature	Elevation
1016.0	1173.1	Sand Spring Trail west to "The General"	1361
1015.8	1173.3	Cold Spring Trail to east	1400
1013.6	1175.5	Spring, campsite	1080
1013.5	1175.6	**Rausch Gap Shelter** (0.3E) 33.0◀24.7◀18.0▶13.4▶17.5▶32.6	1063
1013.0	1176.1	AT on gravel road for 0.2 mile, bridge over Rausch Creek	904
1012.7	1176.4	Cemetery to west	860
1012.5	1176.6	Stony Creek, footbridge	827
1011.4	1177.7	Second Mountain	1362
1009.7	1179.4	Field	650
1009.4	1179.7	Cross two roads: Greenpoint School Rd, then PA 443	575
1008.8	1180.3	Pass under PA72 and cross PA 443 40.4821,-76.5506 **P**	483
		Stream, campsite south of PA 72	
1007.4	1181.7	Swatara Gap, PA 72, **Lickdale, PA** (2.1E) (pg.118)	480
1007.0	1182.1	I-81, AT passes underneath	450
1006.7	1182.4	Gravel road	615
1002.8	1186.3	Abandoned powerline overlook, view	1386
1000.1	1189.0	**William Penn Shelter** (0.1E)(1993)	1409
		38.1◀31.4◀13.4▶4.1▶19.2▶33.9	
		Water and tent sites 0.1W on blue-blazed trail.	
998.0	1191.1	PA 645, Waggoners Gap Rd 40.5066,-76.3768 **P** (pg.118)	1219
		Pine Grove, PA (3.4W)	
996.8	1192.3	Fisher Lookout, view	1310

NoBo		Description	Features	Elev
996.1	1193.0	Kimmel Lookout, view.	📷	1362
996.0	1193.1	PA 501, **501 Shelter** (0.1W)(1975). . . . . 40.5125,-76.3444 🅿 ☽ ⚲ ◐ ◢ (pg.119)		1444
995.5	1193.6	35.5◄17.5◄4.1►15.1►29.8►38.9 **Pine Grove, PA** (4.2W), **Bethel, PA** (4.1E) Trail to Pilger Ruh (Pilgrims Rest), spring to east, Applebee Campsite to west.	◐ ◢	1450
992.9	1196.2	Round Head, Shower Steps Trail, campsite to south on AT. Side trail to view.	◢	1500
990.9	1198.2	Overlook, view.	📷	1404
990.5	1198.6	⚠ NoBo: AT turns east, Boulderfield Trail to west (straight ahead)		1271
990.4	1198.7	Hertline Campsite and picnic table	◐ ⚲ ⛨	1200
989.7	1199.4	Pipeline, road paralleling pipeline, cross twice, then parallel to AT		1516
987.0	1202.1	Fort Dietrich Snyder Monument	◐ (0.2W)	1474
986.7	1202.4	PA 183, Rentschler Marker on side trail 30 yards north of road		1423
986.2	1202.9	Game Commission road (gravel) . . . . 40.5273,-76.2148 🅿		1479
985.4	1203.7	Black Swatara Spring 0.3E.	△	1567
982.8	1206.3	Eagles Nest Trail to east		1601
981.6	1207.5	Sand Spring Trail 0.2E to spring	◐	1510
980.9	1208.2	**Eagles Nest Shelter** (0.3W)(1988), spring on trail to shelter . . . ☽ ◐ ◢ ⊏ (8) 32.6◄19.2◄15.1►14.7►23.8►31.2		1580
979.0	1210.1	Shartlesville-Cross Mtn Rd (overgrown dirt road).		1450

NoBo
SoBo

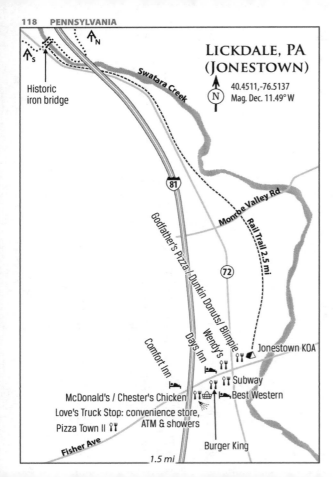

LICKDALE, PA (JONESTOWN)

40.4511,-76.5137
Mag. Dec. 11.49° W

Historic iron bridge

Swatara Creek

Monroe Valley Rd

Rail Trail 2.5 mi

Godfather's Pizza / Dunkin Donuts/ Blimpie

Days Inn

Wendy's

Jonestown KOA

Comfort Inn

McDonald's / Chester's Chicken

Love's Truck Stop: convenience store, ATM & showers

Pizza Town II

Subway

Best Western

Burger King

Fisher Ave

1.5 mi

1181.7   Swatara Gap, PA 72, **Lickdale, PA (Jonestown)** (2.1E)

🛏🏕📶🖥 **Days Inn** 717.865.4064 Cont B, pets $10.

🛏🏕📶🖥 **Best Western** 717.865.4234 $89.99/up, cont B, indoor heated pool, pet fee $15.

🛏🏕📶🖥 **Comfort Inn** 717.865.8080 Call or stop by for rates, includes breakfast, pool. Pets $25

🛏🌢🍴🏧🏕📶 **Jonestown KOA** 877.865.6411 Open 7 days. Summer 5am-9pm. Tentsite $37/up, cabin sleeps 4 $67/up. Pets on leash okay.

🏧🍴💲🗞📶📞 **Love's Travel Stop** with **McDonalds, Chesters** 717.861.7390 $10 showers, ATM, all open 24 hrs.

1191.1   PA 645, **Pine Grove, PA** (3.4W) *(more services on map)*

🍴 **Original Italian Pizza** 570.345.5432 Open Sa-Th 11-10, F 11-11. Delivers to 501 shelter.

🍴🏧💲🗞🏕 **Pilot Travel Center** 570.345.8800, 24hr, other side of 81, **Subway, Dairy Queen** and **Auntie Anne's Pretzel**, shower $12.

🛒 **Bergers Market** 570.345.3663, open 7 days, M-F 8-9, Sa-Su 8-6.

🚌 **Carlin's AT Shuttle Service** 570.345.0474, 570.516.3447. Shuttles anywhere in PA.

       4.8W near intersection of I-81

🛏📶🖥 **Comfort Inn** 570.345.8031 $65/up includes hot breakfast. Hiker friendly, pool, $10/pet.

🛏📶 **Econo Lodge** 570.345.4099 Hiker rate when room available, includes full breakfast. Dogs $10 allowed in smoking rooms only.

🛏📶 **Relax Inn** 570.345.8095 $50-$55, Pets $10. HBO.

1193.1   PA 501, **Bethel, PA** (4.1E) *(services on map)*

⌐ **501 Shelter** Caretaker house nearby, solar shower, water from faucet on shower, no alcohol, no smoking in shelter, pets on leash.

       Pine Grove, PA 17963 (4.2W) *(listings at PA 645 and on map)*

(125) **Pine Grove**

(443)

Ace 570.345.2561

🛒 BG's Market 570.345.0464 (0.5mi from 443 + 125)

Original Italian Pizza,
O'Neals Pub, Do's Pizza 🍴
Turkey Hill Minit Mrkt 🏪

Tri-Valley Pharmacy 570.345.4966

PO (17963): 570.345.4955
M-F 8:30-4:30, Sa 9-12

Action Laundry
Theater 570.345.0426

2.1 mi to (81)

(443) (895)

0.7 mi to P.O.

Pilot Travel Center
with Subway & DQ

(81)

Diner

Hampton Inn

Dollar General

Econo Lodge
Comfort Inn & McDonalds

Knights Inn

Beer Mtn Distributors 570-915-6124

Piece of Cake
Bakery

N

(645) (501)

501 Shelter (0.1W on side trail north of road)

P

2.7 mi to (443)

P

4.2 mi to Pine Grove P.O.

4.1 mi to I-78, P.O. 0.4 further

N

PO (19507):
717.933.8305
M-F 8-12
& 1:15-4:30
Sa 8:30-10:30

S

William Penn Shelter

(501)

Bethel Animal Hospital
717.933.4916 (by appt)

Bethel

(78)

Bethel Library:
717.933.4060
M 10-8
Tu, W, Th 10-6
F 10-5
Sa 10-2

Convenience stores (3) at intersection

8.3 mi

About the Author

David Miller (Awol) thru-hiked the AT in 2003, and is the author of **Awol on the Appalachian Trail.** David is a life member of the Appalachian Trail Conservancy.

SoBo	NoBo	Description		Elev
976.3	1212.8	Phillips Canyon Spring (unmarked, unreliable)	◁	1500
974.3	1214.8	State Game Land Rd		1417
973.7	1215.4	Pipeline clearing, AT crosses multiple times		1413
972.1	1217.0	Schuylkill Trail 2.4E to Hamburg, parking 0.1N	40.5796,-76.0267 **P**	564
971.9	1217.2	**Port Clinton, PA,** Broad St + Penn St	(pg.123)	430
971.6	1217.5	PA 61, Blue Mtn Rd, **Hamburg, PA** (1.7E)	(pg.123)	490
969.1	1220.0	Spring to west, campsite	◦ ● ▲	1184
967.9	1221.2	Minnehaha Spring, frequently dry	◁	1361
966.5	1222.6	Reservoir Rd, stream north on AT	40.5896,-75.9443 **P** ●	878
966.2	1222.9	Parking 0.3E only with permission from Hamburg Borough 610.562.7821 M-F 8-5. **Windsor Furnace Shelter** (0.1W)(1972)	⊃ ● ⊆ (8)	848
965.5	1223.6	33.9◄29.8◄14.7▶9.1▶16.5▶26.5 No swimming, creek south of shelter. Blue-blazed trail to **Blue Rocks Campground** (1.5E)	(pg.123)	997
964.6	1224.5	Pulpit Rock, 30 yards west to privy at Pulpit Rock Astronomical Park.	⊃ ▣	1582
962.8	1226.3	Yellow-blazed trail to **Blue Rocks Campground** (1.5E)	(pg.123)	1594
962.4	1226.7	The Pinnacle, 0.1E to panoramic view, no camping or fires	▣	1615
960.7	1228.4	Furnace Creek Trail to west		1444
960.5	1228.6	Gold Spring, no camping	◁	1372
959.8	1229.3	Blue-blazed trail 1.5W reconnects with AT near Windsor Furnace Shelter		1402
959.5	1229.6	Pinnacle Spur Trail to west		1394
958.9	1230.2	Panther Creek, dependable	●	1090
958.0	1231.1	Parking lot 0.4E on side trail	40.6255,-75.9535 **P**	832

SoBo	NoBo	Description	Elev
957.1	1232.0	Hawk Mountain Rd, **Eckville Shelter** (0.2E) 38.9◄23.8◄9.1◄►7.4►17.4►24.2 Enclosed bunkroom, tent platforms, flush toilet, spigot at side of caretaker's house. ☾ 🚿 ♦ ⌂ ⊏ (6) (pg.123)	692
956.6	1232.5	Footbridge, stream, campsite north on AT ♦	564
955.2	1233.9	Hawk Mtn Trail to west	1364
954.1	1235.0	Dans Pulpit, trail register 📷	1615
953.5	1235.6	Dans Spring 0.1E △	1558
950.9	1238.2	Tri-County Corner, ⚠ AT to west.	1524
949.7	1239.4	**Allentown Hiking Club Shelter** (1997) 31.2◄16.5◄7.4◄►10.0►16.8►33.5 ☾ △ ♦ ⊏ (8)	1488
949.4	1239.7	Unreliable spring downhill in front of shelter 0.2 mile, another 0.1 farther. Springs to east; Blue 100 yards, Yellow 0.3 mi ♦	1331
947.8	1241.3	Fort Franklin Rd (gravel) 40.6943,-75.8419 P	1350
945.9	1243.2	Trail 0.2W to restaurant (closer to AT + PA 309)	1356
945.6	1243.5	PA 309, Blue Mountain Summit 40.7072,-75.8086 P (pg.123)	1360
943.8	1245.3	Powerline, New Tripoli Campsite 0.2W. ♦	1431
942.7	1246.4	Knife Edge, view 📷	1560
942.2	1246.9	Bear Rocks, view 📷	1544
940.7	1248.4	Bake Oven Knob Rd (gravel) 40.7446,-75.7386 P	1450
940.3	1248.8	Bake Oven Knob.	1560
939.7	1249.4	**Bake Oven Knob Shelter** (1937) 26.5◄17.4◄10.0◄►6.8►23.5►37.2 Trail in front leads downhill to multiple water sources, more reliable farther down. △ ♦ ⊏ (6)	1387

NoBo
SoBo

5000 3000 1000

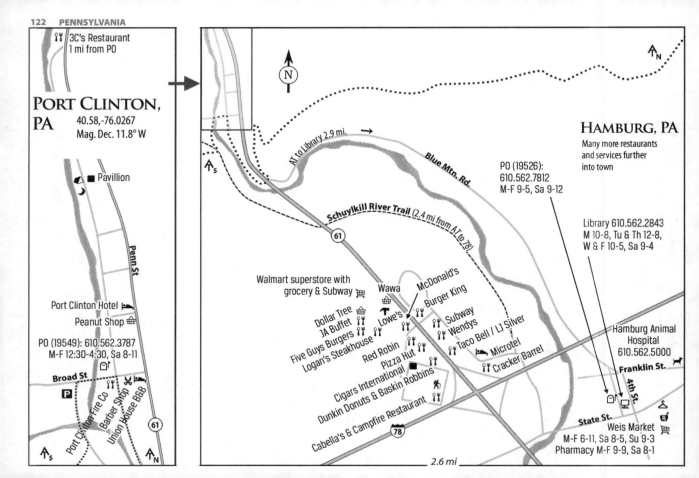

3C's Restaurant
1 mi from PO

PORT CLINTON, PA
40.58,-76.0267
Mag. Dec. 11.8° W

◆ ■ Pavillion

Port Clinton Hotel
Peanut Shop
PO (19549): 610.562.3787
M-F 12:30-4:30, Sa 8-11

Broad St.
P
Port Clinton Fire Co
Barber Shop
Union House B&B
Penn St.
61

N

AT to Library 2.9 mi. →

Blue Mtn. Rd.

Schuylkill River Trail (2.4 mi from AT to '78)

61

HAMBURG, PA
Many more restaurants
and services further
into town

PO (19526):
610.562.7812
M-F 9-5, Sa 9-12

Library 610.562.2843
M 10-8, Tu & Th 12-8,
W & F 10-5, Sa 9-4

Walmart superstore with
grocery & Subway
Wawa
McDonald's
Burger King

Dollar Tree
JA Buffet
Lowe's
Subway
Wendys
Taco Bell / LJ Silver
Five Guys Burgers
Logan's Steakhouse
Red Robin
Pizza Hut
Microtel
Cracker Barrel
Cigars International
Dunkin Donuts & Baskin Robbins
Cabella's & Campfire Restaurant

Hamburg Animal
Hospital
610.562.5000

Franklin St.

4th St.

State St.
Weis Market
M-F 6-11, Sa 8-5, Su 9-3
Pharmacy M-F 9-9, Sa 8-1

78

2.6 mi

1217.2 Broad St, Penn St **Port Clinton, PA 19549**
🛏️🍴⛺ **Port Clinton Hotel** 610.562.3354, 888.562.2626
⟨www.portclintonhotel.net⟩ Call for prices. $10 deposit for room key & towel, limited rooms available. Laundry, dining Tu-Su 11-9, closed Monday. Please shower before use of dining room. CC accepted.
🛏️⛺ **Union House B&B** 610.562.3155 after 5pm 610.562.4076 Open F-Su. Reservations available during week upon request.
🍴📶 **3C's** 610.562.5925 Open daily 6am-2pm.
🍴 **Port Clinton Fire Co** 610.562.5499 Technically membership only; ask about visiting as a guest. Open 3pm-past midnight.
🏠**$ The Peanut Shop** 610.562.0610 Su-F 10-6, Sa 10-8 Soda, candy, dried fruit, trail mixes, ATM.
🔋🚶 **Pavilion Tenting** max 2 nights, no car camping or drive-ins.
✂️ **Port Clinton Barber Shop** Hikers welcome to hang out, coffee, cookies, and phone charging.

1217.5 PA 61, Blue Mtn Rd
Hamburg, PA 19526 (1.7E)
🛏️🍴⛺📶✉️ **Microtel Inn** 610.562.4234 ⟨www.microtelinn.com⟩ **Pappy T's** pub & lounge on-site. Call/stop by for hiker rate, includes cont. b'fast. Mail(for guest w/reservation): 100 Industrial Drive, Hamburg, PA 19526
🏃 **Cabela's** 610.929.7000, M-Sa 8-9, Su 9-8. Largest Cabela's store in the world with 250,000 sq. ft. of retail space. Full line of hiking gear, canister fuel. Pickup from trailhead if staff is available.
🍴 **Campfire Restaurant** Inside Cabela's serves B/L/D, closes a little earlier than the store.
🏪 **Rite Aid** 610.562.9454, **CVS** 610.562.2454
⛺ **Hamburg Coin Laundry** 610.562.4890
🏥 **Hamburg Animal Hospital** 610.562.5000
⟨www.hamburganimal hostpital.com⟩ M-Th 9-7, F 9-5, Sa 9-11.
🚌 **Barta Bus Service** 610.921.0601⟨www.bartabus.com⟩ Routes within Hamburg $1.95 per boarding, stops at Cabellas.
Pottsville, PA 17901 (15W, compass north on PA 61)
🍺 **Yuengling Brewery** 570.628.4890 America's oldest brewery.

Tours M-F 10am-1:30pm, Sa 11am-1pm. Closed-toe shoes required.

1223.6 Blue-blazed trail to campground
1226.3 Yellow-blazed trail to campground
🛏️🔋🍴🏠🎣⛺📶 **Blue Rocks Campground** 610.756.6366 ⟨www.bluerockscampground.com⟩ Tentsite $30/up, cabin $55/up accommodates 2 adults, 2 children. Showers & laundry. Pets allowed in campground, but not cabins. Open year-round with limited days Nov-Mar. **Woody's Filling Station** open F-Su seasonally, sells burgers, shakes, etc. Camp store (sodas, candy bars, snacks) closed Dec-Mar. CC accepted.

1232.0 Hawk Mountain Rd, 1.6W to Hawk Mountain Sanctuary.
🛏️⛺📶🖥️🚌✉️ **Common Ground Farm & Retreat** 610.756.4070 B&B on 50 acre organic farm. Hiker discount $99 for two-person stay includes breakfast & pickup/return from Eckville Shelter. Call about other trailheads. Slackpacking, parking for section hikers, longer shuttles for a fee. Mountain bike available for ride to nearby store. Open year-round, no alcohol or drugs. CC accepted. Mail with reservation: 333 New Bethel Church Road, Kempton, PA 19529.

1243.5 PA 309
🛏️🔋🍴🚌✉️💧 **Blue Mountain Summit B&B** 570.386.2003 ⟨www.bluemountainsummit.com⟩ In view to west. $95–$125D includes breakfast. Open 7 days by appt. No pets. Help yourself to water at outside spigot at southwest corner of building. Please be respectful of non-hiking guests at the B&B and restaurant; okay to hang out in back, but please don't loiter in front or hang clothes to dry. Camping with permission, no fires. Ask about shuttles. Dining (summer) Th 12-9, F 12-10, Sa 11-9, Su 11-8; winter (after Thanksgiving) Th hours 4-9, F-Su same as summer. Live music on Fridays. All major credit cards accepted. Guest maildrops (call first): 2520 W Penn Pike, Andreas, PA 18211.

NoBo		Description	Elev
937.3	1251.8	Lehigh Furnace Gap, Ashfield Rd, Comm tower. . . . . . 40.7696,-75.6949 **P** ♦	1320
		Piped spring 0.5E on Ashfield Road, spring is on the right side of road.	
936.2	1252.9	South Trail 0.3E to view.	1590
934.6	1254.5	North Trail (scenic route) to west, TV tower, AT is over Lehigh Valley Tunnel	1488
934.1	1255.0	Tower access road	1461
933.1	1256.0	North Trail (scenic route) to west	1065
932.9	1256.2	**George W. Outerbridge Shelter** (1965) Reliable piped spring 0.1N ♦ ⊂(6)	948
		24.2◄16.8◄6.8◄►16.7►30.4►61.6	
932.4	1256.7	Lehigh River south bank, PA 873, **Slatington, PA** (2.0E) . . . . (pg.126)	422
931.9	1257.2	PA 248/145 traffic light, **Walnutport, PA** (2.0E) . . . . (pg.126)	481
931.8	1257.3	Superfund Trailhead **Palmerton, PA** (1.5W) 40.7832,-75.6041 **P** (pg.126)	492
		Water 0.4W on blue-blazed trail to Palmerton.	
930.9	1258.2	Superfund Detour south end.	1420

Rocky, steep trail from Lehigh Gap. Deforested ridge due to zinc smelting from 1898-1980. Palmerton Superfund site.

NoBo		Description	Elev
928.3	1260.8	High metallic content spring 0.1W (unmarked 40.8050,-75.5568)	1380
		emergency water source, drinking not recommended.	
928.1	1261.0	Superfund Detour north, powerline	1368
		360 view from pile of rocks east of trail near power line tower.	
927.0	1262.1	Little Gap Rd, **Danielsville, PA** (1.5E) 40.8062,-75.5346 **P** (pg.127)	1100
926.6	1262.5	Tower access road (gravel)	1343
923.2	1265.9	Dirt road, powerline.	1571
922.2	1266.9	Delps Trail to east, ◊(0.4E) 40.8092,-75.4512 **P** (0.7E)⚑	1580
		Campsite near trail intersection, unreliable spring 0.4E	
920.6	1268.5	Stempa Spring 0.6E, reliable ♦	1559
919.7	1269.4	Smith Gap Rd (paved) 40.8255,-75.4143 **P** (pg.128)	1540

NoBo
SoBo

NoBo	SoBo		Elev
916.2	1272.9	**Leroy A. Smith Shelter** (0.2E)(1972) 33.5◄23.5◄16.7◄►13.7►44.9►51.5 Water 0.2 mile down blue-blazed trail; second source 0.2 mile farther. Piped spring 0.5 mile down service road.	⟩♦⟨(8) 1456
916.0	1273.1	Powerline	1489
914.3	1274.8	Pipeline	1487
912.6	1276.5	Hahns Overlook, view	📷 1450
911.8	1277.3	Powerline	1107
911.6	1277.5	PA 33, **Wind Gap, PA** (1.0E) 40.8607,-75.2928 P (pg.128)	980
909.5	1279.6	Private road (gravel)	1591
905.9	1283.2	Campsite	⌂ 1628
905.2	1283.9	Wolf Rocks bypass trail south end to west. Spring 100 yards west (treat)	△ 1584
904.8	1284.3	Wolf Rocks, view	📷 1623
904.2	1284.9	Wolf Rocks bypass trail north end to west.	△ 1539
903.1	1286.0	Fox Gap, PA 191 (paved)	1400
902.5	1286.6	**Kirkridge Shelter** 37.2◄30.4◄13.7◄►31.2►37.8►43.6. 40.9354,-75.1969 P	⟩♦⟨(6) 1440
902.2	1286.9	Campsite, view. Tap 0.1 mi behind shelter, off in winter.	📷♦ 1490
900.6	1288.5	Totts Gap, gravel road, powerline to south	1300
900.3	1288.8	Pipeline	1382
900.0	1289.1	Roadbed	1401

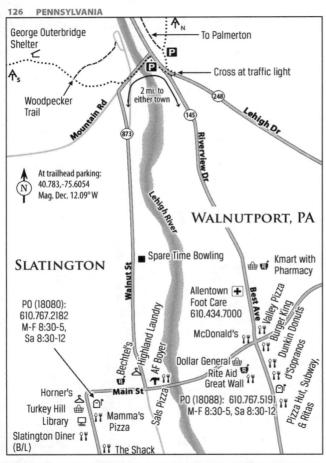

At trailhead parking:
40.783,-75.6054
Mag. Dec. 12.09°W

WALNUTPORT, PA

SLATINGTON

PO (18080):
610.767.2182
M-F 8:30-5,
Sa 8:30-12

Spare Time Bowling

Kmart with Pharmacy

Allentown Foot Care
610.434.7000

McDonald's

Dollar General

Rite Aid
Great Wall

PO (18088): 610.767.5191
M-F 8:30-5, Sa 8:30-12

Valley Pizza
Burger King
Dunkin Donuts
d'Sopranos
Pizza Hut, Subway,
& Ritas

Horner's
Turkey Hill
Library
Slatington Diner (B/L)

Mamma's Pizza

The Shack

Bechtel's
Highland Laundry
AF Boyer
Sals Pizza

Main St

George Outerbridge Shelter

Woodpecker Trail

Mountain Rd

To Palmerton

Cross at traffic light

2 mi. to either town

Lehigh Dr

Riverview Dr

Lehigh River

Walnut St

Best Ave

1256.7　Lehigh River, PA 873, ***Slatington, PA 18080*** (2E)
🦷 **Bechtel's Pharmacy**　610.767.4121 Open M-F 9-8, Su 9-2.
🖥 **Slatington Library**　610.767.6461 M,W: 9-7, Tu 9-3, F 9-5, Sa 8-2.

1257.2　PA 248/145, ***Walnutport, PA 18088*** (2E)
🏪🦷 **Kmart**　610.767.1812, Open daily 8-10, pharmacy hours slightly shorter. Grocery section only has dry goods (no produce).
🍴 **Valley Pizza Family Restaurant**　610.767.9000 L/D, delivers.
➕ **St Luke's Family Practice Center**　610.628.8922 Open M-F.
🦷 **Rite Aid Pharmacy**　610.767.9595
🐾 **Blue Ridge Veterinary Clinic**　610.767.4896
⟨www.blueridgeveterinary.com⟩ Call before coming.

1257.3　Superfund Trailhead
　　　Palmerton, PA 18071 (1.5W)
Town Ordinance: Pets must be kept on leash.
🛏🛁📶 **Sunny Rest Resort**　610.377.2911 *Clothing optional* resort 2 miles outside of town, rides sometimes available. Weekdays: hotel rooms $118-209, camping $75, day visit $46-$56/couple. Prices higher on weekends. Mention trail guide for 20% discount. Addt'l discount for 18-35 y/o. Restaurant (B/L/D), nightclub, two heated pools, pool bar, hot tub, volleyball, nature trails, 425 Sunny Rest Rd, Palmerton, PA. Open May-Sep.
🍴🛏📶 **Bert's Restaurant**　610.826.9921 Open 7am-8pm 7 days, WiFi available in restaurant, ask about overnight stay, shower $5.
🍴 **Palmerton Hotel Restaurant**　610.826.5454 Dining Su-Th 4-10, F-Su 11-10.
🏪 **Country Harvest**　610.824.3663 8am-9pm 7 days.
🍴 **Tony's Pizzeria**　610.826.6161 L/D, no delivery.
🍴 **Joe's Place**　L/D, deli sandwiches.
🐾 **Little Gap Animal Hospital**　610.826.2793 (3.5W) from town.
🧺 **Towne Laundry**　5am-7pm 7 days.

Library 610.826.3424
M, Tu 10-8, W-F 10-5, Sa 9-4

Palmerton Hospital
610.826.3141

1.0 mi

5th St
4th St
6th St

Spillane's Hot Dogs &
Claude's Creamery
Tony's Pizza

Family Dollar
Rite Aid
Dunkin' Donuts
Subway
Palmerton Pizza
Convenient Mart/ATM

Human House

County Harvest
Blue Mtn Family Med
610.826.5110

Joe's Steaks 'n Subs
Gulf Quick Stop
Balch's Soup & Salad
Jan's Barber Shop
Towne Laundry
Bert's Steakhouse

Delaware Ave
C&C Food Outlet
Shipman's Pharmacy
Simply Something Cafe
Palmerton Restaurant

Shea's Hardware

One Ten Tavern
2nd St

PALMERTON, PA

N
40.7996,-75.6156
Mag. Dec. 12.09°W

PO (18071):
610.826.2286
M-F 8:30-5,
Sa 8:30-12

State Rd / Red Hill Dr
248

Lehigh River
path if gate locked
Gate
(1.5 mi.
from PO)

Aquashicola Creek

It is not advisable to walk along shoulderless, fast-moving PA 248. SoBo intending to go to town should do so before reaching PA 248. Go west on the blue-blazed winter trail. The winter trail joins an old railroad bed and veers right uphill. Stay to the left on the railroad bed, and follow it to private parking area at the end of Red Hill Dr. (at bottom left of town map). Cross Red Hill bridge and follow the road into town. If the bridge is gated or access is denied, hop the guardrail to PA 248, cautiously cross Aquashicola Creek on the 248 bridge, then hop the guardrail again to return to Red Hill Drive. The total distance to town is 1.5W miles on level ground.

🚐 **Jason "SoulFlute"** 484.341.3356 Palmerton-area shuttles. Slackpacks Port Clinton to DWG. If call is missed please send text.

🚐 **Brenda** 484.725.9396 Call for pricing. Shuttles ranging from local to bus terminals & airports.

1262.1   Little Gap Rd

🍴⛲ **Slopeside Grill** 0.2W and 0.5mi up driveway. Hikers welcome to get water from outside spigot. Grill hours: Fri 5-11pm, Sat 2-11pm, Sun 2-9pm.

   Danielsville, PA 18038 (1.5E on Blue Mountain Dr, then left on Mountainview Dr to PO and B&B.)

🏤 M-F 9:30-1 & 2-4:30, Sa 8-12, 610.767.6882

🛏⛺🚐📶✉ **Filbert B&B** 610.428.3300 ⟨www.filbertbnb.com⟩ $100S, $150D + tax. Hosted by Kathy in Victorian farmhouse with A/C includes full country breakfast. Will pickup at Little Gap (no charge). Fee for pickup at PA 309, Lehigh Gap, Smith Gap, or Wind Gap. Slackpacking possible DWG-Port Clinton. Parking for section hikers. Call ahead for reservations, no credit cards. Laundry for a fee. Italian restaurant will deliver. Guest only Mail: 3740 Filbert Dr, Danielsville, PA 18038.

🍴💲 (0.8E) **Blue Mountain Restaurant & Ice Cream** 610.767.6379 B/L/D Tu-Su, closed M. Ask about overnighting.

🏪 (1.0E) **Miller's Market**

1269.4   Smith Gap Rd (Point Phillips Rd)

◐🚐⊛♦🍴🅿 (1.0W, blue blazes on telephone poles) Home of John "Mechanical Man" and Linda "Crayon Lady" Stempa (610.381.4606), eponym of the spring 0.7 mile south. Hikers welcome to water from spigot at rear of house (no need to call) and to use outside shower during daylight hours. Pet friendly, ask about dog sitting. Please sign register. For-fee shuttles ranging from Lickdale (Swatara Gap) to Delaware Water Gap, safe place to park your car. *Only with permission*, $10 camp or stay in garage with hot shower & towel, ride to Kunkletown included, and ride back to trail; call in advance. Sodas $1. Ask about stoves, fuel & maildrops.

◐🏠🍴△ (2.7E) **Evergreen Lake** 610.837.6401 East 1.7 on Smith Gap Road, then left one mile on Mountain Road. Tenting $30 for up to 2 adults, 2 children. Snack shop, laundry, free showers.

Kunkletown, PA 18058 (3.0W) See map: west on Smith Gap Rd/ Point Phillips Rd for 2 mi to stop sign, right on Lower Smith Gap Rd for 100 yards, left on Chestnut Ridge Rd for 0.9 mi to Kunkletown Rd.

🛏🍴**Kunkletown Pub** 610.895.4255 Room $50/up, 10% discount on meals (L/D). Pool table. Meal delivery possible, $50 min. order.

🍴⊛ **Penny's Place** 610.381.5350 Pub food & beer; good place to meet up with helpful locals. Free pool for hikers. Sells *The A.T. Guide*.

🏠🅱 **General Store** 610.381.2887 Good selection of packaged foods, deli, ice cream. Summer hours 6:30-8:30 (till 7:30 in winter).

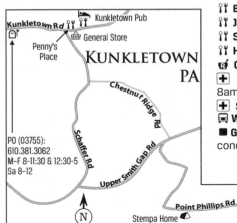

Kunkletown Rd 🍴🍴 Kunkletown Pub
📮 🏠 General Store
Penny's Place
KUNKLETOWN PA
Chestnut Ridge Rd
PO (03755):
610.381.3062
M-F 8-11:30 & 12:30-5
Sa 8-12
Schaffer Rd
Upper Smith Gap Rd
Point Phillips Rd
Stempa Home ◣
Smith Gap Rd→
(N)
2.4 mi

1277.5   PA 33

🛏△🛜(0.1W) **Gateway Motel** 909.524.5369 Renovated at the end of 2015 by hiker-friendly owner. Hikers welcome to get water. Vending machine.

🏥(4W) **Creature Comforts** 610.381.2287, 24/7 emergency care.

Wind Gap, PA 18091 (1E)

📮 M-F 8:30-5, Sa 8:30-12, 610.863.6206

🛏🅱🛜 **Travel Inn** 717.885.3101 $59.99D weekdays, $69.99D weekends. Room for 4 $69.99 weekdays, $79.99 weekends.

🛏🛜 **Red Carpet Inn** 610.863.7782 Stay includes cont. breakfast.

🍴 **Giant Food Store** 24hr, deli with salad bar.

🍴🗝 **K-Mart** with pharmacy

🍴 **Beer Stein** Serves L/D wings, seafood.

🍴 **J&R's Smokehouse** L/D

🍴 **Sal's Pizza** 610.863.7565, delivers.

🍴 **Hong Kong Chinese** L/D buffet.

🗝 **CVS** 610.863.5341

➕ **Priority Care** 610.654.5454 Walk-in clinic M-F 8am-8pm, Sa 10am-5pm, Su 10am-4pm.

➕ **Slate Belt Family Practice** 610.863.3019

🚐 **WGM Taxi** 570.223.9289

■ **Gap Theatre** 610.863.3094 Mostly used for concerts.

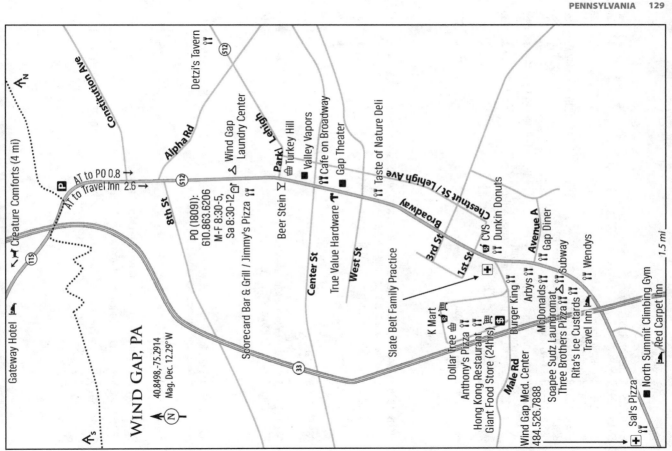

WIND GAP, PA

40.8498,-75.2914
Mag. Dec. 12.29°W

Detzi's Tavern

Constitution Ave

Alpha Rd

Lehigh

Park

Wind Gap Laundry Center

Turkey Hill

Valley Vapors

Cafe on Broadway

Gap Theater

Taste of Nature Deli

Chestnut St / Lehigh Ave

AT to PO 0.8 →
AT to Travel Inn 2.6 →

8th St

512

PO (1809):
610.863.6206
M-F 8:30-5,
Sa 8:30-12

Jimmy's Pizza

Beer Stein

Scorecard Bar & Grill / Jimmy's Pizza

Center St

West St

True Value Hardware

Broadway

Dunkin Donuts

CVS

3rd St

1st St

Avenue A

Gap Diner

Subway

Wendys

Creature Comforts (4 mi)

115

Gateway Hotel

33

Slate Belt Family Practice

K Mart

Dollar Tree

Anthony's Pizza

Hong Kong Restaurant

Giant Food Store (24h[s])

Burger King

Arbys

McDonalds

Soapee Sudz Laundromat

Three Brothers Pizza

Rita's Ice Custards

Travel Inn

Male Rd

Wind Gap Med. Center
484.526.7888

North Summit Climbing Gym

Red Carpet Inn

Sal's Pizza

1.5 mi

SoBo	NoBo	Elev	Feature
898.6	1290.5	1461	Mt Minsi
897.6	1291.5	800	Lookout Rock, view
897.4	1291.7	760	Stream.
896.8	1292.3	536	Council Rock
896.7	1292.4	575	Turn east on gravel road
896.3	1292.8	498	Hiker parking lot .... 40.9798,-75.142 P (pg.132)
896.1	1293.0	386	PA 611, **Delaware Water Gap, PA**
895.8	1293.3	278	**PA-NJ** border, I-80, Delaware River Bridge west bank
894.8	1294.3	290	Kittatinny Visitor Center .... 40.9720,-75.1261 P ⓘ 🏛 🚻
894.4	1294.7	295	NoBo: cross under I-80 and turn left. Parking, V.C. is preferred for overnight parking. 40.9701,-75.1287 P
894.1	1295.0	445	✖ What name, stamped in cursive, is on (non-functioning pump)? Dunnfield Trail to east, reconnects with AT at Sunfish Pond (4 mi)
892.9	1296.2	950	Holly Spring Trail
890.8	1298.3	1327	Backpacker Campsite, Douglas Trail to west, water south of camp. No fires, use bear boxes/poles, leash dogs.
890.0	1299.1	1382	Sunfish Pond south end, no swimming or camping.
889.4	1299.7	1384	Sunfish Pond north end, rock sculptures.
888.5	1300.6	1452	Stream.
887.8	1301.3	1565	Powerline
887.7	1301.4	1532	Kittatinny Mountain, rocky summit
887.1	1302.0	1416	Kaiser Trail to west
885.3	1303.8	1109	Camp Rd (gravel), footbridge **Mohican Outdoor Center** (0.3W) ...... 41.033,-75.004 P (pg.132)
884.1	1305.0	1475	Rattlesnake Swamp Trail, view.
883.2	1305.9	1565	Catfish Lookout Tower, picnic table below the tower.
882.6	1306.5	1260	Rattlesnake Spring on dirt road about 17 yards west of AT
882.3	1306.8	1249	Stream.
882.1	1307.0	1270	Millbrook-Blairstown Rd (paved) ...... 41.0595,-74.9636 P
881.8	1307.3	1252	Millbrook Village (1.1W) historical park with picnic area.
881.5	1307.6	1384	Swamp / Powerline

SoBo	NoBo	Description	Elev
879.4	**1309.7**	Campsite	1487
878.3	**1310.8**	Blue Mtn Lakes Rd, pump disabled, water 0.1E on road No camping in zone from 0.5 mile south of road to 3 mi. north of road.	1350
876.2	**1312.9**	Side trail leads 0.5E to Crater Lake. No camping.	1447
875.2	**1313.9**	Buttermilk Falls Trail, campsites to the north	1557
873.9	**1315.2**	Campsite	1293
873.5	**1315.6**	Rattlesnake Mountain	1492
873.2	**1315.9**	Spring	1365
871.3	**1317.8**	**Brink Shelter** (0.2W)(2013) 61.6◄44.9◄31.2◄▶6.6▶12.4▶15.0 Bear box. Close to road. Water 100 yards to right of old shelter site.	1229
870.1	**1319.0**	Jacobs Ladder Trail	1374
868.3	**1320.8**	Powerline	1260
867.7	**1321.4**	US 206, Culvers Gap, **Branchville, NJ** (3.4E) 41.1797,-74.788 P	935 (pg.132)
867.4	**1321.7**	Sunrise Mountain Rd (paved)	972
865.8	**1323.3**	Culver Fire Tower (locked)	1543
864.8	**1324.3**	Stony Brook Trail 1.0W to free showers at Stony Lake	1344 (see map pg.133)
864.7	**1324.4**	**Gren Anderson Shelter** (0.1W) ☾◆(0.1W) ⊆(8) 51.5◄37.8◄6.6◄▶5.8▶8.4▶13.0 Spring to left of shelter and downhill 70 yards.	1333
863.3	**1325.8**	Tinsley Trail	1446
862.3	**1326.8**	Sunrise Mountain, no camping at pavilion 41.2195,-74.7182 P	1653
861.6	**1327.5**	Roadbed.	1451
860.6	**1328.5**	Stream (slow outflow from pond), treatment recommended.	1384

NoBo
SoBo

5000

3000

1000

1293.0 PA 611, *Delaware Water Gap, PA 18327*

🏕️⊛🚿 **Church of the Mountain Hiker Center** 570.476.0345 or 570.992.3934 Bunkroom, showers, overflow tenting, rides to Stroudsburg when available. Donations encouraged. 2-night max. No drive-ins, no parking, no laundry. Phone numbers of persons who can help are posted in the hostel.

🛏️⛺🛜 **Pocono Inn** 570.476.0000 $65 weekdays, $69 F & Sa + tax. No pets.

🛏️🍴 **Deer Head Inn** 570.424.2000 $90/up weekdays, $120/up weekends. No pets, no TV. Restaurant & lounge open to all. Live music Th-Su, hiker attire okay.

🍴🏠 **Village Farmer & Bakery** 8am-8pm 7 days. Hot dog and slice of pie $2.95. Breakfast sandwiches, salads, sandwiches.

Credit card min. $10.

🍴 **Doughboy's Pizza** open 7 days in summer.

🥾🚪⊠ **Edge of the Woods Outfitters** 570.421.6681 Full line of gear, trail food, footwear. Coleman/alcohol/oz. Shuttles from Little Gap to Bear Mtn. Open 7 days, Memorial - Labor Day. Mail: (FedEx/UPS only) 110 Main St, Delaware Water Gap, PA 18327.

🥾🚪 **Water Gap Adventures** 570.424.8533 Open Apr-Oct.

🚌 **Pocono Pony** 570.839.6862 ⟨gomcta.com⟩ Runs on 2hr-loop through Stroudsburg, $1.50 per boarding.

🚌 **Martz Trailways** 570.421.3040 $66.50 NYC roundtrip.

🚌 **Pocono Cab** 570.424.2800

🚌 **WGM Taxi** 570.223.9289

Stroudsburg, PA 18360 (3.5W)

Large town with all services, including **Walmart** (24hrs w/pharmacy) supermarket, motels, laundry, and movie theater.

🥾 **Dunkleberger's Sports** 570.421.7950 M-Th 9-6, F 9-7, Su 9-5

1303.8 Camp Road

🏕️🛶⊛🍴🏠♦🚿🛜⊠ **Mohican Outdoor Center** (0.3W) 908.362.5670 <www.outdoors.org/lodging/mohican/> Thru-hiker rates (increase expected in 2016) for bunkroom $34.50PP, tenting $13, + tax. Shower/towel for tenters or w/o stay $5. Campfires only in designated areas. Welcome center & camp store hours in peak season are Su-Th 8-7, F 8-9, Sa 8-8. Open 9-5 in winter (Nov-Apr). Water available at the lodge or at spigot near the garage across the street. Deli sandwiches, sodas, candy, Coleman/alcohol/oz, and hiker supplies (footwear, packs, socks, poles). Operated by the AMC. Mail: 50 Camp Mohican Rd, Blairstown, NJ 07825.

1321.4 US 206, Culvers Gap

🛏️🛶🚿 **Stokes SP** 973.948.3820 Tentsites 2 mi from SP office near Rte 206; cabins 4 mi away. Rates: tentsite 1-6 persons $25/up, cabins: $65/up. Rates $5 lower for NJ residents. $5 transaction fee per stay. Snack bar & free showers at Stony Lake Mem-Columbus Day, accessible from 1.0 mile-long Stony Lake Tr.

DELAWARE WATER GAP, PA

40.9831, -75.1406
Mag. Dec. 12.4° W
N

Stroudsburg 3.0 mi
Foxtown Hill Rd
Fuel On 🏠
Water Gap Adventures 🥾 Gulf Mini Mart 🏠💳📞
Broad St
I-80
Martz Trailways / Pocono Pony 📞🚪🏠
Water Gap Diner B/L/D 🍴
Doughboy's Pizza 🍴 🏠
Village Farmer 🍴
Edge of the Woods 🥾🏠
Sycamore Grille 🥾🍴
Zen Fusion
BoTangles Hair Studio
Zoe's Ice Cream
Water Gap Hair Studio
Cherry Valley Rd
Main St
Shepard Ave
Church of the Mountain
Deer Head Inn
Mountain Rd
Lake Rd
Delaware River
PO (18327):
570.476.0304
M-F 8:30-12
& 1-4:45
Sa 8:30-11:30
0.9 mi

▶▲☂✉ **Forest Motel** 973.948.5456, $60S $70D + tax, pets $20, laundry $20. Guest Mail: 104 Rte 206 N, Branchville, NJ 07826.

▶ **Cobmin Ridge Motel** 973.948.3459, 973.652.0780 $50/up.

🍴🏠☂♦✉ **Sunrise Appalachian Trail Deli** 973-948-0045 Open 6-6 with coffee, cold drinks, breakfast & deli sandwiches. Hiker friendly; okay to charge electronics, get water, use WiFi & bathroom. Mail: 15 Rte 206 S. Sandyston, NJ 07826

🍴☂ **Stokes Steakhouse** 908.797.8102 Beer, burgers, fish & chips, WiFi and charging outlets. Closed in winter.

🍴 **Gyps Tavern** Hikers welcome to inside or lakeside seating, charging outlets, economical food choices and packaged goods to go. Open L/D.

🍴 **Jumboland Diner** B/L/D, $2.99 breakfast, Th dinner buffet.

🏠 (1.5E) **Dale's Market** 973.948.3078 M-F 6-9, Sa-Su 7-9

Branchville, NJ 07826 (3.4E)

🏣 M-F 8:30-5, Sa 8:30-1, 973.948.3580

1335.7　NJ 23

⛵⛲👫♦🅿✉ **High Point State Park Headquarters** 973.875.4800 Office open year-round 9am-4pm, Mem-Labor Day extended hours F&Sa 8-8. Bathrooms inside, water spigot outside. Overnight parking 0.25E. **Sawmill Lake Camping Area** 2.5 mile from HQ, tentsites $20 NJ resident/$25 non-resident plus $5.50 walk-in fee. Mail: 1480 State Rte 23, Sussex, NJ 07461.

▶▲🚌☂✉ (1.5E) **High Point Country Inn** 973.702.1860 $89.99D + tax, pets $10, no room phone. Laundry $7. Free pickup/return to trail from NJ 23, longer shuttles for a fee. Guest Mail: 1328 NJ 23, Wantage, NJ 07461.

Port Jervis, NY 12785 (4.4W)

▶☂🖥✉ **Days Inn** 845.856.6611 $79.95D/up + tax, $10EAP, cont B, pets $25. Guest Mail: 2247 Greenville Turnpike, Port Jervis, NY 12771.

🍴 **Village Pizza** 973.293.3364 M-S 10:30am-11pm, Su 10-11

🛒🛒 **Shop Rite Market**, **Price Chopper**

💊 **Rite Aid** 845.856.8342, **Medicine Shoppe** 845.856.6681

➕ **Bon Secours Community Hospital** 845.858.7000

🐾 **Tri-States Veterinary Medical** 845.856.1914

Forest Motel (2.1 from AT)　Stony Lake
Mezza Luna
Stony Lake Tr
1.0 to lake
2 mi. from HQ to tentsites
4 mi. to cabins
Sunrise Mtn Rd
N
Stokes State Park
Stokes Forest Sports
North Shore Rd
Gyp's Tavern
Stokes Steakhouse
Sunrise A.T. Diner
206
N
Kittatinny Lake
Mountain Trail
Culver Lake
S.
BRANCHVILLE, NJ
Lentini Farms　Culver Lake Nursery
County Rd 521
Jumboland Diner
Lakeside Tavern
Dales Market　Jimmy's Pizza (closed Mon.)
Dairy Queen　Bud's Bar
Cobmin Ridge Motel (2.5 from AT)
Yellow Cottage Deli & Bakery (closed Mon.)　Riviera Maya
Union Turnpike
1.9 mi

SoBo	NoBo	Feature		Elev
858.9	1330.2	**Mashipacong Shelter** 43.6◀12.4◀5.8◀▶2.6▶7.2▶19.6 Close to road. ◡ ⊏(8)		1410
		Spring (0.6N) on red-blazed Iris Trail. Sometimes water left in bear box.		
858.7	1330.4	Deckertown Turnpike . . . . 41.2523,-74.6895 **P**		1322
857.8	1331.3	Three intersections with red-blazed trail		1418
856.3	1332.8	**Rutherford Shelter** (0.4E) 15.0◀8.4◀2.6◀▶4.6▶17.0▶28.5 . . . ◡ ⊿ ⬖ ⊏(6)		1488
		Spring 100 yards before shelter on connecting trail. Slow stream. Bear box.		
856.0	1333.1	View.	📷	1481

△ *Camp only in designated sites; fires only in campsite fire rings. Hitchhiking is illegal in NY.*

SoBo	NoBo	Feature		Elev
854.5	1334.6	Intersection with blue-blazed trail.		1601
853.6	1335.5	Iris Trail 0.2E to parking on NJ 23		1504
853.4	1335.7	NJ 23 . . . . 41.3026,-74.6678 **P** ◆ (pg.133)		1500
		High Point State Park Headquarters, **Port Jervis, NY** (4.4W)	📷 ⭍ 🍴 ⛽	
852.4	1336.7	Wooden tower, 0.3W to beach & concessions Mem-Labor Day 12-6		1701
852.2	1336.9	Green-blazed trail 0.3W to 220' tower atop highest point in NJ		1607
851.7	1337.4	**High Point Shelter** (0.1E) 13.0◀7.2◀4.6◀▶12.4▶23.9▶36.0 . . . ◡ ⊏(8)		1298
		Streams on both sides of shelter. Road to privy to right of shelter. Bear box.		
850.4	1338.7	Greenville Rd, County 519 (paved)		1100
849.5	1339.6	Courtwright Rd (gravel), stream on AT 0.1 south of road	●	986
849.0	1340.1	Streams	●	959
848.4	1340.7	Fergerson Rd (gravel), east 20 yards on road.		873
847.8	1341.3	Gemmer Rd (paved)		732
847.5	1341.6	Stream.	●	701
847.1	1342.0	Two footbridges, streams	●	607
846.8	1342.3	Goodrich Rd (paved)		628
846.5	1342.5	Pond	●	673
846.3	1342.8	Murray property 0.2W, gravel driveway	(pg.136)	654
845.9	1343.2	Goldsmith Lane (gravel)		672
845.5	1343.6	Unionville Rd (paved), County Rd 651	(pg.136)	610
845.3	1343.8	Quarry Rd		616
844.6	1344.5	Lott Rd, **Unionville, NY** (0.7W)	(pg.136)	590
843.5	1345.6	NJ 284, **Unionville, NY** (0.7W), stream N of rd 41.2885,-74.5524 **P** ◆ (pg.136)		432
843.1	1346.0	Lower Rd (Oil City Rd)		519
842.6	1346.5	Carnegie Rd, NoBo: follow road 0.2W		404
842.3	1346.8	State Line Rd, NoBo: follow road 0.5E		410
842.1	1347.0	Wallkill River parking. 41.2877,-74.534 **P**		410
841.8	1347.3	AT + State Line Rd north end. NoBo: turn east into Wallkill Reserve		398
841.0	1348.1	90 degree turn on Wallkill perimeter		381
840.6	1348.5	90 degree turn on Wallkill perimeter		395

NoBo
SoBo

SoBo	NoBo	Description	Coordinates		Elev
839.8	1349.3	Liberty Corners Rd (paved).			440
839.7	1349.4	Water to west.			516
839.3	1349.8	**Pochuck Mtn. Shelter** (0.1W) 19.6◀17.0◀12.4▶11.5▶23.6▶37.9		)◆⊂(6)	884
		Bear box. Spigot at vacant house at foot of Pochuck Mountain.			
838.5	1350.6	View.		🏕	1111
837.7	1351.4	Pochuck Mountain		🏕	1147
837.2	1351.9	Lovemma Lane (gravel).			880
837.0	1352.1	Stream.			794
836.6	1352.5	County Rd 565, **Glenwood, NJ** (1.1W), stream south of road		◆(pg.136)	720
		SoBos planning to stay at Pochuck Mtn Shelter should get water here.			
835.9	1353.2	Roadbed.			764
835.1	1354.0	County Rd 517, **Glenwood, NJ** (1.1W).	41.2357,-74.4805	P (pg.136)	428
834.4	1354.7	Pochuck Creek suspension footbridge.			394
		Boardwalk over swamp for (0.6S) and (0.2N) of footbridge.			
833.7	1355.4	Canal Rd.	41.2266,-74.469	P	410
833.5	1355.6	Footbridge, Wawayanda Creek.		◆	401
832.8	1356.3	NJ 94, **Vernon, NJ** (2.4E)	41.2193,-74.4551	P (pg.137)	450
831.8	1357.3	Spring, climb up south side of mtn known as "stairway to heaven"		◆	973
831.4	1357.7	Pinwheels vista 0.1W, Wawayanda Mountain, side trail 0.8E to views		🏕	1340
830.5	1358.6	Footbridge, stream.		◆	994
829.7	1359.4	Barrett Rd (paved), **New Milford, NY** (1.8W)		(pg.137)	1140
828.6	1360.5	Cross stream on Iron Mountain Rd			1060
827.8	1361.3	**Wawayanda Shelter** (0.1W). 28.5◀23.9◀11.5▶12▶26.4▶31.7		)◆⊂(6)	1194
827.6	1361.5	Wawayanda State Park (0.2E) Water from park 0.1N and 0.2E.	41.1981,-74.3975	P ♟♪◆	1149
827.3	1361.8	Warwick Turnpike.	41.2014,-74.3916	P (pg.138)	1140
826.8	1362.3	Footbridge, stream			1107
825.9	1363.2	Long House Dr / Brady Rd	41.1955,-74.3715	P	1115
824.8	1364.3	Long House Creek, footbridge		◆	1085
824.0	1365.1	Ernest Walter Trail (yellow-blazed) to east			1341
823.7	1365.4	**NJ-NY border**, State Line Trail 1.0E to **Lakeside, NJ.**			1385
823.3	1365.8	0.1N on AT is Zig Zag Trail to west. Prospect Rock, highest point on AT in NY. Views of Greenwood Lake to east		🏕	1433
822.4	1366.7	Furnace Brook		◆	1143
822.1	1367.0	Ladder.			1262

NoBo
SoBo

5000
3000
1000

⚠ *Despite the unimposing profile, rocks, abrupt ups & downs make this section challenging.*

1342.8 Murray property driveway

Private cabin open for the use of long distance hikers as it has been for nearly 20 years, tenting, well water, shower & privy. If you feel the need to change your brain chemistry this is probably not your stop but serious hikers welcome. No groups please.

1343.6 Unionville Rd, County Rd 651

1344.5 Lott Rd

1345.6 NJ 284 ***Unionville, NY*** PO is 0.5W from any road crossing.

Village Office 845.726.3681 Tenters check-in at office or at Horler's.

Wit's End Tavern 845.726.3956 Darts, pool table. Open 7 days noon-midnight or later. Great ribs, burgers, wings. Occassional wkend music.

Horler's Store 845.726.3210 M–Sa 6–8, Su 7–7, short-order grill open M-F 6:30-3, Sa-Su 7-1.

End of the Line Grocery 845.726.3228 Deli, M-S 6–8, Sa–Su 6–7.

Annabel's Pizza 845.726.9992 <www.annabelspizza.com> M-Sa 11-10, Su 11-9 burgers, pizza by slice.

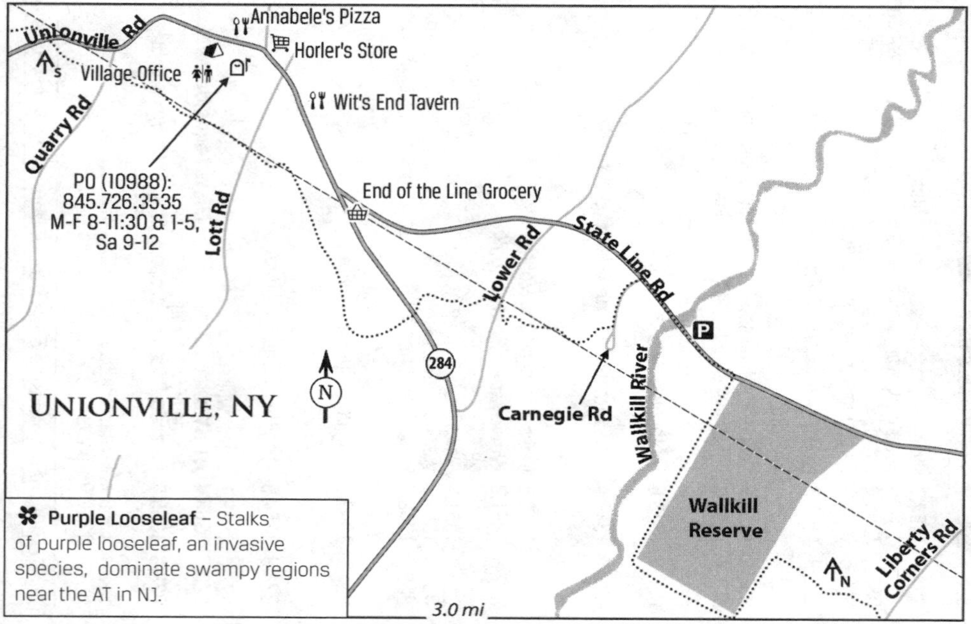
Unionville Rd
Annabele's Pizza
Horler's Store
Village Office
Wit's End Tavern
Quarry Rd
PO (10988):
845.726.3535
M-F 8-11:30 & 1-5,
Sa 9-12
Lott Rd
End of the Line Grocery
Lower Rd
State Line Rd
284
Carnegie Rd
Wallkill River
Wallkill Reserve
Liberty Corners Rd
N
UNIONVILLE, NY
3.0 mi

Purple Looseleaf – Stalks of purple looseleaf, an invasive species, dominate swampy regions near the AT in NJ.

1352.5 County Rd 565

1354.0 County Rd 517 (0.9W to PO and Pochuck Valley Farm)

Glenwood, NJ 07418

(1.1W from either road)

M-F 7:30–5, Sa 10–2, 973.764.2616

Apple Valley Inn 973.764.3735 $145-$160 + tax, includes country breakfast, no pets, shuttles to County Roads 517 & 565 with stay. Guest Mail: PO Box 302, Glenwood, NJ 07418.

Pochuck Valley Farms Market & Deli 973.764.4732 Open daily M–F 6am–6pm, Sa–Su 6am–5pm. B/L, produce, bakery. Water spigot and restroom.

1356.3   NJ 94

🏛 🚶 💲 (0.1W) **Heaven Hill Farm** 973.764.5144 ⟨www.heavenhillfarm.com⟩ Summer hours daily 9–7, Su until 6. Ice cream, bakery, seasonal fruit & vegetables, picnic tables.

🍴 (0.2E) **Mitch's Roadside Grill** Hot dog stand open 11-3 Apr-Oct. Hot dogs, sodas, Italian Ice & potato knishes. Shaded picnic tables, good place from which to hitch.

🛏⛺🛜✉ (1.2E) **Appalachian Motel** 973.764.6070 $70-110D, $10EAP. Call for ride. Pets $20. Laundry $10. Mail (guests only): 367 Route 94, Vernon, NJ 07462.

Vernon, NJ 07462 (2.4E)

🛏◉💦⛺ **St. Thomas Episcopal Church Hostel** 973.764.7506 Sign in on computer within an hour of arrival ⟨www.st-thomas-vernon.org/hiker-hostel---sign-in.html⟩ $10PP donation, capacity 12, one night limit. Hikers only, no guests of hikers. Shower/ towel, fridge, micro. Hikers may have to share space with other groups and are expected to help w/cleanup. Hikers with pets my tent outside. No alcohol, no smoking. Hikers welcome to Sunday service. Open May-Sep. Paypal/CC accepted.

🛒 💳 💲 **Acme Market** 973.764.5350 M-Sa 6-midnight, Su 6-10, **Starbucks** inside.

➕ **Vernon Urgent Care** 973.209.2260 1.0 mile beyond hostel, M–F 8–8, Sa–Su 9–5.

*New Milford, NY (*2.7W from NJ 94, see listings at Barrett Rd.)

VERNON, NJ
41.1984,-74.4829
Mag. Dec. 12.81° W

Appalachian Motel 🛏
1.1 mi
644
94
1.3 mi. from hotel Heaven Hill Farm & Mitch's Grill near trailhead
Vernon Vet Clinic 973.764.3630 🐕
🍴 Vernon Inn
Ming's Asian Bistro
DJ's Barber Shop
China Star
Dunkin Donuts
Mixing Bowl
Church St
St. Thomas Episcopal
🍴 Paesano Pizza
Burger King
Pizza Station
McAfee Vernon Rd
94
Main St
Vernon Rd
➕ Vernon Urgent Care (1.0mi)
Healthy Tyhmes Market 🏪
🍴 Dairy Queen
Rumours Hair ✂
Rite Aid
515
PO (07462) 973.764.9056: M-F 8:30-5, Sa 9:30-12:30
🍴 Lox of Bagels
🛒💳 ACME Market, Pharmacy, Starbucks

1359.4   Barrett Rd

New Milford, NY 10959 (1.8W) 1.6W on Barret Rd, then right 0.2 on NJ 94 to shoe store and post office.

🏤 M-F 8:30-12:30, Sa 9-11:30, 845.986.3557

■ **Sneakers to Boots** 845.986.0333 Open M-F 10-6, Sa 10-5, Su 11-2 Shoes by Merrell, Keen, Oboz and others, merino wool socks. 314 Rt 94 South.

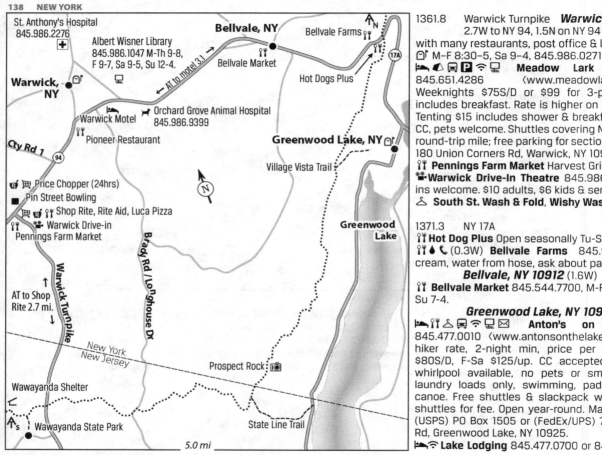

St. Anthony's Hospital
845.986.2276

Albert Wisner Library
845.986.1047 M-Th 9-8,
F 9-7, Sa 9-5, Su 12-4.

Bellvale, NY

Bellvale Farms

Bellvale Market

Hot Dogs Plus

(17A)

Warwick, NY

AT to motel 3.1

Warwick Motel

Orchard Grove Animal Hospital
845.986.9399

Pioneer Restaurant

Greenwood Lake, NY

Cty Rd 1

(94)

Village Vista Trail

Price Chopper (24hrs)

Pin Street Bowling

Shop Rite, Rite Aid, Luca Pizza

Warwick Drive-in
Pennings Farm Market

Greenwood Lake

Brady Rd / Longhouse Dr

N

Warwick Turnpike

AT to Shop
Rite 2.7 mi.

New York
New Jersey

Prospect Rock

Wawayanda Shelter

State Line Trail

Wawayanda State Park

5.0 mi

1361.8   Warwick Turnpike **Warwick, NY 10990**
     2.7W to NY 94, 1.5N on NY 94 to downtown
with many restaurants, post office & library.
⌂ M–F 8:30–5, Sa 9–4, 845.986.0271
🛏🛁🚗🅿🛜🖥 **Meadow Lark Farm B&B**
845.651.4286 ⟨www.meadowlarkfarm.com⟩
Weeknights $75S/D or $99 for 3-person room,
includes breakfast. Rate is higher on Fri-Sa nights.
Tenting $15 includes shower & breakfast. All major
CC, pets welcome. Shuttles covering NJ & NY, $1 per
round-trip mile; free parking for section hikers. Mail:
180 Union Corners Rd, Warwick, NY 10990.
 🍴 **Pennings Farm Market** Harvest Grill, ice cream.
🎬 **Warwick Drive-In Theatre** 845.986.4440 Walk-
ins welcome. $10 adults, $6 kids & seniors.
 ⚒ **South St. Wash & Fold**, **Wishy Washy**

1371.3   NY 17A
🍴 **Hot Dog Plus** Open seasonally Tu-Sa 10:30-3:30.
🍴💧🐾 (0.3W) **Bellvale Farms** 845.988.1818 Ice
cream, water from hose, ask about parking.
       Bellvale, NY 10912 (1.6W)
🍴 **Bellvale Market** 845.544.7700, M-F 7-7, Sa 7-6,
Su 7-4.
     Greenwood Lake, NY 10925 (2E)
🛏🍴⚒🚗🛜🖥✉ **Anton's on the Lake**
845.477.0010 ⟨www.antonsonthelake.com⟩ Thru-
hiker rate, 2-night min, price per night: Su-Th
$80S/D, F-Sa $125/up. CC accepted, rooms w/
whirlpool available, no pets or smoking, small
laundry loads only, swimming, paddle boats &
canoe. Free shuttles & slackpack w/stay, longer
shuttles for fee. Open year-round. Mail for guests:
(USPS) PO Box 1505 or (FedEx/UPS) 7 Waterstone
Rd, Greenwood Lake, NY 10925.
🛏🛜 **Lake Lodging** 845.477.0700 or 845.705.2005.

Good hiker rates. No pets, no credit cards.

🛏🍴🅱🛜✉ **Breezy Point Inn** 845.477.8100 ⟨www.breezypointinn.com⟩ $85+tax room with 2 double beds, no pets, no smoking, L/D dining 7 days. Closed month of January. Guest Mail: (UPS/FedEx) 620 Jersey Ave, Greenwood Lake, NY 10925.

🚐 **Greenwood Lake Taxi** 845.477.0314 ⟨greenwoodlaketaxi.com⟩

Warwick, NY 10990 4.5W to downtown area, see map & more listings on pg. 138.

🛏⛺🛜 **Warwick Motel** (3.1W from NY 17A) 845.986.6656.

1383.3 NY 17 **Southfields, NY 10975** (2.1E) 🏠 M-F 10-12 & 1-5, Sa 8:30-11:30, 845.351.2628

🛏⛺✉ **Tuxedo Motel** 845.351.4747 $54.50S, $59.50D, $10EAP. No pets, no cooking. Food delivery options. Accepts Visa/MC. Mail: 985 Route 17 South, Southfields, NY, 10975.

⛪ **Valero** 0.1 west of PO.

Harriman, NY 10926 (3.7W) Lodging, groceries, restaurants & more.

1383.7 Arden Valley Rd parking
🅿🚐 **Harriman Shuttle** ⟨www.myharriman.com/harriman-shuttle-bus/⟩ Runs Sa, Su & holidays w/ pickup here at 11:43 and Tiorati circle at 11:40. Connects to town of Southfields and Tuxedo Train Station. $5 per ride.

🛏 **Stony Point Center** (see pg. 142)

1388.8 Arden Valley Rd (Tiorati Circle)
🍴🚿⛱🚻👫🏊 **Lake Tiorati Beach** (0.3E) 845.429.8257 Open 9-7 daily mid Jun-mid Aug, weekends only spring & fall. Restrooms, free showers, vending machine, swimming.

Map: Greenwood Lake, NY

⬆ 1.8 mi. ⬆ (17A)

3 Corners Cafe
Friendly Beer & Soda
(17A)
Scoops Ice Cream
Sunrise Diner
Lake Lodging

Village Vista Trail 0.8 mi. from park to ⬆

Lion's Field

PO (10925): 845.477.7328 M-F 8-5, Sa 9-12
Subway
CVS
Frozen Treats
The Grill (B/L)
(210)
Sunoco
Linden Motel
Planet Pizza
Walnut St
Cumberland Farms (Open 24/7)

Elm St
Country Kitchen
Irish Whisper
Mangos
Sing Loong Kitchen
Linden Ave
Ten Eyke Ave

Breezy Point Inn 0.6 mi.
Murphy's
Ashley's Pizza
Village Buzz Cafe
True Value Hardware

Jersey Ave
Country Grocery
NJTransit.com 973.275.5555 (bus to NYC M-F @ $14)
Library: 845.477.8377 M & F 9-5, Tu-Th 9-9, Sa 10-4, Su 11-3
Waterstone Rd

GREENWOOD LAKE, NY
41.2227, -74.2942
Mag. Dec. 12.92° W

Anton's on the Lake

Windermere Ave
0.7 mi
Bridge Inn

Ⓝ

SoBo	NoBo	Feature	Elev.
820.7	1368.4	Cascade Brook ◆	1176
819.9	1369.2	Village Vista Trail, 0.8E to Greenwood Lake	1282
818.3	1370.8	Powerline	1201
817.8	1371.3	NY 17A, **Bellvale, NY** (1.6W) 41.2443,-74.2869 **P** (pg.138) **Greenwood Lake, NY** (2.0E)	1180
817.2	1371.9	Pipeline clearing	1248
816.5	1372.6	Eastern Pinnacles, short bypass trail to west 🖼	1204
816.3	1372.8	Brook 🖼	1050
816.0	1373.1	Cat Rocks, view	1082
815.7	1373.4	**Wildcat Shelter** (0.2W) 36.0◀23.6◀12.1◀▶14.3▶19.6▶22.8 🌙◆◢⊂(8) Spring in front of shelter.	1066
814.4	1374.7	Highlands Trail ◆	763
814.2	1374.9	Lakes Rd (paved), 0.1N powerline, footbridge and stream ◆	680
813.9	1375.2	Fitzgerald Falls ◆	739
812.6	1376.5	Allis Trail, Sterling Fire Tower 5.0E 🖼🔭	1263
811.9	1377.2	Mombasha High Point 🖼	1280
810.8	1378.3	Boardwalk, pond	911
810.7	1378.4	West Mombasha Rd, stream just north on AT 41.2693,-74.2146 **P** ◆	929
809.8	1379.3	Buchanan Mountain	1142
809.0	1380.1	East Mombasha Rd (paved)	840
808.7	1380.4	Little Dam Lake, stepping stones over creek ◆	754
807.6	1381.5	Orange Turnpike 41.2695,-74.181 **P** ◆ (0.5E)	780
806.9	1382.2	Arden Mountain	1180
806.6	1382.5	Sapphire Trail	1137
806.2	1382.9	View 🖼	1024
805.8	1383.3	NY 17, **Southfields, NY** (2.1E), **Harriman, NY** (3.7W) (pg.139)	550
805.4	1383.7	AT on Arden Valley Rd for 0.4 mile, 41.2649,-74.1544 **P** 🚻 (pg.139) Passes over NY State Thruway 87, crosses thru parking area north of bridge.	600
804.1	1385.0	Island Pond Rd (gravel) 0.1E to pond ◆	1006
803.5	1385.6	Lemon Squeezer, Arden-Surebridge Trail to east	1091
803.2	1385.9	Island Pond Mountain	1302
802.8	1386.3	New York Long Path 52.0E to Manhattan 🖼	1065
802.1	1387.0	Surebridge Brook ◆	1087
801.5	1387.6	AT joins Red Dot Trail (south end)	1341

SoBo	NoBo	Description		Elev
801.4	1387.7	**Fingerboard Shelter** 37.9◄26.4◄14.3◄▶5.3▶8.5▶40.7. △ ⌒(8)		1348
		Spring downhill to left unreliable. Water at Lake Tiorati 0.5E on Hurst Trail.		
800.8	1388.3	Fingerboard Mountain		1322
800.3	1388.8	Arden Valley Rd (paved), Tiorati Circle (0.3E) .... 41.2646,-74.1544 **P** (pg.139)		1196
799.6	1389.5	Woods road		1027
798.2	1390.9	Footbridge, stream	♦	836
798.1	1391.0	Seven Lakes Dr		850
796.1	1393.0	**William Brien Memorial Shelter** 31.7◄19.6◄5.3◄▶3.2▶35.4▶44.4 △ ⌒(8)		1076
		Unreliable spring-fed well 80 yards down blue-blazed trail to right of shelter.		
		Yellow-blazed Menomine Trail to east.		
795.2	1393.9	AT joins Red Dot Trail (north end)	📷	915
794.8	1394.3	Black Mountain, views, can see NY City skyline		1193
794.0	1395.1	Palisades Parkway, busy 4-lane divided hwy. NY City 34E. Visitor. **H** 🏛♦⌕		680
		center in median 0.4W, soda & snack machines. △ Watch blazes next 3mi. north.		
793.7	1395.4	Beechy Bottom Brook, footbridge, parking 0.8W	**P** ♦	610
792.9	1396.2	**West Mountain Shelter** (0.6E) 22.8◄8.5◄3.2◄▶32.2▶41.2▶49.0. 📷 ⌒(8)		1221
		Views of Hudson River & NYC.		
792.2	1396.9	Views from ridge of West Mountain	📷	1137
791.1	1398.0	Seven Lakes Dr		610
790.5	1398.6	Perkins Memorial Dr		793
788.7	1400.4	Bear Mountain, Perkins Memorial Tower, ... 41.3112,-74.0072 **P** 📷 🏛		1305
		Vending machines, view of NYC skyline.		
788.1	1401.0	Perkins Memorial Dr (south end of 0.3 mi. roadwalk)		1001
		⚠ NoBo: Upon reaching the park, AT turns left through playground then follows path at edge of lake.		
786.8	1402.3	Bear Mountain Recreation Area, Hessian Lake .... 41.313,-73.989 **P** (pg.142)		189
786.4	1402.7	Tunnel under US 9, Trailside Museum, bear cage is lowest point on AT ... (pg.142)		177
785.9	1403.2	Bear Mountain Bridge, Hudson River, **Fort Montgomery, NY** (1.8W) .... (pg.142)		200
785.4	1403.7	NY 9D, Bear Mountain Bridge north end.		198
784.7	1404.4	Camp Smith Trail, 0.6E to Anthonys Nose, views of Hudson River	📷	727
783.7	1405.4	Hemlock Springs Campsite	♦ 🔥	503
783.5	1405.6	Manitou Rd (gravel). .... 41.3296,-73.9533 **P**		460
782.5	1406.6	Osborne Loop Trail to west (blue-blazed)		774
782.1	1407.0	Curry Pond Trail to west (yellow-blazed)		857

1402.3 Bear Mountain Recreation Area, *Bear Mountain, NY 10911*

1402.7 ⊛**Trailside Museum and Zoo** 845.786.2701 Open 10-4:30; no charge for hiking through. No dogs. Lowest elevation on the AT (124') is within the park. If closed, or if you have a dog, use bypass (see map).

1403.2 Bear Mountain Bridge, *Fort Montgomery, NY 10922* (1.8W)

⚠ Going into town? Consider passing through zoo first; hours are limited.

🛏🍴💲🛜🖥 **Bear Mountain Inn** 845.786.2731 $149/up+tax, cont b'fast. Dining options: **1915, Blue Tapas & Hiker Cafe** in the inn, seasonal concession lakeside.

🛏🛜✉ **Bear Mountain Bridge Motel** 845.446.2472 $75D, no pets, accepts Visa/MC, pickup/return to trail (park, zoo, or bridge) with stay. Wir sprechen Deutsch. Guest Mail: PO Box 554, Fort Montgomery, NY 10922.

🛏🍴⌂🛜🖥🅿✉ **Stony Point Center** (8E) 845.786.5674 Call x100 7:30am-6pm or register on-line ⟨www.stonypointcenter.org/AT⟩ use code "ATHike" for discount: $50S wkdays, $80S wkends $10EAP up to 3. Includes b'fast. Drug free 35 acre retreat with farm and pottery workshop. Shuttle from Rec Area $10 ea. way for up to 9 passengers. Buffet lunch $10, dinner $15. 1 acre-farm. Clean, simple rooms, no TV, common use bathrooms. Laundry $3. Fuel/oz and some hiker foods. Parking for section hikers, slackpacking Arden Valley Rd to Graymoor. Mail w/ reservation: 17 Cricketown Rd. Stony Point, NY 10980.

🛏🛜 **Overlook Lodge** 845.786.2731 $149/up +tax, cont b'fast, some pet rooms.

🛏⛺🛜🖥✉ **Holiday Inn Express** 845.446.4277 $120D+tax $10EAP, full b'fast, indoor pool & sauna, coin laundry, 24-hour business center. Guest Mail: 1106 Route 9 W, Fort Montgomery, NY 10922-0620.

🛏 **Victorian Riverview Inn** 845.446.5479

🍴 **Foodies Pizza** 845.839.0383 B/L/D

Highland Falls, NY (3.8W)

🛏🛜 **Fairbridge Inn & Suites** 845.446.9400 $75D, cont b'fast. Pets $10.

🍴 **Dunkin' Donuts,** and many other restaurants

⌂ **My Town Marketplace** 845.446.3663

🏪 **Rite Aid** 845.446.3170

🖥 **Highland Falls Library** 845.446.3113 M, Th-F 10-5, Tu 10-7, W 10-8, Sa 10-2.

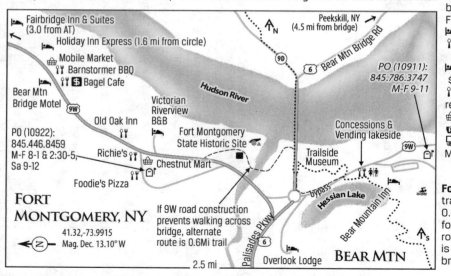

Fairbridge Inn & Suites (3.0 from AT)

Holiday Inn Express (1.6 mi from circle)

Mobile Market
Barnstormer BBQ
Bagel Cafe

Bear Mtn Bridge Motel

PO (10922): 845.446.8459 M-F 8-1 & 2:30-5, Sa 9-12

Old Oak Inn

Richie's

Foodie's Pizza

Victorian Riverview B&B

Fort Montgomery State Historic Site

Chestnut Mart

FORT MONTGOMERY, NY

41.32,-73.9915
Mag. Dec. 13.10° W

If 9W road construction prevents walking across bridge, alternate route is 0.6Mi trail

Hudson River

Peekskill, NY (4.5 mi from bridge)

Bear Mtn Bridge Rd

PO (10911): 845.786.3747 M-F 9-11

Concessions & Vending lakeside

Trailside Museum

bypass

Hessian Lake

Bear Mountain Inn

Overlook Lodge

BEAR MTN

2.5 mi

Fort Montgomery State Historic Site Side trail starting from end of bridge guardrail 0.6W passes through Revolutionary War fort for which the town is named. The side trail is roughly the same length as the roadwalk but is more interesting. View the Hudson River bridge down the barrel of a cannon.

1409.0   US 9, NY 403

🍴🚐 **$** 💧 **Appalachian Market** at trailhead. 845.424.6241 Hiker-friendly, open 24hrs, deli serves B/L/D. Water spigot on north side of building.

🍴 **Stadium Sports Bar** (0.8E) daily 11:30-10, closed M Jan-Feb.
Peekskill, NY 10566 (4.5E) large town
📮 M-F 9-5, Sa 9-4, 914.737.6437

1409.6   Franciscan Way

🛏☂💧🌿♪ **Graymoor Spiritual Life Center** (0.4E) 845.424.2111 Hikers permitted to sleep (free) at monastery's ball field picnic shelter Mar-Nov. Has water, privy & shower. Follow signs & blue-blazes; stay to the left at both forks in the road. Rooms available by reservation (no walk-ins) $45, no A/C or TV, free WiFi, community shower. No pets, no smoking, quiet time after 10pm. Fixed-schedule meals are available to room guests only for $15; B 7:30, L 12:00, D 5:00.

1414.0   Canopus Hill Rd

🍴🏠 **$** (1.6E) **Putnam Valley Market** 845.528.8626 Directions: 0.3E on Canopus Hill Rd, right on Canopus Hollow Rd for 0.1 mi, left on Sunset Hill Rd for 1.2 mi. Pizza, hot food from the grill, ATM, open M-Sa 6-9, Su 6-7.

1421.4   NY 301, Canopus Lake (1E to SP)
1423.4   Side trail entry (0.2E to SP beach)

⚡🍴🚻🌿 **Clarence Fahnestock State Park** 845.225.7207, 800.456.2267 Open mid-Apr to mid-Dec. Thru-hikers get one free night of camping. Concession at beach open wkends only Mem Day - June; open daily July - Labor Day. Hours M-Sa 9-5, Su 9-6.

1428.4   Hortontown Rd, **RPH Shelter** (Ralph's Peak Hiker Cabin) Trail work weekend following July 4. ✖ What word is etched onto the concrete pad outside of the shelter?
🍴 Pizza delivered after 4pm only by **Carlo's Pizza Express** 845.896.6500 and **Gian Bruno's** 845.227.9276.

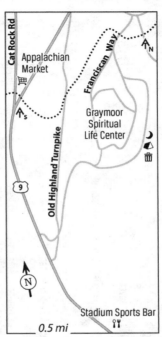

0.5 mi

1433.5   NY 52

🏠🍴☂ **$** 💧📞 (0.4E) **Mountaintop Market Deli** 845.221.0928 Open daily 5-8, ATM, pay phone inside, welcome to water from faucet on side of building & electric outlets. Camping allowed.

🍴 **Danny's Pizzeria** 845.223.5888 pizza by the slice.
Stormville, NY 12582 (1.9W)
📮 M-F 8:30-5, Sa 9-12, 845.226.2627

1440.7   NY 55
(1.5W) Pleasant Ridge Plaza with:
🍴 **Pleasant Ridge Pizza** 845.724.3444 Open 7 days for L/D.
🍴 **A&A Deli** 845.452.4040
💊 (1.2W) **Total Care Pharmacy** 845.724.5757. Open M-F 9-8, Sa 9-3
Poughquag, NY 12570 (3.1W)
📮 M-F 8:30-1 & 2-5, Sa 8:30-12:30, 845.724.4763
🛏📶 **Knights Inn** 845.724.5151 $70S $75D, + tax, no pets, accepts Visa/ MC/Disc.

🍴 **Great Wall** 845.724.5387, **Clove Valley Deli & Café** 845.227.1585
💊 **Total Care Pharmacy, Beekman Pharmacy** 845.724.3200
🐾 **Beekman Animal Hospital** 845.724.8387
Pawling, NY (4.0E, see pg. 148)

1445.9   County Rd 20, West Dover Rd
Dover Oak north side of road, largest oak tree on AT. Girth 20' 4" and estimated to be over 300 years old.
Pawling, NY 12564 (3.1E, see pg. 148)

NoBo	SoBo	Elev	Feature
1408.0	781.1	862	Osborne Loop Trail to west (blue-blazed)
1408.5	780.6	513	Carriage Connector Trail to west (yellow-blazed)
1409.0	780.1	400	US 9 + NY 403, **Peekskill, NY** (4.5E) (pg.143)
1409.3	779.8	461	Old Highland Turnpike (paved)
1409.5	779.5	540	Franciscan Way (paved), **Graymoor Spiritual Life Center** (0.4E)
1409.6	779.4	466	(pg.143)
1409.7			Two gravel roads
1411.5	777.6	900	Blue-blazed trail 0.1W to Denning Hill
1412.3	776.8	607	Old Albany Post Rd (gravel), Chapman Rd
1413.3	775.8	813	Canopus Hill
1413.9	775.2	395	Brook (pg.143)
1414.0	775.1	420	Canopus Hill Rd (paved)
1415.0	774.1	570	South Highland Rd (paved), stream north side of road.
1415.8	773.3	655	Stream.
1416.5	772.6	941	Catfish Loop Trail (red-blazed)
1417.7	771.4	860	Dennytown Rd (paved), Three Lake Trail to west. 41.4206, -73.8689 **P** Water on side of pump building, open late-Apr–Oct.
1417.9	771.2	814	Catfish Loop Trail to east (red-blazed)
1419.3	769.8	800	Sunken Mine Rd (gravel), stream to north.
1420.5	768.6	986	Three Lakes Trail
1421.4	767.7	920	NY 301, Canopus Lake, **Clarence Fahnestock SP** (1.0E) (pg.143)
1422.0	767.1	1101	Fahnestock Trail to west
1423.4	765.7	998	Green-blazed trail to lake, **Clarence Fahnestock SP** (0.2E) (pg.143)
	764.9		View of the lake from AT north of this intersection.
1424.2		1023	Stream
1425.6	763.5	1282	Shenandoah Mountain, view, painted 911 Memorial Flag.
1426.0	763.1	1019	Long Hill Rd (gravel)
1426.5	762.6	1000	Powerline

NoBo
SoBo

SoBo	NoBo	Description		Elev
762.0	**1427.1**	Shenandoah Tenting Area 0.1W, hand pump	⌂ ●	900
761.6	**1427.5**	Brook	●	763
760.8	**1428.3**	Bridge over brook	●	355
760.7	**1428.4**	Hortontown Rd	41.514,-73.7918 🛏 ⟆ ⌂ ⊏ (6) (pg.143)	357
760.4	**1428.7**	RPH Shelter (1982) 40.7◄35.4◄32.2◄►9.0►16.8►25.6 Treat pump water. Footbridge, stream, Taconic State Pkwy underpass	●	515
757.2	**1431.9**	Hosner Mountain Rd, footbridge, stream (do not drink, farm upstream)		500
755.6	**1433.5**	NY 52, **Stormville, NY** (1.9W)	41.541,-73.7328 P (pg.143)	800
755.0	**1434.1**	Stream, footbridge	◁	831
754.4	**1434.7**	AT on Old Stormville Mountain Rd for 0.1 mile		977
754.2	**1434.9**	AT on Stormville Mountain Rd for 0.1 mile, crosses over I-84		950
754.0	**1435.1**	Grape Hollow Rd		935
752.7	**1436.4**	Side trail 0.6W to Indian Pass		1179
751.8	**1437.3**	Mt Egbert	☾ ● ⊏ (6)	1329
751.7	**1437.4**	**Morgan Stewart Shelter.** 44.4◄41.2◄9.0◄►7.8►16.6►20.6		1292
750.6	**1438.5**	Depot Hill Rd, parking 0.1W.	41.5715,-73.6807 P	1230
748.8	**1440.3**	Railroad track, Whakey Lake Stream	●	664
748.7	**1440.4**	Old Route 55		679
748.4	**1440.7**	NY 55, **Poughquag, NY** (3.1W)	41.5897,-73.6592 P (0.1W) (pg.143)	720
748.1	**1441.0**	Beekman Uplands Trail to west		752
747.3	**1441.8**	Footbridge, stream (more streams in this area)		697
747.0	**1442.1**	Nuclear Lake south end, loop trail to east (yellow-blazed).		746
746.1	**1443.0**	Nuclear Lake north end, loop trail to east		775
745.7	**1443.4**	Beekman Uplands Trail to west		854
744.8	**1444.5**	Footbridge, swampy area	●	1041
744.5	**1444.6**	Penny Rd		1121
744.2	**1444.9**	West Mountain	☾ ◁ ⊏ (6)	1200
743.9	**1445.2**	**Telephone Pioneers Shelter** (0.1E), shelter trail crosses stream. 49.0◄16.8◄7.8◄►8.8►12.8►21.2 If dry, get water from residence 0.7N.		910
743.2	**1445.9**	County Rd 20, West Dover Rd, **Pawling, NY** (3.1E)	● (pg.143)	568

5000

3000

1000

NoBo

SoBo

SoBo	NoBo	Description	Elev
741.1	1448.0	Footbridge, stream, boardwalk from here north to RR track	467
740.8	1448.3	NY 22, **Appalachian Trail RR Station** . . . 41.5938,-73.5871 P 🏛 (pg.148)	480
		Wingdale (4W), **Pawling** (2.6E) hot dog stand often here in summer, deli 0.6E	
740.6	1448.5	Hurd Corners Rd, wooden water tower	480
739.9	1449.2	Stream to west	577
739.1	1450.0	Hammersly Ridge	1058
738.9	1450.2	Red Trail	1005
738.4	1450.7	Yellow Trail to east	940
738.1	1451.0	Red Trail to east	970
738.0	1451.1	Green trail west, Red Trail east	987
737.1	1452.0	Pawling Nature Reserve to east	900
736.1	1453.0	Stream	787
735.5	1453.5	Leather Hill Rd (gravel), stream to south	750
735.1	1454.0	**Wiley Shelter** 25.6◄16.6◄8.8◄▶4.0▶12.4▶19.7 pump 0.1N	704
734.9	1454.2	Duell Hollow Rd	563
734.6	1454.5	Footbridge, stream	426
733.9	1455.2	**NY-CT** border, Hoyt Rd . . . 41.6418,-73.5208 P (pg.149)	400
733.6	1455.5	Side trail to parking, brook to north	429
733.3	1455.8	CT 55, **Gaylordsville, CT** (2.5E) . . . 41.6447,-73.5193 P (pg.149)	444
		Wingdale, NY (3.3W)	
732.1	1457.0	Ten Mile Hill, Herrick Trail to east	1000
731.1	1458.0	**Ten Mile River Shelter** (0.1E) 20.6◄12.8◄4.0◄▶8.4▶15.7▶25.7	277
		Water (hand pump) to left. Group campsites across river and up trail to left.	
731.0	1458.1	Ten Mile River, Ned Anderson Memorial Bridge	260
729.8	1459.3	Bulls Bridge Rd (paved) + Schaghticoke Rd . . . 41.6756,-73.5102 P (pg.149)	366
		AT on Schaghticoke Rd (gravel) 0.3 mile	
728.6	1460.5	**CT-NY** Ⓢ Campfires prohibited in CT. Camping only in designated sites.	1030
728.0	1461.1	View to west from exposed slab of rock, many good sitting boulders.	1199
726.6	1462.5	**NY-CT**, stream to north	1226
726.3	1462.8	Indian Rocks, view to east.	1249
725.6	1463.5	Schaghticoke Mountain Campsite & privy 0.1W, stream on AT	904
724.8	1464.3	Stream.	988
723.7	1465.4	Thayer Brook	914

NoBo	SoBo	Features		Elev
722.7	1466.4	**Mt Algo Shelter** 21.2◄12.4◄8.4▶7.3▶17.3▶28.7	☾ ♦ ⌂ (pg.150)	638
722.4	1466.7	CT 341, Schaghticoke Rd, **Kent, CT** (0.8E)		350
722.3	1466.8	Macedonia Brook	●	335
721.8	1467.3	Numeral Rock Trail to east		801
719.6	1469.5	Skiff Mountain Rd (paved), stream to south	●	771
718.9	1470.2	Calebs Peak		1124
718.6	1470.5	St. Johns Ledges, steep stone steps down to Housatonic River	🄿	883
717.7	1471.4	River Rd south end, NoBo: turn west on road for 0.8 mile		382
716.9	1472.2	Kent Rd to west		428
716.7	1472.4	River Rd north end		389
715.4	1473.7	**Stewart Hollow Brook Shelter** (0.1W) 19.7◄15.7◄7.3▶10.0▶21.4▶28.9 Footbridge over SH Brook.	☾ ♦ ⌂ (6)	398
714.8	1474.3	Stony Brook, Campsite to west	● ♦	414
713.3	1475.8	Footbridge, stream		452
713.0	1476.1	River Rd	41.8057,-73.395 🅿	460
712.8	1476.3	Dawn Hill Rd (paved)		583
712.1	1477.0	Silver Hill Campsite 0.1E, pavilion, water from pump (may take many pumps to get water flowing)	♦ △	926
711.3	1477.8	CT 4, **Cornwall Bridge, CT** (0.9E)	● (pg.151)	700
711.1	1478.0	High water bypass 0.5E on CT 4, then left on unpaved Old Sharon Rd for 0.5 mi.		
711.1	1478.0	Old Sharon Rd (gravel), Guinea Brook south of road		756
711.0	1478.1	Breadloaf Trail 0.1E, view	🄿	944
709.9	1479.2	Hatch Brook		880
709.7	1479.4	Pine Knob Loop Trail 1.0E to Housatonic Meadows State Park		1005
709.0	1480.1	Another intersection with Pine Knob Loop Trail to east.		1044
708.7	1480.4	Caesar Rd, Caesar Brook Campsite, stream to north.	♦	798
707.2	1481.9	Stream.		879
706.6	1482.5	Carse Brook, footbridge		810
706.5	1482.6	West Cornwall Rd, **West Cornwall, CT** (2.2E), **Sharon, CT** (4.7W)	♦ (pg.151)	849
706.2	1482.9	Pass through cracked boulder similar to Lemon Squeezer.		1175
705.4	1483.7	**Pine Swamp Brook Shelter** 25.7◄17.3◄10.0▶11.4▶18.9▶20.1	☾ ♦ ⌂ (6)	1087
704.5	1484.6	Mt. Easter Rd		1150
703.9	1485.2	Woods road		1291
703.7	1485.4	Woods road		1287

Pawling, NY (east from NY 55, County Rd 20, or NY 22. If coming from NY 55, veer left on Old Rte 55)

Edward R. Murrow Memorial Park Town allows hikers to camp in park, one night only. One mile from the center of town, park offers lake swimming, no pets.

Vinny's Deli 845.855.1922, **Gaudino's Pizzeria** 845.855.3200, **Mama Pizza II** 845.855.9270, **Great Wall** 845.855.9750

McGrath Restaurant 845.855.0800 L/D.

Pawling Free Library Closed Sundays in July and August.

Martin and Donna 845.505.1671 or 845.546.1832. Nights & weekends only. Shuttle range RPH Shelter to Kent, CT.

1448.3   NY 22, **Appalachian Trail Railroad Station**

MTA Metro-North Railroad (see info box on this page)

Native Landscapes & Garden Center 845.855.7050 Open daily 9-5, please do not loiter after hours. Owner Pete Muroski is hiker-friendly. Free outside shower, charging, use of restrooms. Drinks, snacks, freeze-dried meals and canister fuel sold at the garden center. Mail: 991 Route 22, Pawling, NY 12564.

(0.6E) Tony's Deli 845.855.9540 sandwiches, salads, soda machine outside. Open daily 5am–midnight. Ask about camping.

Pawling, NY (2.5E)
Wingdale, NY 12594 (4W)

Dutchess Motor Lodge 845.832.6400, 914.525.9276 $73S+tax. Ride for a fee when available. A/C, free long distance, guest laundry $7, one pet room. Mail: 1512 Route 22, Wingdale, NY 12594.

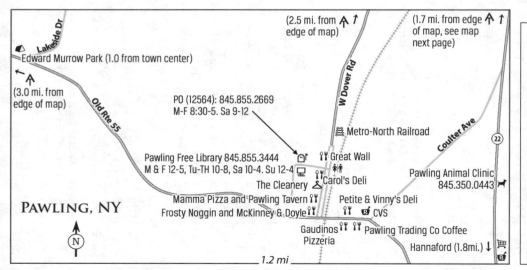

PAWLING, NY

- Lakeside Dr
- Edward Murrow Park (1.0 from town center)
- (3.0 mi. from edge of map)
- Old Rte 55
- (2.5 mi. from edge of map)
- W Dover Rd
- (1.7 mi. from edge of map, see map next page)
- Coulter Ave
- 22
- PO (12564): 845.855.2669 M-F 8:30-5. Sa 9-12
- Metro-North Railroad
- Pawling Free Library 845.855.3444 M & F 12-5, Tu-TH 10-8, Sa 10-4. Su 12-4
- Great Wall
- Carol's Deli
- The Cleanery
- Pawling Animal Clinic 845.350.0443
- Mamma Pizza and Pawling Tavern
- Petite & Vinny's Deli
- Frosty Noggin and McKinney & Doyle
- CVS
- Gaudinos Pizzeria
- Pawling Trading Co Coffee
- Hannaford (1.8mi.)
- N
- 1.2 mi

MTA Metro-North Railroad 212.532.4900 ⟨www.mta.info\mnr\⟩ Stations on the AT and in Pawling & Wingdale/Harlem Valley. Trip to NYC Grand Central Station requires a transfer, costs approx. $27-30 one-way, and takes about two hours. Must pay in cash when boarding at the trailhead; can purchase round trip and pay with credit card if your trip originates at Grand Central Station. Schedule varies by season. Also connects to other cities in NY and CT.

1455.8 CT 55, *Gaylordsville, CT 06755* (2.5E to bridge and country store, 0.6 further south to PO and diner)
⌂ M-F 8-1 & 2-5, Sa 8-12, 860.354.9727
🏠 **⑤ Gaylordsville Country Store**
860.350.3802 deli, grocery M-F 6-6, Sa 6-5, Su 7-1, hours shorter in winter.
🍴 **Gaylordsville Diner** 860.210.1622 B/L/D.
🍴 (1.4W) **Riverview Tavern** Food, pool table, open noon-9pm.
Wingdale, NY (3.3W) see map

1459.3 Bulls Bridge Rd, Schaghticoke Rd
📷 (0.4E) To covered bridge with view of the Housatonic cascading down the backside of a dam. The one-lane bridge was built in 1842. Wooden bridges are covered to protect the wood deck and trusswork from the elements.

0.2 beyond bridge:
🏠 **⑤ Country Market** Fruit, ice cream, soda. M-Sa 5:30-7, Su 6:30-6.
🍴 **Bulls Bridge Inn** 860.927.1000 M-Th 5-9, F 5-9:30, Sa 12-9:30, Su 12-9. American cuisine (dinners $10-26), casual atmosphere, bar.

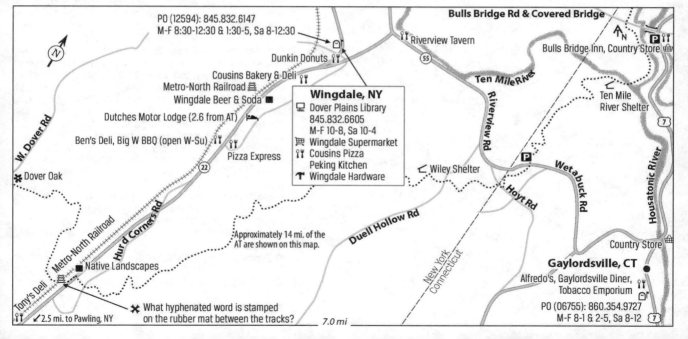

PO (12594): 845.832.6147
M-F 8:30-12:30 & 1:30-5, Sa 8-12:30

Bulls Bridge Rd & Covered Bridge

Riverview Tavern

Dunkin Donuts 🍴

Cousins Bakery & Deli
Metro-North Railroad 🚉
Wingdale Beer & Soda ■

Bulls Bridge Inn, Country Store 🏠

Ten Mile River

Ten Mile River Shelter

Wingdale, NY
🖥 Dover Plains Library
845.832.6605
M-F 10-8, Sa 10-4
🏪 Wingdale Supermarket
🍴 Cousins Pizza
Peking Kitchen
🔧 Wingdale Hardware

Dutches Motor Lodge (2.6 from AT) 🛏

Ben's Deli, Big W BBQ (open W-Su) 🍴 🍴

Pizza Express

W. Dover Rd

❋ Dover Oak

⌐ Wiley Shelter

Riverview Rd

Hoyt Rd

Wetabuck Rd

Housatonic River

Metro-North Railroad

Hurd Corners Rd

Approximately 14 mi. of the AT are shown on this map.

Duell Hollow Rd

New York
Connecticut

Country Store 🏠

■ Native Landscapes

Tony's Deli
🍴 ↙2.5 mi. to Pawling, NY

❋ What hyphenated word is stamped on the rubber mat between the tracks?

7.0 mi

Gaylordsville, CT ●
Alfredo's, Gaylordsville Diner, 🍴
Tobacco Emporium
PO (06755): 860.354.9727 ⌂
M-F 8-1 & 2-5, Sa 8-12 ⑦

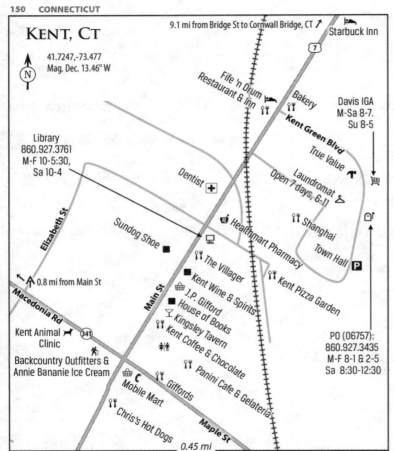

KENT, CT

41.7247, -73.477
Mag. Dec. 13.46° W

N

9.1 mi from Bridge St to Cornwall Bridge, CT ↗

Starbuck Inn

Fife 'n Drum Restaurant & Inn

Bakery

Davis IGA
M-Sa 8-7.
Su 8-5

Kent Green Blvd

True Value

Library
860.927.3761
M-F 10-5:30,
Sa 10-4

Dentist ✚

Laundromat
Open 7 days, 6-11

Healthmart Pharmacy

Shanghai

Sundog Shoe

Town Hall

Elizabeth St

Macedonia Rd

0.8 mi from Main St

The Villager

Kent Wine & Spirits

J.P. Gifford

House of Books

Kingsley Tavern

Kent Coffee & Chocolate

Kent Pizza Garden

PO (06757):
860.927.3435
M-F 8-1 & 2-5
Sa 8:30-12:30

Main St

Kent Animal Clinic

341

Backcountry Outfitters &
Annie Bananie Ice Cream

Giffords

Mobile Mart

Panini Cafe & Gelateria

Chris's Hot Dogs

Maple St

0.45 mi

1466.7 CT 341, Schaghticoke Rd
Kent, CT 06757 (0.8E) (**15% lodging tax**)

🛏️🍴📶✉️ **Fife 'n Drum Inn & Restaurant**
860.927.3509 ⟨www.fifendrum.com⟩ Hiker room rates $140D+tax wkdays, $170D+tax wkends, $25EAP+tax, no pets. Front desk closed Tu, so make prior arrangements for Tu night stays. Guest Mail: (USPS) PO Box 188 or (FedEx/UPS) 53 N Main Street, Kent, CT 06757.

🛏️🚐📶 **Cooper Creek B&B** 860.927.4334 Hiker rate Su-Th $95D+tax. Weekend rates $145-200+tax. 2.5mi. north of town on US 7. Shuttles to/from Kent w/stay, slackpacking and longer shuttles for a fee.

🛏️📶 **Starbuck Inn** 860.927.1788 $207D/up + tax, includes full breakfast & afternoon tea. Sometimes discounted mid-week, accepts credit cards, no pets.

🛏️⛺📶 **Newbury Inn** 203.775.0220 About 20 miles from Kent, Gaylordsville, or Pawling (1030 Federal Rd, Brookfield, CT 06804) but has affordable hiker rate ($60D + tax, $10EAP), deluxe cont. breakfast. Shuttle can be arranged from Backcountry Outfitters.

🚶🍴🚐💲📶✉️ **Backcountry Outfitters**
860.927.3377 ⟨www.bcoutfitters.com⟩ M-Sa 9-6, Su 10-4. In summer hours extended 6am till 8pm weekdays, 9pm Fri & Sat, 6pm Sunday. Sells stamps, ships Priority Mail. Fuel/oz, canisters, selection of gear. **Annie Bananie** ice cream & grill inside serving hot dogs, coffee, snacks, barrels of candy, chocolates. Shuttles anywhere. Mail: 5 Bridge Street, Kent, CT 06757.

⛪🍴 **JP Gifford** Breakfast sandwiches, salads, bakery, coffee and supplies.

■ **Sundog Shoe** 860.927.0009 10% hiker discount on footwear (Salomon, Merrell, High-Tech, Keen), socks (Darn Tough), Dirty Girl Gaiters and footbeds (Superfeet, Power Step).

■ **House of Books** UPS services, open daily 10-5:30.

1477.8   CT 4, **Cornwall Bridge, CT 06754** (0.9E)

🛏🚶🚗📶✉ **Hitching Post Motel** 860.672.6219 $65/up weekdays, $85/up weekends. Pets $10, laundry $5, shuttles $2/mi. Mail: 45 Kent Road, Cornwall Bridge, CT 06754.

🛏⊛🚶📶✉ **The Amselhaus** 860.248.3155 $85S, $100 for couple, $50 EAP. 2-3 bedroom apartments includes laundry, sat. TV, local and long-distance phone. Rides available. Located behind carpet store, check-in at grey house next door to apartments. Mail: C/O Tyler, 7 River Road South, Cornwall Bridge, CT 06754.

🛏 ⚓ ⚘ **Housatonic Meadows State Park** 860.672.6772 Camping and Cabins 1.3 mi. north of town on US 7. Campsite $17 for CT residents, $27 non-residents, $3 walk-in fee for first night. Cabins $60 with 2 night min. No hammocks. Open mid-May to Oct, registration at main cabin by gate, no alcohol.

🛏📶🚗 **Cornwall Inn** 860.672.6884 Su-Th $129D + tax, includes cont. breakfast. Weekends 10% hiker discount. 2.2 miles south on US 7. Pickup/return to trailhead and other shuttles for a fee. Seasonal pool & hot tub. Pet fee. Maildrops with reservation.

🏪⊛💲📶👫 **Cornwall Country Market** 860.619.8199 M-F 6am-6pm, Sa-Su 7-5. Hiker friendly, hot meals, breakfast, groceries, charging stations.

🚶 **Housatonic River Outfitters** 860.672.1010 ⟨www.dryflies.com⟩ Some hiker gear, Aquamira.

⊛ **Cornwall Package Store** 860.672.6645 closed Su, water spigot outside. Stopping to sign their register can be refreshing.

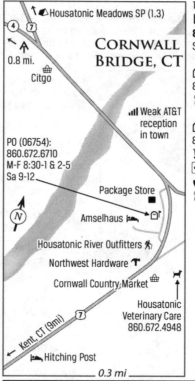

↑🛶 Housatonic Meadows SP (1.3)

④⑦

↖↑

0.8 mi.

⛪ Citgo

CORNWALL BRIDGE, CT

.ıll Weak AT&T reception in town

PO (06754):
860.672.6710
M-F 8:30-1 & 2-5
Sa 9-12

Package Store ■

(N)

Amselhaus 🛏→⌂

Housatonic River Outfitters 🚶

Northwest Hardware 🔨

Cornwall Country Market ⛪

Housatonic Veterinary Care 860.672.4948

Kent, CT (9mi) ⑦

↙🛏 Hitching Post

— 0.3 mi —

1482.6   West Cornwall Rd

📷 **Bearded Woods One-of-a-Kind Bunk & Dine** Will pickup from Falls Village or Salisbury. See details on pg. 152.

West Cornwall, CT 06796 (2.2E)

⌂ M-F 8:30-12 & 2-4:30, Sa 9-12, 860.672.6791

🍴 **Wandering Moose Café** 860.672.0178

Sharon, CT 06069 (4.7W)

⌂ M-F 9:30-4:30, Sa 9:30-12:30, 860.364.5306

🏪 **Sharon Farm Market**

✚ **Sharon Hospital** 860.364.4141

🦷 **Sharon Pharmacy**

🍴 **Stacked Kitchen**

1489.7   US 7, bridge over Housatonic River

🏠◉🏨⛺🚌🖥 **Bearded Woods One-of-a-Kind Bunk & Dine** 860.480.2966 ⟨www.beardedwoods.com⟩ Hudson & BIG Lu offer accommodations in their home to hikers $50pp. Includes: clean bunk with linens, shower with amenities, communal laundry, shuttle to/from trail and PO. Cash only. All guests invited at no cost for family style dinner & breakfast. Please make advance reservation then call or text Hudson for **pickup from West Cornwall Rd, Falls Village or Salisbury** between 12:00 - 5:30. Resupplies available, stove fuel & Aquamira. No pets. Free slackpacking between W. Cornwall Rd and Salisbury with second night stay. Longer shuttles for fee. Not a party place. Open May 15-Sept 1. Limited services may be available outside of those dates. Relax and let your AT experience be fulfilled!

Iron Bridge (Amesville Bridge) replaced in 2016.

FALLS VILLAGE, CT

Hydro Plant

Outdoor shower on wall of vine-covered building. There is also a power outlet.

Library
860.824.7424
Tu, Th 10-5,
Wed 2-8,
Fri 2-6,
Sa 10-2

Main St

Toymakers
Cafe

Warren Turnpike Rd

Railroad St

Package Store

Falls Village Inn

PO (06031):
860.824.7781
M-F 8:30-1 & 2-5
Sa 8:30-12

Prospect St

Miner St

0.4 mi

1491.8   Water Street Parking Area **Falls Village, CT 06031**

🍴◍ **Toymakers Café** 860.824.8168 B/L Thursday-Sunday (Th–F 7–2, Sa–Su 7–4) free tent sites, hiker friendly, knock on upstairs door if closed. Cash only.

🛏◉🍴 **Falls Village Inn** 860.824.0033 $239/up, restaurant & bar.

1498.8   Cobble Rd (0.5W)
1499.2   Undermountain Rd (0.8W) **Salisbury, CT 06068**

🏠✉ **Maria McCabe** 860.435.0593 Beds in home $35PP includes shower, use of living room, shuttle to coin laundry, cash only. Guest Mail: 4 Grove Street.

🏠⛺🚌✉ **Vanessa Breton** 860.435.9577 860.248.5714 Beds in home $40PP, pets $5, laundry $5. Shuttle range 100 mi. Street address is 7 The Lock Up Rd, but send mail to PO Box: ($5 fee for non-guests): PO Box 131, Salisbury, CT 06068.

🛏📶 🍴 **White Hart Inn** 860.435.0030 Rooms $225/up.

🍴 **Chaiwalla** 860.435.9758 W-Su 10-6. Hiker friendly tea room. Closed in Mar, open weekends only in winter.

🛒🍴 **LaBonne's Market** M-Sa 8-7, Su 8-6pm. Grocery, deli, bakery, pizza.

ℹ 🚻📶 **Town Hall** 860.435.5170 M-F 8:30-4 Hikers welcome to use bathrooms and phone (local calls only).

Lakeville, CT (2.0 mi. south of Salisbury)

🍴 **Boathouse** 860.435.2111 Sports bar/restaurant

🍴 **Mizza's Pizza** 860.435.6266

⛺ **Washboard Laundromat** Behind Mizza's

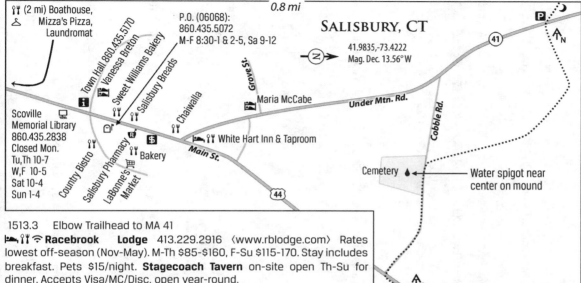

0.8 mi

SALISBURY, CT

41.9835,-73.4222
Mag. Dec. 13.56°W

⛊ (2 mi) Boathouse,
⛺ Mizza's Pizza,
Laundromat

P.O. (06068):
860.435.5072
M-F 8:30-1 & 2-5, Sa 9-12

Town Hall 860.435.5170
Vanessa Breton
Sweet Williams Bakery
Salisbury Breads
Chaiwalla
Grove St.
Maria McCabe
Under Mtn. Rd.
Cobble Rd.

Scoville
Memorial Library
860.435.2838
Closed Mon.
Tu,Th 10-7
W,F 10-5
Sat 10-4
Sun 1-4

Country Bistro
Salisbury Pharmacy
LaBonne's Market
Bakery
Main St.
White Hart Inn & Taproom

44

Cemetery
Water spigot near
center on mound

Ⓝ
⛊ N

⛊ S

1513.3 Elbow Trailhead to MA 41

⛆⛊📶 **Racebrook Lodge** 413.229.2916 ⟨www.rblodge.com⟩ Rates lowest off-season (Nov-May). M-Th $85-$160, F-Su $115-170. Stay includes breakfast. Pets $15/night. **Stagecoach Tavern** on-site open Th-Su for dinner. Accepts Visa/MC/Disc, open year-round.

1517.0 MA 41 *South Egremont, MA 01258* (1.2W)
⌂ M-F 8:15-12 & 12:30-4, Sa 9-11:30, 413.528.1571

ℹ (0.1W) **ATC New England Regional Office** 413.528.8002 in Kellogg Conservation Center. Water from hose, picnic table, 2 charging outlets, no camping/parking.

⛊🏪 **Egremont Market** 413.528.0075 Market & deli 6:30am-7pm 7 days (6pm in winter). Ice cream, trail mix, sodas.

⛊ **Mom's Country Cafe** 413.528.2414 Breakfast/Lunch restaurant open 6:30-3 every day and 5-9pm F-Su. Breakfast all day, free coffee refills, outdoor water spigot, hikers welcome.

> *Gary Monk (trail name "Blaze") counted every white blaze he passed during his 2002 northbound thru-hike. There were 80,900. I wouldn't tell anyone about getting lost.*

SoBo	NoBo	Description	Features	Elev
703.0	**1486.1**	Sharon Mountain Campsite 0.1W, stream nearby.	◆	1134
702.2	**1486.9**	Hang Glider View	[camera]	1103
700.1	**1489.0**	Belters Campsite 0.2W, view.	[camera] ◆) ●	746
699.8	**1489.3**	US 7, CT 112		520
699.4	**1489.7**	US 7, parking, bridge over Housatonic River	◆ 41.9327,-73.3635 P (pg.152)	513
698.8	**1490.3**	Mohawk Trail 0.5E to view	[camera]	554
698.2	**1490.9**	Warren Turnpike, footbridge, stream to north.	●	516
697.3	**1491.8**	Water St parking, **Falls Village, CT**(0.3E) . . . 41.9558,-73.3675 P (pg.152)	) ●	530
697.0	**1492.1**	Iron Bridge (Amesville Bridge) over Housatonic River		507
696.7	**1492.4**	Housatonic River Rd, AT crosses road twice 0.2 mi. 41.9623,-73.374 P [camera]		604
696.1	**1493.0**	apart. In between are two short trails east to views of great falls. Spring	●	793
694.7	**1494.4**	Mt Prospect	) ●	1475
694.0	**1495.1**	**Limestone Spring Shelter** (0.5W), road 0.25 farther. 28.7◄21.4◄11.4◄►7.5►8.7►17.5	) ● ⌂ (6)	1304
693.9	**1495.2**	Rands View (field)		1250
693.5	**1495.6**	Giants Thumb	[camera]	1293
692.7	**1496.4**	Stream.	●	1038
690.6	**1498.5**	AT on US 44 for 0.2W		700
690.3	**1498.8**	AT on Cobble Rd 0.2E, **Salisbury, CT** (0.5W). (pg.152)		706
689.9	**1499.2**	Undermountain Rd (paved) **Salisbury** (0.8W) 41.9941,-73.42685 P (pg.152)	) ◆ ●	720
689.6	**1499.5**	Stream.	●	828
688.4	**1500.7**	Streams (multiple)	●	1110
687.5	**1501.6**	Lions Head Trail 0.5W to Bunker Hill Rd		1496
687.3	**1501.8**	Lions Head, view, bypass trail to west	[camera]	1729
686.5	**1502.6**	**Riga Shelter**, spring. Tent platform behind shelter. 28.9◄18.9◄7.5◄►1.2►10.0►10.1	) ◆ ● ⌂ (6)	1646
685.9	**1503.2**	Ball Brook Campsite, stream.	) ◆	1720
685.3	**1503.8**	**Brassie Brook Shelter**, stream 20 yards north on AT 20.1◄8.7◄1.2◄►8.8►8.9►23.2	) ◆ ● ⌂ (6)	1733
684.8	**1504.3**	Undermountain Trail 1.9E to CT 41		1834
684.6	**1504.5**	Bear Mountain Rd to west		1920

NoBo
SoBo

5000

4000

3000

2000

SoBo	NoBo	Description	Elev
683.9	1505.2	Bear Mountain, rock observation tower, view. North side steep & rocky.	2316
683.5	1505.6	Unmarked trail 0.6W to Mt Washington Rd	1806
683.3	1505.8	Paradise Lane Trail to east, **CT-MA** border 50 yards north (not marked)	1694
683.1	1506.0	Sages Ravine Campsite to west	1527
682.7	1506.4	Sages Ravine, Misplaced border sign at footbridge. AT parallel to stream for 0.3 mile, swimming holes.	1474
681.4	1507.7	Laurel Ridge Campsite 0.1W, spring to south	1608
681.2	1507.9	Stream.	1686
679.4	1509.7	Mt Race, views along ridgeline for 0.6S.	2365
678.3	1510.8	Race Brook Falls Trail 0.3E to campsite	1950
677.6	1511.5	Mt Everett	2602
676.9	1512.2	Guilder Pond Picnic Area, Mt Everett Rd.	2081
676.5	1512.6	**The Hemlocks Shelter** (0.1E) 17.5◀10.0◀8.8◀▶0.1▶14.4▶19.7	1916
676.4	1512.7	**Glen Brook Shelter** (0.1E) 10.1◀8.9◀0.1▶14.3▶19.6▶21.4	1941
675.8	1513.3	Elbow Trail 1.5E to MA 41 near **Racebrook Lodge** (pg.153)	1752
674.3	**1514.3**	Mt Bushnell	1847
673.7	**1515.4**	Jug End, view	1469
673.0	1516.1	Jug End Rd, unreliable piped spring 0.2E 42.1444,-73.4316 **P**	875
672.1	1517.0	MA 41, **South Egremont, MA** (1.2W) (pg.153)	810
671.1	**1518.0**	Footbridge, stream (2 close together).	711
670.5	**1518.6**	Footbridge, stream	694
670.3	1518.8	Sheffield Egremont Rd, Shays Rebellion Monument 42.1471,-73.3867 **P**	700
669.5	1519.6	Gravel road	742
669.2	1519.9	West Rd (paved)	703
668.5	1520.6	US 7, RR to south, soda vending 0.2E at repair shop. **Sheffield, MA** (3.0E), **Great Barrington, MA** (3.0W) (pg.156)	675
668.3	1520.8	Footbridge, stream	664
667.6	**1521.5**	Housatonic River, cross on Kellogg Rd Bridge 42.144,-73.3595 **P**	659
667.2	1521.9	Boardman St	706
665.8	1523.3	June Mtn	1252
665.6	1523.5	Homes Rd (paved)	1150
665.0	1524.1	Footbridge, spring at bottom of cleft	1526
664.6	1524.5	East Mountain, view	1737

NoBo
SoBo

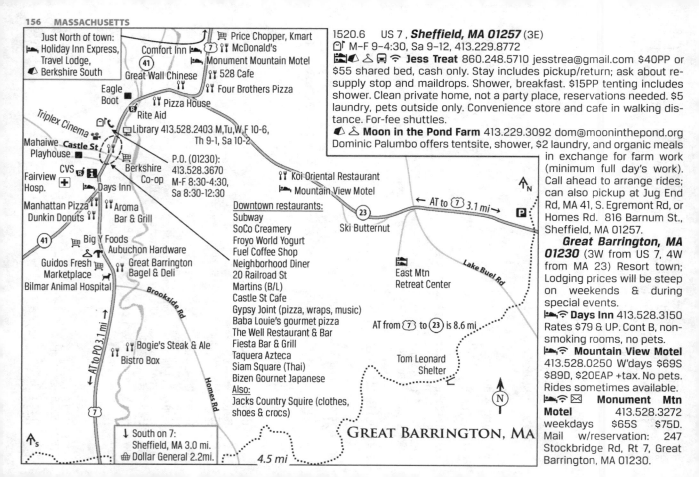

Just North of town:
🛏️ Holiday Inn Express,
Travel Lodge,
⛵ Berkshire South

Comfort Inn 🛏️
(41)
Great Wall Chinese

🏪 Price Chopper, Kmart
(7) 🍴 McDonald's
🛏️ Monument Mountain Motel
🍴 528 Cafe
🍴 Four Brothers Pizza

Eagle
Boot
🍴 Pizza House
Rite Aid

Triplex Cinema

📚 Library 413.528.2403 M,Tu,W,F 10-6,
Th 9-1, Sa 10-2

Mahaiwe **Castle St**
Playhouse

CVS
Fairview
Hosp.
🛏️ Days Inn

P.O. (01230):
413.528.3670
M-F 8:30-4:30,
Sa 8:30-12:30

Berkshire
Co-op

Manhattan Pizza 🍴 🍴 Aroma
Dunkin Donuts 🍴 Bar & Grill

(41)
🏪 Big Y Foods
⚓ Aubuchon Hardware

Guidos Fresh 🏪 🍴 Great Barrington
Marketplace Bagel & Deli
Bilmar Animal Hospital

Brookside Rd.

🍴 Bogie's Steak & Ale
Bistro Box

↑ AT to PO 3.1 mi

Homes Rd.

(7)

↓ South on 7:
Sheffield, MA 3.0 mi.
🏪 Dollar General 2.2mi.

Downtown restaurants:
Subway
SoCo Creamery
Froyo World Yogurt
Fuel Coffee Shop
Neighborhood Diner
20 Railroad St
Martins (B/L)
Castle St Cafe
Gypsy Joint (pizza, wraps, music)
Baba Louie's gourmet pizza
The Well Restaurant & Bar
Fiesta Bar & Grill
Taquera Azteca
Siam Square (Thai)
Bizen Gournet Japanese
Also:
Jacks Country Squire (clothes,
shoes & crocs)

🍴 Koi Oriental Restaurant
🛏️ Mountain View Motel

(23)
Ski Butternut

East Mtn
Retreat Center

Lake Buel Rd.

← AT to (7) 3.1 mi →

P

AT from (7) to (23) is 8.6 mi

Tom Leonard
Shelter

N

4.5 mi

GREAT BARRINGTON, MA

1520.6   US 7 , **Sheffield, MA 01257** (3E)
M-F 9-4:30, Sa 9-12, 413.229.8772
🛏️⛵⛺ **Jess Treat** 860.248.5710 jesstrea@gmail.com $40PP or
$55 shared bed, cash only. Stay includes pickup/return; ask about re-supply stop and maildrops. Shower, breakfast. $15PP tenting includes
shower. Clean private home, not a party place, reservations needed. $5
laundry, pets outside only. Convenience store and cafe in walking dis-
tance. For-fee shuttles.
⛵⛺ **Moon in the Pond Farm** 413.229.3092 dom@mooninthepond.org
Dominic Palumbo offers tentsite, shower, $2 laundry, and organic meals
in exchange for farm work
(minimum full day's work).
Call ahead to arrange rides;
can also pickup at Jug End
Rd, MA 41, S. Egremont Rd, or
Homes Rd. 816 Barnum St.,
Sheffield, MA 01257.

**Great Barrington, MA
01230** (3W from US 7, 4W
from MA 23) Resort town;
Lodging prices will be steep
on weekends & during
special events.
🛏️📶 **Days Inn** 413.528.3150
Rates $79 & UP. Cont B, non-
smoking rooms, no pets.
🛏️📶 **Mountain View Motel**
413.528.0250 W'days $69S
$89D, $20EAP +tax. No pets.
Rides sometimes available.
🛏️📶✉️ **Monument Mtn
Motel** 413.528.3272
weekdays $65S $75D.
Mail w/reservation: 247
Stockbridge Rd, Rt 7, Great
Barrington, MA 01230.

🛏️👤🛜🖥️✉️ **Fairfield Inn & Suites** 413.644.3200 Prices seasonal. Full B, heated pool & hot tub, no pets. Maildrops with advance reservation: 249 Stockbridge Rd, Rt 7, Great Barrington, MA 01230.

🛏️👤🛜 **Travel Lodge** 413.528.2340 Su-Th $50-89D + tax, $10EAP, cont B, coin laundry.

🔌🌿 **Berkshire South Regional Community Center** 413.528.2810 ⟨www.berkshiresouth.org⟩ 15 Crissey Rd north end of town. Free tenting, check-in at front desk. $5PP use of facility (showers, saunas, pool). Free dinner M 5-6pm, donations accepted. No smoking, drugs, alcohol, or pets. On BRTA route (tell driver your destination).

🏪 **Guido's** Organic produce, cold juices, and more.

➕ **Fairview Hospital** 413.528.0790

🚐 **All Points Driving Service** 413.429.7397 Range: Salisbury-Dalton.

1529.0   MA 23

🏨✉️ (1.5W) **East Mountain Retreat Center** 413.528.6617 1.0W from MA 23 or Lake Buel Rd. and 0.5 mile up driveway (where there is a blue sign), $10PP donation, no credit cards. Shower, dryer (no washer), pizzeria delivers to hostel, check-in by 8:30pm, 8:30am checkout. Quiet after 10pm. Open May 15-Aug15. Maildrops (FedEx or UPS only): 8 Lake Buel Rd, Great Barrington, MA 01230.

1540.1   Jerusalem Rd (0.6W to town)
1541.2   Main Rd (0.9W to town)
          Tyringham, MA 01264

📪 M-F 9-12:30 & 4-5:30, Sa 8:30-12:30, 413.243.1225

🛜🖥️ **Library** 413.243.1373 Adjacent to P.O. Tu 3-5, Saturday 10-12

🛏️ **Cobble View** 413.243.2463 Call in advance, mid-week discounts. No pets, no smoking, Visa/MC accepted.

1548.1   **Upper Goose Pond Cabin** (0.5W)

🔺(14)🔌🌂💧🌙 On side trail north of pond. Fireplace, covered porch, bunks with mattresses. Swimming and canoeing. Open daily Sa before Memorial Day - Sa after Columbus Day (dates subject to change). When caretaker not in residence, hikers may camp on porch (no cooking) or tent platforms. Please store food in bear box.

During summer, caretaker brings water; otherwise, pond is water source. Donations welcome.

1549.7   US 20

🛏️🛜✉️💧 (0.1E) **Berkshire Lakeside Lodge** 413.243.9907 Weekdays $60-90, weekends $94-174 2-person room, $10EAP. Cont. breakfast, TV, fridge. No pets. Hikers welcome to get water. Sodas for sale. No services nearby but you can get Italian & Chinese food delivered. Mail (call ahead to arrange pickup): 3949 Jacob's Ladder Rd, Rt 10, Becket, MA 01223.

Lee, MA 01238 (5W) Lodging busy and expensive on weekends and during Tanglewood Music Festival.

📪 M-F 8:30-4:30, Sa 9-12, 413.243.1392

🛏️🛜 **Econo Lodge** 413.243.0501 Apr-May $52-55 Su-Th, $65-75 F-Sa, Jun-Oct $60-79 Su-Th, $110-$195 F-Sa, cont B.

🛏️🛜 **Roadway Inn** 413.243.0813 Jul-Aug Su-Th $79, F-Sa $199, (plus tax). Other months prices vary. Cont B.

🛏️👤🛜 **Pilgrim Inn** 413.243.1328 Peak rates Jun 15-Aug; Su-Th $79D, F-Sa $225D. Non-peak rates $55D-$110D. Cont B, micro, fridge. Pets $20.

🛏️ **Super 8** 413.243.0143

🍴 **Dunkin Donuts, Athena's Pizza House**, **Friendly's, Joe's Diner, McDonalds**, and many more.

🏪 **Price Chopper Supermarket** 413.528.2408

🏥 **Rite Aid**

🐾 **Valley Veterinary Clinic** 413.243.2414

👤 **Lee Coin-Op Laundry**

🚌 **BRTA** 800.292.2782 Commuter bus connects **Great Barrington, Dalton, Cheshire, North Adams, Adams, Williamstown, Pittsfield, Lee** and **Berkshire Mall**. Buses run M-F 5:45am-7:20pm, Sa 7:15pm-7pm. Fare $1.75 for local routes (in-town and adjoining towns), or $4.50 systemwide. "CharlieCard", available from drivers for $5, gives you a discount per ride and allows you to make bus transfers. Drivers cannot make change. Flag bus anywhere on route.

SoBo	NoBo	Feature	Elev.
664.2	1524.9	Woods road	1789
662.1	1527.0	Ice Gulch, **Tom Leonard Shelter** ⊚ ☾ ♦ ▲ ⊏ (10) 23.2◀14.4◀14.3◀▶5.3▶7.1▶ 21.1 Campsite overlooking ravine north of shelter. Stream 0.2 on path to left or 0.3 on path to right.	1561
661.0	1528.1	Lake Buel Rd (paved), parking area with kiosk 42.1745,-73.294 P	1088
660.1	1529.0	MA 23 (paved) 42.1844,-73.2907 P (pg.157) **East Mountain Retreat Center** (1.0W)	1050
658.9	1530.2	Blue Hill Rd (paved), Stony Brook Rd	1550
658.2	1530.9	Beartown Mtn Rd, Benedict Pond, 0.5W on blue-blazed trail to	1598
658.0	1531.1	**Beartown State Forest,** beach, picnic area, phone, tent sites $10.	1624
657.5	1531.6	Benedict Pond Loop Trail to west, footbridge and stream east of AT	1820
657.1	1532.0	The Ledges	1634
656.8	1532.3	Stream. ☾ ♦ ▲ (5) ⊏ (6/12) **Mt Wilcox South Shelters** 19.7◀19.6◀5.3◀▶1.8▶15.8▶ 24.6 Old shelter 0.1E (6), newer shelter 0.2E (12).	1819
655.9	1533.2	Stream (several)	1830
655.8	1533.3	Pond, Swann Brook outlet at south end.	1820
656.0	1534.1	**Mt Wilcox North Shelter** (0.3E) ♦ ⊏ (10) 21.4◀7.1◀1.8◀▶14.0▶22.8▶ 31.6	2067
654.3	1534.8	Motorcycle path	1833
654.2	1534.9	Beartown Mountain-Rd, NoBo: turn east	1796
653.8	1535.3	East Brook, footbridge, more streams north and south	1716
651.2	1537.9	Fernside Rd / Jerusalem Rd (gravel)	1200
650.9	1538.2	Shaker Campsite to east; platforms, bear box, water north on AT	947
649.2	1539.9	Cobble Hill	1279
649.0	1540.1	Jerusalem Rd (paved) **Tyringham, MA 01264** (0.6W) ♦ (pg.157) Water 0.1W on left side of road, water also outside of P.O. 0.6W.	1128
648.5	1540.6	Three streams crossed by footbridges	1001
647.9	1541.2	Main Rd (paved), **Tyringham, MA** (0.9W) N42 14.125 W73 11.667 P ♦ (pg.157) Water, parking to west.	995
646.3	1542.8	Baldy Mtn.	1921
646.1	1543.0	Webster Rd (gravel).	1800
645.5	1543.6	Knee-Deep Pond to west. ♦	1689

5000

3000

NoBo

SoBo

SoBo	NoBo	Description	Elev
644.5	**1544.6**	Spring on side trail 0.1W	1781 ◆
643.7	**1545.4**	Goose Pond Rd (gravel) 42.2743,-73.1838 **P** (0.1E)	1650
643.3	**1545.8**	Cooper Brook, footbridge	1564 ◆
642.8	**1546.3**	Signed trail junction	1727
		⚠ NoBo: this is not the side trail to Upper Goose Pond Cabin.	
641.6	**1547.5**	Higley Brook, footbridge, Upper Goose Pond to west	1495 ◆
641.1	**1548.0**	Old chimney	1480
641.0	**1548.1**	**Upper Goose Pond Cabin** (0.5W) ⊏ (pg.157)	1552
		21.1◄15.8◄14.0◄►8.8►17.6►34.5	
639.8	**1549.3**	MA Turnpike I-90	1400
639.5	**1549.6**	Greenwater Brook, footbridge	1355 ◆
639.4	**1549.7**	US 20, **Lee, MA** (5.0W), hotel 0.1E 42.293,-73.1614 **P** (0.1W) (pg.157)	1400
639.0	**1550.1**	Powerline, stream to north	1583 ◆
638.6	**1550.5**	Tyne Rd / Becket Rd, stream to south	1797 ◆
638.1	**1551.0**	Becket Mountain	2180
637.1	**1552.0**	Walling Mountain	2214 📷
636.5	**1552.6**	Finerty Pond	1940 ◆
634.7	**1554.4**	Washington Mountain Brook	1761 ◆
634.1	**1555.0**	County Rd (gravel)	1850
633.8	**1555.3**	Bald Top	2040
632.2	**1556.9**	**October Mountain Shelter**, intermittent stream, cables.	1907 ☾ ◊ ⚘ ⊏(12)
		24.6◄22.8◄8.8◄►8.8►25.7►32.3	
631.5	**1557.6**	West Branch Rd (gravel)	1960
		⚠ Many of the water sources listed in this book are springs and small streams that can go dry. Never carry just enough water to reach the next water source.	
629.9	**1559.2**	AT joins dirt road and crosses Washington Mtn Rd (paved), **Becket, MA** 01223 (5.0E) 42.377,-73.1507 **P** (pg.160)	2000
627.9	**1561.2**	Streams	1836 ◆
626.8	**1562.3**	Blotz Rd (paved), small parking lot on north side 42.4094,-73.1503 **P**	1850
626.1	**1563.0**	Warner Hill	2050 📷

NoBo
SoBo

1559.2   Washington Mtn Rd

🪰🔥🚐✉ Home of the "**Cookie Lady**" 100 yards east. 413.623.5859 Water spigot near the garage door, please sign register on the steps. Homemade cookies often available. Soda, ice cream, boiled eggs & pick your own blueberries. Camping allowed, ask permission first. Shuttle range from Kent, CT to Manchester Center, VT. Mail: Roy & Marilyn Wiley, 47 Washington Mountain Road, Becket, MA 01223.

Becket, MA 01223 (5E) 🏠 M–F 8–4, Sa 9–11:30, 413.623.8845

🛏️⛺📶(6E) **Becket Motel** 413.623.8888 $95-156+tax, includes shuttle from/to US 20 or Wash Mtn Rd. Tavern next door. Guest Mail: 29 Chester Road, Becket, MA 01223.

1568.7   MA 8 & 9 *Dalton, MA 01227*
12% tax added to lodging prices.

🛏️⛺📶🖥️**Shamrock Village Inn** 413.684.0860 Hiker rates Su-Th are $70.60S, $75D, $85 king bed. F-Sa prices $85.50/$93.60/$99 respectively. Add tax to all prices. Well-behaved pets allowed with $75 deposit. Coin laundry, free use of computer and WiFi.

🍴 **Angelina's Subs** with veggie burgers, **Dalton Restaurant** serves D Th–Sa with live entertainment.

🍴 **SweetPea's** Ice cream, summer hours M-Th 12-9, F-Sa 12-10, Su 1-8

⛺ **Dalton Laundry** M-F 9-6, Sa 10-4, Su 10-2.

🔥 **LP Adams** Coleman/denatured alcohol.

Pittsfield, MA Many stores & restaurants approx. 2.0W from Dalton.

🛏️📶 **Econo Lodge** 413.443.5661 prices seasonal.

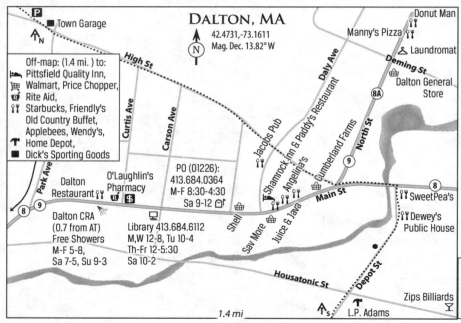

DALTON, MA

42.4731,-73.1611
Mag. Dec. 13.82° W

P Town Garage

High St

Off-map: (1.4 mi.) to:
🛏️ Pittsfield Quality Inn,
🛒 Walmart, Price Chopper,
💊 Rite Aid,
🍴 Starbucks, Friendly's Old Country Buffet, Applebees, Wendy's,
🔥 Home Depot,
⬛ Dick's Sporting Goods

Curtis Ave

Carson Ave

Park Ave

Dalton Restaurant 🍴

O'Laughlin's Pharmacy 💊 💲

Dalton CRA
(0.7 from AT)
Free Showers
M-F 5-8,
Sa 7-5, Su 9-3

PO (01226):
413.684.0364
M-F 8:30-4:30
Sa 9-12 🏠

Library 413.684.6112
M,W 12-8, Tu 10-4
Th-Fr 12-5:30
Sa 10-2

Jacobs Pub

Daly Ave

Shamrock Inn & Paddy's Restaurant

Angelina's

Cumberland Farms

North St

Deming St

Dalton General Store

Manny's Pizza 🍴

Donut Man

⛺ Laundromat

Shell

Sav More

Juice & Java

Main St

8A

9

8

🍴 SweetPea's

🍴 Dewey's Public House

Housatonic St

Depot St

Zips Billiards

🔥 L.P. Adams

1.4 mi

Berkshire Mall on SR 8, 4 mi. north of Dalton & 7 mi. south of Cheshire has:
🏃 **EMS** 413.445.4967 M-Sa 10-8, Su 11-6
🎬 **Regal Cinema 10** 413.499.3106

1577.5   Main St, School St

Cheshire, MA 01225 (pronounced "chesh-er")

St. Mary of the Assumption Church Check-in with the Pastor (west side door near the mailbox). Indoor sleeping space, use of restrooms and outside cooking area. No laundry or showers. No smoking, alcohol or drugs on church property. Welcome to attend service in hiker attire. Please donate. Mail: 159 Church Street, Cheshire, MA 01225.

Diane's Twist Limited hours, deli sandwiches, soda, ice cream.

HD Reynolds 413.743.9512 M-W & F 8-5, Th 8-7, Sa 8-3. General store, hiker snacks, Coleman fuel/oz.

BRTA (pg. 157) stops at AT kiosk; ride to outfitter, Adams, MA, and to Berkshire Mall (has EMS) $1.75.

1578.0   MA 8

(2.2E) **Berkshire Outfitters** ⟨www.berkshireoutfitters.com⟩ 413.743.5900 M-F 10-6, Sa 10-5, Su 11-4, Full service outfitter, Coleman/alcohol/oz and canister fuel, freeze-dried foods, footwear, minor equipment repairs. Often provides return ride to Cheshire.

Adams, MA 01220 (4.2E)

M-F 8:30-4:30, Sa 10-12, 413.743.5177

Big Y Foods Supermarket

Rite Aid, Medicine Shop

Adams Veterinary Clinic 413.743.4000

Thrifty Bundle Laundromat, Waterworks

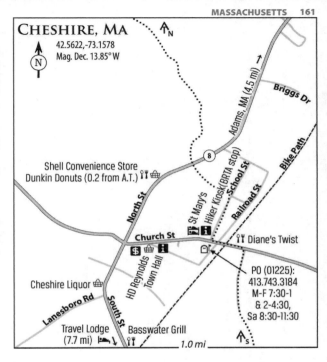

CHESHIRE, MA
42.5622,-73.1578
Mag. Dec. 13.85°W

Adams, MA (4.5 mi)
Briggs Dr
Bike Path
Shell Convenience Store
Dunkin Donuts (0.2 from A.T.)
Hiker Kiosk (BRTA stop)
School St
Railroad St
St Mary's
North St
Church St
Diane's Twist
HD Reynolds
Town Hall
PO (01225):
413.743.3184
M-F 7:30-1
& 2-4:30,
Sa 8:30-11:30
Cheshire Liquor
Lanesboro Rd
South St
Travel Lodge
(7.7 mi)
Basswater Grill
1.0 mi

APPALACHIAN TRAIL
CONSERVANCY®

The ATC works with the National Park Service, 31 volunteer maintaining clubs, and multiple other partners to engage the public in conserving this essential American resource. Their website, www.AppalachianTrail.org, contains information about trail history and protection, hike planning, volunteer opportunities, and trail conditions. Please join or donate to the ATC.

624.5	**1564.6**	Tully Mountain		2082 📷
623.7	**1565.7**	Powerline		1918
623.4	**1565.7**	**Kay Wood Shelter** (0.2E) 31.6◀17.6◀8.8▶16.9▶23.5▶33.4		1757 ☽ ♦ ⛺(10)
623.1	**1566.0**	Grange Hall Rd		1628
622.9	**1566.2**	Barton Brook, footbridge		1543 ♦
621.5	**1567.6**	Woods road		1325
620.9	**1568.2**	Railroad tracks, Housatonic St + Depot St		1220
620.4	**1568.7**	MA 8 & 9, **Dalton, MA**	(pg.160)	1145
619.4	**1569.7**	AT on Gulf Rd / High St for 1.0 mile	42.4818,-73.1783 🅿	1180

❊ **Touch-Me-Not** – Also known as "jewelweed". Trumpet-shaped flowers with a short curled tail hang horizontally like a bug in flight. Yellow with splotches of orange. Salve from crushed stems is a folk remedy for poison ivy's itch.

617.2	**1571.9**	Spring		1920 ♦
616.3	**1572.8**	Powerlines		1906
616.2	**1572.9**	Crystal Mountain Campsite 0.2E, water on AT just north of side trail		1950 ☽ ♦ ⛺(5)
615.4	**1573.7**	Gore Brook, outlet of Gore Pond		2031 ♦
614.3	**1574.8**	Stream.		1986 ♦
613.9	**1575.2**	Stream.		1815 ♦
613.2	**1575.9**	The Cobbles, outcroppings of marble with view of Hoosic River Valley, Mt Greylock, and the town of Cheshire.		1848 📷
612.1	**1577.0**	Furnace Hill Rd (south end)		1046
611.6	**1577.5**	Main St + School St, **Cheshire, MA**	(pg.161)	978
611.1	**1578.0**	MA 8, **Cheshire, MA, Adams, MA** (4.0E)	(pg.161)	992
610.0	**1579.1**	Outlook Ave (paved), stream and powerline to north		1317 ♦
607.4	**1581.7**	Old Adams Rd (dirt)		2341
606.5	**1582.6**	**Mark Noepel Shelter** (0.2E), spring to right of shelter 34.5◀25.7◀16.9▶6.6▶16.5▶23.7 Spring stronger the farther you go.		2823 ☽ ♦ ⛺(10)
606.0	**1583.1**	Jones Nose Trail to west		3233

SoBo	NoBo	Feature	Elevation
604.2	1584.9	Rockwell Rd / Summit Rd to west. . . . . . 42.6311, -73.1783 P	3025
603.8	1585.3	Cross Rockwell Rd twice, side trails to east.	3144
603.2	1585.9	Mt Greylock, highest peak in MA. 🏚(pg.164)	3491
602.8	1586.3	Thunderbolt Trail and Bellows Pipe Trail, 75 yards apart, both to east.	3105
601.2	1587.9	Bernard Farm Trail	2780
600.9	1588.2	Mt Williams	2950
600.1	1589.0	Notch Rd (paved)	2319
599.9	1589.2	**Wilbur Clearing Shelter** (0.3W) on Money Brook Trail 🌙◊⊿⊏(8)	2275
		32.3◄23.5◄6.6◄►9.9►17.1►23.0 Intermittent stream.	
599.6	1589.5	Mt Prospect Trail to west.	2505
598.0	1591.1	Pattison Rd (paved) . . . . . . 42.6876, -73.1598 P	1018
597.4	1591.7	Phelps Ave (south end), on road 0.5 mile.	732
596.9	1592.2	MA 2, Hoosic River, footbridge and RR tracks, **Williamstown, MA** (west), **North Adams, MA** (east) 42.699, -73.1535 P (0.1E) (pg.164)	660
596.8	1592.3	Massachusetts Ave / Hoosac Rd. NoBo: east on road for 0.1 mile. (pg.165)	689
596.5	1592.6	Footbridge, stream.	756
595.3	1593.8	Petes Spring. Sherman Brook Campsite 0.1W 🌙◊⊿	1352
594.6	1594.5	Bad weather bypass trail.	1806
594.2	1594.9	Pine Cobble Trail to west.	2113
594.1	1595.0	'98 Trail to west.	2128
592.8	1596.3	**MA-VT** border, southern end of Long Trail (LT)	2330
592.4	1596.7	The AT and LT are concurrent northbound for the next 105.2 miles. Spring, stream to north.	2154
590.3	1598.8	Stream.	2074
590.0	1599.1	**Seth Warner Shelter** (0.2W) 🌙◊⊿⊏(8)	2229
		33.4◄16.5◄9.9◄►7.2►13.1►21.6 Brook 0.1 left of shelter, known to dry up.	
589.7	1599.4	Country Rd, Powerline	2290
588.0	1601.1	Powerline	2894
587.1	1602.0	Roaring Branch, pond	2479

1585.9 Mt Greylock (3,491') is Massachusetts's highest peak. Veterans War Memorial Tower is on the summit. There are views of the Green, Catskill, and Taconic mountain ranges and surrounding towns. No camping or fires on summit.

🛏🏚🍴🎫📶 **Bascom Lodge** on summit 413.743.1591 private rooms $125/up, bunkroom $35PP. Bunkroom includes use of shower and continental breakfast. Shower & towel w/o stay $5, some snacks in gift shop, restaurant serves B/L/D. Open May 15-Oct 23, 2016, weekends only in May.

1592.2 MA 2

P **Greylock Community Center** Park on grass west of building, leave note with name & vehicle ID in mailbox, donations accepted.

Williamstown, MA 01267 (2.6W) All hotels expensive on peak nights, 11.7% lodging tax.

🛏♿📶🖥✉ **Willows Motel** 413.458.5768, $58-129, fourth night free, elaborate cont. breakfast, free pickup/return with stay, discount at adjacent Olympia restaurant. Laundry $6. Pool, no pets. Mail: 480 Main Street, Williamstown, MA 01267.

🛏♿📶🖥✉ **Williamstown Motel** 413.458.5202 $59S $69D wkdays, $79S $89D wkends; prices higher on high-demand nights. Cont B. Laundry (done for you) $8. Will pickup at Route 2. Major CC accepted. Mail: 295 Main Street, Williamstown, MA 01267.

🛏📶🖥✉ **Howard Johnson** 413.458.8158, Rates seasonal, cont B. Maildrops (fee for non-guests): 213 Main Street, Williamstown, MA 01267.

🛏📶 **Maple Terrace** 413.458.9677 Prices seasonal, call for rates. Heated pool, all rooms non-smoking.

🛏**P** **River Bend Farm** 413.458.3121 $120D includes breakfast. Unique experience in an authentic 1770 colonial farmhouse. Free pickup & return when available, short term parking for guests.

🛏🍴📶 **P** **Williams Inn** 413.458.9371 $155D/up. Non-guests can pay $8 for use of shower, swim and sauna. Restaurant open 7 days 5am-10pm. Short term parking $2/day.

🍴 **Desperado's** is hiker friendly.

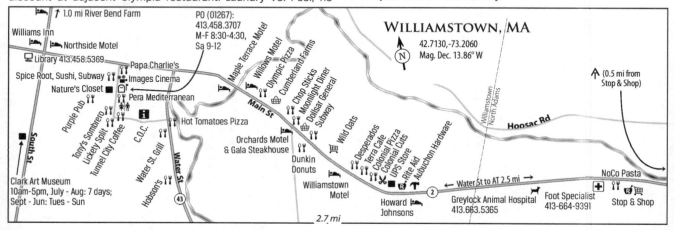

🍴 **Spice Root Indian Cuisine** 10% hiker discount.

🍴 **Water Street Grill** Craft beer, L/D daily.

✉ **Nature's Closet** Apparel, footwear, canister fuel and consignment sales. Mail: 61 Spring St, Williamstown, MA 01267.

🖳 **Milne Public Library** M-F 10-5:30, W 10-8, Sa 10-4

🚌 **Greyhound Bus Service**

North Adams, MA 01247 (services spread east of AT)

🛏🍴⛺🛜🖳 **Holiday Inn** 413.663.6500 Summer rates $169.99/up. Pool, hot tub. **Richmond Grill** on-site.

✈ **Greylock Animal Hospital** 413.663.5365, M-Th 8-7, F 8-5, Sa 8-3, Su 9-3, M-F doctor on call until 11pm.

🚌 **David Ackerson** 413.346.1033, 413.652.9573 daveackerson@yahoo.com Shuttles to trailheads ranging from Bear Mtn Bridge to Hanover, and to/from area airports.

1592.3　Massachusetts Ave / Hoosac Rd

🛏⛺🛜 **The Birches B&B** 413.458.8134 ⟨www.birchesbb.com⟩ $125D/up. Free pickup/return from Massachusetts Ave or MA 2 with stay, advance notice required. Two night min on weekends Jun-Oct. Swimming pond, laundry, big breakfast. Ask about slackpacking (19.3mi to Bennington).

> *Red-spotted newt* is the slow-moving red salamander that can be seen anywhere along the AT. The newt lives on land for the middle stage of its life, which lasts about two years. During this stage, it's also known as a *red eft*. It is a tadpole in its first stage. In its last stage it returns to water and turns green, but retains its red spots.

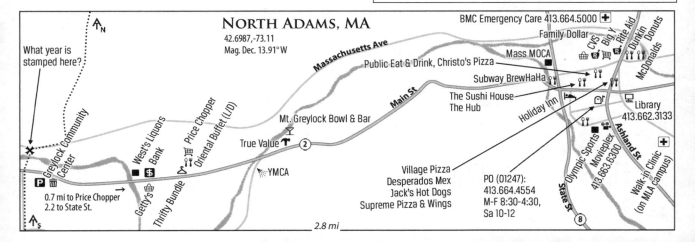

NORTH ADAMS, MA
42.6987,-73.11
Mag. Dec. 13.91°W

What year is stamped here?

0.7 mi to Price Chopper
2.2 to State St.

BMC Emergency Care 413.664.5000
Family Dollar
Mass MOCA
Public Eat & Drink, Christo's Pizza
Subway BrewHaHa
The Sushi House
The Hub
Holiday Inn
Library 413.662.3133
Mt. Greylock Bowl & Bar
True Value
Village Pizza
Desperados Mex
Jack's Hot Dogs
Supreme Pizza & Wings
PO (01247):
413.664.4554
M-F 8:30-4:30,
Sa 10-12
West's Liquors
Price Chopper
Oriental Buffet (L/D)
Getty's
Thrifty Bundle
YMCA
Greylock Community Center
Olympic Sports
Movieplex
413.663.6300
Walk-in Clinic
(on MLA campus)
CVS
Big Y
Rite Aid
Dunkin Donuts
McDonald's
Massachusetts Ave
Main St
Ashland St
State St
2.8 mi

SoBo	NoBo	Feature	Elev.
585.9	1603.2	Consultation Peak	2833 ◆
584.8	1604.3	Woods road, Stamford Stream	2246 ◆
584.4	1604.7	Stream.	2177 ◆
583.9	1605.2	Pond.	2191 ◆
583.5	1605.6	Woods road	2199
582.8	1606.3	**Congdon Shelter,** creek is water source 23.7◄17.1◄7.2◄►5.9►14.4►18.7	2088) ◆ ◗ ⌂(8)
582.0	1607.1	Stream	2223 ◆
580.7	1608.4	Footbridge, stream	2214 ◆
580.3	1608.8	Harmon Hill	2325
579.8	1609.3	Spring	2101 ◆
578.5	1610.6	VT 9, **Bennington, VT** (5.1W) .... 42.8851,-73.1153 **P** ◆ (pg.169) Bridge over City Stream north of road	1359
576.9	1612.2	Brook, **Melville Nauheim Shelter,** stream north of trail to shelter. 23.0◄13.1◄5.9◄►8.5►12.8►17.4	2424 ◆ ⌂(8)
576.4	1612.7	Powerline	2627
576.0	1613.1	Spring	2570 ◆
575.7	1613.4	Stream	2384 ◆
575.3	1613.8	Hell Hollow Brook, footbridge	2350 ⊘
574.3	1614.8	Porcupine Ridge	2816
572.1	1617.0	Little Pond Mtn (wooded summit)	3306
568.4	1620.7	**Goddard Shelter** 21.6◄14.4◄8.5◄►4.3►8.9►19.3 Spring 50 yards south on AT, limited tenting.	3566) ◆ ◆ ⌂(12)
568.1	1621.0	Glastenbury Mountain, lookout tower	3748 ▣ ☗

564.1 1625.0 **Kid Gore Shelter** 8.7◄12.8◄4.3◄▶4.6▶15.0▶19.9 ⬛☾◗◢⊏(8) 2784
Tenting north of shelter, west side of AT.
563.7 1625.4 Stream. ◗ 2855

560.4 1628.7 South Alder Brook. ◗ 2604

559.5 1629.6 **Story Spring Shelter,** spring 50 yards north on AT ☾◗◢⊏(8) 2803
17.4◄8.9◄4.6▶10.4▶15.3▶18.3

557.9 1631.2 USFS 71 (gravel). 43.0536,-72.9905 [P] 2499
557.5 1631.6 Footbridge, stream. ◗ 2390
556.8 1632.3 Black Brook, footbridge. ◗ 2206

555.9 1633.2 Stratton-Arlington Rd / Kelly Stand Rd (gravel) 43.0611,-72.9681 [P]◢◗ 2230
NoBo: east on road across Deerfield River. Daniel Webster Monument 0.3E.
Campsite 100 yards north of road to the east.

554.4 1634.7 Logging road 2584

552.1 1637.0 Stratton Mtn, lookout tower, caretaker cabin. No camping ⊛◉🛈(pg.169) 3936
Summit on which Benton MacKaye was inspired to propose creation of the AT.
551.9 1637.2 Spring to east. ◗ 3817

550.2 1638.9 Logging road ◗ 2680
549.6 1639.5 Footbridge, stream. ◗ 2467
549.1 1640.0 **Stratton Pond Shelter** (0.2W) ☾◢⊏(16) 2622
19.3◄15.0◄10.4◄▶4.9▶7.9▶12.7 Overnight fee, no tenting, no fires.
549.0 1640.1 Lye Brook Trail to west. ◗ 2557
548.9 1640.2 Stratton Pond, North Shore Trail 0.5W to campsite, overnight fee ◢◗ 2562
548.2 1640.9 Stream. ◗ 2498
547.6 1641.5 Stream. ◗ 2447

BENNINGTON, VT

42.8783,-73.197
Mag. Dec. 13.92°W

Hampton Inn
Hannaford
Chili's
Home Depot
China Wok

(279)

Best Western
Price
Chopper
Cinema 7
Dairy Bar
Dunkin Donuts
Pizza Hut
Walmart
Pizza House
Wendys

(67A)

Knotty Pine Motel
Super Shoe Store
CVS
McDonalds
Taco Bell & KFC
Aldi

Park St.

Kocher Dr.

Burger King
Quiznos

Chamber of
Commerce

Benmont Ave.

Bennington Battle
Monument

(7)

Jensen's Home Cooking
Blue Benn Diner

Rattlesnake
Cafe

Laundry

Rite Aid

Family Dollar

Greenberg Hardware

Subway & Dunkin' Donuts
Spice & Nice Natural Foods
The Pharmacy
Your Belly's Deli
Madison Brew Co. & Bennington Pizza House
Green Mountain Express
Lucky Dragon

Lil' Britain

County Rd.

Benner's Bagels, Pizza
Donovan's
Love a Bagel
Laundromat

Bennington Pizza House

Autumn Inn

(279)

Papa Pete's
(B/L)

(9)

Mt. Anthony Veterinary
Hospital 802.442.4324

Elm St.

P.O. (05201):
802.442.2421
M-F 8-5, Sa 9-2

Main St.

Henry's
Market
M-Sa 9-7
Su 10-6

Bakery

(9)

3.4 mi.
from
edge of
map

South St Cafe

Visitor Center

Express Care Walk-in Clinic
SW Vermont Med. Center

Ramunto's

Carmody's
Friendly's

Library

Catamount Motel

Crazy Russian Girls Bakery

2.8 mi

Green Mountain Club (GMC)

⟨www.greenmountainclub.org⟩
Maintains the AT in Vermont. When caretaker is present, there is a $5 overnight fee at or within one half mile of these shelters and tenting areas; Stratton Pond, Peru Peak, Griffith Lake, Little Rock Pond. On your first night stay ask for a dated receipt; it can be used within a week at another GMC fee site.

⚠ There are muddy sections of trail in Vermont. Please walk through the mud; do not trample vegetation bordering the trail.

1610.6   VT 9   *Bennington, VT 05201* (5.1W)

🛏️👣🛜 **Catamount Motel** 802.442.5977, $54S, $65D, $10EAP + tax. Laundry $4. One pet room, accepts credit cards.

🛏️👣🚐🛜🖥️✉️ **Autumn Inn Motel** 802.447.7625 $60S $70D, Pickup or return to trail $10 (each way). Pets $10. Guest Mail: 924 Main Street, Bennington, VT 05201.

🛏️🛜🖥️✉️ **Knotty Pine Motel** 802.442.5487 ⟨www.knottypinemotel.com⟩ 6.5 miles from the AT on VT 9, $88D/up, $8EAP up to 4. Includes cont B, pets free, pool. Mail (guests only): 130 Northside Drive, Bennington, VT 05201.

🛏️👣🛜🖥️ **Best Western** 802.442.6311 $99/up

🛏️👣🛜🖥️ **Hampton Inn** 802.440.9862 rates seasonal, hot b'fast.

🍴 **Lil' Britain** Fish & chips.

🚌 **Green Mountain Express** 802.447.0477 ⟨www.greenmtncn.org⟩ 215 Pleasant St. Free bus route "Emerald Line" passes between Bennington and Wilmington (17E) 3 times a day M-F. Board at town bus station, or flag the bus down at the trailhead. You may also request an unscheduled ride from town to trail for $3.

🚌 **Bennington Taxi** 802.442.9052

🚌 **Vermont Translines** 844.888.7267 ⟨www.vttranslines.com⟩ Routes cover from Albany, NY airport through towns including Bennington, VT, Wallingford, VT, Rutland, VT, and Hanover, NH.

➕ **Express Care Walk-in Clinic** 802.440.4077. No appointment necessary, open daily 8am to 6pm.

➕ **SW Vermont Med. Center** 802-442-6361

🎬 **Cinema 7** 802.442.8170

🏛️ **Bennington Battle Monument** Contains statue of Seth Warner, Revolutionary War leader of the Green Mountain Boys, for whom the shelter is named.

       (3.0E) Prospect Mountain Ski Area

🏕️🍴🛜 **Greenwood Lodge & Campsites** 802.442.2547 Open May 20 - Oct 26. Bunk $33, $30 for Hostelling International members. Tentsite $30 for 2. CC not accepted. Country Store nearby.

1637.0   Stratton Mountain

🛏️ **Stratton Mountain Resort** 802.297.4000 can be reached by taking a 1.0 mi. side trail from the summit to a gondola ride. Gondola has limited days/hours; don't make the walk unless you are certain of gondola operation (or are willing to walk an additional 1.5 miles down ski slopes). The resort has a restaurant, hotel rooms starting at $84 in summer, and **First Run Ski Shop** 802.297.2200 that has limited footwear and snacks.

Leave What You Find

•Leave plants, cultural artifacts and other natural objects where you found them for others to enjoy.

•Don't build structures or dig trenches around tents.

•Do not damage live trees or plants; green wood burns poorly. Collect only firewood that is dead, down, and no larger than your wrist. Leave dead standing trees and dead limbs on standing trees for the wildlife.

•Consider using rubber tips on the bottom of your trekking poles to avoid scratch marks on rocks, "clicking" sounds, and leaving holes along the trail.

•Avoid introducing or transporting non-native species by checking your boots, socks, packs, tents, and clothing for non-native seeds that you could remove before hitting the trail.

Read more of the Leave No Trace techniques developed for the A.T.: www.appalachiantrail.org/LNT

SoBo	NoBo	Description	Elevation
547.1	1642.0	Winhall River, footbridge, stream	2269
545.6	1643.5	Stream.	2209
544.2	1644.9	**William B. Douglas Shelter** (0.5W) 19.9◄15.3◄4.9►3.0►7.8►15.9 Spring to left of shelter.	2286 ⟨(10)
543.3	1645.8	Prospect Rock to west, view. ⚠ NoBo: AT turns east off gravel road.	2099
541.2	1647.9	**Spruce Peak Shelter** (0.1W) 18.3◄7.9◄3.0►4.8►12.9►17.6.	2190 ⟨(14)
540.8	1648.3	Spruce Peak 0.1W.	2040
540.4	1648.7	Stream, powerline.	1819
540.2	1648.9	Stream.	1839
538.9	1650.2	Powerline, footbridge, stream.	1741
538.4	1650.7	VT 11 & 30 **Manchester Center, VT** (5.4W) 43.2068,-72.9707 P (pg.172)	1840
537.5	1651.6	Footbridge, stream.	2134
536.4	1652.7	**Bromley Shelter** 12.7◄7.8◄4.8►8.1►12.8►14.3.	2535 ⟨(12)
535.8	1653.3	Ski slope	3090
535.4	1653.7	Bromley Mountain, no tenting or fires, okay to overnight in ski warming hut, no smoking, please keep hut clean.	3260
532.9	1656.2	Mad Tom Notch, USFS 21 (gravel)	2446
531.3	1657.8	Styles Peak	3394
529.6	1659.5	Peru Peak	3429
528.7	1660.4	Spring.	2801
528.0	1660.8	**Peru Peak Shelter** 15.9◄12.9◄8.1►4.7►6.2►6.4 (fee).	2597 ⟨(10)
528.0	1661.1	Footbridge, stream (two).	2570
527.8	1661.3	Griffith Lake Tenting Area, camping only at designated sites within 0.5 mi.	2600

NoBo
SoBo

SoBo	NoBo	Description		Elev
527.5	1661.6	Old Job Trail to east, Griffith Lake Trail to west	◆	2612
525.7	1663.4	Baker Peak Trail to west, Baker Peak 0.1N on AT	📷	2642
523.6	1665.5	**Lost Pond Shelter** 17.6◀12.8◀4.7◀▶1.5▶1.7▶5.0.	⊃◆⊿⊏(6)	2192
523.1	1666.0	Spring	◆	1956
522.1	1667.0	Old Job Trail to **Old Job Shelter** (1.0E), Lake Brook is water source	⊃◆⊏(8)	1524
521.9	1667.2	14.3◀6.2◀1.5◀▶0.2▶2.5▶8.3 **Big Branch Shelter** 6.4◀1.7◀0.2◀▶3.3▶8.1▶13.2.	⊃◆⊏(8)	1492
		Close to road; heavy weekend use. Water source is Big Branch. Privy uphill.		
520.8	1668.3	Danby-Landgrove Rd., 43.3727,-72.9627 P ⊃ (pg.173)		1517
520.2	1668.9	Big Black Branch Bridge, **Danby, VT** (3.5W) Footbridge, stream	◆	1646
518.7	1670.4	Homer Stone Brook Trail to west.		1854
518.6	1670.5	**Little Rock Pond Shelter & Tenting Area**	⊃◆⊏	1835
517.6	1671.5	5.0◀3.5◀3.3◀▶4.8▶9.9▶13.6 Water source is at the caretaker's platform. Overnight fee. Tenting restricted to designated sites. Footbridge, stream	◆	1938
514.4	1674.7	Trail to White Rocks Cliff 0.2W, blue-blazed trail amid stone cairns	📷	2276
513.8	1675.3	**Greenwall Shelter** (0.2E) 8.3◀8.1◀4.8◀▶5.1▶8.8▶14.9.	⊃◇⊏	2095
		Spring 0.1 mile on side trail behind shelter, prone to fail in dry seasons.		
513.1	1676.0	Bully Brook, Keewaydin Trail to west.	◆	1424
512.4	1676.7	Sugar Hill Rd (gravel)		1222
512.3	1676.8	VT 140, footbridge, stream 43.4567,-72.9329 (0.2E) P ◆ (pg.173)		1105
		Wallingford, VT (2.8W)		
511.3	1677.8	Short side trail to west to Domed Ledge Vista (no longer a view)		1674
510.6	1678.5	Bear Mountain		2228
509.7	1679.4	Patch Hollow		1761
509.3	1679.8	Footbridge, stream (3)	◆	1648
509.1	1680.0	Lake Trail loop to west (yellow blazed), 100 yards north, red-blazed tr to east.		1652
508.7	1680.4	**Minerva Hinchey Shelter** 13.2◀9.9◀5.1◀▶3.7▶9.8▶14.1.	⊃◆⊿⊏(10)	1611
		spring 75 yards in front of shelter.		

NoBo
SoBo

5,000

🚌 **Marble Valley Regional Transit District (MVRTA)** "The Bus" 802.773.3244, ext 117 M-F. ⟨www.thebus.com⟩ Red & white bus can be flagged down; they will stop if it is safe to do so. ***Manchester to Rutland:*** ($2PP) Loops from Rultand to Manchester Center, passing through M-Sa 4 times a day. Stops include Rutland Airport, Clarendon, Wallingford, Danby, and Shaws in Manchester Center.

MANCHESTER CENTER, VT

43.1752,-73.0523
Mag. Dec. 14.07°W

(N)

0.6 mi

PO (05255): 802.362.3070
M-F 8:30-4:30, Sa 9-12

Carriage House (0.6 mi)
Palmer House

Northshire Medical Center
802.362.4440

Library 802.362.2607
M-F 10-6, Sa 10-4

Ye Olde Tavern
Gringo Jack's

Sutton's Place
Roundabout Cafe
Christo's Pizza
Up For Breakfast
Gourmet Cafe
Rite Aid
Maplefields
Cilantro's Burrito

Scoops
Ice Cream

Ship Express
(UPS & FedEx)

Northshire Bookstore
Main St
Mountain Goat
Thai Basil

FroYo
Wyman Ln
McDonalds
Cottage St

Footwear Outlet Stores

Theater
China City
Price Chopper

Depot St

Bakery Works
Starbucks

EMS
Subway
Manchester Pizza
Manchester Laundromat
Mrs Murphy's Donuts

Center Hill Rd

(30)
(11)

Ben & Jerry's
Kilburns

Richville Rd

(5.4 mi from Richville Rd)

(1.4 mi) Red Sled Motel
(1.5 mi) Econo Lodge
(0.3 mi) Green Mtn Vet
802.362.2620

🚌 **Vermont Translines** 844.888.7267
⟨www.vttranslines.com⟩ Routes cover from Albany, NY airport through towns including Bennington, VT, Wallingford, VT, Rutland, VT, and Hanover, NH.

1650.7   VT 11 & 30, ***Manchester Center, VT*** (5.4W)
  East of trail:
🍴**Cilantro Burrito** (0.5E) Burritos, ice cream, sodas. 11-8, 7 days in summer; Th-Su in winter.
  Between trail and town:
🛏🛜⛺✉ **Red Sled Motel** (3.6W) 802.362.2161. Hiker-friendly. $70/room includes tax. Ride to trail when available. Laundry for a fee, swimming pool, trout pond. Motel is 1.5E of town. Some resupply on-site. Mail: 2066 Depot Street Manchester Center, VT, 05255.
🛏🛜✉ **Econo Lodge** (3.4W) 802.362.3333, $79-$139 includes cont. B. Pets $15. Mail: 2187 Depot St, Manchester Center, VT 05255.
🏪 **Dutton Farm Stand** (3.5W) 802.362.3083 9am-7pm 7 days. Produce, sodas, baked goods, ice cream.
  Call for ride:
🛏🦽⛺🛜🖥 **Green Mountain House** 330.388.6478 ⟨www.greenmountainhouse.net⟩ Jeff & Regina Taussig host hikers at their home. Open Jun 7 - Sep 7. Space is limited so reservations are essential. Clean bed with linens, shower, free laundry, WiFi, computer & well equipped hiker kitchen. Private room for couples. Free breakfast supplies; make your own pancakes, eggs, cereal, coffee. Not a party place, no alcohol. Hikers with reservations hitch to town, resupply, then call for pick-up. Check-in from 1pm to 7pm. Free morning shuttle back to the trail for guests. Credit cards accepted. $35+tax per person.

In town: (5.4W)

🛏�📧 **Sutton's Place** 802.362.1165, $75S, $85D, $105(room for 3), pets okay on porch. Accepts MC/Visa. USPS Mail: (USPS) PO Box 142 or (UPS) 50 School St, Manchester Center, VT 05255.

🛏� **Palmer House** 802.362.3600 Ask for hiker discount, $2.50 for cont B, no pets, indoor & outdoor pool. Par-3 golf, tennis courts and trout pond (equipment provided).

🛏� **Carriage House** 802.362.1706 $55PP summer, no pets.

🥾⛽📧 **Mountain Goat Outfitter** 802.362.5159, M-Sa 10-6, Su 10-5, ⟨www.mountaingoat.com⟩ Full-service outfitter, white gas/alcohol/oz canister fuel, footwear. Mail: 4886 Main St, Manchester, VT 05255.

🥾 **EMS** 802.366.8082, 7 days 10-6, full service outfitter, Coleman/alcohol/oz, pole repair, list of shuttlers. Bus stops here.

🚙 **Leonards Taxi** 802.362.7039

🚙 **Northshire Taxi** 802.345.9333

   Peru, VT (Businesses below are to the east)

🛏⛺�📧 **The Lodge at Bromley** (2.1E) 802.824.6941 $99 hiker rate, no pets, tavern with light menu, game room, ride to/from trail w/stay. Mail: (non-guests $5) 4216 VT 11, Peru, VT 05152.

🍴🏪 **Bromley Market** (2.5E) 802.824.4444 7 days 7am-7pm

🛏🚙�📧 **Bromley View Inn** (3.6E) on VA 30, 802.297.1459 ⟨www.bromleyviewinn.com⟩ $85D/up, includes hot breakfast, shuttle to/from VT 11/30 trailhead w/stay. Mail: 522 VT 30, Bondville, VT 05340.

🍴🏪💲� **JJ Hapgood General Store & Eatery** (4.2E) 802.824.4800 On Main St. in Peru, next to PO. Wood-fired pizza, beer and resupply. Open 7-7, call ahead for extended hours on weekends.

1668.3   Danby-Landgrove Rd ***Danby, VT 05739*** (3.5W)
🏤 M-F 7:15–10:15 & 11:15-2:15, Sa 7–10:30, 802.293.5105

🛏🍴⛺�📧 **Silas Griffith B&B** 802.293.5567 ⟨www.silasgriffith.com⟩ Starting at $99D midweek, 2 night min weekends & holidays. Includes full breakfast. Check-in starts at 2pm. Laundry $20/load, pets $25. Dinner with advance reservation. Call ahead to arrange vegan/vegetarian/gluten free/special dietary needs. Hiker friendly, family friendly, pet friendly, no smoking. Maildrops with reservation: 178 South Main St, Danby, VT 05739.

🏪 **Mt. Tabor Country Store** 802.293.5641 M-Sa 5-8, Su 6-7

🏪 **Nichols Store & Deli**

🖥 **Silas Griffith Library** 802.293.5106 W 2-7 (2-5 in summer), Sa 9-noon, one computer.

1676.8   VT 140, ***Wallingford, VT 05773*** (2.8W)
🏤 M-F 8–4:30, Sa 9–12, 802.446.2140

🍴 **Mom's Country Kitchen** 802.446.2606 W-Sa 6:30-2, Su 7-1.

🍴 **Sal's Italian Restaurant & Pizza**

🏪 **Wallingford Country Store & Deli**

🏪 **Cumberland Farms** Bus stop for **MVRTA** (4 times daily) and **Vermont Translines** (see pg. 172)

🔧 **Nail It Down Hardware**

🖥� **Gilbert Library** 802.446.2685 Th-F 10-5, W 10-8, Sa 9-12.

1683.1   VT 103
🍴�🐾♿ (0.5W) **Qu's Whistle Stop Restaurant** 802.772.7012 Open Su, M, Tu 7-3, Th-Sa 7-7, closed Wed (open 7 days July 5 - Aug). Serves breakfast all day, hiker specials, ice cream, beer, charging stations, and bag lunches. Ask about tenting. The Bus ($2 route to Rutland) stops here 3 times a day.

🏪 (1W) **Loretta's Deli** 802.772.7638, M-F 6am-7pm, Sa 9-6. Prepared meals & to-go trail foods. Fuel/oz, water filters.

🚙 **MVRTA** Stops near deli 4/day.
   North Clarendon, VT 05759 (4.2W)
🏤 M-F 8–1 & 2–4:30, Sa 8–10, 802.773.7893

🏪 **Mike's Country Store**
   Rutland, VT (8W of VT 103)

SoBo	NoBo	Feature	Elev	Icons
506.8	1682.3	View to Rutland Airport	1424	📷
506.1	1683.0	Clarendon Gorge, suspension bridge, swimming holes in Mill River	808	♦
506.0	1683.1	VT 103, restaurant 0.5W .... 43.5214,-72.9258 **P** ♦ (pg.173)	860	
505.5	1683.6	**North Clarendon, VT** (4.2W) **Rutland, VT** (8.0W) View, north end of rock scramble	1326	📷
505.0	1684.1	**Clarendon Shelter** (0.1E) 13.6◄8.8◄3.7◄►6.1►10.4►12.9	1244	⊃♦⊘⊏(10)
504.5	1684.6	Beacon Hill	1740	
504.2	1684.9	Lottery Rd (gravel), powerline	1654	
503.7	1685.4	Hermit Spring to east (unreliable)	1791	△
502.6	1686.5	Stream	1586	♦
502.4	1686.7	Keiffer Rd (gravel)	1522	
502.1	1687.0	Cold River Rd / Lower Rd (paved) NoBo east on road 75 yards	1385	⊞
501.3	1687.8	**W.E. Pierce Groceries** in North Shrewsbury (2.4E) Gould Brook to west, AT parallel for 0.5 miles	1480	♦
500.5	1688.6	Upper Cold River Rd (gravel)	1630	
499.7	1689.4	Gravel road, Robinson Brook	1735	♦
498.9	1690.2	**Governor Clement Shelter** 14.9◄9.8◄6.1◄►4.3►6.8►8.7	1903	⊃♦⊘⊏(12)
		⚠ Shelter's proximity to road makes it prone to use by non-hiking crowd.		
498.6	1690.5	AT on gravel road 0.3 miles north of shelter	2049	
497.6	1691.5	Ski trail, blue diamond blazes	2562	
496.6	1692.5	Spring	3321	
496.2	1692.9	Shrewsbury Peak Trail to east, signed	3494	
494.6	1694.5	**Cooper Lodge Shelter** 14.1◄10.4◄4.3◄►2.5►4.4►16.3	3908	📷⊃♦⊏(16)(pg.176)
		Spring 60 yards north on AT. Trail behind shelter 0.2 to summit, view, restaurant.		
494.5	1694.6	Bucklin Trail to west	3787	
494.3	1694.8	Spring	3590	

✳ **Clintonia** – Foot-tall plant with plastic-looking blue berries atop long stems.

SoBo	NoBo	Feature	Elev	Icons
492.1	1697.0	**Pico Camp** (0.5E) 12.9◄6.8◄2.5◄►1.9►13.8►23.7	3465	♦⊏(4)
		Shelter on Sherburne Pass Tr where it leaves the Long Tr/AT south of Pico summit.		
490.9	1698.2	Spring	3133	♦
490.2	1698.9	**Churchill Scott Shelter** (0.1W) 8.7◄4.4◄1.9◄►11.9►21.8►33.4	2602	⊃△⊏
		Composting privy, unreliable water, southern spur from shelter, no fires.		
490.0	1699.1	Stream	2420	△
489.2	1699.9	Stream	2054	♦

NoBo

SoBo

NoBo	SoBo	Description	Elev
488.3	1700.8	US 4, **Rutland, VT** (8.5W) . . . 43.6666,-72.85 **P** (pg.176)	1880
488.2	1700.9	Stream.	1885
487.3	1701.8	Maine Junction, Tucker-Johnson camping area (0.4W).	2239
		⚑ The Long Trail is also white-blazed, it turns to the west.	
487.1	1702.0	Spring, Deer Leap Trail to west.	2290
486.5	1702.6	Deer Leap Trail 0.3E to view	2435
486.4	1702.7	Sherburne Pass Trail 0.5E to **Inn at Long Trail**	2440
485.6	1703.5	Spring.	1850
485.2	1703.9	**Gifford Woods State Park** . (pg.177)	1651
485.0	1704.1	VT 100, **Killington, VT** (0.6E). 43.6743,-72.8096 **P** (pg.177)	1612
484.4	1704.7	Kent Pond, side trail to **Killington, VT** (0.4E) (pg.177)	1554
483.1	1706.0	Thundering Brook Rd (gravel)	1398
482.9	1706.2	Thundering Falls to west.	1232
482.7	1706.4	River Rd (gravel) . 43.6806,-72.7822 **P**	1260
481.4	1707.7	Quimby Mountain.	2515
480.8	1708.3	Powerline, boulder to sit on, view to Pico slopes.	2329
480.5	1708.6	Gravel road	2325
478.3	1710.8	**Stony Brook Shelter** (0.1E) 16.3◄13.8◄11.9 ◄▶9.9▶21.5▶30.3 ☾♦⊂ (8)	1761
		Tent sites behind shelter. Water from stream 0.1N on AT.	
477.7	1711.4	Stony Brook Rd (gravel), Stony Brook and footbridge.	1346
475.4	1713.7	Streams	2013
473.8	1715.3	Chateauguay Rd (gravel), Locust Creek	2003
473.4	1715.7	Stream.	2144
472.9	1716.2	Stream.	2503
470.9	1718.2	The Lookout, 0.1W to cabin and tower, no fires	2365

5000

3000

1000

NoBo
SoBo

1694.5   Trail to Killington Peak (0.2E from Cooper Lodge Shelter) ⛏🍴 (0.2E) **Killington Peak Lodge** 800.621.6867 Food service at the summit lodge, gondola ride ($25 round trip) to the ski resort. Summer hours 10am-5pm.

1700.8   US 4 🛏🔥🚿🍴⛺📶✉

(0.8E) **The Inn at Long Trail** 802.775.7181 or 800.325.2540 ⟨www.innatlongtrail.com⟩ Hiker rates, rooms include full breakfast. Limited pet rooms, reservations recommended on weekends. Overflow camping across street (no facilities). Coin laundry, outside water spigot. Closed mid-April through Mem Day. **McGrath's Irish Pub** L/D 11:30-9pm, live music Fri & Sat. Mail: (FedEx/UPS) 709 US 4, Killington, VT 05751.

🛏📶✉ (1.4W)   **Mendon Mountain View Lodge** 802.773.4311 Hiker rate $69S $15EAP. Breakfast $10. No pets. Heated pool & sauna, bus stops here. Mail: 5654 Route 4, Mendon, VT 05701.

Rutland, VT (8.5W from US 4 trailhead)
⛏🏨🍴🚿⛺📶✉ **Hikers Hostel at the Yellow Deli** 802.683.9378 or 802.775.9800 ⟨www.hikershostel.org⟩ Run by a Twelve Tribes spiritual community. Donation or WFS. Kitchenette, coin laundry ($1 wash $1 dry). No alcohol, no smoking. Free showers even w/o stay. Shuttles sometimes available by donation. Hostel open 24/7. Stay includes breakfast and 15% off at deli and at **Simon the Tanner** (adjacent outfitter, open 10-5 M-Th, F 10-3). Mail: Hiker Hostel, 23 Center Street, Rutland, VT 05701.

🥾 **Mountain Travelers Outdoor Shop** 802.775.0814 Tu–Sa 10-5. All gear, Coleman/alcohol/oz.

🛒 **Rutland Food Co-op** 802.773.0737 7 days, M-Sa 9-7, Su 10-6
🐾 **Rutland Veterinary** 802.773.2779
🚆 **Amtrak** 800.872.7245 Daily routes Rutland to many northeastern cities.
🚌 **Rutland Taxi** 802.236.3133

Killington, VT 05751 (1.8E from US 4, pg.177)

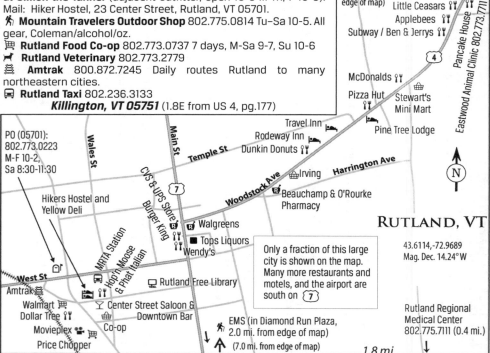

PO (05701): 802.773.0223 M-F 10-2, Sa 8:30-11:30

(6.7 mi. from edge of map)

Big Lots
Home Depot
Mtn Traveler
Little Ceasars
Applebees
Subway / Ben & Jerrys
Pancake House 802.773.7111
Eastwood Animal Clinic

McDonalds
Pizza Hut   Stewart's Mini Mart

Travel Inn
Rodeway Inn   Pine Tree Lodge
Dunkin Donuts

Irving   Harrington Ave
Woodstock Ave   Beauchamp & O'Rourke Pharmacy

Wales St   Main St   Temple St

RUTLAND, VT

43.6114,-72.9689
Mag. Dec. 14.24°W

Hikers Hostel and Yellow Deli

CVS & UPS Store

Hop'n Moose & Phat Italian

Burger King
Walgreens
Wendy's
Tops Liquors

MRTA Station

West St
Amtrak
Walmart
Dollar Tree
Movieplex
Price Chopper

Rutland Free Library

Center Street Saloon & Downtown Bar
Co-op

Only a fraction of this large city is shown on the map. Many more restaurants and motels, and the airport are south on ⑦

EMS (in Diamond Run Plaza, 2.0 mi. from edge of map)
(7.0 mi. from edge of map)

Rutland Regional Medical Center 802.775.7111 (0.4 mi.)

1.8 mi

1703.9 🏕️⚙️🚻📷🪦 The AT passes thru **Gifford Woods State Park** 802.775.5354 Shelters, discounted tent sites for AT hikers in special hiker section, coin-op showers, water spigot. Open Mem Day-Columbus Day. Fills quickly in fall.

1704.1   VT 100

Killington, VT 05751 (0.6E from VT 100, 1.8E from US 4)
🚶📧🛒 **Base Camp Outfitters** 802.775.0166, Summer hours: 9-6 every day. Full service outfitter, alcohol/oz & canister fuel. Also accessible by side trail from Mountain Meadows Lodge. Disc golf. Mail: 2363 Route 4, Killington VT 05751.

🛏️📶 **Greenbrier Inn** 802.775.1575 15% discount for hikers, no pets.
🛏️📶🖥️ **Killington Motel** 802.773.9535 Call for hiker rate, includes cont. B, pool.

🚐 **Apex Shuttle Service** 603.252.8295 AThikershuttle@gmail.com Inn-to-Inn hiking packages between Killington & Franconia Notch, NH. Shuttle, lodging & lunches provided for hikers who want the AT day hiking experience with a comfortable night's lodging.

🍴🍸🧺 **JAX Food & Games** 802.422.5334 Eat/drink while-u-wash (laundry downstairs) 0.8S of US4 on Killington Rd.

1704.7   Kent Pond, AT crosses behind lodge near pond, 0.4E trail to **Base Camp Outfitters** ✖ Dock over lake is supported by metal poles; what letters are on pole caps?
🛏️⚙️🍴⛺🅿️📶🖥️📧 **Mountain Meadows Lodge** 802.775.1010 〈www.mountainmeadowslodge.com〉   Room $69D, single room sometimes available for $59. Open year-round, but meals and lodging are not available most weekends & during events. Okay to charge phones, but please do not loiter when events are being held at the lodge. Occasional WFS. Lunch or dinner $10. No pets inside. Hot tub, sauna, game room and canoe for guests. Parking for section hiking guests. Ask about tenting. Mail free even for non-guests: 285 Thundering Brook Rd, Killington, VT 05751.

🚐 **Marble Valley Regional Transit District (MVRTA)** "The Bus" 802.773.3244, ext 117 M-F. 〈www.thebus.com〉 Red & white bus can be flagged down; they will stop if it is safe to do so. *Rutland Killington Commuter (RKC)* ($2PP) Loops hourly from 5:15-7:15, 7 days from Rutland to Killington, passing AT on US 4. Stops westbound at The Inn at Long Trail.

🚐 **Vermont Translines** (see pg. 172) Stops at Rutland bus station and at Long Trail Inn.

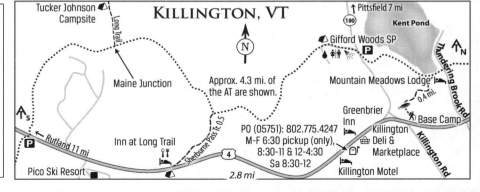

KILLINGTON, VT

Tucker Johnson Campsite
Long Trail
Maine Junction
↑ Pittsfield 7 mi
(100)
Kent Pond
🌲 Gifford Woods SP
🅿️
Mountain Meadows Lodge
0.4 mi.
Thundering Brook Rd
Approx. 4.3 mi. of the AT are shown.
Greenbrier Inn
🛏️ Killington Deli & Marketplace
🛏️ Base Camp
A↑ S
🅿️ ← Rutland 11 mi
Inn at Long Trail
Sherburne Pass Tr. 0.5
(4)
PO (05751): 802.775.4247 M-F 6:30 pickup (only), 8:30-11 & 12-4:30 Sa 8:30-12
🛏️ Killington Motel
Pico Ski Resort
2.8 mi

468.4	1720.7	**Wintturi Shelter** (0.2W) 23.7◀21.8◀9.9◀▶11.6▶20.4▶27.7	)♦⊿⊂(8)	2058
467.7	1721.4	Woods road		1757
466.1	1723.0	Ascutney Mountain	📷	1488
465.0	1724.1	VT 12, Barnard Gulf Rd (paved). 43.6552,-72.5562 P ♦(pg.180) Gulf Stream south of road crossing. **Woodstock, VT** (4.2E)		886
464.3	1724.8	Dana Hill		1550
463.1	1726.0	Woodstock Stage Rd, Barnard Brook, **South Pomfret, VT** (1E)	♦(pg.180)	820
462.8	1726.3	Stream	♦	1035
462.3	1726.8	Totman Hill Rd, footbridge, stream	♦	1007
461.5	1727.6	Bartlett Brook Rd (gravel), footbridge, stream	♦	1001
460.9	1728.2	Pomfret Rd (paved) Pomfret Brook south of road crossing, powerline	♦	906
460.5	1728.6	View	📷	1538
459.7	1729.4	View	📷	1713
459.1	1730.0	Cloudland Rd (gravel), **Cloudland Market** (0.2W) closed M & Su	⛪	1370
458.6	1730.5	Previous AT shelter (Cloudland, 0.5W) now on private land. Owners also own Cloudland Market and hikers are welcome to stay at the shelter.	♦⊂	1617
457.3	1731.8	Thistle Hill		1946
456.8	1732.3	**Thistle Hill Shelter** (0.2E), stream 0.1 further 33.4◀21.5◀11.6◀▶8.8▶16.1▶25.6	)♦⊿⊂(8)	1754
456.5	1732.6	Dimick Brook	♦	1504
455.5	1733.6	Joe Ranger Rd (gravel)		1295
454.9	1734.2	Bunker Hill Rd (dirt)		1406

✿ Queen Anne's Lace – White flower cluster in disk shaped doily 3-5" wide on hairy stem.

453.1	1736.0	Bench, view to east	📷	1134
452.5	1736.6	Stream	♦	535
452.3	1736.6	Quechee West Hartford Rd, ⌂ NoBo west on road 0.4 mi, cross White River.		474
452.0	1737.1	VT 14, White River, **West Hartford, VT**. (pg.180)		392
451.6	1737.5	NoBo: turn west, on road 0.3 mile.		397
451.3	1737.8	Tigertown Rd, NoBo: turn east, on road 0.4 mile. I-89 underpass	43.7208,-72.4132 P	559
450.6	1738.5	Podunk Rd (gravel) Podunk Brook	43.7168,-72.4002 P	860
450.1	1739.0	Woods road		1048
449.7	1739.4	Woods road, stream	♦	998

SoBo	NoBo	Feature	Elev.
448.0	1741.1	**Happy Hill Shelter** (0.1E) 30.3◄20.4◄8.8▼▲7.3►16.8►22.5 . . .) ◊ ∈(8)	1409
		Brook near shelter, known to run dry.	
447.7	1741.4	Tucker Trail 3.1W to Norwich.	1320
446.4	1742.7	Woods road	1127
445.2	1743.9	Powerline	1165
444.7	1744.4	Stream ●	819
444.6	1744.5	Elm Street, NoBo: turn east, on road 1.0 mile	833
443.6	1745.5	Main St, **Norwich, VT**, NoBo: turn east, on road 1.4 miles (pg.181)	512
442.7	1746.4	**VT-NH** border, Connecticut River	380
442.1	1747.0	**Hanover, NH**, Dartmouth College 43.7065,-72.2776 P (pg.183)	520
		NoBo: turn east on SR 10.	
441.4	1747.7	NH 120, trailhead near convenience store.	508
440.7	1748.4	**Velvet Rocks Shelter** (0.2W) 27.7◄16.1◄7.3◄▼▲9.5►15.2►21.9) ● ∈(6)	907
		Spring on northern access to shelter.	
440.1	1749.0	North shelter loop Trail ● (0.2W)	959
438.4	1750.7	Pond, boardwalk ●	800
437.7	1751.4	Trescott Rd (paved)	933
436.4	1752.7	Footbridge, stream (2) ●	851
436.3	1752.8	Etna-Hanover Center Rd (paved), **Etna, NH** (0.8E) (pg.183)	845
		●ıl Cell phone reception at cemetery to west.	
433.8	1755.3	Three Mile Rd (gravel)	1414
433.6	1755.5	Mink Brook, footbridge 43.718,-72.176 P ●	1348
432.0	1757.1	Moose Mountain south peak. [📷]	2290
431.4	1757.7	Woods rd ⚠ NoBo stay on AT for another 250 yards to Moose Mtn Shelter.	2004
431.2	1757.9	**Moose Mountain Shelter** (0.1E)) ◊ ◭ ∈(8)	2113
		25.6◄16.8◄9.5▼▲5.7►12.4►17.7 Loop trail to shelter, water at AT and northern leg intersection, tenting on northern leg of loop.	

WEST HARTFORD, VT

Former site of Village Store
(closed in 2014)

Library 802.295.7992
M 2-8,
Tu 9-12 & 1-6
W 10-12 & 1-7
Th 9-12 & 1-6
Sa 10-1

0.4 mi

White River Junction, VT (8mi)

1724.1   VT 12, Barnard Gulf Rd

⛪ **On The Edge Farm** (0.2W) 802.457.4510 Mid-May to Labor Day 7 days 10-5:30; rest of year Th-M 10-5. Pies, fruit, ice cream, smoked meats and cheese, cold drinks.

Woodstock, VT 05091 (4.2E)

🏠 M-F 8:30-5, Sa 9-12, 802.457.1323
Pricey resort town, several motels & restaurants, movie theater, and bookstore.

🛏🛜 **Shire Woodstock** 802.457.2211 $138/up

🛏🛜 **Braeside Motel** 802.457.1366 $98-$168D

🍴 **Bentley's**, **Pizza Chef**

⛪ **Cumberland Farms**, **Gillingham & Sons**

💊 **Woodstock Pharmacy**

🐾 **Woodstock Vet. Hospital** 802.457.2229

🖥 **Library** 802.457.2295 M-F 10-6, Sa 10-4

1726.0   Woodstock Stage Rd

South Pomfret, VT 05067 (1E)

🏠 M-F 10-2, Sa 8:30-11:30, 802.457.1147 located inside of Teago's

⛪ **Teago's General Store** 802.457.1626 M-Sa 7-6, Su 7-4, B&J ice cream, beer, sandwiches & salads.

1737.1   VT 14, White River

West Hartford, VT 05084

🚌 **Big Yellow Taxi** 802.281.8294 Also covers Woodstock, Norwich, Hanover, Lebanon and White River Junction.

1745.5   Main St, **Norwich, VT 05055** (more services on map)
      Overnight stay may be possible with one of the many trail angels here and in Hanover. Look for list at **Norwich Library**.

🛏🍴🛜🖥✉ **Norwich Inn** 802.649.1143 ⟨www.norwichinn.com⟩ $109D includes a free beer, 2 pet rooms available, no smoking, reservations recommended. **Jasper Murdocks Ale House** W–Su B/L, dinner 7 days, microbrewery. Maildrops for guests: PO Box 908, Norwich, VT 04055, or FedEx to 325 Main St.

🏪 **Dan & Whits General Store** 802.649.1602, 7 days 7-9, 0.1W on Main St. Hikers get free day old sandwiches when available. Small gear items, canister fuel, batteries, ponchos, hardware and grocery.

🖥🛜 **Norwich Library** 802.649.1184, M 1-8, Tu-W-F 10-5:30, Th 10-8, Sa 10-3, Su 12-4.

🚗 **Enterprise Rent-A-Car** 800.736.8227 Car rental w/free pickup/return can be as economical as shuttles. ATC has arranged for hiker discount, use code W15509. Locations include Franklin, NC, Abingdon,VA, Pearisburg,VA, Roanoke,VA, Waynesboro,VA, Front Royal,VA, Charles Town,WV, Carlisle,PA, East Stroudsburg,PA, Warwick,NY, Pittsfield,MA, Bennington,VT, Rutland,VT, Hanover,NH, Gorham,NH.

🚌 **Advance Transit** 802.295.1824 www.advancetransit.com⟩ M-F 6-6, offers FREE bus service connecting Hanover area towns. Detailed schedule and stops are available on-line and at libraries. The routes are indicated on Norwich and Hanover maps and primary bus stops are:
Norwich - Dan & Whits (Brown).
Hanover - Dartmouth Book Store (Orange/Blue), Hanover Inn (Brown).
White River Junction - Amtrak.
West Lebanon - Main St. (Orange/Red), grocery stores, outfitters.
Lebanon - City Hall (Blue/Red).

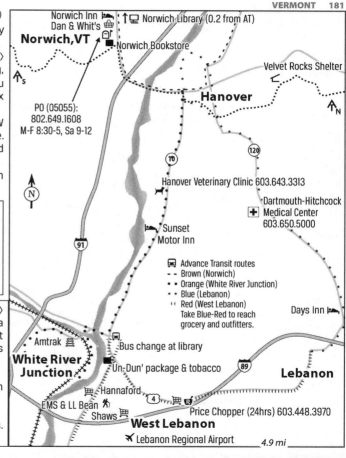

Norwich Inn 🛏
Dan & Whit's 🏪
Norwich,VT
🏛 Norwich Library (0.2 from AT)
Norwich Bookstore
🅿

Velvet Rocks Shelter

Hanover

Ⓝ Ⓝ

PO (05055):
802.649.1608
M-F 8:30-5, Sa 9-12

🔟 ⑫⓪

Hanover Veterinary Clinic 603.643.3313

Dartmouth-Hitchcock
✚ Medical Center
603.650.5000

🅝

🛏 Sunset
Motor Inn
Ⓘ91

🚌 Advance Transit routes
- - Brown (Norwich)
• • Orange (White River Junction)
∗ ∗ Blue (Lebanon)
'' Red (West Lebanon)
Take Blue-Red to reach
grocery and outfitters.

Days Inn 🛏

Amtrak 🚆
**White River
Junction**

🚌 Bus change at library

Un-Dun' package & tobacco

🅘89

Lebanon

🚆 Hannaford 🚆
EMS & LL Bean 🚶
Shaws 🚆

Ⓘ4

Price Chopper (24hrs) 603.448.3970

West Lebanon

✈ Lebanon Regional Airport   4.9 mi

See wide-area map on pg. 181

Baker-Berry Library 603.646.2560

✖ On this road not taken by the AT, an alumnus sits contemplatively on a granite boulder. What words has he written?

Lot A- Call Dartmouth Parking Operations 603.646.2204 with vehicle info & dates car will be left.

"Color" routes shown are a free service of Advance Transit (see pg. 179)

The Green

Thayer Hall

Dartmouth Outing Club (DOC)

Collis Center Student Union

Wheelock St

Crosby St

Park St

Dirt Cowboy

Dartmouth Coach bus stop

Hanover Inn

Take brown route to:
Norwich, VT
1.4 mi. from
Main St. (Hanover)
to Norwich Post Office

Murphys

Canoe Club

EBAs

Allen St

Lou's (free muffin)

Hopkins Center

Hood Museum of Art (free admission)

HANOVER, NH

N

43.7022,-72.2892
Mag. Dec. 14.58°W
town-wide WiFi

Dartmouth Bookstore (and bus stop)

Allen St. Deli

Starbucks

Boloco Burritos

Market Table

Stinsons

Mollys

Morano Gelato

Theater

Salt Hill Pub, Base Camp Cafe & Subway

C&A Pizza

Noodle Station & Frozen Yogurt

Jewel of India

Lebanon St

Maple St

Zimmermans

South St

Irving

(0.7 mi. Hanover Inn to Co-op)

CVS

PO (03755): 603.643.4544
M-F 8:30-5, Sa 8:30-12
Sat pick-up available until 3

School St

Main St

Yama (Asian)

Umpleby's Bakery Cafe

Hanover Hardware

Ramuntos Brick Oven Pizza (free slice for thru-hikers)

Howe Library
603.643.4120
M-Th 10-8, Fr 10-6,
Sa 10-5, Su 1-5

120

Richard W. Black Community Center

Co-op Foodstore
(8am-8pm, 7 days)

Co-op Service Center

Take orange route to:
Hanover Veterinary Clinic (1 mi from Wheelock)
Sunset Motor Inn (2 mi from Wheelock)
West Lebanon, NH (5 mi from Wheelock)

Currier St

Take blue route to:
Dartmouth-Hitchcock Medical Center (2 mi from Co-op)
Days Inn (4 mi from Co-op)
Lebanon, NH (5 mi)

0.8 mi

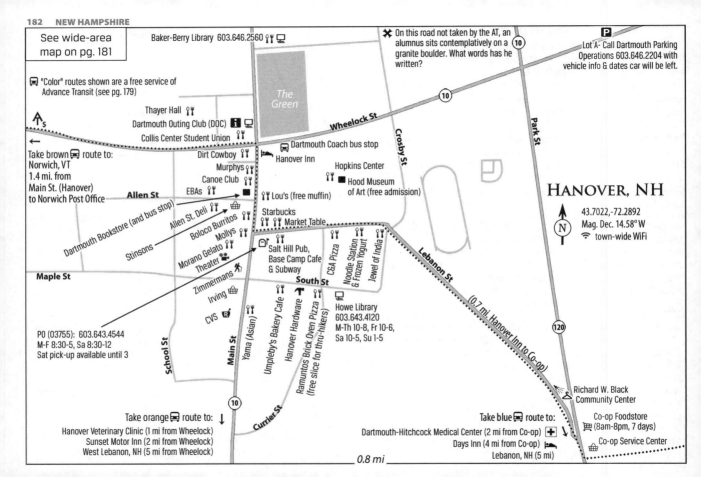

1747.0   Dartmouth College **Hanover, NH 03755**

🔋 **Hanover Friends of the AT** produce a brochure with complete list of hiker services, available at the DOC, PO, libraries, Co-op.

🔋 📶 🖥 **Dartmouth Outing Club (DOC)** 603.646.2428 Unsecured room for pack storage in Robinson Hall & in Howe Library cannot be left overnight. Not available during Dartmouth orientation (mid Aug - mid Sept). Both places have computers for free internet use. There are no hiker accommodations on campus.

🅿 Overnight parking on Wheelock Street Lot A, see map. No parking near Connecticut River Bridge.

🛏🏕📶✉ **Sunset Motor Inn** 603.298.8721, open 8-11, Call ahead for availability; discount for hikers. Will shuttle when bus is not running, free laundry before 6pm, quiet after 10pm, $15 pet fee. Mail (guest only): 305 N Main Street, West Lebanon, NH 03874.

🛏🍴 **Hanover Inn** 603.643.4300 Pricey, discount sometimes avail.

🍴 **EBA's** 603.643.6135 11am-2am, full menu and beer, daily specials. Pizza buffet Tuesday night $7.95.

🍴 **Allen St. Deli** Open 7-4, 7 days. One free bagel for thru-hikers.

🍴 **Jewel of India** buffet Su 11:30-2:30

🏪🍴 **Stinson's** Convenience store with $5 hiker lunch special: deli sandwich, soda & small bag of chips. Good selection of beer & tobacco.

🛒📶 **Hanover Food Co-op** 603.643.4889 8am-8pm 7 days year-round. Deli and food bar in-store. Please use member #7000 at check-out to help fund AT related initiatives.

🚿🏕📶 **Richard W. Black Recreation Center** 603.643.5315 M-F 9am-5pm. Open Saturdays Sept-June. Shower w/soap & towel $3, laundry w/soap $2, must finish either by 4:30pm. Pack storage.

🥾✉ **Zimmerman's** 603.643.6863 Hiker-friendly, canister fuel, Aquamira, socks & outdoor clothes. Mail: 63 Main St, Hanover, NH 03756

🔧 **Hanover Hardware** Coleman/alcohol/oz

🚌 **Advance Transit** (see pg. 181)

🚌 **Vermont Translines** 844.888.7267 ⟨www.vttranslines.com⟩ Routes cover from Albany, NY airport through towns including Bennington, VT, Wallingford, VT, Rutland, VT, White River Junction, NH, and Hanover, NH.

🚌 **Big Yellow Taxi** 603.643.8294

🚌 **Dartmouth Coach** 603.448.2800 ⟨www.dartmouthcoach.com⟩ Routes to Boston, to Logan Airport, and to NY. See schedules on website.

🚌 **Apex Shuttle Service** 603.252.8295 AThikershuttle@gmail.com (Steve "Stray Cat" Lake) To/from anywhere if originating or ending in the Hanover area.

🐾 **Hanover Veterinary** 603.643.3313

White River Junction, VT

🚃 **Amtrak** 800.872.7245 Vermonter line travels north as far as St. Albans, VT, and south through New York, Philadelphia, Baltimore and Washington, DC. There is no ticket office at this station, but you can reserve on the phone and pay when you board.

Lebanon & West Lebanon, NH (see map pg. 181)

🛏📶🖥 **Days Inn** 603.448.5070, 4 mi. south of the Co-op on Rte 120 on free bus route, cont. B, pets $20.

🥾 **EMS** 603.298.7716, **LL Bean** 603.298.6975

🛒 **Shaw's** 603.298.0388 7am-10pm, 7-9 Sunday

1752.8   Etna-Hanover Center Rd, **Etna, NH 03750** (0.8E)

🏠♿🏕 **Tiggers Tree House** 603.643.9213 Private home; not a party place. No drive-ins. Advance notice ensures a place to stay. Call from trailhead, Etna General Store (will let you use phone) or Dartmouth Outing Club for pickup. Pets allowed, donations accepted or buy laundry soap or work for stay. Rides to grocery store, Walmart, EMS.

🏪🍴 (0.8E) **Etna General Store** 603.643.1655, M-F 6-7, Sa, Su 8-7. Deli, hot meals, open 7 days.

1764.5 Grafton Turnpike, Dorchester Rd, Dartmouth Skiway

◑ ☽ **Bill Ackerly** Welcomes hiker visits. Help yourself to water, rest, chat, paint a picture, or play a game of croquet. Porta-potty on-site. Ask about camping. ✖ What does Bill have in his right hand?

Lyme Center, NH 03769 (1.3W) ☖ M–F 8–10, Sa 8–11:30, 603.795.4037
Lyme, NH 03768 (3.2W)

☖ M–F 7:45–12 & 1:30–5:15, Sa 7:45–12, 603.795.4421

🍴 ☏ **Stella's Italian Kitchen & Market** 603.795.4302 ⟨www.stellaslyme.com⟩, M–Th 10–9, F–Sa 10–10, Su closed.

🛏🛜🖥✉ **Dowd's Country Inn B&B** 603.795.4712 ⟨www.dowdscountryinn.com⟩ Call in advance & let them know you are a hiker. Pickup/return available. Rates fluctuate; mid week starting at $85S, $100D + NH taxes, wkends through Sep 20 $125S, $140D + taxes. Includes full breakfast & afternoon tea. Pets $15, allowed in some rooms. Mail: 9 Main Street, Lyme, NH 03768.

🏛🍴☏ **Lyme Country Store** (3.3W) ice cream, produce, deli, 7 days.

🐾 **Lyme Veterinary Hospital** (2.8W) bear right onto High St and hospital is 50 yards up on the left, 603.795.2747 M–F 8–5, Sa 8–noon.

Appalachian Mountain Club (AMC) 603.466.2727
⟨hutsblog.outdoors.org/2014/06/thru-hiker-to-thru-hiker-hows-and-whys.html⟩ Maintains AT from Kinsman Notch, NH to Grafton Notch, ME & operates 8 walk-in only huts with space for 30-90 people (no pets). Huts use alternative energy sources and composting toilets. There is no heat or showers. Huts are closed in winter. In spring & fall huts are open to "self-serve" use. Rates (member/ nonmember): $26/$31 Su–F; $40/$49 Sa. See White Mtn map for dates. "Full serve" season includes bunk, dinner & breakfast, starting at $125PP for non-members. Don't count on Hut stays without reservations, & camping is not allowed near huts, except at Nauman Tentsite. Reservations can be made by phone or with any AMC caretaker. *Work-for-stay* is available to 2 thru-hikers (4 at LOC), no reservations. Arrive after 3pm and please put sincere effort into your work. WFS hikers get floor space for sleeping, feast on leftovers, and are typically asked to work 2 hours after breakfast. Limit WFS to 3 nights in the Whites to give other hikers the opportunity. Lakes of the Clouds Hut has 4 WFS spots and a $10 thru-hiker bunkroom called *"The Dungeon"*.

🍴 Thru-hikers can stop in at lunchtime for $2 bottomless bowl of soup.

🚌 **AMC Hiker Shuttle** (see pg. 191)

White Mountain National Forest (the "Whites")

Passage through the Whites should be planned carefully. It is one of the more heavily visited sections of the AT, and campsites are limited. The trail is rugged, so your pace may be slowed. Weather is dynamic, adding to the dangers of hiking on stretches of trail above treeline.

Take adequate cold-weather gear, check weather reports, carry maps, and know your options for overnighting. The AMC and Randolph Mountain Club (RMC) maintain camps, which are detailed in the following pages. Most have fees. Have cash on hand even if you do not plan to use them; your plans may change.

There are many trails in the Whites. The AT is the only white-blazed trail, but blazes are scant. There are no blazes in the Great Gulf Wilderness Area. The AT is always coincident with another named trail, and the other trail name may be the one you see on signs. Wherever the AT changes from one trail to another, this book uses the notation: "AT: Town Line Tr◀▶Glencliff Tr." This means that the AT to the south of this point is coincident with the Town Line Trail; to the north, the AT joins the Glencliff Trail.

The area within a quarter mile of all AMC and RMC facilities and everything above treeline (trees 8' or less) are part of the Forest Protection Area (FPA). Trails are often marked where they enter or leave the FPA. Do not camp within a FPA, and camp at least 200' from water and trails. Rocks aligned to form a trail boundary (scree walls) are an indication that you should not leave the treadway. Doing so damages fragile plant life.

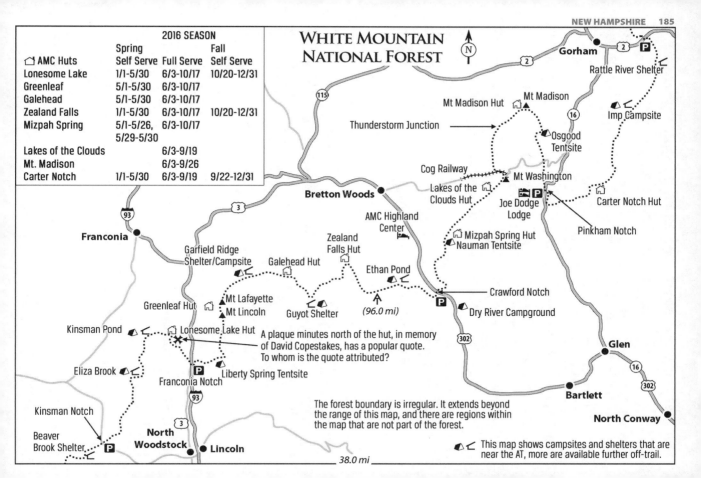

WHITE MOUNTAIN NATIONAL FOREST

AMC Huts	2016 SEASON Spring Self Serve	Full Serve	Fall Self Serve
Lonesome Lake	1/1-5/30	6/3-10/17	10/20-12/31
Greenleaf	5/1-5/30	6/3-10/17	
Galehead	5/1-5/30	6/3-10/17	
Zealand Falls	1/1-5/30	6/3-10/17	10/20-12/31
Mizpah Spring	5/1-5/26, 5/29-5/30	6/3-10/17	
Lakes of the Clouds		6/3-9/19	
Mt. Madison		6/3-9/26	
Carter Notch	1/1-5/30	6/3-9/19	9/22-12/31

Gorham

Rattle River Shelter

Mt Madison Hut — Mt Madison

Thunderstorm Junction

Imp Campsite

Osgood Tentsite

Cog Railway

Mt Washington

Lakes of the Clouds Hut

Joe Dodge Lodge

Carter Notch Hut

Pinkham Notch

Bretton Woods

AMC Highland Center

Franconia

Zealand Falls Hut

Garfield Ridge Shelter/Campsite

Galehead Hut

Ethan Pond

Mizpah Spring Hut
Nauman Tentsite

Crawford Notch

Greenleaf Hut — Mt Lafayette
Mt Lincoln

Guyot Shelter

(96.0 mi)

Dry River Campground

Kinsman Pond

Lonesome Lake Hut

A plaque minutes north of the hut, in memory of David Copestakes, has a popular quote. To whom is the quote attributed?

Glen

Eliza Brook

Liberty Spring Tentsite

Franconia Notch

Kinsman Notch

North Woodstock

Lincoln

Bartlett

North Conway

Beaver Brook Shelter

The forest boundary is irregular. It extends beyond the range of this map, and there are regions within the map that are not part of the forest.

This map shows campsites and shelters that are near the AT, more are available further off-trail.

38.0 mi

NoBo	Mile	Description	Elev
430.0	1759.1	Moose Mountain north peak	2293
428.4	1760.7	South fork of Hewes Brook	1023
428.2	1760.9	Goose Pond Rd (paved), parking to east . . . 43.7528, -72.1233 🅿	945
426.1	1763.0	Holts Ledge, precipitous drop-off, views 📷	1915
425.5	1763.6	**Trapper John Shelter** (0.2W) ⚠ Side Tr to shelter is white blazed ☽ ♦ ⊏ (6) 22.5◄15.2◄5.7◄►6.7►12.0►27.7 privy behind shelter	1501
424.6	1764.5	Grafton Turnpike(paved), Dorchester Rd . . . 43.79, -72.1 🅿 ♦ (pg.184) **Lyme Center, NH** (1.3W), **Lyme, NH** (3.2W) ⚠ NoBo east on wedge of land between fork in road side trail to Bill Ackerly home 0.1 north of intersection.	880
423.2	1765.9	Grant Brook ♦	1211
422.9	1766.2	Concrete milepost ♦	1127
422.6	1766.5	Lyme-Dorchester Rd (gravel) . . . 43.79, -72.1029 🅿	1107
421.8	1767.3	Lambert Ridge, multiple views from quartzite ridge 📷	1901
419.4	1769.7	Smarts Ranger Trail to east . . . 📷 ☽ △ ⊏ (12)	2713
418.9	1770.2	Campsite, weak spring to east, fire tower north of camp, west of AT 🏕 △ ♦	3230
418.8	1770.3	Smarts Mountain, **Fire Wardens Cabin.** 21.9◄12.4◄6.7►5.3►21.0►27.9 Shelter is cabin north of summit, west of AT. Spring 0.2 in front of cabin. Clark Pond Loop Trail to east.	3218
414.9	1774.2	South Jacobs Brook ♦	1450
414.3	1774.8	Eastman Ledges 📷	1897
413.9	1775.2	North Jacobs Brook ♦	1917
413.5	1775.6	**Hexacuba Shelter** (0.3E) 17.7◄12.0◄5.3►15.7►22.6►31.6 ☽ △ ⊏ (8) Shelter on steep side trail, unreliable stream at intersection with side trail.	2051
411.9	1777.2	Mt Cube south peak, cross Rivendell Trail to west 📷	2911
411.8	1777.3	Side trail 0.3W to Mt Cube north peak. 📷	2878

❈ **Cattail** – A tall (head-high) plant that grows in swampy areas. Characteristic part of the plant looks like a fuzzy cigar impaled lengthwise on a spear.

5000

3000

1000

NoBo
SoBo

SoBo	NoBo	Description	Elev
410.2	1778.9	Brackett Brook	1506
409.3	1779.8	Stream.	1295
409.1	1780.0	Woods road	1197
408.5	1780.6	NH 25A (paved) NoBo east on road 300 yards . . . 43.9013,-71.9838 **P** (pg.190) **Wentworth, NH** (4.8E)	911
406.7	1782.4	Cape Moonshine Rd (gravel) . . . . 43.9158,-71.9646 **P** (pg.190) AT northbound joins Ore Hill Trail.	1431
406.0	1783.1	Ore Hill Campsite Muddy spring 100 yards downhill from tentsites.	1878
404.0	1785.1	Ore Hill.	1827
403.3	1785.8	Lake Tarleton Rd, NH 25C, **Warren, NH** (4E) . . . 43.9537,-71.9448**P** ◆ (pg.190) AT on road past parking area & power lines, Ore Hill Brook north of road.	1543
401.3	1787.8	Mt Mist	2200
401.0	1788.1	View.	1873
400.7	1788.4	Webster Slide Trail 0.7W to summit, view.	1678
398.7	1790.4	NH 25, Oliverian Brook north of road. . . . . . . 43.9899,-71.8895**P** (pg.191) AT: Ore Hill Tr ◆▶ Wachipauka Pond Tr, **Glencliff, NH** (0.3E), **Warren, NH** (5.0E)	1043
397.8	1791.3	**Jeffers Brook Shelter,** Jeffers Brook, footbridge 0.1 south . . . ◗ ◆ ⌒ (10)	1308
		27.7◀21.0◀15.7▶6.9▶15.9▶19.9	
397.7	1791.4	Long Pond Rd ⚠ NoBo 0.1E on road AT: Wachipauka Pond Tr ▲▶ Town Line Tr	1329
397.6	1791.5	High St (paved) ⚠ NoBo: 0.2W on road. AT: Town Line Trail ▲▶ Glencliff Trail	1344
397.2	1791.9	Stream.	1493
396.9	1792.2	Hurricane Trail to east	1661
396.1	1793.0	Stream.	2484
395.6	1793.5	Spring.	3005
393.2	1795.9	Mt Moosilauke, Gorge Brook Trail to east	4802
392.9	1796.2	AT: Glencliff Trail ▲▶ Beaver Brook Trail, Benton Trail to west	4561
391.3	1797.8	Ridge Trail to east	4048

⚠ The notation "AT: Ore Hill Tr ▲▶ Wachipauka Pond Tr" indicates that the AT to the south is coincident with the Ore Hill Tr; the AT to the north joins the Wachipauka Pond Tr.

SOBO	NOBO	Description	Elev.
390.9	1798.2	**Beaver Brook Shelter** 27.9◄22.6◄6.9▲▶9.0▶13.0▶28.1 . . . ☽ ◆ ♨ ⌂(10)	3732
		Shelter on Beaver Brook trail. Beaver Brook just past shelter.	
389.6	1799.5	Beaver Brook, footbridges, streams	1880
389.4	1799.7	Lost River Rd, NH 112, Kinsman Notch . . . 44.0398,-71.7921 **P** (pg.191) ◆	1870
		North Woodstock, NH (5.0E), **Lincoln, NH** (6.0E)	
388.7	1800.4	AT: Beaver Brook Trail ◄▶ Kinsman Ridge Trail	2662
		Dilly Cliff Trail to east	
386.1	1803.0	Gordon Pond Trail to east	2682
384.8	1804.3	Mt Wolf east peak, summit to west	3478
382.9	1806.2	Reel Brook Trail to west	2624
382.5	1806.6	Powerline	2602
381.9	1807.2	**Eliza Brook Shelter** 31.6◄15.9◄9.0▲▶4.0▶19.1▶24.6 . . . ☽ ◆ ♨(4) ⌂(8)	2386
		3 single tentpads, one double. Water source is brook.	
381.1	1808.0	Eliza Brook, parallel to AT for 0.8 mi	2861
380.5	1808.6	Harrington Pond	3411
379.4	1809.7	South Kinsman Mountain	4358
378.5	1810.6	North Kinsman Mountain	4293
378.0	1811.1	Mt Kinsman Trail to west.	3842
377.9	1811.2	**Kinsman Pond Shelter** 19.9◄13.0◄4.0▲▶15.1▶20.6▶29.6 . . . ☽ ◆ ♨(4) ⌂(16)	3746
		Caretaker, fee $8PP. Treat pond water. Kinsman Ridge Tr to west, Kinsman Pond Tr to east. AT: Kinsman Ridge Trail ◄▶ Fishin' Jimmy Trail	
377.0	1812.1	Stream.	2821
376.1	1813.0	Lonesome Lake Hut. . . . ☽ ◆ ⛺ (see AMC notes, pg.184)	2747
		AT: Fishin' Jimmy Tr ◄▶ Cascade Brook Tr (east), many other trail intersections	
375.1	1814.0	Kinsman Pond Trail to east.	2302
374.6	1814.5	Cascade Brook	2106
373.6	1815.5	Whitehouse Brook	1649
373.3	1815.8	US 3, I-93, AT underpass. Town east on US 3; better to take side trail (next entry)	1477
373.1	1816.0	Franconia Notch . . . 44.1002,-71.6825 **P** (pg.192)	1432
		Paved trail (1.0E) to Liberty Springs trailhead parking. **North Woodstock, NH** (4.8S) left from parking area on US 3. **Lincoln, NH** (1.0E) of North Woodstock. AT: Cascade Brook Trail ◄▶ Liberty Springs Trail	
372.4	1816.7	Flume side trail to east.	1843
371.9	1817.2	Streams	2067

NOBO
SOBO

NoBo	Mile	Description	Elev
370.4	1818.7	Liberty Spring Campsite. Overnight fee $8PP, caretaker, 7S and 3D platforms.	3905
370.2	1818.9	AT: Liberty Springs Tr ◀▶ Franconia Ridge Tr to west	4283
368.4	1820.7	Little Haystack Mountain, Falling Waters Trail to west. NoBo: AT above treeline for next 2.0 miles.	4800
367.7	1821.4	Mt Lincoln, Franconia Ridge	5089
366.7	1822.4	Mt Lafayette, Greenleaf Hut (1.1W). Greenleaf Hut visible from summit of Mt Lafayette. Located down steep Greenleaf Trail. AT: Franconia Ridge Trail ◀▶ Garfield Ridge Trail	5263
365.9	1823.2	Skookumchuck Trail to west	4727
363.6	1825.5	Garfield Pond	3880
363.2	1825.9	Mt Garfield	4458
363.0	1826.1	Garfield Trail to west	4249
362.8	1826.3	**Garfield Ridge Shelter/Campsite** (0.2W), reliable water. 28.1◀19.1◀15.1◀▶5.5▶14.5▶56.5 Overnight fee $8PP, caretaker.	3933
362.3	1826.8	Franconia Brook Trail to east goes steeply down 2.2mi to 13 Falls Campsite.	3435
360.7	1828.4	Gale River Trail to west	3418
360.1	1829.0	Frost Trail to Galehead Hut. ◀▶ Twinway Trail. AT: Garfield Ridge Trail ◀▶ Twinway Trail	3800
359.3	1829.8	South Twin Mountain, North Twin Spur Trail to west	4902
357.3	1831.8	**Guyot Shelter** 0.7E on Bondcliff Tr, plus 0.3 left on spur trail. 24.6◀20.6◀5.5◀▶9.0▶51.0▶57.1 Overnight fee $8PP, caretaker.	4515
357.2	1831.9	Mt Guyot, view to east.	4580
356.2	1832.9	Trail west to summit of Zeacliff Ridge	4037
354.9	1834.2	Zeacliff Pond to east	3788
354.5	1834.6	Zeacliff, Zeacliff Trail to east.	3758
354.3	1834.8	View to east.	3661
353.8	1835.3	Whitewall Brook, many streams leading to falls	3195
353.4	1835.7	Lend-A-Hand Trail to west	2667
353.2	1835.9	Zealand Falls Hut, next to falls	2617
353.0	1836.1	Ethan Pond Trail to west, AT: Twinway Trail ◀▶ Ethan Pond Trail	2462

NoBo
SoBo

1780.6   NH 25A, Gov. Meldrim Thomson Scenic Hwy

◭ **Mt Cube Sugar Farm** (1.9W) 603.353.4111 Owned by the Thomson family, for whom the road is named. Store is not manned, but caretaker makes frequent stops. Hikers may tent outside or may be allowed to stay in the sugar house. Sometimes more is offered. Open year-round, pets welcome.

Wentworth, NH 03282 (4.3E on NH 25A, then right 0.5 on NH 25)

⌂ M–F 9:30–12:30 & 1:30–4:30, Sa 7:15–12, 603.764.9444
🛒📞 **Shawnee's General Store** 603.764.5553 Open daily 5-8.

1782.4   Cape Moonshine Rd

◭ 🌫 **Dancing Bones Intentional Community** (1.4E) 802.440.1612 ⟨www.dancingbones.net⟩ Hot outdoor showers, open-air kitchen, tenting, composting toilets and good conversation. This is a residential community, so please be respectful when using shared facilities. Smoking is permitted in designated areas. Pets are welcome on a case by case basis.

1785.8   Lake Tarleton Rd, NH 25C
         Warren, NH 03279 (4E)

⌂ M-F 7:30-9:30 & 3-5, Sa 7:30-12, 603.764.5733
🍴 **Calamity Jane's Restaurant** 603.764.5288 Breakfast/Lunch W-Su, Dinner F-Sa

🍴 **Greenhouse Food & Spirits** 603.764.5708 Th,F 3-11pm, Sa 12-10, Su 12-8pm. Open mic Thursdays, band on Fridays.

🍴📶 **Moose Scoops** 603.764.9134 Open seasonally. Ice cream, hot dogs, soda, & hiking shirts. Free WiFi, wireless cell signal extender.

🛒 **Tedeschi Food Shop** 603.764.9002 Open daily 5-11. Grocery w/produce, deli w/sandwiches & pizza, deli closes 7pm Su-Th, 8pm F-Sa.

⚒ **Laundry** M-Su 8:30-8:30

🖥📶 **Library** 603.764.9072 M 9-1, Tu 1-5, W 3-7, Sa 10-1. No WiFi password, so you can use it after hours.

🔨 **Burning Bush Hardware** 603.764.9496 Open 7 days.

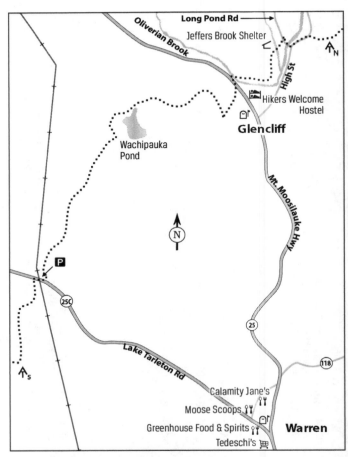

1790.4   NH 25   **Glencliff, NH 03238** (0.3E)
🏠 M-F 12-2, Sa 7-1, 603.989.5154
🏨🛅⊕🌐🔥⛺🛏📶🖥📧 **Hikers Welcome Hostel** 603.989.0040
Open early May to Oct 1. Bunk ($20) and camping ($15) includes shower. Shower only w/towel $2.50, laundry $2.50 wash, $2.50 dry. Snacks, sodas, and ice cream. All hikers (even non-guests) are welcome to hang out and enjoy huge DVD library. Slackpacking & shuttles (5 miles to resupply in Warren). Coleman/alcohol/oz. Tools to help with gear repair, and selection of used gear available, particularly winter wear. Pet Friendly. Both guests and non-guests are welcome to send maildrops (USPS/FedEx/UPS): c/o Hikers Welcome Hostel, 1396 NH Rt 25, PO Box 25, Glencliff, NH 03238

Warren, NH (5E) see entry pg. 190

1799.7   Lost River Rd, NH 112, Kinsman Notch
🏛 **Lost River Gorge** (0.5E) 603.745.8031 ⟨www.findlostriver.com⟩ Tourist attraction featuring a boulder jumble similar to Mahoosuc Notch. Gift store with microwavable food (and microwave), snacks, coffee, soda. Open early May - late Oct.
🛅💲🌐⛺🔥📧 **Lost River Valley Campground** (3.0E)
603.745.8321, 800.370.5678 ⟨www.lostriver.com⟩ cabin $60S, 70D, camping primitive sites $21, pets allowed but not in cabins. Showers, coin laundry, pay phone, open mid-May to Columbus Day 8-9, quiet 10pm-8am, owner Jim Kelly. Mail: 951 Lost River Rd, North Woodstock, NH 03262.
🏨📶 (16E) **Wise Way Wellness Center** 603.726.7600 Open May-Oct. $65 for 1-2 persons in cabin, includes light breakfast. $10PP for pickup & return from Franconia Notch, Kinsman Notch, North Woodstock, or Lincoln. Cabin is 10 miles south of Lincoln in Thornton, NH. This is a serene rustic cabin with no TV/phone. Bathroom and shower inside adjacent building. Amenities include pool, mini-fridge & grill. Licensed Massage Therapist on-site $35/30 min. Additional services: sauna and outdoor Epsom salt bath. No smoking or pets. Cash/checks/PayPal.

North Woodstock, NH (5E), **Lincoln, NH** (6E)
(See pg. 192)

Randolph Mountain Club (RMC)

Maintains the section of the AT from Edmands Col to Madison Hut and four shelters in the Northern Presidentials. Per-person fees for non-members: Gray Knob or Crag Camp $20, The Perch or Log Cabin $10. Fees must be paid in cash for stays at Gray Knob, Crag Camp and The Perch. Persons without cash can stay at the Log Cabin and will receive a receipt to mail in their fee. There is a caretaker year-round at Gray Knob if you need assistance or have questions. During the summer months, a second caretaker is in residence at Crag Camp. A caretaker visits Crag Camp and The Perch every evening throughout the year.

Shelter use is first-come, first-served; no reservations. Weekends are busy. If space is not available, be prepared to camp. Camping is not permitted within a quarter mile of RMC shelters.

There is no trash disposal. Carry in, carry out. Please keep noise to a minimum after 10pm. The use of cell phones and portable TVs is not permitted. Group size is limited to ten. There is no smoking inside RMC facilities. When a camp is full, all guests are asked to limit their stay to two consecutive nights. Outdoor wood campfires are not allowed at any of the camps. Dogs are allowed at RMC's facilities, but they should be under voice control at all times.

🚌 **AMC Hiker Shuttle** 603.466.2727 Schedule on-line: ⟨www.outdoors.org/lodging/lodging-shuttle.cfm⟩ Operates June - mid Sept daily, and weekends and holidays through mid Oct. Stops at Lincoln, Franconia Notch (Liberty Springs Trailhead), Crawford Notch (Webster Cliff Trailhead), Highland Center, Pinkham Notch, and Gorham; $23 for non-members. Walk-ons if space available.

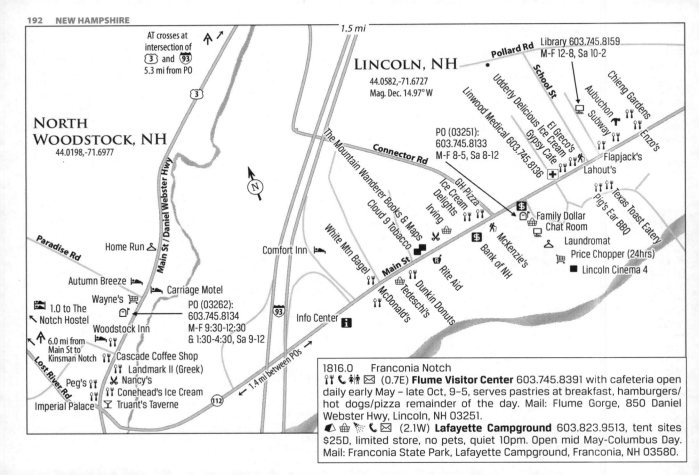

1.5 mi

AT crosses at intersection of ③ and ⑨③ 5.3 mi from PO

LINCOLN, NH
44.0582,-71.6727
Mag. Dec. 14.97° W

Pollard Rd

Library 603.745.8159
M-F 12-8, Sa 10-2

School St

Chieng Gardens

Udderly Delicious Ice Cream

Linwood Medical 603.745.8136

Aubuchon

Subway

Enzo's

NORTH WOODSTOCK, NH
44.0198,-71.6977

The Mountain Wanderer Books & Maps

Connector Rd

PO (03251):
603.745.8133
M-F 8-5, Sa 8-12

El Greco's
Gypsy Cafe

Flapjack's

Lahout's

Texas Toast Eatery
Pig's Ear BBQ

GH Pizza
Ice Cream Delights
Irving

Paradise Rd

Home Run

Main St / Daniel Webster Hwy

Cloud 9 Tobacco

White Mtn Bagel

Comfort Inn

Family Dollar
Chat Room

McKenzie's

Bank of NH

Laundromat
Price Chopper (24hrs)

Lincoln Cinema 4

Autumn Breeze

Carriage Motel

Wayne's

PO (03262):
603.745.8134
M-F 9:30-12:30
& 1:30-4:30, Sa 9-12

Rite Aid

Main St

Info Center

Dunkin Donuts

Tedeschi's

McDonald's

1.0 to The Notch Hostel

6.0 mi from Main St to Kinsman Notch

Woodstock Inn

Cascade Coffee Shop

Landmark II (Greek)

Nancy's

Peg's

Conehead's Ice Cream

Imperial Palace

Truant's Taverne

Lost River Rd

1.4 mi between POs

1816.0   Franconia Notch
(0.7E) **Flume Visitor Center** 603.745.8391 with cafeteria open daily early May – late Oct, 9-5, serves pastries at breakfast, hamburgers/hot dogs/pizza remainder of the day. Mail: Flume Gorge, 850 Daniel Webster Hwy, Lincoln, NH 03251.
(2.1W) **Lafayette Campground** 603.823.9513, tent sites $25D, limited store, no pets, quiet 10pm. Open mid May-Columbus Day. Mail: Franconia State Park, Lafayette Campground, Franconia, NH 03580.

📪📶✉ (1.2E) **Profile Motel & Cottages** 603.745.2759
Fridge & microwave in room, grills & tables outside, open 7am-10pm, closed Nov-Mar. Mail: 391 US 3, Lincoln, NH 03251.

📪⛺📶✉ (3.0E) **Mt. Liberty Motel** 603.745.3600
⟨www.MtLibertyMotel.com⟩ Open May-Oct. $85+ in season, $59+ off season includes pickup/return from Kinsman/Franconia Notch and town shuttle. Laundry $5. No smoking or pets. CC accepted. Mail: 10 Liberty Road, Lincoln, NH 03251.

🚐 **AMC Hiker Shuttle** (pg. 191)

🚐 **The Shuttle Connection** 603.745.3140 Shuttles between town & Kinsman or Franconia Notch or to bus terminals and airports ranging from Portland, ME to NY. Can handle large groups.

🚐 **Notch Taxi Service** 603.991.8777 Reservations recommended, runs 7 days. Hikers welcome.

North Woodstock, NH (4.8S of Franconia Notch)

🏕️⛲⛺🚐📶🖥️✉ **The Notch Hostel** 603.348.1483
⟨www.notchhostel.com⟩ Bunk in large, white farmhouse on Rt. 112 (Lost River Rd). 1.0W of North Woodstock / Lincoln. Ideally situated for slackpack between Kinsman & Franconia Notch. $30pp includes bunk, fresh linens, towel, shower, laundry service, coffee/tea, make-your-own pancake breakfast, AM trailhead drop-off (Kinsman or Franconia Notch), WiFi, computer, guest kitchens and fridges, large yard. Check-in 4-9pm (earlier OK, call ahead). Rental bikes available for town trips. Beer & wine OK in moderation. No liquor. Small camp store including pizza, ice cream, soda. Mail drops: c/o The Notch Hostel, 324 Lost River Rd, North Woodstock, NH 03262.

📪🍴📶 **Woodstock Inn** 603.745.3951, 800.321.3985
⟨www.woodstockinnnh.com⟩ 10% discount for thru-hikers, prices seasonal, stay includes full breakfast. Pet rooms available. **Woodstock Station** restaurant, outdoor bar, and a micro-brewery on-site.

📪⛺📶 **Autumn Breeze** 603.745.8549
⟨www.autumnbreezemotel.com⟩ Open year-round, hiker friendly. $60 hiker rate includes kitchenette, laundry, shuttle to/from trail. One pet room. Shuttle to town if available. CC accepted.

📪📶✉ **The Carriage Motel** 603.745.2416

⟨www.carriagemotel.com⟩ $69/up, no pets, game room, pool, grills. Mail: PO Box 198, 180 Main St, North Woodstock, NH 03262.

🍴🍴💲 **Wayne's Market** 603.745.8819 Deli, ATM, cheap sandwiches, large beer selection. Open year-round, daily 5-10.

🏪 **Fadden's General Store & Sugar House** 603.745.8371 Ice cream, fudge and more. Open year-round, daily 9-5.

Lincoln, NH (5.8S of Franconia Notch)

📪 **Wise Way Wellness Center** 10S of Lincoln, listing pg. 191.

🧍 **Lahout's Summit Shop** ⟨www.lahouts.com⟩
603.745.2882 M-F 9:30-5:30, Sa 9-5:30, Su 9-5, full service outfitter, packs, Coleman/alcohol/oz, canister fuel, freeze-dried foods.

🖥️ **Chat Room Coffee House & Books** M-Sa 10-6.

⬛ **Mountain Wanderer** 603.745.2594 Open most days 10-5:30. Book and map store has everything you need to navigate the Whites.

Franconia, NH 03580 (11W of Franconia notch)

🏤 M-F 8:30-1 & 2-5, Sa 9-12, 603.823.5611

📪⛺🚐📶🖥️✉ **Gale River Motel** 603.823.5655 800.255.7989
⟨www.galerivermotel.com⟩ $50–$200, pets with approval, laundry wash $1, dry $1, Coleman/oz. Free pickup/return to trail w/stay, longer shuttles for a fee. Open year-round. CC accepted. Mail (fee for non-guest): 1 Main Street, Franconia, NH 03580.

🍴 **Mac's Market** 603.823.7795 Open daily 7-8.

🏪🍴 **Franconia Village Store** 603.823.7782 Open M-Sa 6-9, Su 6:30-7, deli.

📶🖥️ **Abbie Greenleaf Library** 603.823.8424 M-W 2-6, Th 10-12 & 2-5, F 2-5, Sa 10-1.

Littleton, NH (17W)

🧍📶 **Badass Outdoors Gear Shop** 603.444.9445 Full service outfitter 17 miles west (compass north) from Franconia Notch. Thru-hiker discount. Hiker food, canister fuel & experienced staff. Open Tu-Th 11-5, F-Sa 10-6, Su 11-5. Sometimes rides are available.

SoBo	NoBo	Description	Elev.
351.6	1837.5	Zeacliff Trail to east.	2445
350.8	1838.3	Stream, Thoreau Falls to east.	2464
350.6	1838.5	Footbridge, stream.	2464
350.3	1838.8	Stream, Shoal Pond Trail to east	2509
349.6	1839.5	Footbridge, stream.	2626
348.3	1840.8	**Ethan Pond Campsite** (0.2W), Ethan Pond, inlet brook to pond. 29.6◄14.5◄9.0►42.0►48.1►61.8 Overnight fee $8PP, caretaker, 3S and 2D platforms.	2855
347.2	1841.9	Willey Range Trail to west, stream north on AT	2621
347.0	1842.1	Kedron Flume Trail to west.	2457
345.9	1843.2	Ripley Falls 0.5E	1558
345.7	1843.4	RR tracks, parking, AT: Ethan Pond Trail ►road walk. 44.1771,-71.3861 [P]	1436
345.4	1843.7	Crawford Notch, US 302. AT: road walk ►Webster Cliff Trail (pg.196)	1277
345.3	1843.8	Saco River (treat), Saco River Trail to east, Sam Willey Trail to west.	1261
344.6	1844.5	Stream.	1939
343.0	1846.1	Webster Cliffs, views from many spots along 0.5 mile traverse	3288
342.1	1847.0	Mt Webster, Webster Jackson Trail to west, NoBo: AT to east	3910
340.7	1848.4	Mt Jackson, Webster Jackson Trail to west. SoBo hikers turn east (left)	4052
339.0	1850.1	Mizpah cutoff to west, Mizpah Spring Hut to east, Nauman Campsite Tent site next to hut, overnight fee $8PP.	3800
338.2	1850.9	Mt Pierce (Mt Clinton)	4312
338.1	1851.0	AT: Webster Cliff Trail ►Crawford Path	4258
337.0	1852.1	Mt Eisenhower Loop Trail west to summit.	4448
336.4	1852.7	Mt Eisenhower Loop Trail west to summit.	4464
336.3	1852.8	Mt Eisenhower Trail to east	4494
335.4	1853.7	Mt Franklin	5004
335.1	1854.1	Mt Monroe Loop Trail west to summit	5080
334.7	1854.7	Mt Monroe Loop Trail west to summit	5095
334.4	1854.7	Lakes of the Clouds Hut. See map, several trails in area (pg.196)	5047
333.5	1855.6	Davis Path to east, Westside Trail to west	5592
333.1	1856.0	AT: Crawford Path ►Trinity Heights Connector	6172
332.9	1856.1	Mt Washington (pg.197)	6288
332.7	1856.4	AT: Trinity Heights Connector ►Gulfside Trail	6104
332.5	1856.6	Cross Cog Railroad, stay west on Gulfside Trail.	5933

NoBo

SoBo

NOBO	SOBO	Description	Elev
332.0	1857.1	Westside Trail to west	5504
331.7	1857.4	Mt Clay Loop Trail to east.	5441
330.9	1858.2	Mt Clay Loop Trail to east, Sphinx Trail to east	5021
330.1	1859.0	Mt Jefferson Loop Trail, summit 0.3W	5405
329.7	1859.4	Six Husband Trail 0.4W to Mt Jefferson	5336
329.2	1859.9	Edmands Col, Gulfside Spring 50 yards east on Edmands Col cutoff, Randolph Path & Mt Jefferson loop to west.	4947
328.6	1860.5	Israel Ridge Path to RMC Perch Shelter (0.9W), $7 fee.	5269
328.5	1860.6	Peabody Spring to east near boulder	5251
328.1	1861.0	Thunderstorm Junction, RMC cabins to west (pg.197)	5500
327.5	1861.6	Airline Trail, King Ravine Trail to west	5150
327.2	1861.9	Madison Spring Hut, Valley Way Trail 0.6W to VW Tent Site, no fee	4800
		AT: Gulfside Trail ▼ ▶ Osgood Trail	
326.7	1862.4	Mt Madison, Watson Path to west.	5366
326.4	1862.7	Howker Ridge Trail to east	5113
326.1	1863.0	Parapet Trail to east, Daniel Webster Trail to west.	4878

There are no blazes in the Great Gulf Wilderness area, approx. Mt. Madison to Auto Rd

NOBO	SOBO	Description	Elev
324.1	1865.0	Osgood Tent Site to west, no fee. AT: Osgood Trail ▼ ▶ Osgood Cutoff.	2555
323.9	1865.2	Stream.	2542
323.5	1865.6	AT: Osgood Cutoff ▼ ▶ Great Gulf Trail to east. (see map pg.197)	2341
323.5	1865.6	Parapet Brook, AT: Great Gulf Trail ▼ ▶ Madison Gulf Trail to west	2329
323.4	1865.7	West branch of Peabody River, suspension bridge. Great Gulf Tr to east	2300
322.9	1866.2	Stream.	2412
322.5	1867.1	Stream.	2582
321.5	1867.6	Lowes Bald Spot 0.1W	2849
321.4	1867.7	Mt Washington Auto Rd 44.2815,-71.2534 P	2734
		AT: Madison Gulf Trail ▼ ▶ Old Jackson Rd	
321.2	1867.9	Nelson Crag Trail and Raymond Path to east	2679
320.4	1868.7	George's Gorge Trail to west	2570
320.1	1869.0	Peabody River, four other trails cross the AT from here to Pinkham Notch	2271
319.4	1869.7	NH 16, Pinkham Notch 44.2569,-71.2526 P (pg.196)	2050
		Gorham, NH (10.7W), AT: Old Jackson Rd ▼ ▶ Lost Pond Trail	
318.4	1870.7	AT: Lost Pond Trail ▼ ▶ Wildcat Ridge Trail	2009
318.0	1871.1	View.	2860
317.4	1871.7	Rocky crevasse, stairs	3273
316.7	1872.4	Wildcat Mountain peak E.	4066
316.4	1872.7	Wildcat Mountain peak D, observation tower, ski gondola 0.1 north. Gondola rides to/from the AT, $12 round trip, restaurant at base, open Jul-Oct.	3990
315.3	1873.8	Wildcat Mountain peak C.	4278
314.4	1874.7	Wildcat Mountain peak A.	4422
313.9	1875.2	Spring.	3675
313.7	1875.4	AT: Wildcat Ridge Trail ▼ ▶ Nineteen Mile Brook Trail to east.	3401
313.5	1875.6	AT: Nineteen Mile Brook Trail ▼ ▶ Carter Moriah Trail, Carter Notch Hut (0.1E).	3303
312.8	1876.3	Spring to west	4308

1843.7　Crawford Notch, US 302

¶ℓ (1W) **Willey House** 603.374.0999 Snack bar open 9:30-5, 7 days, weekend before Memorial Day - weekend after Columbus Day.

◢ ⚑ ⌂ (1.8E) **Dry River Campground** 603.374.2272 〈www.nhstateparks.com/crawford.html〉 Tent sites $25 for 2 adults and children. Shelter $30D, $10EAP. Pets allowed, coin laundry & showers, sometimes rides avaiable, quiet 10pm-8am. Open May-late Oct, reduced services through Nov.

▭ 🏠¶ℓ ⚑ ₪ ⌖ ✉ (3.5W) **AMC Highland Center** 603.278.4453 〈www.outdoors.org〉 Rates seasonal and are highest in summer and during holidays. Lodge $50-$150PP/up includes dinner & breakfast. Shapleigh Bunkhouse $81 with dinner & breakfast, $54 with B only. Rates lower for AMC members. No pets, no smoking. AMC Shuttle stops daily mid-Jun to Columbus Day, afterwards only weekends and holidays. Restaurant open to all for B/L/D. Store sells snacks, sodas, some clothing and canister fuel. Mail (include ETA): Route 302, Bretton Woods, NH 03574.

▭ ◢ ⚑ (E3.3) **Crawford Notch General Store & Campground** 603.374.2779 〈www.crawfordnotch.com〉 Cabins $75-95, tent sites (hold 2 tents) $30. 9% lodging tax. Store carries hiker foods, ice cream and beer. Open mid May - mid Oct.

🚌 **Notch Taxi Service** 603.991.8777 Covers northern NH. Hikers welcome.

🚌 **AMC Hiker Shuttle** (pg. 191)

Bretton Woods, NH (8.0W)

¶ℓ **Fabyan's Station** 603.278.2222 Open year-round 11:30-9 (limited hours in winter).

🏃 **Drummonds Mountain Shop** 603.278.7547 Open year-round, 7 days. Boots, packs, rain gear, hiking foods, stoves and fuel. 〈www.drummondsmountainshop.com〉

Bartlett, NH (13.0E from Crawford Notch)
Resort town has unique mountain roller coaster and water slide at **Attitash Resort** 800.223.7669 〈www.attitash.com〉.

1854.7　Lakes of the Clouds Hut

▭ 🏠◗ ☽ Lodging and WFS (see AMC notes, pg. 184). Also "The Dungeon," a bunkroom available to 6 thru-hikers for $10PP with access to hut restroom and the common area. When the hut is closed, The Dungeon serves as an emergency shelter.

1856.2　Mt Washington, NH

⌂(03589) M-S 10-4 For outgoing mail; do not send maildrops.

¶ℓ ⚑ 🏃ℓ Second highest peak on the AT. **Sherman Adams Bldg** (part of Mt. Washington State Park) 603.466.3347 Open 8am-6pm mid-May to Columbus Day, sometimes opens earlier on wkends in season. Snack bar 9am-6pm, sometimes closes earlier.

🚂 **Cog Railway** 603.278.5404 〈www.thecog.com〉 Runs hourly Apr-Nov. One-way tickets $46 (if space-available) sold at summit station. Base station 3 miles away near Bretton Woods, NH.

1861.0　Thunderstorm Junction

🏠 **Crag Camp Cabin** (1.1W) on Spur Trail, **Gray Knob Cabin** (1.2W) on Lowe Path; $20 fee for either. If you camp along these side trails, it must be at least 0.25mi. from either cabin.

1869.7　NH 16, Pinkham Notch

🏠¶ℓ 🏃ℓ ⚑ ℓ⌖✉ **Pinkham Notch Visitor Center & Joe Dodge Lodge** 603.466.2721 〈www.outdoors.org〉 Rates seasonal and are highest in summer and during holidays. Bunkroom starting at $63PP w/o meals; $69 with breakfast; $89 with dinner & breakfast. Private rooms also available. Rates on lodging and meals discounted for AMC members. Meals available to non-guests; AYCE breakfast 6:30-9 daily, a la carte lunch, family-style dinner Sat-Thurs at 6pm, Friday dinner buffet. Open year-round. Coin-op shower available 24hrs, $2 towel rental. No pets. Vending machines, Coleman/alcohol/oz, canister fuel. Shuttle 7:30am daily. Accepts credit cards. Mail: AMC Visitor Center, c/o Front Desk, 361 Rte. 16, Gorham, NH 03581.

Gorham, NH (10.7W from Pinkham Notch)

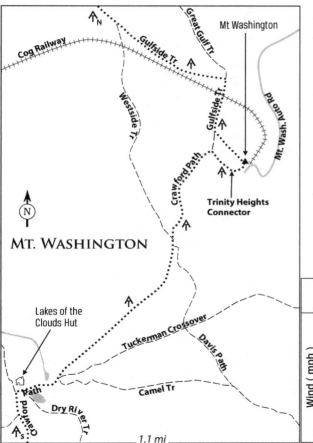

Mt Washington

Cog Railway

Gulfside Tr

Great Gulf Tr

Westside Tr

Gulfside Tr

Mt. Wash. Auto Rd

Crawford Path

Trinity Heights Connector

N

MT. WASHINGTON

Lakes of the Clouds Hut

Tuckerman Crossover

Davis Path

Path

Camel Tr

Crawford Path

Dry River Tr

N
s

1.1 mi

1865.0 - 1866.2 Map of trail intersections

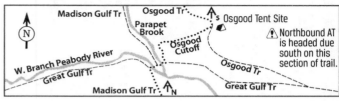

Madison Gulf Tr

Osgood Tr

Osgood Tent Site

Parapet Brook

⚠ Northbound AT is headed due south on this section of trail.

Osgood Cutoff

W. Branch Peabody River

Osgood Tr

Great Gulf Tr

Madison Gulf Tr

Great Gulf Tr

N
s

N

National Weather Service Wind Chill Chart

		Temperature (°F)												
		35	30	25	20	15	10	5	0	-5	-10	-15	-20	-25
Wind (mph)	5	31	25	19	13	7	1	-5	-11	-16	-22	-28	-34	-40
	10	27	21	15	9	3	-4	-10	-16	-22	-28	-35	-41	-47
	15	25	19	13	6	0	-7	-13	-19	-26	-32	-39	-45	-51
	20	24	17	11	4	-2	-9	-15	-22	-29	-35	-42	-48	-55
	25	23	16	9	3	-4	-11	-17	-24	-31	-37	-44	-51	-58
	30	22	15	8	1	-5	-12	-19	-26	-33	-39	-46	-53	-60
	35	21	14	7	0	-7	-14	-21	-27	-34	-41	-48	-55	-62
	40	20	13	6	-1	-8	-15	-22	-29	-36	-43	-50	-57	-64

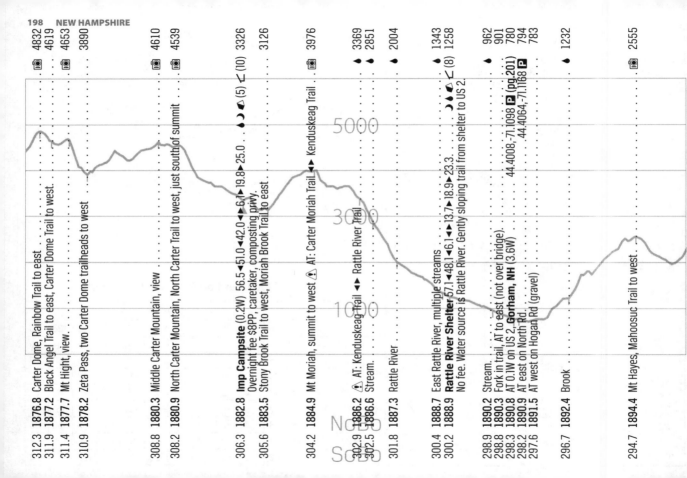

NoBo	Mile	Description	Features	Elev
312.3	1876.8	Carter Dome, Rainbow Trail to east	📷	4832
311.9	1877.2	Black Angel Trail to east, Carter Dome Trail to west.		4619
311.4	1877.7	Mt Hight, view.	📷	4653
310.9	1878.2	Zeta Pass, two Carter Dome trailheads to west		3890
308.8	1880.3	Middle Carter Mountain, view	📷	4610
308.2	1880.9	North Carter Mountain, North Carter Trail to west, just south of summit	📷	4539
306.3	1882.8	**Imp Campsite** (0.2W) 56.5◀51.0◀42.0◀▶6.1▶19.8▶25.0 Overnight fee $8PP, caretaker, composting privy.	◑ ♦ (5) ⓒ (10)	3326
305.6	1883.5	Stony Brook Trail to west, Moriah Brook Trail to east		3126
304.2	1884.9	Mt Moriah, summit to west ⚠ AT: Carter Moriah Trail ◆ Kenduskeag Trail	📷	3976
302.9	1886.2	⚠ AT: Kenduskeag Trail ◆▶ Rattle River Trail	♦	3369
302.5	1886.6	Stream.	♦	2851
301.8	1887.3	Rattle River	♦	2004
300.4	1888.7	East Rattle River, multiple streams	♦	1343
300.2	1888.9	**Rattle River Shelter** 57.1◀48.1◀6.1◀▶13.7▶18.9▶23.3. No fee. Water source is Rattle River. Gently sloping trail from shelter to US 2.	◑♦◆ ⓒ (8)	1258
298.9	1890.2	Stream.	♦	962
298.8	1890.3	Fork in trail, AT to east (not over bridge).		901
298.3	1890.8	AT 0.1W on US 2, **Gorham, NH** (3.6W) 44.4008,-71.1098 🅿 (pg.201)		780
298.2	1890.9	AT east on North Rd. 44.4064,-71.1168 🅿		794
297.6	1891.5	AT west on Hogan Rd (gravel)		783
296.7	1892.4	Brook	♦	1232
294.7	1894.4	Mt Hayes, Mahoosuc Trail to west.	📷	2555

SoBo

293.1	**1896.0**	View	🏕	2341
292.5	**1896.6**	Cascade Mountain		2631
291.4	**1897.7**	Trident Col Campsite (0.2W), no fee, spring on side trail	🌙◐	2020
291.1	**1898.0**	Spring	◐	1909
290.4	**1898.7**	Page Pond	◐	2220
289.8	**1899.3**	Wocket Ledge, view	🏕◐	2642
289.3	**1899.8**	Stream	◐	2589
288.6	**1900.5**	Dream Lake, Peabody Brook Trail to east	◐	2610

◀ ME camping: AT hikers are encouraged to use designated campsites. Dispersed camping is permitted except for specific prohibitions. Look for local postings at signposts and shelters; prohibitions listed in this guidebook are not comprehensive. Camping at non-designated locations is prohibited above treeline (where trees are less than 8' tall).

286.5	**1902.6**	**Gentian Pond Shelter/Campsite** (0.2E)	🌙◐◁⊏ (14)	2162
		61.8◄19.8◄13.7◄►5.2►9.6►14.7 Junction of Mahoosuc Trail (AT) and Austin Brook Trail, inlet brook of Gentian Pond. 3S and 1D platforms.		
285.5	**1903.6**	Stream	◐	2246
285.1	**1904.0**	Stream	◐	2505
283.7	**1905.4**	Mt Success	🏕	3565
283.1	**1906.0**	Success Trail to west		3171

⚐ Camp fires are only allowed along the AT in ME within fireplaces at designated campsites.

281.8	**1907.3**	**NH-ME** border		2972
281.3	**1907.8**	**Carlo Col Shelter and Campsite** (0.3W), on Carlo Col Trail	🌙◐◁⊏ (16)	3191
		25.0◄18.9◄5.2◄►4.4►9.5►16.4 Platforms 3S and 2D, bear box, no fee.		
280.9	**1908.2**	Mt Carlo		3565
279.5	**1909.6**	Goose Eye Mountain west peak; Goose Eye Mtn Trail to west	🏕	3810
279.1	**1910.0**	Goose Eye Mountain east peak		3790
278.8	**1910.3**	Wright Trail to east		3452
277.9	**1911.2**	Goose Eye Mountain north peak	🏕	3672
276.9	**1912.2**	**Full Goose Shelter and Campsite** 3S and 1D platforms	🌙◐◁⊏ (12)	2948
		23.3◄9.6◄4.4◄►5.1►12.0►15.5 No Fee, stream behind shelter.		
276.4	**1912.7**	Fulling Mill Mountain south peak		3395
275.3	**1913.8**	Mahoosuc Notch south end, Mahoosuc Notch Trail to west	◐	2492
		Most difficult or fun mile of the AT. Make way through jumbled pit of boulders.		
274.2	**1914.9**	Mahoosuc Notch north end, Bull Branch, campsite	◐◁	2165

NoBo
SoBo

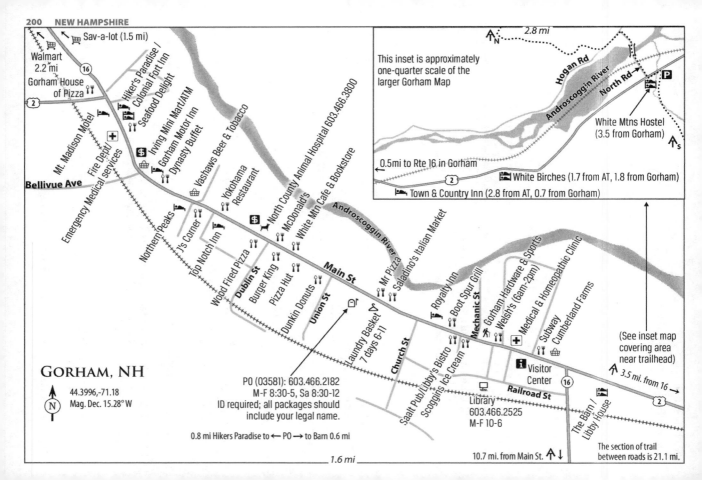

← Sav-a-lot (1.5 mi)

Walmart 2.2 mi

(16)

Gorham House of Pizza

(2)

Hiker's Paradise / Colonial Fort Inn

Seafood Delight

Mt. Madison Motel

Fire Dept/ Emergency Medical services

Irving White Mart/ATM

Gorham Motor Inn

Dynasty Buffet

Bellivue Ave

Vashaws Beer & Tobacco

Northern Peaks

1's Corner

Top Notch Inn

Yokohama Restaurant

North County Animal Hospital 603.466.3800

McDonald's

White Mtn Cafe & Bookstore

Dublin St

Wood Fired Pizza

Burger King

Pizza Hut

Dunkin Donuts

Union St

Main St

Androscoggin River

Mr Pizza

Saladino's Italian Market

Royalty Inn

Boot Spur Grill

Mechanic St

Gorham Hardware & Sports

Welsh's (8am-2pm)

Medical & Homeopathic Clinic

Subway

Cumberland Farms

Laundry Basket 7 days 6-11

PO (03581): 603.466.2182
M-F 8:30-5, Sa 8:30-12
ID required; all packages should include your legal name.

Church St

Saalt Pub/Libby's Bistro

Scoggins Ice Cream

GORHAM, NH

(N) 44.3996,-71.18
Mag. Dec. 15.28° W

0.8 mi Hikers Paradise to ← PO → to Barn 0.6 mi

i Visitor Center

(16)

Railroad St

Library
603.466.2525
M-F 10-6

The Barn / Libby House

(2)

(See inset map covering area near trailhead)

3.5 mi. from 16 →

The section of trail between roads is 21.1 mi.

10.7 mi. from Main St.

— 1.6 mi —

Inset map

2.8 mi

N

Hogan Rd

Androscoggin River

North Rd

P

White Mtns Hostel (3.5 from Gorham)

S

This inset is approximately one-quarter scale of the larger Gorham Map

0.5mi to Rte 16 in Gorham

(2)

White Birches (1.7 from AT, 1.8 from Gorham)

Town & Country Inn (2.8 from AT, 0.7 from Gorham)

1890.8   US 2, Rattle River Trailhead

ⓘⒶⓂⓎⓍⒶ🚐🛜🖥✉🅿 **White Mountains Lodge & Hostel**
603.466.5049   ⟨www.whitemountainslodgeandhostel.com⟩
Directly on AT at the northern Gorham trailhead (Rte. 2 & North Rd).
Clean, B&B style rooms, some private, w/fresh linens & towels.
$35PP includes, huge gourmet breakfast, laundry, loaner clothes,
showers, computer, town & resupply shuttles. Liquid and canister
fuel, sodas, ice cream, snacks for sale. Shuttle and slackpack
(21 mi) from Pinkham Notch (Gorham 1 exit) free w/2 nights stay.
Parking for section hikers. Open June 1-Oct 8. Maildrops (also free
for non-guests): 592 State Rte. 2, Shelburne, NH 03581

ⓘⒶⓂⓍⒶ🛜✉ (1.7W) **White Birches Camping Park**
603.466.2022 ⟨www.whitebirchescamping.com⟩ bunks $15, tent
sites $13PP, pool, air hockey, pool table, pets allowed, Coleman/
alcohol/oz and canister fuel. Free shuttle from/to trail and town
with stay, open May-Oct. CC accepted. Guest mail ($5 fee for non-
guest): 218 US 2, Shelburne, NH 03581.

   Gorham, NH 03581 (3.6W from US 2 RR Trailhead)
🏠 ID required; all packages should include your legal name.
🛏🍴🛜🖥 (2.6W) **Town and Country Inn** 603.466.3315 Open year-
round. ⟨www.townandcountryinn.com⟩ $64-129 seasonal, pets
$10. Breakfast 6-10:30, dinner 5-9, cocktails. Indoor pool, sauna.

🛏ⓘⒶⓂⓎ🚐Ⓐ🛜✉ **Libby House B&B & The Barn Hikers Hostel**
603.466.2271 Bunks $22, tenting $15PP, B&B rooms available,
Hot country b'fast available. Fast, free pickup & return to Rte 2
trailhead for guests. Shuttle from Pinkham Notch free with 2 night
stay to facilitate slackpacking. Celebrating more than 30 years of
professional services, located within walking distance of shops &
restaurants in town; shuttle to Walmart. Clean beds with linens,
full kitchen with cookware & refrigerator, lounge with big screen
TV. Laundry $5, No pets. Visa MC accepted. Open year-round. Mail
free for guests, $15 fee for non-guests: 55 Main Street, Gorham,
NH 03581.

🛏ⓘⒶⓂⓎⒶ🛜 **Hiker's Paradise** at Colonial Fort Inn
603.466.2732 ⟨www.hikersparadise.com⟩ bunks $24 (includes
tax) with linen, tub/shower, kitchen. Private rooms available. Coin

laundry for guests. Restaurant serves breakfast. Coleman/alcohol/
oz. Free shuttle with stay from/to Route 2, other limited shuttles.
CC accepted. Smoking only on outside porch. No pets or maildrops.

🛏🍴Ⓐ🛜 **Royalty Inn** 603.466.3312 ⟨www.royaltyinn.com⟩ Hiker
rate $79 wkday, $89 wkend (subject to change). Indoor pool,
sauna, A/C. **Guldies Restaurant** on site serves B/L.

🛏Ⓐ🛜✉ **Top Notch Inn** 603.466.5496
⟨www.topnotchinn.com⟩ Guest laundry, limited shuttles, pool, hot
tub, behaved dogs under 50 lbs okay, no smoking, CC accepted.
10% local restaurant discount. Open May-mid Oct. Guest mail: 265
Main St, Gorham, NH 03581.

🛏🛜 **Northern Peaks Motor Inn** 603.466.2288
⟨www.northernpeaksmotorinn.com⟩ $70/up + tax. A/C, pets $5, no
smoking, all major credit cards accepted, hiker friendly.

🛏🛜 **Gorham Motor Inn** 603.466.3381 $58-$158 Open May-Oct.

🚶Ⓜ **Gorham Hardware & Sports** 603.466.2312 Open M-F 8-5:30,
Sa 8-4, Su 8-1. Close Su after Columbus Day. Hiking poles, Water
treatment, hiking food, cold-weather clothes, White gas/alcohol/
oz & canisters. Visa/MC/Disc.

🚐 **Trail Angels Hiker Services** 978.855.9227 Shuttles covering NH
& ME.

🚐 **Concord Coach** 800.639.3317 Bus service 7:50am daily from
Irving Mini Mart to Pinkham Notch. $7 one-way, $13 round-trip.

   Berlin, NH (10W from US 2)
➕ **Androscoggin Valley Hospital** 603.752.2200
   Lancaster, NH (28W from US 2)

🚶ⒷⓘⒶⓎⓌⒶ🚐🛜✉ **Hikers Hostel at the Yellow Deli**
603.788.3031 ⟨www.hikershostel.org⟩ Run by a Twelve Tribes
spiritual community. Shuttle times (for Crawford Notch, Pinkham
Notch, and Rattle River trailheads): 8:30am and 6:30pm. $20
suggested donation, WFS when available. Kitchenette and
laundry. No alcohol, no smoking. Stay includes breakfast and 15%
off at **Simon the Tanner** (adjacent footwear and clothing Outfitter,
open 9-5 S-Th, F 9-3). Mail: Hiker Hostel, 65 Main Street, Lancaster,
NH 03584.

273.2	1915.9	Spring	3291
272.7	1916.4	Mahoosuc Arm	3770
272.0	1917.1	Speck Pond brook	3414
271.8	1917.3	**Speck Pond Shelter & Campsite.** ☽♦⚑⌂ (8)	3419
		14.7◄9.5◄5.1◄►6.9►10.4►20.9 Overnight fee $8PP, caretaker. Spring down	
		Speck Pond Trail just beyond caretaker's yurt. 3S and 3D platforms	
270.7	1918.4	Intersection, AT north on Old Speck Tr., south on Mahoosuc Tr. 🅿📷🗼	4023
		Side Trail 0.3E to Old Speck summit and observation tower.	
268.4	1920.7	Eyebrow Trail to west	2508
268.1	1921.0	Stream. ♦	2376
267.3	1921.8	Eyebrow Trail to west	1522
267.2	1921.9	Grafton Notch, ME 26 44.5897, -70.9467 🅿 🏛 ☽ (pg.206)	1495
266.4	1922.7	Stream, Table Rock Trail to east ♦	2105
264.9	1924.2	**Baldpate Lean-to** (0.1E), stream next to lean-to ☽♦⚑ (8)	2665
		16.4◄12.0◄6.9◄►3.5►14.0►26.8	
264.1	1925.0	Baldpate west peak 📷	3662
263.2	1925.9	Baldpate east peak, Grafton Loop Trail 📷	3810
261.4	1927.7	**Frye Notch Lean-to,** Frye Brook in front of lean-to ☽♦⚑ (6)	2283
		15.5◄10.4◄3.5◄►10.5►23.3►31.6	

📶 **(NoBo)** Poor cell reception at East B Hill Rd, consider calling ahead if you need ride.

257.6	1931.5	Dunn Notch and Falls. ♦	1249
256.9	1932.2	East B Hill Rd (paved), stream 44.6683, -70.8932 🅿 ♦ (pg.206)	1485
		Andover, ME (8.0E)	
256.6	1932.5	Stream. ♦	1684
255.0	1934.1	Surplus Pond. Two woods roads 100 yards apart. ♦	2080
		0.1W on southernmost road to spring near pond.	

5000

3000

1000

NoBo
SoBo

.ıll (SoBo) Poor cell reception at East B Hill Rd, consider calling ahead if you need ride.

Mile	Elev.
252.2 **1936.9** Wyman Mountain	2920
250.9 **1938.2** **Hall Mountain Lean-to** 20.9◀14.0◀10.5◀▶12.8▶21.1▶32.3	2629
Spring south of lean-to on AT, tenting and view behind shelter.	
249.5 **1939.6** Sawyer Notch, Sawyer Rd (dirt)	1095
249.4 **1939.7** Sawyer Brook, campsite	1073
249.0 **1940.1** View	2059
248.6 **1940.5** Moody Mountain, view	2440
246.8 **1942.3** South Arm Rd (paved), **Andover, ME** (9.0E)	1410
246.3 **1942.8** Black Brook on south side of road, campsite. View	2198
244.0 **1945.1** Old Blue Mountain	3600
242.4 **1946.7** Unnamed Gap, mileage sign, water to west	3005
241.1 **1948.0** Spring	3166
240.8 **1948.3** Bemis Stream Trail to east	3350
239.8 **1949.3** Bemis Mountain	3550
239.3 **1949.8** View	3295
238.1 **1951.0** **Bemis Mountain Lean-to**, small spring to left of lean-to 26.8◀23.3◀12.8◀▶8.3▶19.5▶28.4	2826
236.8 **1952.3** Bemis Mountain Second Peak	2905
234.6 **1954.5** Dirt road, campsite and stream north of road	1559

NoBo
SoBo

Mile	Feature	Elev.
234.4	Bemis Stream (ford) ♦	1501
233.6	**ME 17, Oquossoc, ME** (11.0W) 44.8364,-70.711 **P** 📷 (pg.206)	2206
	Height of Land view, bench and boulder seating	
232.5	Woods road	2368
231.9	Moxie Pond ♦	2333
229.8	**Sabbath Day Pond Lean-to** 31.6◄21.1◄8.3◄►11.2►20.1►28.1 ☾♦◣⌂⊏(8)	2377
	Pond in front of lean-to. Sandy beach 0.3S on AT, swimming.	
229.3	Houghton Fire Rd	2388
228.2	Powerline	2792
225.2	Little Swift River Pond Campsite ☾♦◣	2460
	Spring house next to pond.	
224.0	Chandler Mill Stream, pond ♦	2184
222.9	Stream. ♦	2305
222.5	South Pond ♦	2174
220.4	**ME 4, Rangeley, ME** (9.0W) 44.8869,-70.5405 **P** (pg.207)	1613
220.2	Sandy River, footbridge ♦	1664
219.7	Old County Rd (gravel)	1867
218.9	Stream ♦	1978
218.6	**Piazza Rock Lean-to,** stream through campsite ☾♦◣⊏(8) (pg.207)	2088
	32.3◄19.5◄11.2◄►8.9►16.9►35.5 Two-seat privy and cribbage board.	
217.8	Ethel Pond ♦	2365
217.6	Saddleback Stream ♦	2453
216.8	Eddy Pond, woods road passes near north bank, no camping near pond ♦	2643

5000

3000

1000

Mile	Feature	Icons	Elevation
214.7	**1974.4** Saddleback Mountain, trail 2.0W to ski lodge.	📷	4120
213.1	**1976.0** The Horn.	📷	4021
212.4	**1976.7** Redington Campsite to west, water 0.2W on side trail	☾◆▲(8)	3154
211.1	**1978.0** Saddleback Junior	📷◆	3655
210.7	**1978.4** Stream.	◆	3230
209.7	**1979.4 Poplar Ridge Lean-to** (1961) 28.4◄20.1◄8.9◄►8.0►26.6►36.8 Some tenting at lean-to, more on knoll to the north. Stream in front.	☾◆▲⊏(6)	2948
207.0	**1982.1** Orbeton Stream (ford)	◆	1550
206.9	**1982.2** Woods road, NoBo: walk a short distance east on road	◆	1627
206.2	**1982.9** Sluice Brook.	◆	2088
205.6	**1983.5** Barnjam Rd, private gravel road	◆	2321
205.1	**1984.0** Perham Stream, logging road to north (not accessible by car)	◆	2300
203.9	**1985.2** Lone Mountain		3260
202.7	**1986.4** Mt Abraham Trail, 1.7E to summit above treeline, remnants of lookout tower .	📷	3247
201.7	**1987.4 Spaulding Mountain Lean-to**, spring on north shelter loop trail 28.1◄16.9◄8.0◄►18.6►28.8►36.5	☾◆⊏(8)	3122
200.7	**1988.4** Crest NW shoulder of Spaulding Mountain Side trail 0.1E to summit.	▲	3894
200.0	**1989.1** Bronze plaque Completion of the last section of the AT from GA-ME.		3544
198.9	**1990.2** View to east.	📷	3617
198.6	**1990.5** Sugarloaf Mountain, stream 0.2E, Sugarloaf Mountain Trail 0.6E to summit	📷	3645
196.6	**1992.5** South Branch Carrabassett River (ford), tenting on north side of river	◆▲	2147
196.5	**1992.6** Caribou Valley Rd (gravel)	◆	2220
196.0	**1993.1** Spring.	◆	2440
195.5	**1993.6** Crocker Cirque Campsite (0.2E), stream	☾◆▲	2730

5000

3000

1000

NoBo
SoBo

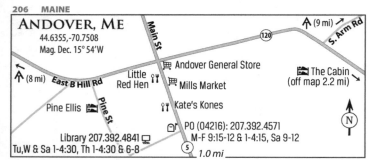

ANDOVER, ME
44.6355,-70.7508
Mag. Dec. 15°54'W

Main St

120

↑ (9 mi) ↗ S. Arm Rd

↑ (8 mi) East B Hill Rd

Pine St

Little Red Hen

Andover General Store

Mills Market

Kate's Kones

Pine Ellis

PO (04216): 207.392.4571
M-F 9:15-12 & 1-4:15, Sa 9-12

The Cabin
(off map 2.2 mi)

N

Library 207.392.4841
Tu,W & Sa 1-4:30, Th 1-4:30 & 6-8

5

1.0 mi

1921.9   Grafton Notch, ME 26

(12.8E) Stony Brook Camping 207.824.2836 ⟨www.stonybrookrec.com⟩ tent site $28 for 4, lean-to $32 for 4. Shuttles from Grafton Notch for a fee. Pool, miniature golf, zip line, rec room, campstore. 12.0E on Hwy 26, then left 0.8 mile on Route 2. Mail: 42 Powell Place, Hanover, Maine, ME 04237.

Bethel, ME 04217 (12E to Rt 2, right 5 miles on Rt 2)

M-F 9-4, Sa 10-12:30, 207.824.2668

Chapman Inn 207.824.2657 ⟨www.chapmaninn.com⟩ Bunk space $35 includes shower & full breakfast, $25 without breakfast. Rooms $79/up include breakfast. Kitchen privileges, $6 laundry. Mail: PO Box 1067, Bethel, ME 04217.

Bethel Outdoor Adventure 207.824.4224 About 20 minutes by car from Grafton Notch or US 2 trailheads. $22 campsites near river within walking distance of Bethel stores. Shuttle one-way to/from Grafton Notch tailhead $45/group.

Pat's Pizza 7 days 11-9

Sudbury Inn Restaurant & Pub, Tu-Su 5:30-9, pub 7 days 4:30-9.

Bethel Shop 'n Save

True North Adventurewear 207.824.2201 Full line of gear, M-Th 10-6. F-Sa 9-6, Su 10-5. Leki repair, Coleman/alcohol/oz & canisters, freeze-dried foods.

Bethel Animal Hospital 207.824.2212

1932.2   East B Hill Rd   **Andover, ME 04216** (8E)

Pine Ellis Lodging 207.392.4161 ⟨www.pineellislodging.com⟩ Bunks $25PP, private rooms $45S, $60D, $75 triple. Stays include kitchen privileges, laundry & morning coffee. Trailhead pickup for a fee, call in advance, slackpack Grafton Notch to Rangeley, and shuttles to nearby towns, airport and bus station. No dogs. Full resupply includes on-trail snacks & meals, Coleman/ denatured/oz and canister fuel. Hiker-friendly hosts Ilene Trainor. Guest Mail: (USPS) PO Box 12 or (UPS) 20 Pine Street, Andover, ME 04216.

Paul's AT Camp for Hikers Contact Pine Ellis for stay at rustic cabin $60 for 4. Located 3 miles from Andover. Stay includes shower one round trip shuttle from the hostel.

Andover General Store 207.392.4172   Short-order food & pizza, **Sweet Treats** ice cream. Open M-Sa 5-8, Su 6-8, in summer until 9pm daily.

Mills Market Open 7 days 5am-9pm.

Little Red Hen 207.392.2253 Open (summer hours) Tu-Th 6:30am-2pm, F-Sa 6:30-8pm, Sun 7-2, closed Monday. AYCE Pizza on Sat. July b'fast buffet on Sun. Ask about tenting.

Donna Gifford massage therapist, 207.357.5686, call for rates. Free pickup/return to Andover.

The Cabin 207.392.1333 Alumni hikers welcome; by reservation only ⟨www.thecabininmaine.com⟩.

1942.3   South Arm Rd

(3.5W) South Arm Campground 207.364.5155 ⟨www.southarm.com⟩ Tent sites, camp store, no credit cards, pets okay, open May 1–Oct 1.

Andover, ME (9E from South Arm Rd)

1955.5   ME 17   **Oquossoc, ME 04964** (11W)

M-F 8–10 & 2:15–4:15, Sa 9–12, 207.864.3685

Oquossoc Grocery deli, bakery, Coleman fuel

Gingerbread House B/L/D, vegetarian specials.

Four Seasons Café 7 days 11–9 L/D vegetarian specialties.

1968.7 ME 4 **Rangeley, ME** (9W) Safest to hitch from end of guardrail 0.3W, in front of Hiker Hut. Rangeley is halfway between equator and the north pole (3107 miles from either).

🏕◐🚌✉ **The Hiker Hut** (0.3W) 207.897.8984, 207.670.8095 hikerhut@gmail.com. Quiet, restful sanctuary along the Sandy River with Artisan jewelry maker and massage therapist on-site. $25PP includes bunk w/mattress, pillows, sheets, home cooked meal & shuttle into Rangeley. Private couples hut $50. Shuttles/slackpacking available. Mail ($5 non-guest fee) C/O Steve Lynch 2 Pine Rd. Sandy River Plantation, ME 04970.

🛏🏕⛰⛺📶✉ **Farmhouse Inn** 207.864.3113 Hiker bunkroom for $30PP, includes shower w/towel and return to Rte 4 trailhead. Private rooms avail. Not a party place. Laundry $5. Hiker supplies, Coleman/Denatured/oz, slackpacking. Nice clean facility with use of a kitchen, bikes for riding into town. 0.5 south of IGA. Mail: 2057 Main St, Rangeley, ME 04970.

🛏📶✉ **Town & Lake Motel** 207.864.3755 Call for hiker rate. Pets $5. Canoes for guest use. Mail: PO Box 47, Rangeley, ME 04970.

🛏🍴📶 **Rangeley Inn & Tavern** 207.864.3341 ⟨www.therangeleyinn.com⟩ Rates start at $135 in summer, $115 in fall (after Sept 1). Includes cont. breakfast. Senior discount, free calls to US and Canada.

🛏🍴📶 **Rangeley Saddleback Inn** 207.864.3434 $135D, pets $10 includes cont. B. Ride sometimes available. **Pub 45th Parallel** on-site.

🛏📶 **North Country Inn B&B** 207.864.2440 ⟨www.northcountrybb.com⟩ info@northcountrybb.com $99-149 includes full b'fast, specials mid-week and off-season. Multi-night discount.

🏛🍴 **Moose Loop Cafe** 207.864.3000 Open 7am-2pm daily.

🍴 **Sarge's Sports Pub & Grub** L/D and bar, 7 days 11-1, house bands on Friday and Saturday.

🍴 **Moose Alley** 207.864.9955 Bowling, billiards, darts, dance floor, food. Just west of The Shed BBQ on Main St.

🛒 💲 **IGA Supermarket** 207.864.5089 ATM 7 days 7-8.

RANGELEY, ME

44.9664, -70.6447
Mag. Dec. 15.68° W

🏃⛺🏛🚌✉ **Ecopelagicon** 207.864.2771 Hiker friendly nature store White gas/alcohol/oz, canister fuel, freeze-dried foods, water filters, clothes, Leki poles and does warranty work. Ask about shuttles. Mail: PO Box 899, 7 Pond St, Rangeley, ME 04970.

🏃 **Alpine Shop** 207.864.3741 M-S 9-7, Su 10-6, some hiking gear, fuel/oz.

🏃 **Back Woods** 207.864.2335 Gear, clothes.

➕ **Rangeley Health** 207.864.3303 **& Wellness Center** 207.864.3055 On Dallas Hill Rd south of IGA. $5 shower, towel provided. M-Th 5am-8pm, F 5am-7:30pm, Sa-Su 8-2.

1970.5 **Piazza Rock Lean-to** Two side trails north of shelter; 100 yards north: west to Piazza Rock; 0.1 north: To "The Caves", blue-blazed trail through boulders & caves.

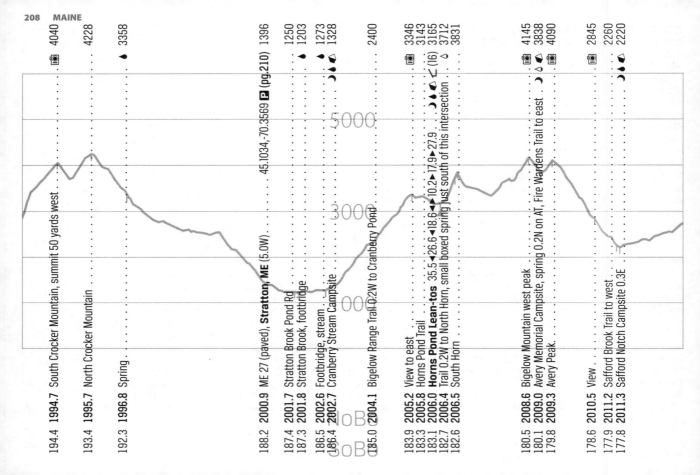

Mile		Feature	Elevation
194.4	**1994.7**	South Crocker Mountain, summit 50 yards west	🄿📷 4040
193.4	**1995.7**	North Crocker Mountain	4228
192.3	**1996.8**	Spring	⧫ 3358
188.2	**2000.9**	ME 27 (paved), **Stratton, ME** (5.0W). 45.1034,-70.3569 🄿 (pg.210)	1396
187.4	**2001.7**	Stratton Brook Pond Rd	1250
187.3	**2001.8**	Stratton Brook, footbridge	⧫ 1203
186.5	**2002.6**	Footbridge, stream	⧫ 1273
186.4	**2002.7**	Cranberry Stream Campsite	◗⧫◗ 1328
185.0	**2004.1**	Bigelow Range Trail 0.2W to Cranberry Pond	2400
183.9	**2005.2**	View to east	🄿📷 3346
183.3	**2005.8**	Horns Pond Trail	3143
183.1	**2006.0**	**Horns Pond Lean-tos** 35.5◀26.6◀18.6◀▶10.2▶17.9▶27.9	◗⧫◗⊑(16) 3165
182.7	**2006.4**	Trail 0.2W to North Horn, small boxed spring just south of this intersection	△ 3712
182.6	**2006.5**	South Horn	3831
180.5	**2008.6**	Bigelow Mountain west peak	🄿📷 4145
180.1	**2009.0**	Avery Memorial Campsite, spring 0.2N on AT, Fire Wardens Trail to east	△ 3838
179.8	**2009.3**	Avery Peak	🄿📷 4090
178.6	**2010.5**	View	🄿📷 2845
177.9	**2011.2**	Safford Brook Trail to west	◗⧫◗ 2260
177.8	**2011.3**	Safford Notch Campsite 0.3E	◗⧫◗ 2220

Mile	Feature	Elevation
175.6	2013.5 View	🔲📷 2915
174.6	2014.5 Little Bigelow Mountain, view	🔲📷 3010
172.9	2016.2 **Little Bigelow Lean-to** 36.8◄28.8◄10.2◄►7.7►17.7►27.4 . . . 〉◆◔⊏(8) 1792 Plenty of tent sites at lean-to. Swimming in "the Tubs" along AT.	
171.5	2017.6 East Flagstaff Rd, ...45.1346,-70.1714 **P** (0.1W) 〉(pg.211) 1200 AT east on road for 0.1mile	
171.3	2017.8 Bog Brook Rd, Flagstaff Lake outlet, footbridge . . . . ◆ 1196
170.6	2018.5 Hemlock Trail to east	1257
170.3	2018.8 East Flagstaff Lake tentpads, 2 beaches, 2 firepits . . . . . 〉◆◔(9) 1208
169.8	2019.3 Two intersections with Hemlock Trail	1244
168.7	2020.4 Long Falls Dam Rd (paved) . . . . (pg.211) 1225
168.6	2020.5 Jerome Brook . . . . ◆ 1236

"Carry" ponds are so named because they were used for portage.
✖ Find a commemorative orange disk nailed to a tree or post. How many men are in the boat?

Mile	Feature	Elevation
165.8	2023.3 Connector trail to Great Carrying Pond Portage Trail. 1319
165.2	2023.9 **West Carry Pond Lean-to** 36.5◄17.9◄7.7◄►10.0►19.7►28.7 . . . 〉◆◔⊏(8) 1325 Swimming in pond. Water at spring house to left of lean-to or at West Carry Pond.
164.5	2024.6 Unmarked trail 0.5W to Arnolds Point on West Carry Pond. 1322
162.7	2026.4 Gravel road, AT to west over Sandy Stream . . . . ◆ 1276
161.8	2027.3 Gravel road	1290
161.5	2027.6 East Carry Pond, beach at north end . . . . ◆ 1261
159.5	2029.6 Scott Rd (gravel) 1337
158.7	2030.4 North branch of Carrying Place Stream . . . . ◆ 1200

NoBo
SoBo

5000
3000
1000

STRATTON, ME
45.1408, -70.4436
Mag. Dec. 15.82° W

Stratton Plaza
Fotter's Market
Old Mill Laundry
School St
PO (04982): 207.246.6461
M-F 8:30-1 & 1:30-4, Sa 8:30-11
Limited cash-back

Main St
Stratton Motel & Hostel
White Wolf Inn, Restaurant & Bar
Flagstaff General Store
Sargent Ave

Library M,W,F 10-5; Tu,Th 1-5; Sa 9-1

(5.0 mi from PO)

Looney Moose
Spillover Motel (0.6 mi from PO)

0.8 mi

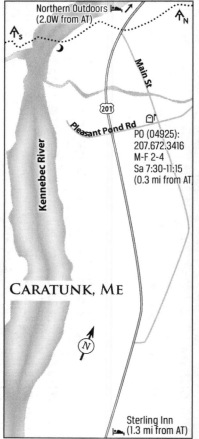

Northern Outdoors (2.0W from AT)

Main St
201
Pleasant Pond Rd
PO (04925): 207.672.3416
M-F 2-4
Sa 7:30-11:15
(0.3 mi from AT)

Kennebec River

CARATUNK, ME

Sterling Inn (1.3 mi from AT)

2000.9   ME 27

(2E) **Mountainside Grocers** 207.237.2248 Open M-Sa 7:30–8, Su 7:30-6.

Stratton, ME 04982 (5W)

Stratton Motel 207.246.4171 or 207.670.5507 ⟨www.thestrattonmotel.com⟩ $25 bunk, $60 private room, Cash Only. Shuttle from trailhead $5PP (when available). Same owners as Farmhouse Inn of Rangeley, who facilitate supply bumps from town to town and slackpacking in area. Shuttle range Gorham to Monson and to airports, train, bus and car rental hubs in Portland, Bangor, Farmington, Augusta and Waterville. Canister fuel & fuel/oz. Mail: PO Box 284, Stratton, ME 04982; FedEx & UPS 162 Main St.,Stratton, ME 04982.

White Wolf Inn 207.246.2922 $59D, $65D on weekends, $10EAP + tax. Pets $10. Visa, M/C accepted $20 min. Restaurant (closed Tu) serves L/D. Breakfast on weekends. Home of the 8oz Wolf Burger; Fish Fry Friday; **Wolf Den Bar** on-site. Guest Mail (non-guest fee): Main Street, PO Box 590, Stratton, ME 04982.

Spillover Motel 207.246.6571 ⟨www.spillovermaine.com⟩ $79/up. Pets $10, cont B. Full kitchen for use by guests, gas grill. Mail: PO Box 427, Stratton, ME 04982.

Stratton Plaza Hotel 207.246.2000 Dining, some rooms.

Fotter's Market 207.246.2401 M-Th 8-7, F-Sa 8-8, Su 9-5. Coleman/alcohol/oz.

Flagstaff General Store 207.246.2300 Deli, pizza, subs, sodas, coffee, protein bars, beer, canister fuel. M-F 5:30am-9pm, Sa 7-9, Su 7-7.

2017.6   East Flagstaff Rd
2020.4   Long Falls Dam Rd
     Kingfield, ME (18E from either Rd)
🛏�︎🛜🖥✉ **Mountain Village Farm B&B** 207.265.2030 Hiker rate of $60PP for room with fridge, microwave & private bath. Includes breakfast. Round-trip shuttle $40 for up to 4 persons from either trailhead. Pets welcome. Bed & Breakfast on an organic farm; inquire about work-for-stay. Town center within walking distance has grocery, laundry & restaurants. Slackpack the Bigelows (Stratton to East Flagstaff Rd, either direction) $40/carload. Mail: PO Box 216, Kingfield, ME 04947.

2033.9, 2034.3   Trails to camp, dam bypass
🛏🍴 **Harrison's Pierce Pond Camps** 207.672.3625, 207.612.8184 May-Nov, 7 days. Bed, shower, and 12-pancake breakfast $40. For breakfast only, ($9-12 served 7am), reserve a seat the day before. Cash only, no reservations for overnight stay. Okay to get water at camp and dispose of trash. Shortest route to camp is west from the north end of blue-blaze shelter loop trail.

2037.5   Kennebec River. The ferry is the official AT route. Do not ford; current is unpredictable due to an upstream dam.
🚤 **Fletcher Mountain Outfitters** 207.672.4879 (David Corrigan) Contracted by ATC to provide free ferry service seasonally. Ferry holds 1 or 2; hikers are required to sign a release form. ⚠️***2015 dates/times specified below for reference***; 2016 dates/times not available in time for this edition. Some after hour & off-season ferries available for a fee.

Before May 1	No service
May 1 - May 21	on-call service $50 time & weather permitting
May 22 - July 9	9am-11am, 7 days
July 10 - Sept 30	9am-11am and 2pm-4pm, 7 days
Oct 1 - Oct 12	9am-11am, 7 days
Oct 13 - Oct 31	on-call service $50 time & weather permitting
After Oct 31	No service

🚤 **Cheryl Anderson** 207.672.3997 Pivately run for-fee ferry service.

2037.9   US 201   ***Caratunk, ME 04925*** (0.3E)
🏤 Post office accepts debit cards with limited cash back. Note limited hours; consider businesses below for maildrops.
🛏🏠⊕🍴📶🚿⛺🛜🖥✉ (1.3E)   **The Sterling Inn** 207.672.3333 ⟨www.mainesterlinginn.com⟩ Bunk room $25, private $40S, $55D (shared bed), $90/4. All include breakfast buffet. Multi-night discount, credit/debit cards accepted, pets welcome, open year-round. **Stephen's resupply** has everything a hiker needs, including fuel/oz, canister fuel, batteries & candy bars, ice cream, sodas, and cook-yourself options and more. Free shuttle to/from trail, PO, and nearby restaurants. Resupply, showers ($2.50) and laundry ($5) available even if you are not staying. Address: 1041 Route 201. Maildrops & shipping (also free for non-guests): PO Box 129, Caratunk Maine 04925.
🛏🏠⊕🍴💲🚿⛺🛜🖥✉ (2W)   **Northern Outdoors** 800.765.7238   ⟨www.northernoutdoors.com⟩   Hikers welcome, free shuttle (coincides with ferry schedule), use resort facilities with or without stay; hikers receive 30% lodging discount; prices vary, call for rates. No pets in campground. Coin laundry, hot tub, free WiFi, full hiker resupply store, food & ale in **Kennebec River Brewpub**, Home of the exterminator burger challenge! Finish the meal in 30 min, get it free. Mail: C/O Northern Outdoors, 1771 Route 201, The Forks, ME 04985.
🏠⊕🍴🛒💲📶✉ (4W)   **Three Rivers Trading Post** 207.663.2104 Store open year-round carries variery of packaged food, beer & wine. Bunks, tenting & restaurant open May-mid Sept. Bunk $25PP, tenting $12PP. Rafting trips by reservation. **Boatman's Bar & Grill** on-site open 4pm-1am. Mail: 2265 US Route 201, The Forks, ME 04985.
🛒 **Berry's General Store** (7.5W) 207.663.4461 4:30am-7pm daily, year-round. Open till 8 in summer.

Trails to Harrison's, before and after the dam, can be used to bypass the dam.

SoBo	AT Mile	Feature	Elev
155.2	**2033.9**	**Pierce Pond Lean-to**, 27.9◀17.7◀10.0◀▶9.7▶18.7▶22.8 ⊃♦⊂(6) (pg.211)	1207
155.1	**2034.0**	Blue-blazed loop trail west to Pierce Pond	1140
154.8	**2034.3**	Wooden dam, outlet of Pierce Pond. From north end of loop, Harrison's is 0.3E.	1100
154.6	**2034.5**	Trail 0.1E to Harrison's Pierce Pond Camps, boat landing to west (pg.211)	1056
154.1	**2035.0**	Otter Pond Rd (gravel)	980
154.0	**2035.1**	Pierce Pond Stream Falls 0.1E	955
		Waterfall 0.1E	
153.5	**2035.6**	Otter Pond Stream, footbridge ♦	864

⊘ Camping on either shore of Kennebec River is prohibited.

SoBo	AT Mile	Feature	Elev
151.6	**2037.5**	Kennebec River. Do not ford. Use ferry service. ♦(pg.211)	485
151.2	**2037.9**	US 201, **Caratunk, ME** (0.3E) ...... 45.2384,-69.9963 P (pg.211)	520
150.9	**2038.2**	Woods road	674
148.6	**2040.5**	Holly Brook ♦	901
147.2	**2041.9**	Grove Rd (gravel)	1220
146.7	**2042.4**	Holly Brook ♦	1292
146.0	**2043.1**	Boise-Cascade Logging Rd to west (gravel), Pleasant Pond Rd to east.	1430
145.5	**2043.6**	**Pleasant Pond Lean-to** 27.4◀19.7◀9.7◀▶9.0▶13.1▶22.0 ⊃♦⊂(6)	1373
		Stream left of lean-to. Beach 0.2 on side trail beyond lean-to.	
145.3	**2043.8**	Pleasant Pond Beach to east	1339
144.2	**2044.9**	Pleasant Pond Mountain 📷	2470

❋ **Blueberries** – Abundant on open summits like Pleasant Pond Mountain and north peak of Moxie Bald.

SoBo	AT Mile	Feature	Elev
139.7	**2049.4**	Stream. ♦	1034
139.3	**2049.8**	Moxie Pond south end (ford), road, powerlines .... 45.2497,-69.83 P	970
139.1	**2050.0**	Baker Stream ♦	972
138.8	**2050.3**	Powerline ♦	1015

NoBo				SoBo
136.5	2052.6	**Bald Mountain Brook Lean-to** (0.1E) ☽◆⌂(8)	1312
		28.7◀18.7◀9.0◀▶4.1▶13.0▶25.0 Bald Mountain Brook in front of lean-to. "AT Road" (gravel) 75 yards north of shelter.	
135.1	2054.0	Summit bypass trail to west	2151
134.5	2054.6	Moxie Bald Mountain [icon]	2629
134.2	2054.9	Summit bypass trail to west ☽	2414
133.5	2055.6	Trail to Moxie Bald north peak (0.5W) [icon]	2212
132.4	2056.7	**Moxie Bald Mountain Lean-to** ☽◆⌂(8)	1224
		22.8◀13.1◀4.1◀▶8.9▶20.9▶28.3 Bald Mountain Pond in front of lean-to.	
131.3	2057.8	Gravel road	1259
130.8	2058.3	Gravel road	1234
130.4	2058.7	Bald Mountain Stream (ford) ◆	1216
128.5	2060.6	Bald Mountain Rd (gravel) 45.2762,-69.6885 P ◆	1116
		bridge and stream to west	
127.0	2062.1	Marble Brook ◆	985
126.5	2062.6	West Branch of Piscataquis River (ford) ◆	964
		River normally knee deep. During heavy rain periods, fording can be dangerous.	
123.5	2065.6	**Horseshoe Canyon Lean-to** 22.0◀13.0◀8.9◀▶12.0▶19.4▶24.1 ☽◆⌂(8)	780
		On blue-blazed trail. Stream at northern AT junction or river in front and below.	
123.1	2066.0	Stream. ◆	740
121.2	2067.9	East Branch of Piscataquis River (ford) ◆	588
120.9	2068.2	Gravel road	741
120.8	2068.3	Shirley-Blanchard Rd (paved) 45.2845,-69.5871 P	850
119.7	2069.4	AT on woods road for 0.5 mile	977
119.3	2069.8	Gravel road	895
117.8	2071.3	Historic AT route near Lake Hebron. 45.2907,-69.5333 P (pg.218)	900
		0.2E on woods road to Pleasant St & parking, then left 1.6 mi to **Monson, ME.**	
117.4	2071.7	Dirt road	1033

NoBo
SoBo

115.9	2073.2	Side trail to Doughty Ponds (0.1W), 180' footbridge built in 2014	◆ 1229
115.8	2073.3	Stream.	1251
115.2	2073.9	Gravel road	1386
114.5	2074.6	ME 15 (paved) **Monson, ME** (3.6E) .... 45.3309,-69.5354 **P** (pg.218)	1215
114.4	2074.7	South end of 100-Mile Wilderness.	1180
113.6	2075.5	Old Stage Rd (dirt) Once a stagecoach road and part of the original AT	1291
113.3	2075.8	Bell Pond	1278
112.6	2076.5	Lily Pond	1130
111.5	2077.6	**Leeman Brook Lean-to** 25.0◀20.9◀12.0◀▶7.4▶12.1▶16.1 Stream in front of lean-to.	☽◆∈(6) 1062
110.7	2078.4	North Pond outlet	1013
110.4	2078.7	North Pond Tote Rd	1090
109.3	2079.8	Mud Pond	1031
108.9	2080.2	Bear Pond Ledge	1208
108.5	2080.6	James Brook	946
108.1	2081.0	Woods road	938
108.0	2081.1	Little Wilson Falls, west 30 yards	844
107.7	2081.4	Little Wilson Stream (ford), campsite	750
107.3	2081.8	Follow gravel road for 100 yards, pond	925
105.4	2083.7	Big Wilson Tote Rd	566
105.2	2083.9	Thompson Brook	563
104.8	2084.3	Big Wilson Stream (ford)	600
104.5	2084.6	Railroad tracks	883
104.1	2085.0	**Wilson Valley Lean-to** (1993) 28.3◀19.4◀7.4◀▶4.7▶8.7▶15.6 Spring on opposite side of AT.	☽◆∈(6) 951
103.4	2085.7	Woods road	1180
102.1	2087.0	Stream	924
101.8	2087.3	Stream	914
101.0	2088.1	Wilber Brook	595
100.8	2088.3	Vaughn Stream	617
100.3	2088.8	Bodfish Farm/Long Pond Tote Rd (gravel), ford Long Pond Stream north of road	638
99.4	2089.7	**Long Pond Stream Lean-to** 24.1◀12.1◀4.7◀▶4.0▶10.9▶20.8	☽◆∈(8) 914
99.2	2089.9	Trail 0.8E to Otter Pond parking	**P** 1059
98.2	2090.9	Barren Slide to east, view	1971
98.1	2091.0	Barren Ledges	2017

SoBo	Mile	Description	Features	Elev
96.3	**2092.8**	Barren Mountain, remnants of tower		2660
95.4	**2093.7**	Side trail to **Cloud Pond Lean-to** (0.4E) 16.1◄8.7◄4.0◄►6.9►16.8►24.0 Cloud Pond is water source.	☽♦⊏(6)	2483
93.9	**2095.2**	Fourth Mountain Bog		1931
93.3	**2095.8**	Fourth Mountain		2380
92.1	**2097.0**	Mt Three and a Half		1958
91.7	**2097.4**	Third Mountain Trail to west		1800
90.8	**2098.3**	Third Mountain, Monument Cliff	📷	2097
90.2	**2098.9**	Trail 0.1E to West Chairback Pond, stream crosses AT north of side trail	♦	1770
89.3	**2099.8**	View	📷	2150
89.2	**2099.9**	Spring	♦	2237
88.9	**2100.2**	Columbus Mountain		2325
88.5	**2100.6**	**Chairback Gap Lean-to** 15.6◄10.9◄6.9◄►9.9►17.1►20.7 Spring on AT north of shelter.	☽♦⊏(6)	1960
88.0	**2101.1**	Chairback Mountain	📷	2180
85.9	**2103.2**	0.2W to East Chairback Pond	♦(0.2W)	1709
85.3	**2103.8**	Spring	♦	1460
84.7	**2104.4**	Katahdin Ironworks Rd (gravel) 45.4772,-69.2851 **P** (0.4E)	♦	783
84.2	**2104.9**	West Branch Pleasant River (ford). Wide ford with slick rocky bottom. Campsites to south; no camping/fires for 2.0N.	♦	663
83.3	**2105.8**	Stream.	♦	748
82.8	**2106.3**	Gulf Hagas Trail to west, 5.2 mile loop trail whose ends intersect the AT 0.7 mile apart. Features narrow, deep gorge with many waterfalls.	♦	875
82.1	**2107.0**	Gulf Hagas Trail to west	♦	1050
78.6	**2110.5**	**Carl A. Newhall Lean-to** 20.8◄16.8◄9.9◄►7.2►10.8►18.9. Gulf Hagas Brook, south of shelter, is water source.	☽♦⊏(6)	1923

⚠ All 100 M.W. roads are privately owned, gated, and have fees. Road names vary on maps and in local use. Both roads that pass by Logan Brook & Cooper Brook Shelters may be referred to as "B Pond Road". If getting shuttles or drops be clear about the destination.

Mile (NoBo)	Mile (SoBo)	Feature	Elevation
77.7	2111.4	Gulf Hagas Mountain	2681
76.8	2112.3	Sidney Tappan Campsite, water 0.1E ● ◆	2434
76.1	2113.0	West Peak	3178
74.5	2114.6	Hay Mountain	3244
73.7	2115.4	White Brook Trail to east	3004
72.8	2116.3	White Cap Mountain ▣ ●	3650
71.9	2117.2	View of Katahdin from north side of mountain ▣	2730
71.4	2117.7	**Logan Brook Lean-to** 24.0◀17.1◀7.2◀▶3.6▶11.7▶23.1 ☾●◆⊆(6) Some tent sites; better sites 0.1N on AT. Logan Brook in front of lean-to; cascades upstream.	2386
69.8	2119.3	Logan Brook Rd (dirt) Piped spring 50 yards south of road, west of AT ☾◆⊆(6)	1602
67.8	2121.3	**East Branch Lean-to**, Pleasant River in front 20.7◀10.8◀3.6◀▶8.1▶19.5▶29.6	1242
67.5	2121.6	East branch of Pleasant River (ford). ●	1208
65.9	2123.2	Mountain View Pond outlet ●	1574
65.6	2123.5	Spring to east ●	1561
64.3	2124.8	Side trail 100 yards to Little Boardman Mountain.	1980
63.0	2126.1	Kokadjo-B Pond Rd (gravel) ●	1222
62.7	2126.4	West to beach on Crawford Pond (no camping) ●	1249
62.1	2127.0	Cooper Brook ●	1206
60.2	2128.9	Stream ●	1000
59.7	2129.4	**Cooper Brook Falls Lean-to** 18.9◀11.7◀8.1◀▶11.4▶21.5▶29.6 ☾●◆⊆(6) Brook, falls, swimming hole in front of lean-to. Privy across trail and up hill.	928
59.1	2130.0	Large tributary to Cooper Brook ●	821

5000
3000
1000

✻ **Indian pipe** – A plant without chlorophyll that grows in moist duff. Translucent white candy cane shape 3-4" tall, grows in clusters. Scale-like leaves/petals.

NoBo	Mile	Feature	Elev
56.0	2133.1	Jo-Mary Rd . . . . 45.6515,-69.0317 🅿 ♦ (pg.219)	625
54.6	2134.5	Footbridge, snowmobile trail . . . . ♦	585
53.5	2135.6	Side trail 0.2E to north shore of Cooper Pond . . . ♦	516
53.1	2136.0	Mud Pond to west, footbridge over Mud Brook . . . ♦	508
51.8	2137.3	Antlers Campsite . . . . ☽ ♦ ◢	500
		Campsites on edge of Jo-Mary Lake. Fort Relief two seat privy.	
50.3	2138.8	Potaywadjo Ridge Trail 1.0W	514
50.1	2139.0	East to sandy beach on lower Jo-Mary Lake . . . . . ♦	499
48.3	2140.8	**Potaywadjo Spring Lean-to** (1995) . . . . ☽ ♦ ◢ ⊏ (8)	637
		23.1◀19.5◀17.4◀•10.1▶18.2▶29.7 Potawadjo Spring to right.	
48.0	2141.1	Tirio Access Rd (gravel).	555
47.7	2141.4	Twitchell Brook, footbridge, east to Pemadumcook Lake, view of Katahdin. . 🔲 ♦	493
46.5	2142.6	Deer Brook . . . . ♦	502
45.8	2143.3	Woods road.	510
45.7	2143.4	Mahar Tote Tr, Blue-blazed tr 0.2E **White House Landing** pickup . . . . (pg.219)	510
45.6	2143.5	Tumbledown Dick Stream (ford) . . . . ♦	501
45.1	2144.0	High water trail to west . . . . ♦	496
44.5	2144.6	Ford branch of the Nahmakanta Stream . . . . ♦	512
44.0	2145.1	Nahmakanta Stream Campsite . . . . ☽ ♦ ◢	520
42.0	2147.1	Stream. . . . . ♦	616
41.2	2147.9	Gravel Road near south end of Nahmakanta Lake . . . . 45.736,-69.1035 🅿	638
		Camping on shore of Nahmakanta Lake is prohibited.	
40.0	2149.1	Prentiss Brook . . . . ♦	661

NoBo

SoBo

2071.3   Historic AT route, side trail 0.2E to Pleasant St., then left 1.7 to **Monson**

2074.6   ME 15   **Monson, ME 04464** (3.6E)

Strictly enforced: No stealth camping in town

🛏️🏠⊛🍴🎿⛺🚗📶🖥️✉️🅱️🅿️ **Lakeshore House Lodging & Pub** 207.997.7069, 207.343.5033 〈www.thelakeshorehouse.com〉 Bunkroom $25PP cash or $32.40PP with credit card. Private rooms $45S/$60D w/shared bath. Well-behaved dogs okay. Reservations appreciated, packs out by 10:30am; full check-out/vacate by noon please, unless otherwise arranged. Accepts credit cards, ATM on-site. Free for guests: trailhead pickup & return (only till 11:00am for return), loaner laptop, loaner clothing, WiFi, kayaks, paddleboat, swimming. Parking $1/day. Laundry $5 & shower $5 available to non-guests. Pub hours: Tu-Sa 12-9, Su 12-9, bar open later, closed M. Live music Su 3-6pm. House quiet by 10:00pm and NO BINGE DRINKING, social drinking okay. Guests welcome at Shaws for breakfast. Maildrops for guests (non-guests $5): PO Box 215, C/O Lakeshore House, Monson, ME 04464 or UPS/FedEx (no Sat delivery): 9 Tenney Hill Rd.

🛏️🏠⛵⊛🍴🎿⛺🚗📶🖥️✉️ **Shaw's Lodging** 207.997.3597 shawslodging@gmail.com 〈www.shawslodging.com〉 Mid-May through Oct, bunks $25, private room $50S $60D, $12 tenting. Free pickup/return with stay. $9 breakfast, $5 laundry, $5 shower & towel (w/o stay), internet. Food drops, liscened & insured slackpacking & shuttles all over Maine. Full resupply including gear, Coleman/alcohol/oz, canister fuel & Aquamira, freeze-dried and packaged food. Gear repair and shakedowns. Credit cards accepted. Maildrops (non-guests $5): PO Box 72 or 17 Pleasant St, Monson, ME 04464.

🚗 **Charlie Anderson** 207.965.5678 or 207.997.7069 Statewide shuttles/slackpack/food drops, call for prices.

🍴⊛🚋 **Pete's Place** 207.997.3400 Open May 1 thru Nov 1; Mon. 5am-7pm, Tu-F 5am-5pm, weekends 7am-5pm. Restaurant, bakery, ice cream. Resupply: hiker foods, small gear items, dog food. Coleman/denatured/oz, canisters.

🍴🏠🅱️ **A.E. Robinson's** 207.997.3700 4am-10pm 7 days. ATM fee $2. Country Cafe Deli inside serves burgers, pizza, breakfast.

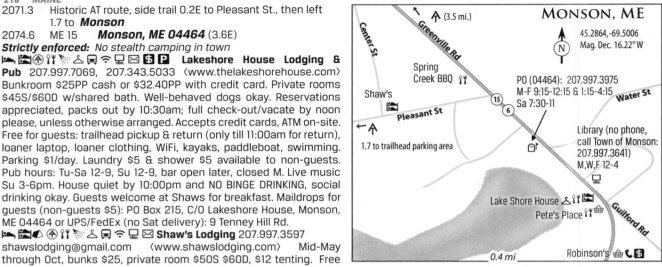

MONSON, ME
45.2864, -69.5006
Mag. Dec. 16.22°W
(3.5 mi.)
Greenville Rd
Center St
Spring Creek BBQ 🍴
Shaw's
Pleasant St
← ⋀
1.7 to trailhead parking area
PO (04464): 207.997.3975
M-F 9:15-12:15 & 1:15-4:15
Sa 7:30-11
Water St
15
6
Library (no phone, call Town of Monson: 207.997.3641)
M,W,F 12-4
Lake Shore House ⛺🍴🏠
Pete's Place 🍴🚋
Guilford Rd
Robinson's 🏠📞🅱️
0.4 mi

🍴 **Spring Creek Bar-B-Q** 207.997.7025 Th-Sa 11am-8pm, Sunday 11am-6pm.

Greenville, ME 04485 (10W from ME 15)

🛏️📶 **Kineo View Motor Lodge** 207.695.4470 $79-$99D, $10EAP includes continental breakfast. Clean, quiet motel with a nice view, 7.5 mi. from trailhead.

🛏️📶 **Indian Hill Motel** 207.695.2623 In center of town, call for rates.

🍴 **Kelly's Landing** 207.695.4438 7 days 7-9, Su AYCE breakfast.

🍴 **Dairy Bar** ice cream

🕸️🍴 **Harris Drug Store** 207.695.2921 dining counter inside.

🏃🚋 **Indian Hill Trading Post & Supermarket** 207.695.2104 Open 7 days 8-8.

⛺ **Jamieson's Store** supplies, pizza and subs.
🏂🍴📶🖥 **Northwoods Outfitters** 207.695.3288
⟨www.maineoutfitter.com⟩ Full service outfitter with fuel/oz and canister fuel. Expresso bar, pastries, internet. 7 days, 8-5.
✚ **Charles Dean Memorial Hospital** 207.695.5200
Also: two banks with ATMs

2133.1   Jo-Mary Rd. (little traffic on road) 12.0E to ME 11.
◣ 🌾⛺ (9.0E) **Jo-Mary Campground** 207.723.8117   Campsites $17 per person for ME residents, $24 non-residents. Pets welcome, coin operated showers and laundry. Open mid May - Mid Sep.

2143.4   Mahar Tote Trail, 0.2E to boat pickup, good cell signal
🛏🏠🍴 **White House Landing** 207.745.5116 By advance reservation only, 2 person/ 1 night min for pickup/return, arrival date flexible. Open MemDay-Oct 15. Bunk $35PP, semi-private $45S, $75D + tax. Shower, towel, pillowcase included; linens extra. AYCE breakfast, Dinner menu includes burgers, pizza & more. Free use of canoes. CC accepted. Mail for 2-night guests only: PO Box 1, Millinocket, ME 04462.

There is another edition of this book, made specifically for southbound hikers, available from the website:
www.theATguide.com

Manufacturers & Retailers

AntiGravityGear	910.794.3308	Ex Officio	800.644.7303	Merrell	800.288.3124
Arc'Teryx	866.458.2473	Feathered Friends	206.292.2210	Montbell	877.666.8235
Asolo/Lowe Alpine	603.448.8827	First Need	800.441.8166	Montrail	800.826.1598
Backcountry.com	800.409.4502	Frogg Toggs	800.349.1835	Mountain Hardwear	800.953.8398
Big Agnes	877.554.8975	Garmin	800.800.1020	Mountainsmith	800.551.5889
Black Diamond	801.278.5552	Garmont	800.943.4453	Mystery Ranch	406.585.1428
CamelBak	800.767.8725	Gossamer Gear	512.374.0133	NEMO	800.997.9301
Campmor	888.226.7667	Granite Gear	218.834.6157	North Face	866.715.3223
Camp Trails	800.345.7622	Gregory	877.477.4292	Osprey	866.314.3130
Cascade Designs	800.531.9531	Hi-Tec	800.521.1698	Outdoor Research	888.467.4327
(MSR/Therm-a-Rest/Platypus)		Hyperlite Mountain	800.464.9208	Patagonia	800.638.6464
Cedar Tree (Packa)	276.780.2354	Gear		Peak 1/Coleman	800.835.3278
Columbia	800.547.8066	Jacks 'R' Better	757.643.8908	Petzl	877.807.3805
Dana Designs	888.357.3262	JanSport	800.552.6776	Photon	877.584.6898
Danner	877.432.6637	Katadyn/PUR	800.755.6701	Primus	307.857.4700
Eagle Creek	800.874.1048	Keen	866.676.5336	Princeton Tec	800.257.9080
Eastern Mountain	888.463.6367	Kelty	866.349.7225	REI	800.426.4840
Sports		Leki	800.255.9982	Royal Robbins	800.587.9044
Etowah Outfitters	770.975.7829	Limmer	603.694.2668	Salomon	800.654.2668
Eureka!	800.572.8822	LL Bean	800.441.5713	Sierra Designs	800.736.8592
		Marmont	888.357.3262	Sierra Trading Post	800.713.4534
				Six Moon Designs	503.430.2303
				Slumberjack	800.233.6283
				SOTO Outdoors	503.314.5119
				Speer Hammocks	252.619.8292
				Suunto	800.543.9124
				Tarptent /	650.587.1548
				Henry Shires	
				Tecnica	800.258.3897
				Teva	800.367.8382
				The Underwear Guys	570.573.0209
				ULA	435.753.5191
				Vasque	800.224.4453
				Warmstuff/	570.573.0209
				Adventurelite	
				Western	408.287.8944
				Mountaineering	
				Zip Stove	800.594.9046

SoBo	NoBo	Description	Coordinates	Features	Elev
38.6	2150.5	Side trail east to sand beach on shore of Nahmakanta Lake		◢	657
38.2	2150.9	**Wadleigh Stream Lean-to,** stream can be dry during summer 29.6◄21.5◄10.1►8.1►19.6►33.0		⌂ ⊂ (6)	685
37.2	2151.9	Spring		◢	819
36.3	2152.8	Nesuntabunt Mountain, short side trail east to view of Katahdin, 16 mile line-of-sight distance to Katahdin summit from here.		📷	1520
35.7	2153.4	View		📷	1181
35.1	2154.0	Wadleigh Pond Rd (gravel)			1022
34.3	2154.8	Crescent Pond west end		◢	1000
33.6	2155.5	Pollywog Gorge, side trail overlooking gorge		📷	891
32.6	2156.5	Pollywog Stream Cross stream on logging road bridge.	45.7796,-69.172	P ◢	668
30.6	2158.5	Outlet stream from Murphy Pond		◢	954
30.1	2159.0	**Rainbow Stream Lean-to,** baseball bat floor. 29.6◄18.2◄8.1►11.5►24.9►0.0 Tenting on hill behind lean-to. Excellent swimming hole upstream.		◑ ◢ ⌂ ⊂ (6)	1002
28.2	2160.9	West to Rainbow Lake dam		◢	1100
28.0	2161.1	Stream.		◢	1062
26.3	2162.8	Rainbow Lake Campsite, spring west 30 yards.		◑ ◢ ◮	1100
25.1	2164.0	Stream.		◢	1079
24.8	2164.3	Unmarked trail leadS 0.2W to Rainbow Lake Camps (private)			1125
24.5	2164.6	Trail 0.7E to Rainbow Mountain			1145
22.9	2166.2	Side trail 0.1E to Little Beaver Pond, 0.7E to Big Beaver Pond		◢	1085
21.1	2168.0	Rainbow Ledges, view of Katahdin		📷	1517

5000

3000

1000

NoBo

SoBo

		Description	Features	Elev
18.6	2170.5	**Hurd Brook Lean-to,** baseball bat floor	☾ ◆ ⊏ (6)	701
		29.7◀19.6◀11.5◀▶13.4▶0.0▶0.0		
18.1	2171.0	Small spring	◆	774
15.9	2173.2	Bog bridge		606
15.4	2173.7	Golden Rd (paved), NoBo east on road, **Millinocket, ME** (19E) (pg.222)		591
15.1	2174.0	Abol Bridge crosses west branch 45.8352,-68.9693 P 📷 (pg.222)		560
		of Penobscot River. Parking on east side of road between bridge and trailhead.		
14.7	2174.4	End of Golden Rd, NoBo veer left on dirt road.		603
14.6	2174.5	Abol Stream Trail to east, footbridge, Baxter State Park Boundary	◆	589
14.3	2174.8	Information board, Abol Pond Trail east, registration for The Birches Campsites.		577
14.0	2175.1	Footbridge, Katahdin Stream, Foss and Knowlton Trail to east	◆	573
13.2	2175.9	Foss and Knowlton Brook, footbridge	◆	580
10.5	2178.6	Lower fork of Nesowadnehunk Stream	◆	606
		Both forks of this stream may require fording. There is a highwater bypass.		
9.5	2179.6	Upper fork of Nesowadnehunk Stream	◆	790
8.7	2180.4	Short side trail to view of Big Niagara Falls	📷	930
8.4	2180.7	Side trail west to Toll Dam and Little Niagara Falls	◆	1042
7.7	2181.4	Daicey Pond Nature Trail to west, parking area and privy north of trailhead P		1078
6.9	2182.2	Tracy and Elbow Pond Trails to west, Daicey Pond Nature Trail to east	◆	1100
6.2	2182.9	Grassy Pond Trail to west (two intersections)		1063
5.8	2183.3	Footbridge, stream	◆	1040
5.3	2183.8	Perimeter Rd	◆	1073
5.2	2183.9	Katahdin Stream Campground	◆ ⊏ (12)	1089
		The Birches Lean-tos & Campsite (0.2E) thru-hikers only, $10PP pay at KSC		
		ranger station or info board (9.1S). 33.0◀24.9◀13.4◀▶0.0▶0.0▶0.0		
4.0	2185.1	Owl Trail to west, footbridge, stream	◆	1548
3.9	2185.2	Katahdin Stream Falls. ✖ How many benches are in the privy waiting area?	☾	1634
3.0	2186.1	Spring	◆	2392
2.6	2186.5	Pass "The cave" small slab cave	◆	2842
1.6	2187.5	The Gateway, The Tableland		4522
1.0	2188.1	Thoreau Spring, Abol Trail to east	◆	4620
0.0	2189.1	**Katahdin,** Baxter Peak, Northern Terminus of the AT (pg.222)		5268

NoBo

SoBo

2173.7, 2174.0   Golden Rd, Abol Bridge

🏠◐🍴�🌲⛺🚆✉ Abol Bridge Campground & Store 207.447.5803 〈www.abolcampground.com〉 Store hours 7-7. Open summer (May 15-Oct 15), winter (Jan 15-Mar 15). Campsites $15PP, minimum $30 per site + tax. Bunkroom $30PP, $60 minimum + tax. Visa/MC accepted. Breakfast sandwiches & subs, sodas, ice cream, long-term resupply. Coin laundry. Shower 50 cents for 6 min, non-guests pay additional $5. Satellite Pay phone available. ⚠ $10 maildrop fee, call before sending and send well in advance: P.O. Box 536 Millinocket, ME 04462

🍴 The Northern Restaurant adjacent to Abol Bridge Store, open Jun 1-Sep 30 11am-8pm. Homemade food, full bar with selection of local and micro-brewed beer.

◐ Abol Pines $8+tax ($4+tax ME residents) self-register tent sites and shelters across the street from Abol Bridge Store, south of Golden Road. Provided by Maine Dept. of Conservation.

🐕 Connie McManus 207.723.6795, 207.731.3111 Privately run kennel service; pickup/drop-off at Abol Bridge.

2189.1   Katahdin, Baxter Peak

Between Baxter & Millinocket (16E from Katahdin Stream Campground (KSC), 8 miles north of Millinocket)

🏠 🔢 🍴 North Woods Trading Post 207.723.4326 Open Memorial Day - mid-Oct. 8-8 most days; hours vary. Good selection of trail foods, many gear items. Sandwiches and excellent pizza made on-site.

🏠◐ ⌐🍴 Big Moose Inn 207.723.8391 〈www.bigmoosecabins.com〉 Open Memorial Day - Columbus Day, prices listed include tax. Rooms with shared baths for $60.48PP, suites with private baths $151.20/up, cabins $105.84/up. Tenting $11.88PP, lean-to $15.12PP. WiFi in lobby, pets allowed at campsites only and must be attended at all times. **Fredericka's** restaurant on-site open W-Sa 5:30pm-close. **Loose Moose Bar & Grill** open every night 5pm-10pm. B available Sa–Su.

Millinocket, ME 04462 (24E from KSC)

Trail's End Festival Second weekend after Labor Day (Sept. 16-18) with vendors, food & entertainment. Hardcore trail work on Friday.

Millinocket: Paul (OleMan) & Jaime (NaviGator) Renaud 207.723.4321 〈www.appalachiantraillodge.com〉 Provide services in this text block from Mem Day-Oct 24. Credit cards accepted.

🏠◐❄⛺🚆🅿 ☎🖥✉ The Appalachian Trail Lodge Bunkroom $25, private room $55, family suite $95D $10EAP. Showers for nonguests $3. Coin laundry. Free daily shuttle from Baxter SP from Sept 1 - Oct 24, between 3:30pm – 4:30pm. Licensed and insured shuttle service for hire to and from bus in Medway, into 100-Mile Wilderness or Monson, food drops. Slackpack in 100-Mile Wilderness, other shuttles by arrangement, free parking. No pets. SoBo special: pickup in Medway, bed in bunkroom, breakfast at AT Cafe, and shuttle to KSC. $70pp, by reservation. Mail (guests only): 33 Penobscot Avenue, Millinocket, ME 04462.

🧍 Ole Man's Gear Shop Full line of gear; ULA & Hyperlite packs, bags, fuel, stoves, poles, Southbound A.T. Guide and more. No clothing or shoes.

🍴 ♿ The Appalachian Trail Cafe Serves B/L/D

🦌☎🖥 Trail Connection Computer, wireless, specialty coffee.

🛏🍴☎✉ Katahdin Cabins 207.723.6305 〈www.katahdincabins.com〉 Skip & Nicole Mohoff run eco-friendly cabins with continental breakfast, TV, DVD, fridge & mwave. $65 up to 3 persons, $85 up to 5. Cafe on-site with coffee and baked goods. No smoking. Gas grill, bikes free for use, community room, accepts CC/cash/checks. Mail: 181 Medway Rd, Millinocket, ME 04462.

🛏☎✉ Parks Edge Inn 207.447.4321 or 207.227.2692 Good for large groups & families: Rooms for 2-8 guests ranging from $65 to $85. All rooms have kitchen, bath, TV & DVD players. Mail with reservation: 19 Central St, Millinocket, ME 04462.

🛏🍴☎✉ Pamola Motor Lodge 800.575.9746 $69S $10EAP up to 4 (price may change in 2016). Pets $10. Cont. breakfast. **Hang Wong**